Alternative Conceptions of Phrase Structure

Alternative Conceptions of Phrase Structure

EDITED BY

Mark R. Baltin and Anthony S. Kroch

THE UNIVERSITY OF CHICAGO PRESS
CHICAGO AND LONDON

MARK R. BALTIN is associate professor of linguistics at
New York University.

ANTHONY S. KROCH is associate professor of linguistics at the
University of Pennsylvania.

The University of Chicago Press, Chicago 60637
The University of Chicago Press, Ltd., London

Library of Congress Cataloging-in-Publication Data

Alternative conceptions of phrase structure / edited by Mark R. Baltin
　　and Anthony S. Kroch.
　　　　p.　cm.
　　Outgrowth of a conference held at New York University in July
1986.
　　Bibliography: p.
　　Includes index.
　　ISBN 0-226-03641-3 (alk. paper). — ISBN 0-226-03642-1 (pbk. :
　alk. paper)
　　1. Phrase structure grammar—Congresses.　I. Baltin, Mark R.
　(Mark Reuben), 1950–　.　II. Kroch, Anthony S.
　P158.3.A48　　1989
　415—dc19　　　　　　　　　　　　　　　　　　88-34327
　　　　　　　　　　　　　　　　　　　　　　　　　　CIP

⊗ The paper used in this publication meets the minimum
requirements of the American National Standard for
Information Sciences—Permanence of Paper for Printed
Library Materials, ANSI Z39.48-1984

Contents

Introduction

MARK R. BALTIN AND ANTHONY S. KROCH

The last few years have seen questions from various fronts about the nature of phrase structure, that grouping of the linguistic elements of a sentence that supports statements of distribution and interpretation. The view predominant in formal grammar at one time, the one in Chomsky (1957), was that phrase-markers were generated by context-free rewriting rules. This view required constituents to be continuous, with dominance and precedence relations complementary. For both empirical and formal reasons, much recent research has focused on revising this view and has had to confront two main questions: (i) What are the formal mechanisms that generate the infinite set of phrase-markers in natural language? (ii) What properties are required of empirically adequate structured representations? The answers to these questions are, of course, interdependent, in that the properties of a given mechanism for generating phrase-markers will restrict the set of possible representations. Thus, although context-free rewriting rules require continuous constituents, other mechanisms, like McCawley's (1968, 1982a) node-admissibility conditions, allow for discontinuous ones.

A number of proposals have been made concerning the properties of phrase-markers and the nature of the mechanisms that generate them. For instance, a resurgence of interest in Categorial Grammar, proposed originally by Ajdukiewicz (1937), has taken place. In this formalism, the traditional proliferation of categories—noun, verb, adjective, preposition, determiner, etc.—gives way to the postulation of a small set of atomic categories, with the others defined by the composition of these basic categories. Categorial Grammar competes with X-bar theories of phrase structure, currently more standard. Another issue in discussions of phrase structure is the degree of specification of the phrase-structure component. Some theories of grammar, most notably Generalized Phrase-Structure Grammar (Gazdar et al. 1985) and Lexical-Functional Grammar (Bresnan 1982a), rely on relatively detailed specifications of phrase-structure rules, while other theories, such as Government-Binding (GB) theory (Chomsky

1981), rely on a general phrase-structure schema and supplant the specification of phrase structure rules with an interaction of constraints from a number of distinct modules of grammar.

Finally, yet another question about phrase structure in current grammatical theory is the extent to which it is possible to utilize that mechanism universally to mediate syntactic and semantic representations. This question is posed as the distinction between configurational and nonconfigurational languages (Hale 1983). In other words, the claim has been made that some languages may lack articulated phrase structure.

Given these and many other questions surrounding the study of phrase structure, it is not surprising that the field of formal grammar contains so many proposals about its nature. And at some point it will be necessary for detailed and critical comparison of these approaches to be undertaken. As a first step toward facilitating this comparison, and to encourage interaction among the proponents of distinct points of view, one of the editors of this volume (Baltin) organized a conference entitled Alternative Conceptions of Phrase Structure at New York University in July 1986. The papers in this volume grew out of that conference.

Mark Baltin's paper provides evidence that syntactic selection is a relationship between heads, rather than between heads and maximal projections. Given the currently received view of phrase-markers as being direct reflections of phrase-structure rules, the paper then argues that, in the unmarked case, heads do not appear exhaustively dominated by higher projections and provides an argument for this view based on the distribution of verbal particles.

In their paper, Ronald Kaplan and Annie Zaenen argue, on the basis of data from Icelandic, that the well-known difference in acceptability between long-distance extraction from arguments and from adjuncts cannot be captured by assigning different phrase-structure contexts to the two kinds of phrase. Instead they propose an analysis of long-distance dependencies within the framework of Lexical-Functional Grammar (LFG) in which the constraints on extraction are stated at the level of functional structure. To formalize this analysis they extend LFG to include a mechanism for handling unbounded uncertainty concerning the role of the preposed elements in predicate-argument structure.

Lauri Karttunen's paper is one of two in this volume (the other is Mark Steedman's) that explore the use of extended versions of Categorial Grammar for linguistic analysis. The paper argues that a marriage of the categorial formalism with the unification operation allows a categorial treatment of long-distance dependencies that does not require type-raising or function composition. The formalism is applied to the treatment of certain long-distance dependencies in Finnish that seem to involve scrambling across clause boundaries.

The paper by Anthony Kroch is an extension of his earlier work on capturing subjacency effects in a Tree-Adjoining Grammar (TAG). That work showed subjacency to be a theorem of TAG when reasonable assumptions were made about the character of the theory's elementary structures. The present discussion extends this analysis to certain well-known exceptions to subjacency, in particular, the acceptability of certain extractions from NP and from indirect questions. Kroch argues that, given a version of the Empty Category Principle and a proper treatment of the distinction between complements and adjuncts, the pattern of exceptions to subjacency found in English and other languages is derivable in a TAG without further stipulation.

The paper by Alec Marantz presents, from a GB perspective, an organization of phrase structure motivated by the behavior of clitics. As is well known, clitics do not respect X-bar phrase-structure organization in their phonological dependencies, often attaching across phrasal boundaries. To account for this behavior without special stipulations, Marantz proposes to do away with phrase-structure rules and to eliminate linear order from D- and S-structure syntactic representations. Hierarchical organization is to be imposed on syntactic structure by an extended version of Chomsky's Projection Principle, and linear order by the mapping from S-structure to the level of structure (often called "surface structure") that serves as the input to phonological interpretation.

James McCawley's paper deals with a number of cases in English and Japanese syntax that seem to necessitate relaxation of the requirement that all the elements within an apparently single sentence must be connected to the same root node in the phrase-marker and must have unique mothers.

Ivan Sag and Carl Pollard's paper deals with the appropriate treatment of subcategorization within the framework of Head-driven Phrase-Structure Grammar, developed originally by Pollard (1984) and developed further in Pollard and Sag (forthcoming).

Mamoru Saito develops further the view expressed in Saito (1985) that the apparently free word order exhibited by Japanese is not due to Japanese being a nonconfigurational language as proposed, for example, by Farmer (1980), but rather is due to the ability of Japanese to tolerate multiple adjunctions to S. He distinguishes the insensitivity of Logical Form to the effects of these adjunctions in Japanese, as opposed to English, by positing a distinction between D-positions, in which an NP can appear and be licensed as a nonoperator, and non-D-positions, in which D-structure NPs cannot appear and be licensed as nonoperators.

Mark Steedman's paper, the only one in this collection that does not derive from a presentation at the New York University conference, revises and extends earlier work of his on capturing the grammar of coordination in a Categorial Grammar. In particular, Steedman shows how the approach can be made to handle gapping in verb-medial (SVO) languages like English, as well as in verb-initial and verb-final languages. By adding the operations of functional composition and type-raising to standard Categorial Grammar's function application, Steedman is able to provide derivations for so-called nonconstituent as well as simple constituent coordination. A consequence of this approach is that the grammar gives a quite nonstandard account of surface constituent structure.

Tim Stowell explores the implications of a view of syntactic categories and semantic types that places them in a one-to-one correspondence. In particular, he proposes that referential nominal phrases are actually DPs, headed by determiners, as proposed by Abney (1986), while predicative nominal phrases are NPs.

Lisa Travis's paper argues that the traditional X-bar parameter of head-initial versus head-final is too coarse to capture all the word-order regularities found in the world's natural languages and proposes that this parameter can be overridden by parameters specifying the directionality of Case assignment and θ-role assignment. Her analysis is based on past and present stages of Chinese and Kpelle.

Edwin Williams argues that, despite important parallelisms between morphology and syntax, there is a deep distinction between the two which prevents a theoretical unification of the two domains. The similarities include (1) the use of rules of formation based on concatenation, (2) crucial reference to distinguished elements called "heads," and (3) a common notion of argument structure. According to Williams, the domains differ, however, in that morphology lacks the notion "maximal projection," and from this difference Williams derives the absence of case-marking, predication, reference, and opacity in morphological domains.

We would like to thank several people who helped us to bring this project to fruition. We first thank the National Science Foundation, in particular its grants officer for linguistics, Dr. Paul Chapin, for funding the original conference of which the present volume is an outgrowth, through grant #BNS-8607743 to New York University. In addition, Terry Langendoen, in his capacity as director of the 1986 Linguistic Institute held at the Graduate Center, City University of New York, graciously allowed us to capitalize on the success of his Institute in order to publicize the conference.

The NYU Faculty of Arts and Sciences, in particular Dean C. Duncan Rice, provided generous support for the conference, and the secretarial staff of the NYU Linguistics Department, especially Elana Oberlander, proved to be invaluable. Roberta Baltin provided sage advice and much more, helping with virtually every aspect of the conference and the manuscript of this book, and deserves special thanks.

1

Heads and Projections

MARK R. BALTIN

In this paper I propose a new conception of the principles governing the construction of phrase-markers and a reinterpretation of the principles of X-bar theory, a reinterpretation which, I believe, unifies a number of facts about subcategorization (or categorial selection, as it were) and constraints on grammar that ultimately depend upon subcategorization, such as the Empty Category Principle of Chomsky's (1981) Government-Binding theory.

In particular, I argue that subcategorization is always for a lexical category, and that principles of X-bar theory determine the way phrases can be projected from lexical categories, but that no superfluous nonbranching structure occurs in a phrase-marker. Therefore, the structure of (1) would be (2) rather than (3), but the structure of (4) would be (5).

(1) *Birds eat.*

(2) $[_{C'} [_{I'} [_N \textit{birds}][_I][_V \textit{eat}]]]$

(3) $[_{C'} [_{I'} [_{N''} [_{N'} [_N \textit{birds}]]][_I][_{V'} [_V \textit{eat}]]]]$

(4) *The birds eat the worms.*

(5) $[_{C'} [_C \textit{that}][_{I'} [_{N''} \text{Det } \textit{the}][_{N'} [_N \textit{birds}]]][_I][_{V'} [_V \textit{eat}][_{N''} [\text{Det } \textit{the}] [_{N'} [_N \textit{worms}]]]]]$

I further assume, following Stowell (1981), that Comp is the head of S′ and that Infl is the head of S, so that, in Chomsky's (1986) terminology, S′ = CP and S = IP.[1]

Heny (1979), in reviewing Chomsky 1975, made a very insightful point in noting that the phrase-structure (PS) component of most work in generative grammar up to that point seemed otiose, in that it specified structures that also needed to be specified anyway in particular lexical entries. For instance, a PS rule such as (6) collapses such rules as (7)–(17).

I would like to thank Ed Batistella, Noam Chomsky, Tony Kroch, and Tom Wasow for their helpful comments.

1

(6) VP → V (NP) $\left\{\begin{array}{l} S' \\ NP \\ VP \\ AP \\ PP \end{array}\right\}$

(7) VP → V
(8) VP → V NP
(9) VP → V NP S'
(10) VP → V S'
(11) VP → V NP NP
(12) VP → V NP VP
(13) VP → V VP
(14) VP → V NP AP
(15) VP → V AP
(16) VP → V NP PP
(17) VP → V PP

However, the eleven subcategorization frames collapsed into rule (6) still need to be individually specified in the subcategorization frames of individual verbs in the lexicon, so that we still need such lexical entries as the following:

(18) *elapse*, V, +[____#]
(19) *like*, V, +[____NP]
(20) *persuade*, V, +[____NP S']
(21) *give*, V, +[____NP NP]
(22) *see*, V, +[____NP VP]
(23) *begin*, V, +[____VP]
(24) *call*, V, +[____NP AP]
(25) *grow*, V, +[____AP]
(26) *complain*, V, +[____S']
(27) *put*, V, +[____NP PP]
(28) *talk*, V, +[____PP]

Thus, the PS rules in (7)–(17) are completely redundant, since the individual subcategorization frames must be specified anyway. Two different tacks have been taken in response to Heny's observation. One, that of Chomsky (1981) and Stowell (1981), has been to completely eliminate PS rules (except for the expansion of S), in favor of the individual subcategorization frames, which, together with principles of X-bar theory and Case assignment, will do the work of an elaborated PS component.

The second, that of Generalized Phrase-Structure Grammar (Gazdar et al. 1985), has been to introduce the subcategorization frames individually, together with an identifying number on the subcategorizing element to re-flect which subcategorization frame is the appropriate one for that element. In this case we have such rules as (29)–(31), and such lexical entries as (32)–(34).

(29) VP → H[1]
(30) VP → H[2], NP
(31) VP → H[3], NP, PP
(32) *elapse*, V[1]
(33) *put*, V[3]

Generalized Phrase-Structure Grammar relies on elaborate feature-transmission mechanisms to pass features up and down the tree, so that these mechanisms will ensure identity of categorial features between the mother in a phrase-structure rule and the head.

1. Selection

Both Government-Binding theory and Generalized Phrase-Structure Gram-mar thus rely essentially on subcategorization frames to provide the input to the construction of phrase-markers for individual sentences. Every the-ory of X-bar syntax with which I am familiar also employs the following generalization:

(34) Only maximal projections can appear in complement position.

Thus, we will never find a verb that can take only a bare lexical noun as object, but not a noun plus modifiers, so that such patterns of acceptability as the following are never found:

(35) *John glorped books.*
(36) **John glorped his books.*

For the most part, subcategorizational domains must respect sisterhood, so that the subcategorized element must be a sister to the subcategorizer (Chomsky 1965). Bresnan (1970), in discussing the intricacies of comple-mentizer selection, noted that the choice of complementizer in a sentential complement often depends on the matrix predicate, so that some predicates permit only a *that*-complementizer, some only a *for–to* complementizer, and some a null complementizer. Examples are the following:

(37) *John declared* { *that Sally was insane.*}
                   {**for Sally to be insane.*}
(38) *I was waiting* {**that Sally left.*}
                   { *for Sally to leave.*}

Bresnan's proposal involved subcategorization for particular complementizers, so that the verbs *declare* and *wait* would have the following subcategorization frames:

(39) *declare*, V, +[_____ [$_{S'}$ [$_{Comp}$ *that*]]
(40) *wait*, V, +[_____ [$_{S'}$ [$_{Comp}$ *for–to*]]

As Bresnan notes, her proposal entails that the theory of subcategorization must be weakened to allow subcategorization of nonsisters, so that the subcategorization frames in (39)–(40) are "arboreal," in Postal's (1976) terms. However, assuming that subcategorization of nonsisters is necessary in the cases discussed by Bresnan, we still do not find unlimited subcategorization of nonsisters, so that we find no instances of, for instance, verbs that take NP objects but require a particular determiner in the NP.

The point is highlighted by an observation about the set of syntactic features in Gazdar et al. 1985, which treats selectional phenomena in great detail. They include such features as PFORM, VFORM, and NFORM, but have no features such as DETFORM.

I therefore propose the following generalization:

(41) Subcategorization is for either a maximal projection or a head.

As it stands, however, (41) is simply a descriptive generalization, something to be explained. I would like to propose a mechanism for subcategorization, and therefore, for the reasons noted above, for the construction of phrase-markers, which entails (41). The principle of subcategorization that I propose is as follows:

(42) Subcategorization is always for a head.

I would also like to amend (34), the statement that only maximal projections can appear as complements, to (43):

(43) Wherever a head can appear, its maximal projection can appear.

These principles will account for many of the restrictions on head movement noted in Chomsky 1986. I am proposing that the principles of X-bar theory operate in a "bottom-up" fashion reminiscent of Categorial Grammars (but not totally bottom-up, as we shall see). In a sense, our claim is that, apart from marked statements in grammars for exocentric constructions, in the sense of Bloomfield (1933), maximal projections only appear as the fullest "adornments" of their heads. Therefore, instead of viewing X-bar principles as (44), we can view them as (45):

(44) a. $X'' \rightarrow$ Spec X'
    b. $X' \rightarrow X\ Y_{max}$

(45) a. X + Y = X'
    b. Spec + X' = X''

Note that, in (45), I am not stating that Y is Y_{max}, since that is predictable from (43). Therefore, the subcategorization frames for *wait* and *declare* will be, instead of (39) and (40), (46) and (47).

(46) *declare*, V, +[___ [$_C$ *that*]]
(47) *wait*, V, +[___ [$_C$ *for*]]

Now, complementizers are all "transitive," so that they each take I as a complement, so that the lexical entries for the complementizers are (48) and (49):

(48) *that*, C, +[___ [$_I$ + fin]]
(49) *for*, C, +[___ [$_I$ − fin]]

The various realizations of I would have the lexical entries in (50) and (51):

(50) *Tense*, I, +[N___V]
(51) *Will*, I, +[N___V]

The proposed mechanism for c-selection makes a striking prediction that is confirmed. In this system, the tense of a clausal complement is not directly selected by a matrix predicate; rather, the complementizer is directly selected by the matrix predicate, and it is the complementizer that selects the tense of its own complement. Therefore, if we find a complementizer that cooccurs with both finite and infinitival Ss, we predict that any predicate that selects said complementizer will not be able to require a particular finiteness value for the complement.

As Ed Battistella (pers. comm.) points out, an example of such a complementizer is the +*Wh* complementizer for questions in English. For example, both (52) and (53) are acceptable:

(52) *I don't know whether or not to work on that.*
(53) *I don't know whether or not I should work on that.*

In fact, the prediction is accurate. There are absolutely no matrix predicates in English that take embedded questions and restrict the finiteness value of the embedded question. Embedded questions can always be either finite or infinitival, and the proposed mechanism requires this, while a c-selection mechanism that directly selects the finiteness value of a clausal complement by a matrix predicate cannot explain this. Incidentally, we can provide an interesting generalization about major and minor lexical categories, based on the differences between such lexical entries as those of

(48)–(49) and (50)–(51), on the one hand, and subcategorization frames for nouns and verbs on the other. A MINOR LEXICAL CATEGORY is *a category all of whose members have the same subcategorization frame with respect to grammatical categories.* Another example of this generalization is provided by degree words in English (Baltin 1987), all of which have the following subcategorization frames:

(54) *so*, Q, +[____ [c *that*]]
(55) *too*, Q, +[____ [c *for*]]
(56) *enough*, Q, +[____C]

This notation receives some support from the phenomenon of idiomatization, assuming idiomatization to be a special case of subcategorization (Chomsky 1981; Marantz 1984). As noted by Marantz, there seem to be no clear cases of idioms consisting of the subject and verb, leaving the direct object free. This is explained if we view the subject as an "external argument" of the verb, in the sense of Williams (1981a, 1982, 1984). If we view idiomatization as a species of subcategorization, generalization (41) receives additional support by noting that the participants in the idiom always involve the head of a phrase and the head of one of its complements (examples: *make headway, keep track of, keep tabs on*).[2] A natural way to represent the above three idioms is as follows:

(57) *keep*, V, +[____ [N *track*][P *of*]]
(58) *keep*, V, +[____ [N *tabs*][P *on*]]
(59) *make*, V, [____ [N *headway*]]

Again, a striking fact about idioms is the nonexistence of idioms which consist of the main verb plus the determiner of a direct object, leaving the head noun of the direct object free. Given the mechanisms for subcategorization that I am proposing, such idioms would be impossible to store in the lexicon.

The identification of idiomatization with subcategorization leads to another confirmation of the view presented here, when we examine an interesting class of idioms first discussed, to my knowledge, by Langendoen (1970). Two idioms in English are the idioms *can afford to* and *can help but:*

(60) *John can afford to do that.*
(61) *John can't help but notice that.*

Substitution of the near-synonymous *be able to* for *can* leads to unacceptability:

(62) *John is able to afford to do that.
(63) *John isn't able to help but notice that.

We notice that the participants in these idioms are not superficial sisters, since *can*, a modal, is outside the VP, while the main verbs *afford* and *help but* are the heads of their respective VPs:

(64) $[_{C'} [_C][_{I'} [_N$ *John*$]][_I$ *can*$][_{V'} [_V$ *afford*$][_{C'}$ *to do that*$]]]]$

In this sense, the idioms *can afford to* and *can help but* are analogous to the idiom *make headway*, since in each case, the idiom consists of a head (*can, make*) followed by a complement (*help but, afford to, headway*). In this system, the subcategorization frames might look like this:

(65) *can*, I, $+[\underline{\quad} [_V$ *afford*$][_C$ *for*$]]$
(66) *can*, I, $+[\underline{\quad} [_V$ *help but*$][V]$
(67) *afford*, V, $+[\underline{\quad} [_C$ *for*$]]$
(68) *help but*, V, $+[\underline{\quad}V]$

Another consequence of principles (42) and (43) is that subcategorization for a gerund and, indeed, for any exocentric construction will be impossible. Stowell (1981) originally noted that no predicate subcategorizes for a gerund and provided an account in terms of the feature decomposition of categories. Therefore, we find no pattern such as the following, where *gok* is a nonsense verb:

(69) *Bill goks* { *John's working on that.*}
              {**John's work.*}

If we can only subcategorize for a lexical category, and maximal projections are simply projections of their heads, then whatever lexical category might be taken to head a gerund will automatically project up to its normal X-bar endocentric construction. I assume that the grammar of English (or perhaps Universal Grammar) contains such marked rules as the following (Schachter 1976):

(70) $N'' = N \ V$

Given that wherever a head can appear, its maximal projection can appear, subcategorization for an N will permit an N'' to appear, and rule (70) will therefore permit a gerund to occur in the position of an N''.

2. Definition of Projection

Viewing subcategorization as obtaining between lexical categories allows us to provide a solution to a little-remarked problem concerning the difficulties involved in providing a formal characterization of the notion of a projection. Many constraints in grammar currently rely heavily on the notion of a maximal projection, but the algorithm for determining one node's being a maximal projection of another are woefully inadequate. An example of a constraint which makes use of this notion is Aoun and Sportiche's (1983) definition of c-command, given in (71):

(71) *A* c-commands *B* iff *A* does not dominate *B* and *B* is contained within the first maximal projection dominating *A*.

A widely accepted constraint on anaphoric binding (Chomsky 1981) requires that an antecedent must c-command an anaphor in order to bind it. With this in mind, consider cases such as (72), discussed by Aoun and Sportiche:

(72) * *their mother's pictures of each other*

Such NPs would have the structure shown in (73):

(73)

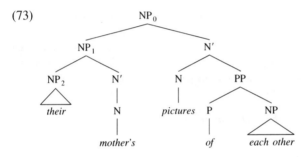

Because the first maximal projection dominating NP_2 is NP_1, and NP_1 does not dominate the reciprocal phrase, bound anaphora between *their* and *each other* is ruled out in (73).

The problem lies in establishing a formal algorithm to ensure that NP_1 is taken to be the maximal projection of NP_2, and not NP_0. Given that Government-Binding theory and Generalized Phrase-Structure Grammar are essentially configurational theories, the notions employed in grammatical processes and representations should be deducible from phrase-marker configurations (recall the discussion in Chomsky 1965 about configurational definitions of grammatical relations). One might view the notion of a projection in a manner akin to the way in which such theories as Lexical-Functional Grammar and Relational Grammar view grammatical relations, as primitives; but while these theories view grammatical relations as primitives, the system in which they are employed is articulated to a much greater degree.

Therefore, let us continue the quest for an algorithm to determine when one element is a projection of another. One proposal for such an algorithm is that of Gazdar et al. (1985: ex. (3.18)):

(74) In a rule of the form: $\{\langle N, a\rangle, \langle V, b\rangle, \langle BAR, n\rangle\}, \ldots$
where $n <$ or $= m$ (sometimes: $n < m$),
$\{\langle N, a\rangle, \langle V, b\rangle, \langle BAR, n\rangle\}$ is the head of $\{\langle N, a\rangle, \langle V, b\rangle, \langle BAR, m\rangle\}$

In essence, the algorithm provided in (74) states that, when node A dominates node B, and nodes A and B are identical with respect to categorial features, and node B has the same number of bars as A or fewer, take node B to be the head of node A.

Clearly, this algorithm will not, by itself, pick out the correct head of NP_0 in a genitive construction, as in (73), nor will it pick out the correct head in cases where a verb takes a VP complement, as in the verbs of temporal aspect (Baltin 1982, 1985; Emonds 1985). An example is (75), with the structure in (76):

(75) *John began eating steak.*
(76) $[_{CP} [_C][_{IP} [_N John][_{VP} [_V began][_{VP} eating steak]]$

One solution would require that the head of a projection be one level lower in bar level than the projection, dropping the equals signs in (74), but this requirement seems too strong, in light of Vergnaud's (1974) convincing arguments for the structure (77) for relative clauses:

(77) $[_{NP} [_{NP} the man][_{S'} who saw Sally]]$

For such structures as relative clauses, we wish to claim that the innermost NP is the head of the NP immediately dominating it.

We might revise (74) along lines suggested by Tony Kroch (pers. comm.), who proposes that the head of a projection be that node which the projection immediately dominates which is identical to the projection in terms of categorial features, and which has the lower integer for bar level when there are two such nodes. Thus, since the lexical category V is really V_0, having fewer bar levels than VP, which is either V_2 or V_1 (depending on one's theory), the V in (76) will be taken to head the outermost VP. Similar considerations will hold in (73) to make the N' immediately dominated by NP_0 into the head of NP_0, rather than making NP_1 the head of NP_0.

This revision will fail for such exocentric constructions as the ones generated by rule (70), however. Let us therefore adopt a mechanism originally suggested by Rouveret and Vergnaud (1980), to register satisfaction of the head–complement relation. Suppose we adopt a convention whereby a head will index each of its complements. Since we are assuming that sub-categorization is for lexical categories, the lexical category which is a complement will receive the head's index, and any elaboration of the lexical category complement will copy the lexical category's index, along with categorial features, onto its projection. Therefore, in a sentence such as (78), the mechanism will work as follows:

(78) *I saw John's picture of Sally.*

The lexical entry for *see* is (79):

(79) *see*, V, +[____N]

The pre–D-structure representation of (78) will be (80):

(80) $[_{CP} [_C] [_{IP} [_N I] [_I] [_{VP} [_V see^i] [_{N^i} picture]$

Since the noun *picture* can itself take a complement, having the lexical entry in (81), an N′ will be built up in accordance with rule (45):

(81) *picture*, N, +[____ ($[_P of]$)

(82) $[_{CP} [_C] [_{IP} [_N I] [_I] [_{VP} [_V see^i] [_{N'_i} [_{N_i} picture] [_{P_i} of]$

Since *of* is transitive, having the lexical entry in (83), the next representation will be (84):

(83) *of*, P, ____N

(84) $[_{CP} [_C] [_{IP} [_N I] [_I] [_{VP} [see^i] [_{N^{'i}} [_{N^i} picture] [_{P^{'i}} [_{P^i} of] [_{N^i} Sally]]]]]]$

Finally, by rule (45b), we will arrive at (85):

(85) $[_{CP} [_C] [_{IP} [_N I] [_I] [_{VP} [_V see^i] [_{N^{''i}} [_N John] [_{N^{'i}} [_{N^i} picture] [_{P^{'i}} [_{P^i} of]$
     $[_{N^i} Sally]]]]]]]$

We are now in a position to reconstruct heads and projections from a phrase-marker:

(86) Node *A* is a projection of node *B* iff they are identical wrt categorial features and argument index.

Since a genitive NP, being a specifier, will not receive an argument index from the lexical category which is the original head, it will not bear the same argument index as the NP which immediately dominates it, and hence the dominating NP will not be a projection of the genitive NP, by (86).

Thus, the mechanisms proposed in this paper for subcategorization receive a natural extension in providing for a configurational reconstruction of the notions HEAD and PROJECTION.

3. Proper Government

The mechanisms provided in this paper for marking satisfaction of sub-categorization domains will account for another apparent disjunction in a theoretical principle found within the theory of government and binding. Lasnik and Saito (1984, ex. (22)) state their version of Chomsky's (1981) Empty Category Principle as follows:

(87) A nonpronominal empty category must be properly governed.

Proper government and government are defined as (88) and (89); antecedent-government is defined as (90) (Lasnik & Saito 1984, exx. (23), (24), (55)):

(88) α properly governs β if α governs β and
    a. α is a lexical category X^0 (lexical government)
  or b. α is coindexed with β (antecedent government)
(89) α governs β if every maximal projection dominating α also dominates β and conversely.
(90) α antecedent-governs β if
    a. α and β are coindexed
    b. α c-commands β
    c. there is no γ (γ an NP or S$'$) such that α c-commands γ and γ dominates β, unless β is the head of γ

It has frequently been remarked that the Empty Category Principle, as stated above, is not a single principle but really two principles, requiring that a trace be either lexically governed or antecedent-governed. Obviously, it would be desirable to try to unify these two cases of proper government.

The clue to unification comes from the proviso in (90c), *unless β is the head of γ*. We again note that NPs and Ss, maximal projections, are barriers to proper government, with the same special designated position, the head, that was a distinguished position with respect to subcategorization domains. By the mechanism proposed above for assignment of argument indices to heads, we can formulate the ECP as (91):

(91) A trace must bear the same argument index as its antecedent.

Lexical government is commonly taken to be not a purely structural relationship, but rather government by a head of its complements. Chomsky (1986) builds the requirement of θ-role assignment into the definition of proper government and takes θ-role assignment to be a consequence of subcategorization. Therefore, the mechanisms proposed in this paper for

subcategorization will automatically supply the same argument index to
the head and its maximal projection, for the reasons discussed in connection with (73), and so heads and their maximal projections form a natural
class.

4. Government

Belletti and Rizzi (1981) discuss an extremely interesting distribution of
quantified Ns in Italian and propose the following definition of government
(their ex. (10)):

(92) α governs γ in a configuration like $[_B \ldots \gamma \ldots \alpha \ldots \gamma \ldots]$
       where: (i) $\alpha = X^0$ (= a lexical element)
               (ii) where ϕ is a maximal projection, if ϕ dominates γ,
       then either ϕ dominates α, or ϕ is the maximal projection of γ.
               (iii) α c-commands γ.

Note that the same disjunction discussed above (maximal projection and
head) appears in (92ii), when one views maximal projections as barriers
to government, except when the head is the position that one wishes to
govern. This emendation of Chomsky's (1981) definition of government is
motivated by the requirement in that work that PRO appear in ungoverned
positions, together with an analysis of the distribution of superficially
headless Ns in Italian. The distribution is exemplified below (Belletti &
Rizzi 1981, exx. (Ib), (Ib), (12)):

(93)   Tre ____ passano rapidamente. (Three ____ pass rapidly.)
(94)   *Gianni trascorrera tre ____ a Milano.
       G. will spend three ____ in Milano.
(95)   (Di libri) [TOP [NP Tre PRO]], credo che li leggero domani.
       (Of books) Three, I think I them will read tomorrow.

In Italian, according to Belletti and Rizzi, NPs consisting of bare quantifiers (i.e. superficially headless) appear in subject position and left-
dislocated position, but not in object position. Assuming X-bar theory, a
lexically empty head N must be posited within these NPs, and Belletti and
Rizzi assimilate this lexically empty head N to the element PRO. By viewing the subject position and left-dislocated position as ungoverned, but the
object position as governed (by V), the distribution of this empty head N is
accounted for. However, we must assume that the head position is susceptible to government from a source external to the maximal projection.
Hence, the disjunction of maximal projection and head.

The mechanisms for co-superscripting heads and complements advocated in §2 will register the government relation along the lines suggested in the previous section, if we define government in the following fashion:

(96) A governs B if B is contained within the first maximal projection dominating A, and A and B bear the same argument index.

5. Particle Movement

In this section I discuss the formulation of the phenomenon known in generative grammar as particle movement (Emonds 1972; Fraser 1965) and demonstrate that the conception of phrase structure advanced in this paper leads to a natural account of the process. The verb–particle construction in English is exemplified in the following sentence pair:

(97) a. *I picked the ball up.*
      b. *I picked up the ball.*

Following Emonds (1972), I assume that the grammar of English does not contain a separate category of verbal particles. The elements termed verbal particles are actually intransitive prepositions. Furthermore, (97a) is closer to the underlying representation, which would be as in (98):

(98)

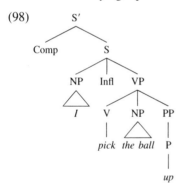

The rule of particle movement would then be formulated as in (99):

(99) NP–P
      1–2 > 2–1

The rule fits Emonds' (1976, ex. (I.5)) criterion for a LOCAL TRANS-FORMATION:

(100) A transformation or a transformational operation that affects only an input sequence of a single nonphrase node C and of one adjacent constituent C' that is specified without a variable, such that

> the operation is not subject to any condition exterior to C and C',
> is called a "local transformation."

It will be noted that the two constituents mentioned in a local transformation need not be sisters. However, the definition of local transformation given above will not rule out movement of a preposition that takes an underlying complement, and yet such an application of rule (99) is impermissible. An example is the contrast in (101) vs. (102):

(101) a. *I put my coat on.*
      b. *I put on my coat.*
(102) a. *I put my coat on the table.*
      b. **I put on my coat the table.*

I would like to propose a slightly different analysis of particle movement, in which no movement occurs at all. In line with Stowell (1981), let us assume that phrase-structure rules, which specify linear order and hierarchical relations simultaneously, do not exist, but rather that whatever ordering restrictions exist are due to independent principles of grammar. Therefore, a lexical entry for the so-called verb–particle verbs, such as *put,* will be as follows:

(103) *put,* V, +[____ N P]

We can further assume a Case Filter (Chomsky 1980; Rouveret & Vergnaud 1980) along the following lines:

(104) *N, if N is lexical and does not receive Case.

The standard view is that Infl assigns nominative case, verbs assign accusative case, and prepositions assign oblique case (perhaps a syncretism has occurred in Modern English, so that the distinction between accusative and oblique case has been merged, as suggested by Richard Kayne (1981b)). In this view (Chomsky 1981), Case assignment takes place under government. Recall that under the government relation, *A* and *B* govern one another when they are both dominated by the same maximal projections. Furthermore, Stowell (1981) argues that in English (but not in such languages as Italian), an adjacency requirement for Case assignment holds, such that the Case assigner and the Case assignee must be adjacent.

These assumptions, together with the view advanced in this paper that maximal projections only occur in phrase-markers when their heads are fully modified, permits us to take a rather different view of the verb–particle construction. Since P is a Case assigner, nothing forces it to appear after the direct object within the VP. It can appear between the verb and the object, since the P can assign Case to the object. Therefore, one could not view either (101a) or (101b) as basic while the other is derived.

Note that this view of the verb–particle alternation requires that the intransitive preposition not be dominated by the PP node. If it were, as in (105), the PP node would block government of the N by the preposition.

(105) $[_S [_N I] [_{VP} [_V put] [_{PP} [_P on]] [_{NP} my coat]]$

We therefore have an explanation for the requirement that one of the elements be nonphrasal. Sentences such as (106) or (107) are unacceptable because of the Case Filter:

(106) *I sent right up a wrench.
(107) *I put on the table a book.

The unacceptable (102b), problematic for the local transformation account, is handled without further ado under this proposal. No movement takes place under the view of free generation. However, heads and complements will be generated as constituents by the mechanisms proposed here. Therefore, (102b) could never be generated.

One might rule out (102b) by imposing a further requirement on local transformations, to the effect that all the elements affected must be sisters. This requirement, as pointed out by Tony Kroch (pers. comm.), will still require the view advanced in this paper that a head that is unmodified will not be dominated by a maximal projection in the phrase-marker.

6. Conclusion

In this paper I have tried to provide a mechanism to eliminate the disjunctive statement "maximal projection and head" which has appeared, albeit in disguised form, in various theories of grammar. Ross (1969), in discussing the analysis of the English auxiliary, noted that the disjunctive curly bracket notation essentially surrendered the idea of finding a property that the elements within the braces shared, so that the braces essentially allowed one to list elements without finding a generalization. Ross's objection to disjunctions is no less applicable to other uses of the brace notation, in the statement of the functioning of more general principles of grammar than those governing the distribution of the English auxiliary.

NOTES

1. In a recent paper, Abney (1986) has argued that determiners within NP, rather than being specifiers, are actually the heads, so that what has traditionally

been called NP should really be viewed as DP. Part of Abney's claim is based on an assumed parallelism between determiners, complementizers, and inflectional elements. Since complementizers and inflectional elements are in fact selected by category-external sources, but determiners are not, I reject the claim of parallelism and continue to analyze determiners as specifiers.

2. Tom Wasow (pers. comm.) claims that Subject–Verb–Object constructions do exist in which the subject and verb are idiomatic while the object is free; he cites such examples as *Heaven help us* and *The Devil take you*. However, these examples have a jussive interpretation (to borrow a term from Latin grammar) and are extremely frozen in form. Therefore, I would be inclined to view Wasow's examples as examples of what Jespersen (1924) termed FORMULAS, rather than free expressions.

2

Long-Distance Dependencies, Constituent Structure, and Functional Uncertainty

RONALD M. KAPLAN AND ANNIE ZAENEN

Tree representations are used in generative grammar to represent several very different types of information. Whereas in structuralist practice (at least as reconstructed by early transformationalists), phrase-structure markers were used to represent surface cooccurrence patterns, transformational grammar extended their use to more abstract underlying structures, where they represent, for example, "grammatical relations." The claim embodied in this extension is that the primitives of a tree representation, namely linear order, dominance (but not multi-dominance) relations, and syntactic category labels, are adequate to represent several types of information that seem quite dissimilar in nature. They have been used, for example, to represent the dependencies between predicates and arguments needed for semantic interpretation, and also the organization of phrases that supports phonological interpretation.

Lexical-Functional Grammar (LFG), like Relational Grammar, rejects this claim[1] and proposes to represent information about predicate argument dependencies in structures that allow multi-dominance and ignore linear order. Moreover, these frameworks claim that the primitives in these representations are not categories like Noun or Sentence. Rather they are of a different nature that approximates the more traditional functional notions of Subject, Object, etc. In a certain sense LFG formalizes a more traditional approach than the one found in transformational grammar. The use of tree representations, called constituent structures (c-structures) in LFG, is restricted to the surface structure, which is assumed to be the input to the

Joan Bresnan, Per-Kristian Halvorsen, Lauri Karttunen, and John Maxwell are thanked for comments on earlier versions of this paper; Joan Maling and Höskuldur Thráinsson for help with the Icelandic data; and the students of the Lexical-Functional Grammar course at Stanford University, winter 1987, and the participants of the conference for reactions to oral presentations.

17

phonological component; information about predicate–argument dependencies and the like is represented in the functional structure (f-structure).

Given this view of the use of phrase-structure representations, it is a bit of
an anomaly that the original formulation of LFG (Kaplan & Bresnan 1982)
used c-structures to state generalizations about so-called long-distance dependencies of the type illustrated in (1):

(1) *Who did Bill claim that Mary had seen?*

Most previous accounts of long-distance phenomena, done in generative
frameworks where no other explanatory devices are available, were stated in
phrase-structure terms. The early LFG proposals (Kaplan & Bresnan 1982;
Zaenen 1980, 1983) in effect incorporated and developed such c-structural
notions without seriously examining the assumptions underlying them. But
given that LFG makes a clear distinction between the functional and phrasal
properties of an utterance and encodes predicate–argument relations specifically in f-structure, this approach embodies the claim that these relations are not directly relevant to long-distance dependencies. This is a
surprising consequence of this approach, given that so many other syntactic phenomena are more sensitive to properties and relations of f-structure
than to those of c-structure. Indeed, a deeper investigation of long-distance
dependencies reveals that they too obey functional rather than phrase-
structure constraints. This motivates the revision to the LFG treatment of
long-distance dependencies that we propose in this paper. This treatment
depends on a new formal device for characterizing systematic uncertainties
in functional assignments.

The organization of the paper is as follows: in §1 we give an argument
based on data from Icelandic that functional notions are necessary to account for generalizations about islands in that language. In §2 we sketch
the mechanism of functional uncertainty that is needed to formalize these
generalizations (for a more extensive discussion of the mathematical and
computational aspects of this mechanism, see Kaplan and Maxwell 1988).
In §3 we show how the system handles some rather recalcitrant data from
English, and in §4 we discuss a case in which multi-dominance (or a similar many-to-one mechanism) is needed to get the right result.

1. The Relevance of Functional Information:
   Icelandic Island Constraints

It is well known that long-distance dependencies involving adjuncts are
more restricted than those involving arguments. To give an example from

English, we can contrast (1), where the initial *who* is interpreted as an argument of the predicate *see* within the sentential complement of *claim*, with (2):

(2) *Which picture did they all blush when they saw?*

In (1) the embedded *see*-clause is an argument of the matrix verb *claim*, whereas in (2) the embedded clause is an adjunct to the main proposition. This contrast cannot be accounted for simply in terms of node labels, because in both (1) and (2) S and/or S' appears in the "syntactic binding domain" (as defined in, for example Zaenen 1983). In English, it can plausibly be claimed that these sentences differ in the configurations in which the nodes appear, so that a c-structure account of the contrast is not implausible. A similar contrast in acceptability is found in Icelandic. In the Icelandic case, however, it can be shown that no difference in surface phrase-structure configuration can plausibly support an account of this kind of contrast.

To show this, we will first quickly summarize the arguments given for surface structure in Thráinsson (1986) and then consider how they bear on the issue of extraction out of sentences dominated by PPs. Thráinsson (1986)[2] shows that sentences with an auxiliary or a modal have a surface structure that is different from those that have no auxiliary or modal. The two types are illustrated in (3a) and (3b) respectively:

(3) a. *Hann mun stinga smjörinu í vasann.*
        he   will put   butter-the in pocket-the
        'He will put the butter in his pocket.'
     b. *Hann stingur smjörinu í vasann.*
        he   puts   butter-the in pocket-the.
        'He puts the butter in his pocket.'

A first place where the difference shows up is when a so-called wandering adverb is added to either of these sentences: whereas for (3a) there are only two possible positions for such an adverb, as illustrated in (4), for (3b) there are the additional possibilities illustrated in (5):

(4) a. *Hann mun **sjaldan** stinga smjörinu í vasann.*
        he   will seldom put   butter-the in pocket-the
        'He will seldom put the butter in his pocket.'
     b. **Hann mun stinga **sjaldan** smjörinu í vasann.*
        he   will put   seldom butter-the in pocket-the
     c. **Hann mun stinga smjörinu **sjaldan** í vasann.*
        he   will put   butter-the seldom in pocket-the

    d. *Hann mun stinga smjörinu í vasann*   **sjaldan.**
        he   will put   butter-the in pocket-the seldom
(5) a. *Hann stingur* **sjaldan** *smjörinu í vasann.*
        he   puts   seldom butter-the in pocket-the
        'He seldom puts the butter in his pocket.'
    b. *Hann stingur smjörinu* **sjaldan** *í vasann.*
        he   puts   butter-the seldom in pocket-the
    c. *Hann stingur smjörinu í vasann*   **sjaldan.**
        he   puts   butter-the in pocket-the seldom

This is not the only contrast between the two types of sentences; indefinite subjects and "floating" quantifiers show the same placement contrasts. We refer to Thráinsson (1986) for examples of these two latter phenomena.

Rather than proposing that these three types of elements are introduced by different rules in sentences with and without auxiliaries, Thráinsson proposes that it is the constituent structure of the clause that differs while the constraints on the distribution of the adverbs, indefinite subjects, and quantifiers remain the same. The generalization is that the adverbs, indefinite subjects, and quantifiers are daughters of S but can appear in any linear position. Thus they can be placed between each pair of their sister constituents (obeying the verb-second constraint, which prohibits them from coming between the first constituent of the S and the tensed verb). This will give the right results if we assume that the c-structure for sentences with an auxiliary is as in (6) whereas sentences without an auxiliary have the structure in (7):

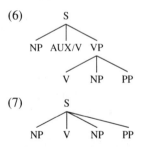

(6)

(7)

To be a bit more concrete, we propose to capture this insight in the following partial dominance and order constraints; these account for word order and adverb distribution in the sentences above:

(8) Dominance Constraints:
        S can immediately dominate {V, VP, NP, PP, Adv};
        VP can immediately dominate {V, VP, NP, PP};
        V is obligatory both in S and in VP.

(9) Ordering Constraints:
    for both S and VP: V < NP < PP < VP;
    for S: XP immediately precedes V[+tense] (verb-second con-
    straint).

These constraints (given here in partial and informal formulation), together
with LFG's coherence, completeness, and consistency requirements, provide the surface structures embodying the generalization proposed by
Thráinsson.

    Given this independently motivated difference in c-structure, let us now
return to the difference between arguments and adjuncts. Icelandic differs
from English in allowing Ss in PPs, as shown in (10)–(13):[3]

(10) *Hann fór   eftir að ég lauk   verkinu.*
    he   went after that I finished work-the
    'He left after I finished the work.'
(11) *Jón var að þvo golfið   eftir að María hafði skrifað bréfið.*
    John was at wash floor-the after that Mary had   written letter-the
    'John was washing the floor after Mary had written the letter.'
(12) *Þu vonaðist til að   hann fengi   bíl.*
    you hoped   for that he   will-get car
    'You hope that he will get a car.'
(13) *Jón var að hugsa um   að María hefði líklega   skrifað*
    John was at think about that Mary had   probably written
    bréfið.
    letter-the
    'John was thinking that Mary had probably written the letter.'

Sentences (10) and (11) illustrate cases in which the PP clause is an adjunct; (12) and (13) are examples in which the PP clause is an argument.
We will use these complex embedded structures because they allow a
straightforward illustration of the patterns of long-distance dependencies:
we find cases that exhibit the same local categorial configurations (PP over
S') but differ in their long-distance possibilities:

(14) **Hvaða verki fór   hann eftir að ég lauk?*
    which job   went he   after that I finished
    'Which job did he go after I finished?'
(15) **Þessi bréf var Jón að þvo golfið   eftir að María hafði*
    this letter was John at wash floor-the after that Mary had
    skrifað.
    written
    'This letter John was washing the floor after Mary had written.'

(16) *Hvaða bíl vonaðist þú til að hann fengi?*
      which car hoped   you for that he   will-get
      'Which car did you hope that he would get?'
(17) *Þessi bréf var Jón að hugsa um   að María hefði líklega*
      This letter was John at think about that Mary had   probably
      skrifað.
      written
      'This letter John was thinking that Mary had probably written.'

What these examples illustrate is that extractions are allowed from the
PP–S' configuration only when it is an argument; it forms a *wh-* island
when it functions as an adjunct.[4]

In defining the original c-structure formalization for long-distance dependencies, Kaplan and Bresnan (1982) noted that the correlation of extraction constraints with categorial configurations is far less than perfect.
They allowed bounding-node specifications in individual phrase-structure
rules to characterize the variations of long-distance dependency restrictions across languages and across different nodes of the same category in a
particular language. Indeed, the formal devices they introduced are sufficient to accurately describe these Icelandic facts: The argument and adjunct PPs can be introduced in separate phrase-structure expansions, with
only the PP receiving the ADJunct function assignment boxed as a bounding
node. But it is clear that the boxing device is used to import functional
distinctions into the c-structure. Looking back at the discussion in Kaplan
and Bresnan (1982), one realizes that it is always the case that when one
instance of a given category is boxed as a bounding node and another
is not, those instances also have different functional schemata attached
(ADJ vs. one of the oblique argument functions in the Icelandic example, or
the COMP vs. RELMOD functions that distinguish English *that*-complement
Ss from relative clauses). Kaplan and Bresnan, while realizing that extraction domains cannot be defined in terms of obvious natural classes of
c-structure categories or configurations, did not then recognize that natural
classes do exist at the functional level.

They actually considered but quickly rejected the possibility of defining
long-distance dependencies in terms of f-structure configurations, partly
because no rigorous functional formalization was at hand and partly because examples like (18) (their ex. (134)) seemed to indicate the long-
distance relevance of at least some categorial information that would not be
available in f-structure:

(18) a. *She'll grow that tall/*height.*
     b. *She'll reach that *tall/height.*

c. *The girl wondered how tall she would grow/*reach.*
d. *The girl wondered what height she would *grow/reach.*

These examples suggest that adjective phrases can only be extracted from AP positions and noun phrases only from NP positions, and, more generally, that fillers and gaps must have matching categories. Thus their theory ignored the apparently functional constraints on long-distance extractions and defined special formal mechanisms for encoding those constraints in c-structure terms. In this it remained similar to other structure-oriented theories of the day.

The Icelandic data given above, however, suggest that a more functional approach would capture the facts more directly. In §3, we show that the data in (18) can also be naturally analyzed in functional terms. In fact, constraints on extraction that in LFG terms are functional in nature have also been proposed by syntacticians working in a completely structure-oriented theory. The Icelandic data discussed above can be seen as a case of the Condition on Extraction Domain proposed in Huang (1982), which can be interpreted as an emerging functional perspective formulated in structural terms. It states:

(19) No element can be extracted from a domain that is not properly governed.

Intuitively the distinction between "governed" and "nongoverned" corresponds to the difference between "argument" and "nonargument." But it is clear from Thráinsson's arguments for the difference in structure between sentences with and without an auxiliary that the correct notion of government cannot be merely defined over c-structures. To represent the difference between the two types of PPs as in (20) would go against Thráinsson's generalization.

(20) a.

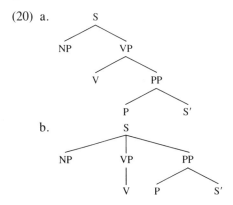

Indeed, adverb placement shows that both adjunct and argument PPs are sisters of S when there is no auxiliary, but are both in the VP when an auxiliary is present: [5]

(21)   *Ég vonaðist **alltaf** til að hann fengi   bíl.*
       I hoped   always for that he   will-get car
       'I always hoped that he would get a car.'
       *Ég hef **alltaf** vonast til að hann fengi   bíl.*
       I   have always hoped for that he   will-get car
       'I have always hoped that he would get a car.'
       * *Ég hef   vonast **alltaf** til að hann fengi   bíl.*
       I   have hoped always for that he   will-get car

(22)   *Hann fór   **alltaf** eftir að ég lauk   verkinu.*
       he   went always after that I finished work-the
       'He always went after I finished the work.'
       *Hann hefur **alltaf** farið eftir að ég lyk   verkinu.*
       he   has   always gone after that I finished work-the
       'He has always gone after I finished the work.'
       * *Hann hefur farið **alltaf** eftir að ég lyk   verkinu.*
       he   has   gone always after that I finished work-the

This pattern does not change when in the context of a long-distance dependency, as the following contrast illustrates:

(23) a. * *Hvaða verki fór   hann alltaf eftir að ég lauk?*
           which job   went he   always after that I finished
           'Which job did he always go after I finished?'
      b. *Hvaða bíl vonaðist þú alltaf til að hann fengi?*
           which car hoped   you always for that he   will-get
           'Which car did you always hope he would get?'

Thus in Icelandic the same c-structure configuration allows for extraction when the PP is an argument but not when the PP is an adjunct.[6] Netter (1987) draws a similar conclusion from data concerning extraposition of relative clauses in German. Given these facts, an adequate structurally based account will have to appeal to stages in a derivation and assume different tree structures for these sentences at the moment the relevant movement takes place. Whether this is feasible or not will depend on one's view of principles like cyclicity and the like, and we leave it to practitioners of structural approaches to elaborate these accounts. From our nonderivational perspective, the most straightforward approach seems also the most reasonable one: we will assume that long-distance dependencies are sensitive to functional information and investigate further how such constraints can be formulated in functional terms.[7]

2. The Formal Account: Functional Uncertainty

When we stand back from the details of particular constructions or particular languages, long-distance dependencies seem difficult to characterize because they involve rather loose and uncertain connections between the superficial properties of local regions of a string and its more abstract functional and predicate-argument relations. For many sentences this connection is very direct and unambiguous. If, for example, the first few words of an English sentence have the internal organization of an NP, it is often the case that those words also function as the subject of the sentence. Of course, there are uncertainties and ambiguities even in simple sentences: in a garden-path sentence such as (24), just exactly which words make up the initial NP is not clear from the local evidence alone, and the first words thus are compatible with two different functional configurations. This local ambiguity is resolved only when information about the later words is also taken into account.

(24) *The cherry blossoms in the spring.*

Local uncertainties of this sort have never seemed difficult to describe, since all grammatical theories admit alternative rules and lexical entries to account for all the local possibilities and provide some method of composition that may reject some of them on the basis of more global contextual information. What distinguishes the uncertainties in long-distance dependencies is that the superficial string properties local to, say, a fronted English topic are compatible with an unbounded number of within-clause functional or predicate-argument relations. The infinite set of possibilities cannot be specified in any finite number of alternatives in basic rules or lexical entries, and which of these possibilities is admissible depends on information that may be available arbitrarily far away in the string.

Structural approaches typically handle this kind of unbounded uncertainty through conspiracies of transformations that introduce empty nodes and prune other nodes and thereby destroy the simple connection between the surface and underlying tree structures. Our solution to the uncertainty problem is much more direct: we utilize a formal device that permits an infinite set of functionally constrained possibilities to be finitely specified in individual rules and lexical entries.

Kaplan and Bresnan (1982) observed that each of the possible underlying positions of an initial phrase could be specified in a simple equation locally associated with that phrase. In the topicalized sentence (25), the equation (in LFG notation) (↑ TOPIC) = (↑ OBJ) specifies that *Mary* is to be interpreted as the object of the predicate *telephoned*.

(25) *Mary John telephoned yesterday.*
(26) *Mary John claimed that Bill telephoned yesterday.*

In (26), the appropriate equation is (↑ TOPIC) = (↑ COMP OBJ), indicating that *Mary* is still the object of *telephoned*, which because of subsequent words in the string is itself the complement (indicated by the function name COMP) of the top-level predicate *claim*. The sentence can obviously be extended by introducing additional complement predicates (*Mary John claimed that Bill said that . . . that Henry telephoned yesterday*), for each of which some equation of the general form (↑ TOPIC) = (↑ COMP COMP . . . OBJ) would be appropriate. The problem, of course, is that this is an infinite family of equations, and hence impossible to enumerate in a finite disjunction appearing on a particular rule of grammar. For this technical reason, Kaplan and Bresnan abandoned the possibility of specifying unbounded uncertainty directly in functional terms.

Instead of formulating uncertainty by an explicit disjunctive enumeration, however, a formal specification can be provided that characterizes the family of equations as a whole. A characterization of a family of equations may be finitely represented in a grammar even though the family itself has an infinite number of members. This can be accomplished by a simple extension of the elementary descriptive device in LFG, the functional-application expression. In the original formalism, function-application expressions were given the following interpretation:

(27) $(f s) = v$ holds if and only if f is an f-structure, s is a symbol, and the pair $\langle s, v \rangle \in f$.

This notation was straightforwardly extended to allow for strings of symbols, as illustrated in expressions such as (↑ COMP OBJ) above. If $x = sy$ is a string composed of an initial symbol s followed by a (possibly empty) suffix string y, then

(28) $(f x) \equiv ((f s) y)$
$(f \varepsilon) \equiv f$, where ε is the empty string.

The crucial extension to handle unbounded uncertainty is to allow the argument position in these expressions to denote a set of strings. The interpretation of expressions involving sets of strings is derived in the following way from the interpretation (28) for individual strings. Suppose α is a (possibly infinite) set of strings. Then we say

(29) $(f\,\alpha) = v$ holds if and only if $((f\,s)\ \text{Suff}(s,\ \alpha)) = v$ for some symbol
       s, where $\text{Suff}(s,\ \alpha)$ is the set of suffix strings y such that $sy \in \alpha$.

In effect, an equation with a string-set argument holds if it would hold for a string in the set that results from a sequence of left-to-right symbol choices. For the case in which α is a finite set, this formulation is equivalent to a finite disjunction of equations over the strings in α. Passing from finite disjunction to existential quantification captures the intuition that unbounded uncertainties involve an underspecification of exactly which choice of strings in α will be compatible with the functional information carried by the surrounding surface environment.

We of course impose the requirement that the membership of α be characterized in finite specifications. More particularly, it seems linguistically, mathematically, and computationally advantageous to require that α in fact be drawn from the class of regular languages. The characterization of uncertainty in a particular grammatical equation can then be stated as a regular expression over the vocabulary of grammatical function names. The infinite uncertainty for the topicalization example above can now be specified by the equation given in (30):

(30) $(\uparrow \text{ TOPIC}) = (\uparrow \text{ COMP* OBJ})$,

involving the Kleene closure operator. One remarkable consequence of our functional approach is that appropriate predicate-argument relations can be defined without relying on empty nodes or traces in phrase-structure trees. This allows us to make the phrase-structure representations much more faithful to the sentence's superficial organization. Note that a particular within-clause grammatical function can be assigned by a long-distance dependency only if the phrase-structure rules optionally introduce the nodes that would normally carry that function in simple clauses.[8] This formulation is possible only because subcategorization in LFG is defined on f-structure via the Completeness and Coherence conditions (see Kaplan & Bresnan 1982) and is independent of phrase-structure configurations.

The mathematical and computational properties of functional uncertainty are discussed further in Kaplan and Maxwell (1988). Here we summarize the mathematical characteristics briefly: It is clearly decidable whether a given f-structure satisfies a functional description that includes uncertainty specifications. Since a given f-structure contains only a finite number of function-application sequences, it contains only a finite number of strings that might satisfy an uncertainty equation. The membership problem for the regular sets is decidable, and each of those strings can therefore be tested to see if it makes the equation hold.

It is less obvious that the satisfiability problem is decidable. Given a set of equations describing a functional structure for a sentence, can it be determined that a structure satisfying all the equations does in fact exist? For a trivial description with a single equation, the question is easy to answer. If the equation has an empty uncertainty language, containing no strings whatsoever, the description is unsatisfiable. Otherwise, it is satisfied by the f-structure that meets the requirements of any string in the language, say the shortest one. The difficult case arises when the functional description has two uncertainty equations, say $(f\alpha) = v_\alpha$ and $(f\beta) = v_\beta$. If α contains (perhaps infinitely many) strings that are initial prefixes of strings in β, then the strings that will be mutually satisfiable cannot be chosen independently from the two languages. For example, the choice of x from α and xy from β implies a further constraint on the values v_α and v_β: for this particular choice we have $(f x) = v_\alpha$ and $(f xy) = ((f x) y) = v_\beta$, which can hold only if $(v_\alpha y) = v_\beta$. Kaplan and Maxwell (1988) show, based on a state-decomposition of the finite-state machines that represent the regular languages, that there are only a finite number of ways in which the choice of strings from two uncertainty expressions can interact. The original equations can therefore be transformed into an equivalent finite disjunction of derived equations whose remaining uncertainty expressions are guaranteed to be independent. The original functional description is thus reducible to a description without uncertainty when each of the remaining regular languages is replaced by a freely chosen member string. The satisfiability of descriptions of this sort is well established. A similar proof of satisfiability has been developed by Mark Johnson (1987).

If the residual uncertainties include an infinite number of strings, then an infinite number of possible f-structures will satisfy the original description and are thus candidates for the f-structure that the grammar assigns to the sentence. This situation closely resembles the general case that arises for descriptions without uncertainties. As Kaplan and Bresnan (1982) noted, if a description is consistent then an infinite number of f-structures will satisfy it. These f-structures are ordered by a subsumption relation, and Kaplan and Bresnan defined the subsumption-minimal satisfying structure to be the grammatically relevant one. The family of f-structures that satisfy the residual uncertainties is also ordered, not just according to subsumption but also according to the lengths of the strings that are chosen from the regular set. We extend the minimality condition of LFG by requiring that the f-structure assigned to a sentence include only the shortest strings realizing a particular uncertainty. In this way we follow the general LFG strategy of excluding from consideration structures that involve arbitrarily redundant information. See Kaplan and Maxwell 1988 for further discussion.

This is a general formalism that may apply to phenomena that are traditionally not thought of as falling into the same class as long-distance dependencies but that nevertheless seem to involve some degree of uncertainty. Johnson (1986) and Netter (1986) have used it in the analysis of Germanic infinitival complements, and Karttunen (this volume) discusses how similar extensions to Categorial Unification Grammar can account for related facts in Finnish that would otherwise require type-raising. Halvorsen (1987) has extended its use to the semantic domain, where it offers a simple characterization of various kinds of quantifier-scope ambiguities. In this paper we illustrate the formalism by showing how it can be used to represent different conditions on long-distance dependencies. Consider the multi-complement sentence (31), whose c-structure and f-structure are given in (32) and (33):

(31) *Mary John claimed that Bill said that Henry telephoned.*

(32)

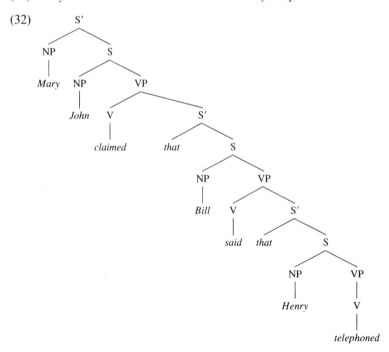

(33)
$$
\begin{bmatrix}
\text{TOPIC} & [\text{PRED } `Mary'] \\
\text{PRED} & `claim<(\uparrow \text{ SUBJ}) (\uparrow \text{ COMP})>' \\
\text{SUBJ} & [\text{PRED } `John'] \\
\text{COMP} & \begin{bmatrix}
\text{PRED} & `say<(\uparrow \text{ SUBJ}) (\uparrow \text{ COMP})>' \\
\text{SUBJ} & [\text{PRED } `Bill'] \\
\text{COMP} & \begin{bmatrix}
\text{PRED} & `telephone<(\uparrow \text{ SUBJ}) (\uparrow \text{ OBJ})>' \\
\text{SUBJ} & [\text{PRED } `Henry'] \\
\text{OBJ}
\end{bmatrix}
\end{bmatrix}
\end{bmatrix}
$$

Note that the tree (32) has no empty NP node in the embedded clause. The link in the functional structure (33) indicates that the relation between the topic and the object of the most deeply embedded complement is one of functional identity, just like the relation between a functional controller in a raising or equi construction and its controllee (see the discussion of functional control in Kaplan & Bresnan 1982). Thus the same subsidiary f-structure serves as the value of both the TOPIC function and the OBJ function in the complement. The linguistic conditions on the linkages in functional control and long-distance dependencies are quite different, however. The conditions on functional uncertainty in long-distance dependencies can be subdivided into conditions on the potential functions at the end of the uncertainty path (the "bottom," OBJ in this example) and conditions on the functions in the middle of the path (the "body," here COMP*).

In the example above, the bottom is the function OBJ. Of course, there is a variety of other within-clause functions that the topic can have, and the equation might be generalized to

(34) $(\uparrow \text{ TOPIC}) = (\uparrow \text{ COMP}^* \text{ GF})$,

where GF denotes the set of primitive grammatical functions. As we discuss in §3, this is too general for English, since the topic cannot serve as a within-clause complement. A more accurate specification is

(35) $(\uparrow \text{ TOPIC}) = (\uparrow \text{ COMP}^* (\text{GF} - \text{COMP}))$

where GF − COMP denotes the set of grammatical functions other than COMP. This might appear to be still much too general, in that it permits a great number of possible bottom functions, most of which would be unacceptable in any particular sentence. But whatever bottom function is chosen will have to be compatible with all other requirements that are imposed on it, not only case-marking and agreement, etc., but also the general principles of consistency, completeness, and coherence. Although phrase-structure rules no longer play a role in insuring that the topicalized constituent will be linked to the right place within the sentence, these functional conditions will rule out unacceptable sentences like (36):

(36) *Mary, he said that John claimed that Bill saw Peter.

(This sentence does have an interpretation with *Mary* as a vocative, but we ignore that possibility here.) If OBJ is chosen as the bottom function and the body reaches down to the lowest clause, the features of *Mary* will be inconsistent with the features of the local object *Peter*. An inconsistency would arise even if *Peter* were replaced by a repetition of the word *Mary* because of the instantiation property of LFG's semantic forms (Kaplan & Bresnan 1982:225). If the body does not reach down to the lowest clause, then one of the intermediate f-structures will be incoherent: neither of the predicates *claim* or *say* takes objects. The f-structure would also be incoherent if some other function, say OBJ2, were chosen as the bottom or if the body were extended below the lowest clause.

The following sentence has the same c-structure as (36) but is grammatical, and even ambiguous, because the function ADJ can be chosen as the bottom:

(37) *Yesterday, he said that Mary claimed that Bill telephoned Peter.*

This is acceptable because ADJ is in GF but is not one of the "governable" grammatical functions, one that can serve as an argument to a lexical predicate, and thus is not subject to the coherence condition as defined by Kaplan and Bresnan (1982).

Similarly, restrictions on the sequence of functions forming the body can be stated in terms of regular predicates. The restriction for Icelandic that adjunct clauses are islands might be expressed with the equation

(38) $(\uparrow \text{TOPIC}) = (\uparrow (\text{GF} - \text{ADJ})^* \text{GF})$.

This asserts that the body of the path to the clause-internal function can be any sequence of non-adjunct grammatical functions, with the bottom being any grammatical function that may or may not be ADJ. For English the body restriction is even more severe, allowing only closed and open complements (COMP and XCOMP in LFG terms) on the path, as indicated in (39):

(39) $(\uparrow \text{TOPIC}) = (\uparrow \{\text{COMP}, \text{XCOMP}\}^* (\text{GF} - \text{COMP}))$.

Given this formalism, the theory of island constraints becomes a theory of the generalizations about the body of possible functional paths, expressible as regular predicates on the set of uncertainty strings. For example, if RELMOD is the function assigned to relative-clause modifiers of noun phrases, that function would be excluded from the body in languages that obey the complex NP constraint.

Other conditions can be stated in the phrase-structure rules that introduce the uncertainty expression. These rules are of the general form indicated in (40):

(40) S′ →   Ω   Σ
                    (↑ DF) = ↓
          (↑ DF) = (↑ body bottom),

where Ω is to be realized as a maximal phrasal category, Σ is some sentential category, and DF is taken from the set of discourse functions (TOPIC, FOCUS, etc.). This schema expresses the common observation that constituents introducing long-distance dependencies are maximal projections and are sisters of sentential nodes. Restricting the introduction of discourse functions to rules of this sort also accounts for the observation that discourse functions need to be linked to within-clause functions (see Fassi Fehri 1988 for further discussion). Rule (39) for English topicalization is an instance of this general schema:

(41) S′ →   XP or S′   S
                    (↑ TOPIC) = ↓
          (↑ TOPIC) = (↑ {COMP, XCOMP}* (GF − COMP))

In English, S′ and any XP can occur in topic position. Spanish, on the other hand, seems to be a language in which some topic constructions allow NPs but not PPs (Grimshaw 1982).

3. Illustrations from English

As mentioned above, Kaplan and Bresnan (1982) noticed an apparent category-matching requirement in sentences like (18c–d), repeated as (42)–(43):

(42) a. *The girl wondered how tall she would grow.*
     b. **The girl wondered how tall she would reach.*
(43) a. *The girl wondered what height she would reach.*
     b. **The girl wondered what height she would grow.*

The verb *grow* seems to subcategorize for an AP and *reach* for an NP. But subcategorization in LFG is done in functional terms, and it turns out that independently motivated functional constraints also provide an account of these facts. First observe that *reach* but not *grow* governs the OBJ function, as indicated by the contrast in (44):

(44) a. *That tall has been grown.
     b. That height has been reached.

Grimshaw (1982) shows that passivization is not dependent on syntactic category but on whether the verb takes an OBJ.[9] The verb *grow,* on the other hand, establishes a predicational relationship between its subject and its adjectival complement and thus governs the XCOMP function. The relevant lexical entries for *reach* and *grow* are as follows:

(45) a. *reach:* $(\uparrow \text{PRED}) = \text{'reach} \langle (\uparrow \text{SUBJ})(\uparrow \text{OBJ}) \rangle$'
     b. *grow:* $(\uparrow \text{PRED}) = \text{'grow} \langle (\uparrow \text{SUBJ})(\uparrow \text{XCOMP}) \rangle$'
             $(\uparrow \text{SUBJ}) = (\uparrow \text{XCOMP SUBJ})$

Sentence (42a) is acceptable if XCOMP is chosen as the bottom function: XCOMP makes the local f-structure for *grow* complete. *Tall,* being a predicative adjective, also requires a local subject, and that requirement is satisfied by virtue of the control equation $(\uparrow \text{SUBJ}) = (\uparrow \text{XCOMP SUBJ})$. The choice of XCOMP in (42b) is unacceptable because it makes the local f-structure for *reach* be incoherent. Choosing OBJ satisfies the requirements of *reach,* but the sentence is still ungrammatical because the f-structure for *tall,* in the absence of a control equation, does not satisfy the completeness condition. In (43a) the choice of OBJ at the bottom satisfies all grammaticality conditions. If OBJ is chosen for (43b), however, the f-structure for *grow* is incoherent. If XCOMP is chosen, the f-structure for *grow* is complete and coherent, and the sentence would be acceptable if *what height* could take the controlled subject. Although some noun phrases can be used as predicate nominals (*She became a doctor, She seems a fool*), others, in particular *what height,* cannot (*She became that/a height, *She seems that height, *I wonder what height she became/seemed*). Whether or not the restrictions ultimately turn out to be functional or semantic in nature, it is clear from the contrasts with *become* and *seem* that they have nothing to do with syntactic categories.

   Not only is category-matching unnecessary, it does not always yield the correct result. Kaplan and Bresnan (1982) discussed the examples in (46) (their ex. 136), where a simple category-matching approach fails:

(46) a. That he might be wrong he didn't think of.
     b. *That he might be wrong he didn't think.
     c. *He didn't think of that he might be wrong.
     d. He didn't think that he might be wrong.

In these examples the category of a fronted S' can only be linked to a within-clause position that is normally associated with an NP. Kaplan and Bresnan complicated the treatment of constituent control to account for

these cases by allowing the categories of the controller and controllee both
to be specified in the topicalization rule. A closer look at the lexical requirements of the verbs involved, however, gives a more insightful account. Bresnan (1982b) proposes association principles between syntactic
categories and grammatical functions. These principles lead to the following VP rule for English:

(47) VP → V   (NP)   (NP)   PP*
            ($\uparrow$ OBJ) = $\downarrow$ ($\uparrow$ OBJ2) = $\downarrow$ ($\uparrow$ ($\downarrow$ PCASE)) = $\downarrow$
        . . .   (S')
                ($\uparrow$ COMP) = $\downarrow$

This rule embodies the claim that in English the OBJ function is only associated with NPs and the COMP function only with S'. Adopting these
principles, we propose the following partial lexical entries for *think* and
think-of:[10]

(48) a. *think:* ($\uparrow$ PRED) = '*think* $\langle$($\uparrow$ SUBJ)($\uparrow$ COMP)$\rangle$'
      b. *think:* ($\uparrow$ PRED) = '*think* $\langle$($\uparrow$ SUBJ)($\uparrow$ OBL$_{OF}$)$\rangle$'

The difference between the grammatical and ungrammatical sentences in
(46) follows if COMPs cannot be the bottom of an uncertainty in English
(whereas OBJ, OBJ2, and obliques such as OBL$_{OF}$ can). For (46a) the choice
of OBL$_{OF}$ for the bottom is compatible with the semantic form in (48b), so
the sentence is acceptable. Since COMP cannot be the bottom, OBL$_{OF}$ and
(48b) are also the only possible choices for (46b), but with this string the
requirement that the preposition *of* be present is violated (this requirement
is similar to the conditions on idiosyncratic case-marking, the details of
which do not concern us here).[11]

It is true that the OBL$_{OF}$ slot in (46a) is filled in a way that would be
impossible in sentence-internal position (46c), but this follows simply from
the phrase-structure rules of English. There is no rule that expands PP as a
preposition followed by an S', no matter what functional annotations might
be provided; as we have seen in §1, this is a very language-specific restriction. But as far as the functional requirements of *think-of* go, nothing in the
f-structure corresponding to an S' prevents it from serving as the OBL$_{OF}$.

Under this account of long-distance dependencies, then, there is no
need to parameterize them in terms of particular phrase-structure categories. This proposal also easily handles the following contrasts, discussed in
Stowell (1981):

(49) *Kevin persuaded Roger that these hamburgers were worth buying.*
(50) **That these hamburgers were worth buying, Kevin persuaded Roger.*

(51) *Louise told me that Denny was mean to her.*
(52) *That Denny was mean to her Louise told me (already).*

They can be compared to

(53) **Kevin persuaded Roger the news.*
(54) *Louise told me the story.*

Example (53) shows that *persuade* does not subcategorize for an OBJ2, while (54) shows that *tell* does take an OBJ2 as an alternative to the COMP assignment in (51). The relevant lexical information is given in (55).[12]

(55) *tell:* (↑ PRED) = '*tell* ⟨(↑ SUBJ)(↑ OBJ)(↑ OBJ2)⟩'
            or
        (↑ PRED) = '*tell* ⟨(↑ SUBJ)(↑ OBJ)(↑ COMP)⟩'
      persuade: (↑ PRED) = '*persuade* ⟨(↑ SUBJ)(↑ OBJ)(↑ COMP)⟩'.

The ungrammaticality of (50) follows again from the fact that the bottom cannot be a COMP, whereas (52) is acceptable because an OBJ2 is permitted.

   Our proposal is different from the one made in Stowell (1981) in that adjacency plays no role for us, so we do not need incorporation rules to account for (51)–(52). This is in keeping with our view that phrase-structure rules and functional structure are in a much looser relation to each other than in the theory that Stowell assumes. The fact that the incorporation analysis of (51) is not independently motivated is in turn a confirmation for this view.

   Both the present proposal and the one elaborated in Stowell (1981) can be seen as accounts of a generalization made in phrase-structure terms by Higgins (1973), namely, that S′ topicalization is only possible from an NP position. Indeed, the present functional approach covers the cases Higgins himself discusses. These include contrasts involving extraposition like those in (56):

(56) a. *That Susan would be late John didn't think was very likely.*
      b. **That Susan would be late John didn't think it was very likely.*

Extraposition is a lexical rule that, for each extraposable entry of the form in (57a), adds a lexical entry of the form shown in (57b) (where R is a variable over this type of verb):

(57) a. (↑ PRED) = 'R ⟨(↑ SUBJ) . . . ⟩'
      b. (↑ PRED) = 'R ⟨(↑ COMP) . . . ⟩(↑ SUBJ)'
         (↑ SUBJ PERS) = 3

(↑ SUBJ NUMB) = sg
(↑ SUBJ GEND) = neuter

This rule applied to the lexical entry for *likely* yields (58) and accounts for the alternation in (59):

(58) *likely:* (↑ PRED) = '*likely* ⟨(↑ COMP)⟩(↑ SUBJ)'
        (↑ SUBJ PERS) = 3
        (↑ SUBJ NUMB) = sg
        (↑ SUBJ GEND) = neuter
(59) a. *That Susan will be late is likely.*
    b. *It is likely that Susan will be late.*

Since a PRED value must be linked to a thematic function, either directly or by a chain of functional control, expletive *it* as in (60) is the only possible realization of the nonthematic SUBJ in (59b):

(60) *it:* (↑ PERS) = 3
      (↑ NUMB) = sg
      (↑ GEND) = neuter
       (↑ PRED)

With the extraposition entry in (58), the ungrammaticality of (56b) easily follows. The function COMP is not a legal uncertainty bottom, so that with this entry a complete functional structure cannot be assigned. Choosing SUBJ as the uncertainty bottom would be compatible with the entry corresponding to (57a), but this choice would result in the subject having a sentential PRED value, which the features for expletive *it* do not allow.

The lexical extraposition rule also interacts with the phrase-structure rule that introduces sentential subjects to exclude (61):

(61) **John didn't think (that) that Susan would be late was very likely.*

Whereas the phrase-structure rule for embedded clauses is as given in (62a), main clauses also allow the one given in (62b):

(62) a. S →   (NP)   VP
            (↑ SUBJ) = ↓
    b. E →   XP   VP
            (↑ SUBJ) = ↓

E is the category for a root-node expression, and XP can be any phrase that can bear the subject function, namely S', PP (as in *Into the room jumped a rabbit,* see Levin 1986 for discussion), and NP. In embedded position, however, we only find NP.[13]

Our discussion ignores embedded questions, but it is clear that some contrasts like the one exemplified in (63) can be treated along the same lines:

(63) a. *Whether John would come early she didn't wonder.
     b.   Whether John would come early she didn't know.

Translating the observations of Grimshaw (1979) into our framework, we would hypothesize that *wonder* takes a COMP only, whereas *know* allows for a COMP and an OBJ. But the general problem of embedded questions needs further study; it is well known that in some cases they are more OBJ-like than *that*-clauses. We have not studied their behavior in enough detail to propose a general treatment.

We have shown in this section that a functional approach can account for the basic correspondences that characterize long-distance dependencies just as well as previous category-matching approaches do, and also for a variety of additional facts that have seemed rather puzzling under a categorial analysis.

4. Interactions with Functional Control: Japanese Relatives

There are no multiply dominated substructures in phrase-structure trees, and, hence, any two nodes are connected by just one path. This is not the case with paths in functional structure. The following example shows such a multiple-path configuration:

(64) *Mary John expected to walk.*

(65)
$$
\begin{bmatrix}
\text{TOPIC} & [\text{PRED } `Mary'] \\
\text{PRED} & `expect<(\uparrow \text{ SUBJ})(\uparrow \text{ XCOMP})>(\uparrow \text{ OBJ})' \\
\text{SUBJ} & [\text{PRED } `John'] \\
\text{OBJ} & \\
\text{XCOMP} & \begin{bmatrix} \text{PRED } `walk<(\uparrow \text{ SUBJ})>' \\ \text{SUBJ} \end{bmatrix}
\end{bmatrix}
$$

The matrix OBJ and the XCOMP SUBJ in this example are identified by an equation of functional control. This means that there are two equivalent ways of resolving the topic uncertainty in this construction, if XCOMP is allowed in the body and OBJ and SUBJ are both allowed at the bottom. Although there appears to be no need for both of these uncertainty paths in English, this formal possibility offers a simple account for certain interactions between coordination and long-distance dependencies in Japanese.

Saiki (1985) observes that some relative clauses in Japanese are constrained so that in a coordinate structure, when a SUBJ is bound in one conjunct, a SUBJ must also be bound in the other. When there is a nonsubject in the one there has to be a nonsubject in the other conjunct too. The pattern is illustrated by the following examples:

(66) *Takashi ga   kat-te Reiko ga   tabeta ringo*
      Takashi SUBJ bought Reiko SUBJ ate   apple
      'the apple which Takashi bought and Reiko ate'
(67) *Hon o   yon-de rekoodo o kiita   gakusei*
      book OBJ read   record OBJ listened-to student
      'the student who read a book and listened to a record'
(68) **Ookiku-te Reiko ga   katta suika*
      big   Reiko SUBJ buy   watermelon
      'the watermelon which was big and which Reiko bought'
(69) **Takashi ga   nagut-te Reiko o   ketobashita otoko*
      Takashi SUBJ hit   Reiko OBJ kicked   man
      'the man whom Takashi hit and who kicked Reiko'

Bresnan, Kaplan, and Peterson (in preparation) present a functionally-based theory of coordination within the LFG framework. According to this theory, coordinate structures are represented formally as a set in f-structure, with the elements of the set being the f-structures corresponding to the individual conjuncts. LFG's function-application primitive is extended in a natural way to apply to sets of f-structures: a set is treated as if it were a function with the properties that are common to all its f-structure elements. As Bresnan, Kaplan, and Peterson show, this simple extension, which is orthogonal to the extension (29) that we are proposing here, is sufficient to provide elegant accounts for the wide variety of facts that coordinate-reduction rules and across-the-board conventions attempt to handle. The theory of coordination also interacts properly with the present theory of long-distance dependencies: a path of functional uncertainty that passes into a set will be resolved independently for each of the set's elements. Thus, for (70a) the topic uncertainty will be resolved as XCOMP OBJ for the first conjunct and as XCOMP OBL$_{TO}$ for the second.

(70) a. *Mary John expected to see and give the book to.*
      b. **Mary John expected to see Bill and give the book to.*

But even though the paths are allowed to differ from one conjunct to the other, it must be the case that if an uncertainty is resolved inside one of the functions it must also be resolved inside the other, as illustrated by (70b).

The fact that uncertainties are resolved independently for each conjunct, as required for the English example (70a), may seem incompatible with the Japanese pattern in (66)–(69). Indeed, if the within-clause role of the relative clause head is specified by a single uncertainty expression whose bottom allows either SUBJ or non-SUBJ functions, the constraint against mixing functions would not be satisfied. There is an obvious way of describing these facts, however, by specifying the within-clause function as a choice between two uncertainties, one with a SUBJ bottom and one with GF − SUBJ, as in the following rule for Japanese relative modifiers, adapted from Saiki (1985):

(71) NP →   S'   NP
     (↑ RELMOD) = ↓ (↑ RELMOD {XCOMP, COMP}* SUBJ) = ↓
                                    or
                      (↑ RELMOD {XCOMP, COMP}* (GF −
                                    SUBJ)) = ↓

The analysis of these examples does not depend on the fact that f-structures can contain separate but equivalent paths. But there are other Japanese examples that contain two equivalent paths, one of which ends in a SUBJ and the other in a non-SUBJ. This situation arises in causatives, which, following Ishikawa (1985), are assumed to have the following lexical schemata:

(72) (↑ PRED) = 'cause ⟨(↑ SUBJ)(↑ OBJ2)(↑ XCOMP)⟩'
     (↑ XCOMP SUBJ) = (↑ OBJ2)

The functional control equation identifies the XCOMP's SUBJ with the OBJ2 of the matrix. Saiki (1985) noticed that in this situation our formalization predicts that either of the uncertainties in (71) can lead to the common element, so that causative phrases ought to be conjoinable with other clauses in which either a SUBJ or a non-SUBJ is relativized. That this prediction is correct is shown by the acceptability of the following phrases (Saiki 1985):

(73) *Takashi o   nagutte, Reiko ga   Satoru o   ketobas-ase-ta otoko*
     Takashi OBJ hit,   Reiko SUBJ Satoru OBJ kick CAUS   man
     'the man who hit Takashi and who Reiko caused to kick Satoru'
(74) *Takashi ga   nagutte, Reiko ga   Satoru o   ketobas-ase-ta otoko*
     Takashi SUBJ hit,   Reiko SUBJ Satoru OBJ kick CAUS   man
     'the man who Takashi hit and who Reiko caused to kick Satoru'

Within a classical transformational framework, the causative could be analyzed as a raising or equi construction, but at the moment of *wh-* movement, the information about the "deep structure" subjecthood of the noun phrase would be unavailable. It would thus be expected to behave only as an object. With Trace theory and other enrichments of phrase-structure approaches, one can imagine stating the right conditions on the long-distance dependency. Again, however, there is no convergence of surface structure configuration and the configuration that must be postulated to account for these cases.

5. Conclusion

LFG proposes a distinction between functionally conditioned and c-structure–dependent phenomena. We have argued that long-distance *wh*-constructions are in fact functionally conditioned, contrary to what was previously assumed, and hence should be accounted for in the f-structure. The Icelandic facts show that c-structure dominance relations are not always relevant, the English facts show that node labels alone do not allow the proper distinctions to be made, and the Japanese causative illustrates a case in which multi-dominance is necessary. In short, the primitives of phrase-structure representation are much less adequate than those of functional structure.

Of course, phrase-structure accounts of these phenomena are possible if several (successive) tree structures are admitted to encode different types of information and if traces and/or reconstruction are introduced to give the effect of multi-dominance. It is clear, though, that these accounts are not more economical than the LFG approach: besides the succession of tree structures and abstract traces, further principles must be defined to govern the mapping from one tree representation to another (such as the pruning convention proposed in Thráinsson 1986 and distinctions between case-marked and non–case-marked position as in Stowell 1981). We are not suggesting that such representations and principles are incapable of yielding the right empirical results. But for the claim that functional generalizations can be stated in terms of structural primitives to be interesting, it has to be shown that the postulated phrase structures are independently motivated. As the Icelandic case illustrates, there are clear cases where they are not. Given this lack of convergence, we conclude that phrase-structure accounts obscure the basically functional nature of long-distance dependencies. In part this is because they do not formally distinguish them from purely distributional generalizations such as those concerning the ordering of adverbs in Icelandic.

NOTES

1. In recent work in phrase-structure–based frameworks there has been some weakening of this claim. For example, almost all proposals now separate linear

order from dominance relations and represent grammatical functions mainly in terms of the latter and not the former. See Pullum (1982) for an early proposal separating these two aspects.

2. Thráinsson's paper is written in a transformational framework, but his generalizations translate in an obvious way into the framework used here. We use his analysis because it gives a very intuitive account of the data, but of course our remarks apply to all phrase-structure accounts that hypothesize that the two types of PP discussed below have the same attachment at some moment of the derivation.

3. These constructions are analyzed as PPs in Icelandic because in all these cases the S' alternates with a simple NP:

(i) *Jón kom eftir kvöldmatinn.*
'John came after dinner.'
(ii) *Jón var að hugsa um Maríu.*
'John was thinking about Maria.'

In general, the simplest hypothesis about Icelandic phrase structure rules is that an S' is permitted wherever an NP can appear (if the meaning allows it).

4. This is true for tensed clauses, but we have not yet investigated infinitives. It is well known that they tend to be less strong as islands, but further studies are needed to understand fully the influence of tense on island constraints.

5. Zaenen (1980) proposes that the extractability from an S is determined by a lexical property of the complementizer that introduces it. Under that hypothesis the adjunct/argument contrast discussed here would be unstatable, since the same complementizer appears in both constructions.

6. A reanalysis of the verb and the prepositions as one unit would not obviously account for this contrast, and in any event, such an analysis has no independent motivation. Maling and Zaenen (1985) argue explicitly that there is no such reanalysis in Icelandic, and the fact that an adverb cannot be placed between the preposition and the following clause is further evidence against such a proposal:

*Ég vonaðist til alltaf að hann fengi bíl.

7. As far as we can see, the Icelandic data also do not allow for a syntactic account in frameworks like Generalized Phrase-Structure Grammar that define "government" solely on the surface structure.

8. Thus a constraint like the one proposed in Perlmutter (1971) that (tensed) clauses must have local surface subjects (and hence that question movement of the subject is not allowed) would follow in a straightforward way from making the NP constituent bearing the Subject equation obligatory in the phrase-structure rule.

9. Jacobson (1982) points out that the verbs *ask* and *hope* are not susceptible to this analysis.

10. This analysis assumes an unlayered f-structure representation of oblique objects related to the proposal of Bresnan (1982) and slightly different from the two-level approach discussed by Kaplan and Bresnan (1982). The only change necessary to accommodate the two-level representation would be to allow the bottom

to be a two-element sequence such as OBL$_{OF}$ OBJ, the same sequence that *think-of* would subcategorize for under that approach.

11. One kind of sentence that is not ruled out on syntactic grounds is:

That John saw Mary Bill kissed.

We assume that this is out for semantic reasons: *that*-clauses, regardless of their grammatical function, correspond to semantic propositions and propositions are not kissable.

12. Note that according to our proposal the grammaticality of (i) does not license (ii):

(i) *John persuaded Roger.*
(ii) **That these hamburgers were worth buying, John persuaded.*

Arguments slots in LFG are reserved for certain semantically restricted types, as the following unacceptable string illustrates:

(iii) **John persuaded the fact.*

One way to achieve this is to assume that each GF is associated with a thematic role and that lexical rules do not change these associations. For instance, a verb like *give* takes a goal and a theme, and in the OBJ, OBL$_{goal}$ realization the theme is linked to the OBJ and the goal to the OBL$_{goal}$. In the OBJ, OBJ2 construction, however, it is the goal that is linked to the OBJ and the theme to the OBJ2. For different ways to formulate this correspondence that preserve thematic role assignments, see Bresnan (1982b) and Levin (1986). With *persuade,* the goal argument is obligatory and the prepositional argument is optional, as is shown by (iv):

(iv) **John persuaded that Bill had left.*

13. These rules also allow us to account for the ungrammaticality of (i) and (ii):

(i) **That John will be late seems.*
(ii) **That John will be late Bill doesn't think seems.*

We simply assume that *seem* has only the "derived" lexical entry in (57b) not the one in (57a). Thus the thematic argument with *seem* is always a COMP and never a SUBJ, and indeed there are no sentences like (iii) that might lead to (ii):

(iii) **John/The fact seems.*

3

Radical Lexicalism

LAURI KARTTUNEN

1. Introduction

The kind of grammar I discuss here is a marriage of Bay Area unification formalism (Kaplan et al. 1986) with a much older, distinguished partner called Categorial Grammar (CG). A number of people are currently exploring categorial unification grammars, but very little has appeared in print so far (Pareschi 1986, Uszkoreit 1986, Whitelock 1986, Wittenburg 1986). This framework seems particularly suited to the description of a language like Finnish, in which the morphology provides a lot of information about the syntactic role of constituents and in which the word order is relatively uninformative in this regard. The aim of this paper is to explore a radical lexicalist view of syntax. In many current approaches to syntax, much of the information about how words are combined into phrases is encoded in the lexicon. What I try to do is to merge techniques for lexical encoding developed in such frameworks as Lexical-Functional Grammar (LFG), HPSG, and the PATR project at SRI with the combinatorial principles of categorial grammar, thus doing away with phrase-structure rules altogether.

Because the framework of this paper is unfamiliar to many linguists, I start with a brief review of categorial grammars and explain how such grammars can be encoded in a unification-based grammar formalism. (For an excellent introduction to unification, see Shieber 1986.) I then present some basic facts about Finnish word order and give an account of the data within a very simple fragment of categorial unification grammar. I review some more problematic data concerning nonlocal dependencies and explain how the simple analysis can be extended to such cases.

This paper, made possible in part by a gift from the Systems Development Foundation, was also supported by a grant from the Nippon Telegraph and Telephone Company. I am grateful to Annie Zaenen and John Bear for their help on the form and content of this paper.

43

1.1. Classical Categorial Grammar

A characteristic feature of CG is that the lexical entries of words encode virtually all the information about how words are combined into phrases; there is no separate component of syntactic rules, as is found in most other grammatical frameworks. The combinatorial properties of a word are indicated by the name of its lexical category. There are two types of categories: BASIC and DERIVED (= FUNCTOR). Basic categories are designated by atomic labels; the names of derived categories are complex expressions. In a prototypical CG, common nouns and noun phrases are regarded as basic categories; the set of functor categories includes determiners and intransitive verbs.

(1) *Basic Categories*   *Derived Categories*
    CN (common noun)   NP/CN (determiner)
    NP (noun phrase)   S\NP (intransitive verb)

The labels of derived categories play the same role in CG as syntactic rules do in a phrase-structure grammar. By assigning determiners to the category NP/CN, the grammarian indicates that determiners combine with common nouns to form noun phrases. In effect, the name of this category encodes the phrase-structure rule NP → Det CN. More generally, the category labels for derived categories are of the form

(2) (result direction argument),

where "result" and "argument" are category labels, either simple or complex, and "direction" is either / or \, depending on whether the functor comes before (/) or after (\) its argument. An example of the latter type is the label for intransitive verbs, S\NP, which indicates that phrases of this category form sentences by combining with a preceding noun phrase. Transitive verbs are commonly assigned to the category (S\NP)/NP, adverbs to (S\NP)\(S\NP). Under this analysis, transitive verbs combine with a noun phrase on their right, while adverbs attach to an intransitive verb phrase on their left. In both cases, the resulting expression is an intransitive verb phrase. A standard CG analysis tree for *John greeted Mary warmly* is:

(3)

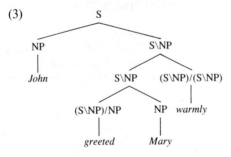

In CG, expressions that belong to nonbasic categories, such as S\NP, are commonly called FUNCTORS. In this context, the term simply means that their category label encodes a combinatorial rule; there is no necessary connection between this technical notion of functor and some semantic or syntactic distinction between functors and arguments. All that distinguishes functors from arguments in the terminology we are using here is that, when a functor is combined with an argument, it is the former that determines what the constraints on the combination are and what the result will be. From the point of view of a parser, functors are syntactically "active," in the sense that they enable the parser to form new constituents, whereas basic expressions are syntactically "inert."

In a prototypical CG, the only combinatorial principle is that of FUNCTIONAL APPLICATION: an expression of a derived category can combine with an adjacent phrase, provided that the latter qualifies as the argument. A categorial grammar of this kind is equivalent to a standard phrase-structure grammar. In recent work on CG, Steedman (1988), Dowty (1988), and others have made use of more powerful combinatorial principles. Binary rules of FUNCTIONAL COMPOSITION allow functors to combine with other functors; unary rules of TYPE-RAISING convert basic expressions to functors; or functors of one type are converted to functors of another type. Functional composition and type-raising are used in Dowty's (1988) treatment of nonconstituent coordination and in Steedman's (1988) account of *wh*-questions and relative clauses. Such rules can be expressed easily in our formalism (Uszkoreit 1986). Although we do not use them here, we consider them briefly in §5. The phenomena covered in our grammar—word order variation and long-distance dependencies—can be described simply in terms of functional application. We take advantage of the fact that our unification-based formalism enables us to construct functors that cannot be expressed in the original CG notation consisting of atomic category labels and slashes. Because type-raising and functional composition, in their most general form, are difficult to constrain, it is a welcome result not to have to invoke them in this case.

1.2. Categorial Unification Grammar

In the last few years, the notion of unification has emerged as a common descriptive device in many linguistic theories (LFG, Functional Unification Grammar (FUG), Head-Driven-Phrase-Structure Grammar (HPSG). Unification is an operation that merges partial information as long as it is consistent; it fails when the information becomes incompatible. A simple example of unification involves the merging of features. In (4), *A* and *B* are feature sets containing information about agreement and case. The unification of *A* and *B* is a feature set that results from merging *A* and *B* into a single set of features.

(4) A $\quad = \begin{bmatrix} \text{agreement [number plural]} \\ \text{case} \qquad \text{nominative} \end{bmatrix}$

$\quad B \qquad = \begin{bmatrix} \text{agreement [person 3d]} \end{bmatrix}$

$\quad A \cup B = \begin{bmatrix} \text{agreement} \begin{bmatrix} \text{number plural} \\ \text{person 3d} \end{bmatrix} \\ \text{case} \qquad \quad \text{nominative} \end{bmatrix}$

In (4), the three feature sets are displayed as matrices. They can also be represented as directed graphs, as we shall do from now on. The graph (5) represents the same information as the last of the three matrices in (4):

(5)
agreement $\underset{\displaystyle \text{person — 3d}}{\overset{\displaystyle \text{number — plural}}{<}}$

case — nominative

A sequence of attributes in a graph is called a PATH. In the case at hand, the path ⟨agreement number⟩, for example, has the value "plural."

One advantage of unification is that it gives a precise meaning to rules stated in terms of attributes and values. A unification-based formalism leads to DECLARATIVE descriptions of syntactic structure. It is not compatible with the notion of a derivational process that changes structure by inserting, deleting, or reordering constituents. Unification-based descriptions are MONOTONIC in the sense that whatever is true of a constituent at some stage of the analysis remains true when new information has been accumulated.

In a unification grammar, it is convenient to express syntactic rules in the form of feature sets. In the case of phrase-structure rules, the left-hand side of the rule and the constituents on the right-hand side are each represented by an attribute whose value is a feature set for that constituent (Shieber 1986, Karttunen 1986). To express the principle of functional application in this format, we introduce five attributes: *cat, left, right, argument,* and *result*. For all basic expressions, the value of *argument* is NONE. This ensures that they cannot act as functors. The attribute *cat* is used to record the category label. The values for *left, right,* and *result* are relevant only for nonbasic expressions. The attributes *left* and *right* distinguish between backward- and forward-looking functors. A forward-oriented functor, such as a determiner in English, has an indeterminate value (indicated by [ ]) for *right*, and NONE as the value of *left*; a backward-looking functor has the features *left:* [ ], *right:* NONE. The attributes *argument* and *result* are used to encode what kind of expression the functor combines with and what the result will be. The value of *argument* is unified with the feature set of the expression the functor combines with. If this unification fails, the two expressions cannot be combined; if it succeeds, the feature set of the consequent expression is the same as the value of *result*.

In our framework, the forward-oriented version of functional application is analogous to the phrase-structure rule

(6) Result → Functor Argument.

A detailed statement of the rule is given in graph (7). The paths ⟨Functor⟩ and ⟨Argument⟩ lead to the feature sets of the two expressions that are combined, ⟨Result⟩ points to the feature set of the concatenated phrase, while the converging lines denote unifications.

(7)

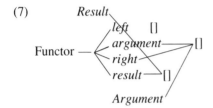

The backward-oriented rule is the same except that the paths ⟨Argument⟩ and ⟨Functor argument⟩ are unified with ⟨Functor left⟩ rather than ⟨Functor right⟩.

To see how this version of functional application works, consider the following simple example of a determiner combining with a common noun to form a noun phrase. We use here the standard CG analysis of determiners, shown in 8a. The feature *cat* in 8a is actually redundant here because its content is spelled out in the values of the other features; it is included only for its mnemonic value. The feature set for the argument—a common noun—is shown in the graph 8b, while the result of the combination appears in the graph 8c:

(8)   cat — NP
                        c. Result: argument — NONE

      cat — NP/CN

      argument — — cat — CN

      result — < cat — NP
                  argument — NONE

      left — NONE   cat — CN
a. Functor: right — []   b. Argument: argument — NONE

When the determiner and the common noun are combined by functional application, the determiner's values for the paths ⟨*argument*⟩ and ⟨*right*⟩ are successfully unified with the features of the common noun. The value of the determiner's *result* attribute becomes the feature set of the noun phrase so formed. This example is oversimplified, as it ignores all the features that are specific to particular lexical items—nor have we indicated how the semantics of the noun phrase is determined by its composition. In a real grammar, all three feature sets have more content than is shown here. As the later examples show, parts of the feature sets of the argument and the functor may be incorporated in the result through unification. On the other hand, in one respect the example could be even simpler, since it is possible to encode the same categorial information by using fewer features. For example, instead of *left* and *right* we could just have a single feature, *direction*, with LEFT, RIGHT as possible values. The advantage of using more features is that we can also introduce two-sided functors that combine to both left and right, possibly with different constraints on their arguments. In this respect, the notation used here is a generalization of the standard CG convention.

2. A Fragment of a Categorial Unification Grammar for Finnish

In this section, we develop a grammar for a subset of Finnish. The purpose is to give a concrete example of a categorial grammar in unification-based formalism with enough coverage to illustrate the problems of word order and long-range dependencies. In particular, we cover simple noun phrases functioning as subjects and objects, auxiliary verbs, and some types of main verbs and infinitival complements. In constructing this grammar, we concentrate on developing an account for the following simple generalizations about Finnish word order:

(9) a. In declarative sentences, subjects and objects may occur in any order with respect to the verb and to one another.
   b. In yes/no questions and imperatives, the finite verb comes first.
   c. The negative auxiliary (*e-*) precedes the temporal one (*ole-*), and both precede the main verb, but the three types of verbs need not be adjacent.

After accomplishing this task, we move on to confront a much harder problem:

(10) Elements of participial and infinitival clauses can be interspersed among the constituents of a superordinate clause.

This problem is similar to the case of English topicalization, in that the clause to which a dislocated constituent syntactically and semantically belongs can be arbitrarily distant. Yet it differs in that the migrant phrase is not in a special syntactic position, as a topicalized phrase is, that identifies it as possibly being a dependent of some distant subordinate clause. Another difference is that, while there is only one topic position per clause, any number of constituents from an embedded clause can occur in a superordinate clause. In §5, we discuss three possible solutions to this type of nonlocal dependency.

2.1. Noun Phrases

In a major departure from CG tradition, we make verbs serve as basic expressions and define noun phrases as functors. This is a natural choice for languages in which word order is relatively free and case-marking provides information about the syntactic role played by noun phrases with respect to verbs. (Whitelock 1986 suggests a similar analysis for Japanese.) To keep our examples as simple as possible, we pretend here that the syntactic roles of noun phrases are determined unambiguously by case. In particular, let us assume that a noun phrase in the nominative case always functions as a subject with respect to some verb and that accusative NPs are always objects. In a real grammar for Finnish, the mapping from case to syntactic roles is of course many-to-many, rather than the one-to-one relationship we are stipulating here. For now, we define a nominative NP in Finnish as an expression that combines with an adjacent verb phrase to yield a verb phrase in which it plays the role of the subject. In terms of a feature set, this combinatorial property is expressed as follows:

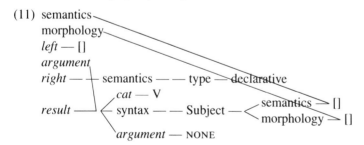

(11) semantics
    morphology
    left — []
    argument
      right — | — semantics — — type — declarative
            ,cat — V
      result — < syntax — — Subject — < semantics — []
                             morphology — []
            'argument — NONE

As graph (11) shows, according to our definition subjects are two-sided functors; they can combine either to the left or to the right, but under different conditions. The graph for a partitive NP is the same as above except that it has the object role. Because the value of ⟨*left*⟩ is indeterminate, there is no constraint on leftward combination; however, the rightward combination requires that the verb be declarative. This constraint is designed to account for the pattern shown in (12). The ungrammaticality of (12d) is due to the constraint that prohibits the subject from combining to the right with an interrogative verb.

(12) a. *Liisa nukkui.*
        'Lisa slept.'
     b. *Nukkui Liisa.*
        'Lisa did sleep.'
     c. *Nukkuiko Liisa?*
        'Did Lisa sleep?'
     d. **Liisa nukkuiko?*
        'Lisa slept?'

Because the value of *argument* is unified with the value of *result* in the feature sets of nominative NPs, the phrase *Liisa nukkui* in our grammar is of Category V just as *nukkui* 'slept' is; in this respect the analysis is reminiscent of Dependency Grammar (Tesnière 1959).

2.2. Main Verbs

All types of main verbs belong to the same basic category but have different valences. In this fragment, verbs are subcategorized with respect to three possible syntactic roles: subject, object, and vcomp (verbal complement). The valence of a simple intransitive verb, such as *nukkui,* is indicated in the following manner:

(13)   subject — []
         syntax — < object — NONE
                              vcomp — NONE

In this graph, the value of the path ⟨syntax subject⟩ is indeterminate; consequently, any subject NP can contribute its content to this position. For example, when the subject NP *Liisa* is combined with *nukkui* by functional application, the above graph is unified with

(14)   semantics — Lisa
      syntax — — subject — <
                                      morphology — — case — nominative

On the other hand, because the value of ⟨syntax object⟩ is NONE for intransitive verbs, such verbs cannot combine with an object NP. The atomic value NONE does not unify with any nonempty set of features.

As far as semantics is concerned, we follow tradition in assigning to each verb a relation that links the semantic values of those constituents that make it syntactically complete. For example, the feature set for the transitive verb *rakastaa* 'love' assigns the subject to the first and the object to the second position in the "love" relation:

(15)
$$
\text{semantics} \text{ — — } \text{issue} \text{ — } \begin{cases} \text{relation — love} \\ \text{arg1} \\ \text{arg2} \end{cases}
$$
$$
\text{syntax} \text{ — } \begin{cases} \text{subject — — semantics — []} \\ \text{object — — semantics — []} \\ \text{vcomp — NONE} \end{cases}
$$

The attribute *issue* in the above graph is used to distinguish the basic semantic relation expressed by the verb stem. The complete semantic description of a fully inflected verb contains a number of other semantic properties that are contributed by inflectional suffixes, clitics, and auxiliary verbs. We use the following traditional attributes: *polarity* (positive, negative), *tense* (present, past), *tenseaspect* (simple, perfect), *mood* (indicative, conditional, potential), and *type* (declarative, imperative, interrogative). For example, in the graph for the word *rakasti* 'loved', the value of ⟨semantics⟩ is

(16)
$$
\text{issue} \text{ — } \begin{cases} \text{relation — love} \\ \text{arg1 — []} \\ \text{arg2 — []} \end{cases}
$$
mood — indicative
polarity — positive
tense — past
tenseaspect — simple
type — declarative

2.3. Auxiliary Verbs

Unlike main verbs, which are basic expressions, auxiliary verbs are forward-oriented functors in our system. The tense auxiliary combines with the past participle form of a verb, the negative auxiliary with either a past participle or a special negation form. The resulting construction is of the same type as the argument: a basic expression of category V. Its morphological properties and some of its semantic features (*tense, polarity*) come from the functor; the argument contributes the syntactic features as well as the rest of the semantics. For example, the past tense form of the tense auxiliary *oli* 'had' combines verb phrases that unify with the following graph:

(17) cat — V

    semantics — < issue — []
                       polarity — positive

    morphology — < case — nominative
                       form — participle

    syntax — []

    argument — NONE

In other words, the argument must be a participial form of a basic verb in the nominative case. The result of the combination has the feature set shown below:

(18) cat — V   issue — []

                  mood — indicative

    semantics — < polarity — positive
                  tense — past
                  tenseaspect — perfect
                  type — declarative

                  form — finite
    morphology — < number — sg
                  person — 3

    syntax — []

    argument — NONE

In this graph, the paths ⟨syntax⟩ and ⟨semantics issue⟩ are actually unified with the corresponding paths in the previous graph; the values of these paths derive from the argument. To show this graphically, we need to view the two subgraphs in the context of the complete graph for the auxiliary. Except for the value of ⟨semantics tenseaspect⟩, which is a special contribution of the tense auxiliary, all the other features under ⟨semantics⟩ and the value of ⟨morphology⟩ are inherited from the functor directly. Thus *oli rakastanut* 'had loved' is a declarative singular 3d person verb phrase with past tense because *oli* 'had' by itself has these features.

Because the negative auxiliary does not have a participial form, it can never follow the tense auxiliary. The fact that both types of auxiliaries are forward-oriented functors means that they must precede the main verb to find their argument. Consequently, the three types of verbs must come in a fixed order:

(19) NegAux < TenseAux < MainVerb.

2.4. Infinitival Complements

Like all other types of main verbs, predicates that take verbal complements (VComp) are basic expressions in our system. There are many types of infinitival and participial complements in Finnish. In this paper, we cover only complements in which the verb is either in the 1st or 3d infinitive form. In our system, infinitives are backward-oriented functors seeking to combine with a verb of the appropriate type. The resulting combination has the feature set of the argument with the infinitival complement unified in as the value of the path ⟨syntax vcomp⟩. For example, 1st infinitive form of *nukkua* 'sleep' has the following value for the path ⟨argument syntax⟩:

(20)

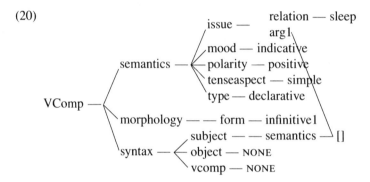

As an example of a verb that qualifies as the argument—that is, takes complements of this type—consider the verb *halusi* 'wanted'. Its lexical representation specifies the following value for ⟨syntax⟩:

(21)

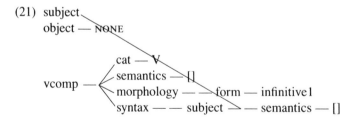

This graph indicates that the complement of *halusi* must be a 1st infinitive and that the subject roles of the two verbs are unified. Consequently, in a sentence such as *Liisa halusi nukkua* 'Liisa wanted to sleep', the subject of the main verb is also the subject of the infinitive. An analysis tree for this sentence and the resulting semantic representation are shown in (22):

(22) a.

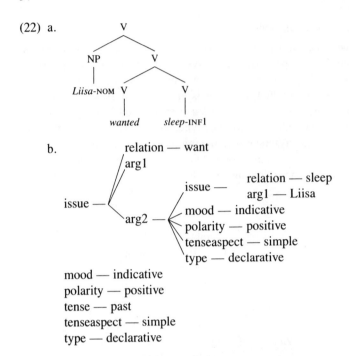

3. Word-Order Variation

In terms of classical CG, the main idea in the grammar of Finnish we have
sketched in the preceding section is that auxiliary verbs, infinitival complements, subjects, and objects are functors of type V/V or V\V. They combine with a basic verb phrase to yield a verb phrase that is the same as the
original except that the content of the functor has been merged with the
argument in a manner that is determined by the functor. This aspect of
the analysis, of course, can only be expressed in a unification-based formalism. In a more complete fragment, the same treatment would be extended to adverbs. Because all the relevant information is expressed in the
lexical entries, a program that uses the grammar for parsing has no need for
phrase-structure rules. The parsing algorithm can be extremely simple: *Always try to combine a functor with an adjacent argument.*

This grammar allows for considerable freedom in word order. For example, because the result of combining a subject with the main verb is a
basic verb phrase, the subject NP may occur between an auxiliary and the

main verb. The same is true of objects. Consequently, there are four ways of saying that Lisa has not slept:

(23) a. *Liisa ei ole nukkunut.*
    b. *Ei Liisa ole nukkunut.*
    c. *Ei ole Liisa nukkunut.*
    d. *Ei ole nukkunut Liisa.*

The resulting set of features is the same regardless of the position of the subject:

(24) *cat* — V

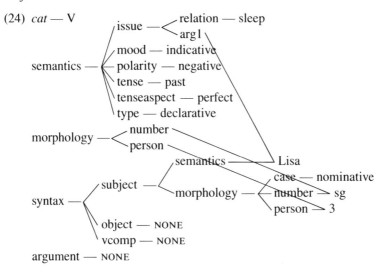

The grammar also places no constraints on the order of the subject with respect to the object. Any of the six possible orderings of the three-word sentence 'John loved Lisa' is allowed; the set of features assigned to the sentence remains the same regardless of the order.

(25) a. *Jussi rakasti Liisaa.*
    b. *Jussi Liisaa rakasti.*
    c. *Liisaa Jussi rakasti.*
    d. *Liisaa rakasti Jussi.*
    e. *Rakasti Jussi Liisaa.*
    f. *Rakasti Liisaa Jussi.*

The only explicit constraint on the ordering of noun phrases is that, when they combine to the right, the argument must be declarative. As we pointed out in §2.1, a verb that is marked with the interrogative enclitic *-ko*

fails this condition: such a verb cannot be preceded by any of its dependents. Another way of forming interrogative verb phrases in our system is
to combine an interrogative noun phrase with an ordinary verb phrase. In
Finnish, interrogative noun phrases are of two types: ordinary noun phrases
suffixed with the interrogative clitic, e.g. *Liisaako,* and phrases containing
an interrogative pronoun, e.g. *ketä* 'who'. In our grammar, both types of
interrogative NPs are forward-oriented functors; they combine only to the
right and yield an interrogative verb phrase as the result. Because noninter-
rogative functors in our system combine to the right only if the argument is
declarative, this analysis correctly predicts that the constituent that makes
the sentence interrogative is always in the initial position:

(26) a.   *Rakastiko Jussi Liisaa?*
           'Did John love Lisa?'
      b.   **Jussi rakastiko Liisaa?*
      c.   *Liisaako Jussi rakasti?*
           'Was it Lisa that John loved?'
      d.   **Jussi Liisaako rakasti?*
      e.   *Ketä Jussi rakasti?*
           'Who did John love?'
      f.   **Jussi ketä rakasti?*

By treating subject and object noun phrases syntactically as functors we
have accounted for the three generalizations about Finnish word order in
(9) by using only function application. In a categorial grammar of a more
traditional sort, in which the verb is responsible for linking up with its syntactic dependents, type-raising and functional composition must be introduced to achieve the same result.

4. Multiple Analyses

It is convenient to represent the analysis of a phrase as a tree that shows
how the resulting feature set was derived. However, the structure of the
tree has no linguistic significance in our system; in this respect our trees are
different from phrase-structure trees. All that matters is the resulting feature set. Because no functor has any priority over others with respect to
order of application, the same result can often be obtained in more than one
way. This is potentially troublesome from a computational point of view.
For example, the sentence *Jussi rakasti Liisaa* has two possible analysis
trees in our grammar:

(27) a.

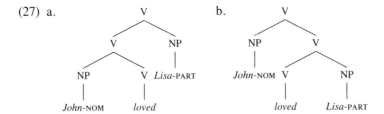

Tree (27a) shows an analysis in which the subject combines with the verb first and the object takes the result as its argument. In (27b), the object is combined with the verb before the subject is joined. A parsing algorithm that always tries to combine adjacent phrases by functional application inevitably produces both analyses for the sentence. From the parser's point of view, this is a "spurious ambiguity," because the two analyses yield exactly the same set of features. In a more complicated sentence, spurious ambiguities multiply very quickly. For example, there are four possible ways of analyzing *Jussi ei ole rakastanut Liisaa* 'John has not loved Lisa', three of which differ only with respect to how much of the verb string has been assembled before it is combined with the object.

Fortunately, it is a simple matter to eliminate such spurious ambiguities. In the D-PATR system (Karttunen 1986), with the help of which this sample grammar was produced, the parser maintains a chart on which it stores all the information about possible analyses of the input phrase and its parts. It is possible to instruct the parser to apply an equivalence test that prevents redundant analyses from being entered on the chart. When an analysis is created, the parser checks whether the chart already contains an equivalent analysis for the same string of words. If one is found, the new analysis is discarded. This policy guarantees that multiple analysis trees for the same string are produced only if there is a genuine syntactic or semantic ambiguity.

5. Nonlocal Dependencies

In Finnish, an infinitival and participial clause can blend with the superordinate clause containing it in the sense that some or all of the dependents of the embedded verb can be interspersed among the constituents of the higher clause. To illustrate this phenomenon, we use an example borrowed from Maria Vilkuna's recent study (1986). Most of the examples in this section are variants of the following simple sentence:

(28) *Minä pelaan näissä   tennistä.*
I   play   these-in tennis
'I play tennis in these (clothes).'

To show what happens in infinitival complements, we use two additional verbs: *ruveta* 'start' and *aikoa* 'intend' along with the negative and tense auxiliary verbs. The verb *ruveta* takes complements in which the verb is the 3d infinitive in the illative case; *aikoa* requires the 1st infinitive:

(29) *En minä ole   aikonut ruveta pelaamaan näissä   tennistä.*
not I   have intend start   play   these-in tennis
'I did not intend to start to play tennis in these.'

In this case, the infinitival complement, *pelaamaan näissä tennistä* 'play tennis in these', forms a contiguous phrase. However, the adverbial *näissä* 'in these' and the object *tennistä* 'tennis' can be scrambled to any of the six possible positions in the superordinate structure consisting of *En minä ole aikonut ruveta* 'I did not intend to start'. Of the 42 possible variants, some are much less acceptable than others, but—because the judgments vary—it is not clear that a grammar should absolutely exclude any of them. The three examples in (30) are acceptable to a great majority of speakers. The discontinuous infinitival phrase is in bold type.

(30) *En minä **näissä** ole   **tennistä** aikonut   ruveta **pelaamaan.***
Not I   these-in have tennis   intended start   play
*En minä **tennistä näissä** ole   aikonut   ruveta **pelaamaan.***
Not I   tennis   these-in have intended start   play
*En minä **tennistä** ole   aikonut **näissä** ruveta **pelaamaan.***
Not I   tennis   have intended these-in start   play

The link from an embedded infinitive to its dependents can in principle extend over an arbitrarily long chain of intervening predicates. In this respect, the phenomenon in Finnish is similar to English topicalization. The difference is that there do not seem to be any structurally defined slots—such as the topic position in English—for the elements of a broken infinitival clause; these elements can be freely interspersed in the host clause.

The grammar that we outlined in §2 cannot handle these cases. According to our definition, a partitive NP needs to find, on one side or the other, a verb that can accept it as its object. The object NP and the verb can be separated only by phrases that are themselves dependents of the same verb. This locality condition is clearly too strong. Some mechanism must be introduced to allow linkage over an unbounded chain of nested complements.

In the next section, we discuss three possible solutions to this problem, two of which appear to be successful. The first is a replay of our analysis of auxiliaries in §2.3, the second is based on augmenting functional application with a type-changing rule, and the third relies on functional application but allows functors to have "floating type." This idea is a variant of Ronald Kaplan's notion of "functional uncertainty" (Kaplan and Zaenen, this volume).

5.1. Clause Union

Before we turn to the successful solutions, let us briefly consider an idea that fails although it may appear promising in the light of the examples we have seen so far. We can make verbs like *aikoa* 'intend' and *ruveta* 'start' combine with an infinitival complement in such a way that the resulting combination inherits its syntactic valence from the complement. Syntactically, the infinitival clause becomes fused with the superordinate clause, but semantically the two clauses of course remain distinct: the object of *ruveta pelaamaan* 'start to play' is interpreted as a dependent of the infinitive. This is the same solution that we adopted in §2.3 for auxiliary verbs.

This solution works well for auxiliary verbs, but it fails here. Auxiliary verbs have no syntactic valence of their own and cannot be modified by adverbial phrases; verbs that take infinitival complements are different in this respect. For example, consider the verb *pyytänyt* 'asked' in the following example:

(31) *Liisaa minä en ole   pyytänyt Jussia auttamaan.*
     Lisa   I   not have asked   John   help

In a neutral context, most people take this example to mean 'I did not ask Lisa to help John', but the interpretation 'I did not ask John to help Lisa' is also possible. Because *pyytänyt* 'asked' and *auttamaan* 'help' both require an object, it is not possible, in our framework, for them to enter into a syntactic clause union. We cannot specify a valency with two distinct object roles for the same verb phrase.

5.2. Type-Changing

If clause union is not a viable solution, our problem is to find a way for an NP or an adverbial phrase to combine with a verb phrase so that the functor acts as a dependent of a verb in a complement clause. Consider the example

(32) *En   minä **tennistä** rupea **pelaamaan**.*
     Not I   tennis   start   play
     'I will not start to play tennis.'

The desired analysis tree for the sentence is:

(33)

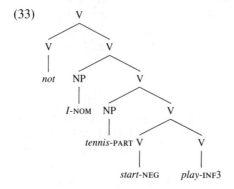

At the point where the partitive NP *tennistä* 'tennis' is combined with the verb phrase *rupea pelaamaan* 'start to play', the feature set of *pelaamaan* 'play' has been unified with the value of the path ⟨syntax vcomp⟩ in the representation of *rupea,* the negative form of 'start'. The value of the path ⟨syntax⟩ in the feature set of *rupea pelaamaan* is thus as follows:

(34) subject
     object — NONE
                    cat — V   relation — play
                                          issue — < arg1
                                                    arg2
                                          mood — indicative
                          semantics — < polarity — positive
                                          tenseaspect — simple
     vcomp —   type — declarative
                                          case — illative
                          morphology — < form — infinitive3
                                          subject — semantics — []
                          syntax — — object — < cat — NP
                                                 semantics — []
                          vcomp — NONE

If the feature set of the partitive NP *tennistä* 'tennis' is of the type in (11), it cannot combine with *rupea pelaamaan.* As the graph above shows, the top-level verb has no place for an object. In order for the operation to succeed, the value of ⟨argument syntax⟩ in the NP's feature set should be (35a), not (35b), as originally given.

(35) a.

$$\text{vcomp} - - \text{syntax} - - \text{object} - \Big\langle \begin{array}{l} \text{semantics} - \text{tennis} \\ \text{morphology} - \Big\langle \begin{array}{l} \text{case} - \text{partitive} \\ \text{number} - \text{sg} \\ \text{person} - 3 \end{array} \end{array}$$

b.

$$\text{object} - \Big\langle \begin{array}{l} \text{semantics} - \text{tennis} \\ \text{morphology} - \Big\langle \begin{array}{l} \text{case} - \text{partitive} \\ \text{number} - \text{sg} \\ \text{person} - 3 \end{array} \end{array}$$

The type-raising mechanism discussed in Steedman (1986) and Dowty (1986) provides a way out of the problem. We can write a rule that takes as its input an NP of the basic type and yields a new functor by splicing the sequence 'vcomp syntax' into the beginning of the path that constrains the argument. This rule must of course be stated in such a way that it can apply to its own output; in the case of

(36) *En minä **tennistä** aio   ruveta **pelaamaan**.*
     not I   tennis   intend start play
     'I do not intend to start to play tennis.'

the rule must be applied twice in order to make *tennistä* its argument's ⟨vcomp syntax vcomp syntax object⟩.

In a parsing system, a recursive type-changing rule leads to an infinite loop unless its application is carefully constrained. In this case, the constraint is easy to find: the rule should be applied only if the NP in question is adjacent to a verb phrase that in fact has a complement at the right level of embedding. In the case at hand, the first application of the type-changing rule is licensed by the fact that *aio ruveta pelaamaan* 'intend to start to play' has the complement *ruveta pelaamaan* 'start to play'; the reapplication in turn is permitted because the latter phrase contains the complement *pelaamaan* 'to play'. At this point, the rule can no longer be applied because the verb *pelaamaan* 'play' does not have a slot for a complement clause. The output of the second round of type-changing is then successfully combined with the adjacent verb phrase *aio ruveta pelaamaan* 'intend to start to play'.

The constraint needed to prevent infinite recursion of the type-changing rule is difficult to express in a formalism that relies on unification. We have worked out a solution to this problem but we will not discuss it here because the details are rather complicated and because we regard the approach discussed in the next section more attractive.

5.3. Functors with Floating Type

In this volume, Kaplan and Zaenen describe a novel solution for the problem of linking an initial *wh-* or topic phrase to a verb in an embedded clause. This solution is in some respects very similar to the idea of type-changing discussed in the preceding section, but it is conceptually more elegant, even though it requires a substantial change in the way unification is implemented in most current systems (including D-PATR). In this section, we describe the essential features of the proposal within our framework; the original version is stated in terms of LFG.

So far we have assumed that functors have a fixed type, for example, a partitive NP as defined in §2.1 combines only with arguments whose feature set contains a suitable value for the path ⟨syntax object⟩. The type-changing rule discussed in the preceding section generates from it—by repeated applications—a set of functors whose type specifications constitute a series:

(37)   ⟨syntax object⟩
       ⟨syntax vcomp syntax object⟩
       ⟨syntax vcomp syntax vcomp syntax object⟩

       . . .

In intuitive terms, this is simply a way of stating that a partitive NP is the object of some verb in the adjacent verb phrase that can be reached by way of one or another path in this set. The basic insight in Kaplan's notion of functional uncertainty is that this kind of open-ended disjunction can be coded directly in the formalism. If we let path specifications be regular expressions, the above set of paths can be represented by a single specification:

(38)   ⟨[syntax vcomp]* syntax object⟩.

This is clearly more elegant from a technical point of view than type changing, and Kaplan and Zaenen argue that, in the context of LFG, it is also motivated by linguistic evidence. The use of regular expressions in equations makes it possible to associate initial topic and *wh-* phrases to predicates directly in functional structure without reference to phrase-structure trees. Kaplan and Zaenen discuss several examples that are difficult to handle in terms of constituent structure and show how the data can be described more adequately with the new technique.

In our framework, the proposal eliminates the need to use type-changing to describe nonlocal dependencies. A partitive NP can combine directly with a verb phrase that has a place for an object at some level of embedding. In effect, NPs and adverbial phrases become functors with "floating type." The combination of such a functor with an argument can yield more than one result as all of the alternative ways of successful unification are tried out. This is the case in the following example:

(39) *Ketä Liisaa pyydettiin auttamaan?*
     who Liisa they-asked help

Although the preferred interpretation is clearly 'Whom did they ask Lisa to help?', the reading 'Whom did they ask to help Lisa?' cannot be excluded. Consequently, when the NP *Liisaa* is combined with the verb phrase *pyydettiin auttamaan* 'they asked to help', two instances of *Liisaa pyydettiin auttamaan* are produced: one for the path ⟨syntax object⟩, the other for the path ⟨syntax vcomp syntax object⟩. The interrogative phrase *ketä* 'who' will then assume whichever object role remains unfilled as it combines with the two verb phrases.

The use of regular expressions in path specifications raises many formal and computational issues that require further study (Johnson 1986). A computer implementation of unification for this type of grammar formalism has been developed by Kaplan.

6. Function of Word Order

The purpose of the preceding section is to sketch an account of Finnish syntax that reflects the intuition that hierarchical structure and word order have relatively little to do with the syntactic roles of constituents in this language. The analyses that our grammar produces are feature structures in which the syntactic dependents of a verb are labeled in a traditional way; a part of that representation is intended to serve as input to semantic interpretation. However, many important aspects of meaning, such as quantifier scope, have intentionally been left unresolved. Because we have focused on the problem that constituents can appear in many different orders without changing the grammatical relations they express, we have not paid any attention to the fact that the alternative orderings of the same constituents differ with respect to some aspects of meaning, such as quantifier scope and discourse function.

Although the derivation of a categorial analysis for a sentence can be recorded in the form of the tree, the analysis trees do not represent any aspect of sentence structure. As we have developed it so far, the grammar simply assigns to a sentence an unordered set of features that does not even express the linear order of constituents. This does not mean that constituent structure cannot be represented in a categorial analysis. On the contrary, because we distinguish between forward and backward application of functional composition, it is a simple matter to augment the system in such a way that some designated attribute will have as its value a list that consists of all the constituents in the order in which they appear. It is also possible to construct a more hierarchical structure; in fact, we could easily arrange the feature system in such a manner that a phrase-structure tree of a traditional sort is constructed as a side effect of applying categorial rules.

This state of affairs has certain advantages that we intend to exploit in future work. By not being committed to any constituent structure in advance, we are free to build as little or as much structure as the data about discourse meaning warrant. Although there are many studies of word order in Finnish (Hakulinen 1976, Heinämäki 1980, Karttunen and Kay 1985, Vilkuna 1986), they have produced very little insight into the principles that are involved. What little is known indicates that there is a close connection between word order and intonation. There appear to be no phenomena that support the assumption that hierarchical structure is involved in determining conversational meaning; it is commonly assumed that conversational structures are flat and consist of only a few elements. Vilkuna (1986), for example, describes discourse functions in terms of a simple template

(40) $P_2 P_1 V X$,

where P_2 and P_1 are positions in front of a finite verb and X covers the rest of the sentence. It is possible that a special role must also be assigned to sentence-final position (Hakulinen 1976). The P_1 role has also been called THEME or TOPIC; the optional P_2 element could be called CONTRASTIVE FOCUS. As Vilkuna points out, the assignment of constituents to these roles is not constrained by category or syntactic function.

The pivotal role of the finite verb in discourse structure is one of the few facts about Finnish word order on which there is common agreement. Another well-attested phenomenon is the contrastive focus in sentences like

(41) *Tennistä Liisa ei   aio   pelata.*
       Tennis I   not intend play
       P_2 P_1 V   X
       'Tennis Lisa does not intend to play.'

It is interesting to note that the $P_2 P_1 V$ order may be inverted just in case the finite verb is the negative auxiliary:

(42) *Ei   Liisa tennistä aio   pelata.*
       Not Lisa tennis   intend play
       V P_1 P_2 X

The initial position of the negative verb implicates that the opposite assumption is being contradicted; in other respects the two variants are very similar. In either case, the normal intonation peak naturally falls on *tennistä* 'tennis', which is perceived as the focus of negation.

The purpose of these inconclusive remarks is simply to point out that the kind of constituent structure that is generated by phrase-structure rules of the type S → NP VP, VP → V NP, and the like appears to be just as irrelevant for the description of conversational meaning in Finnish as it is for the account of grammatical relations. There is no reason to believe that a categorially based description is inferior to a transformational or a phrase-structure grammar with respect to expressing regularities about word order and conversational meaning.

7. Conclusion

This paper is an exploration of unification-based categorial syntax. We have constructed a grammar for a fragment of Finnish that accounts for word-order variation in simple sentences using only functional composition. This is possible because, in departure from CG tradition, we treat subjects, objects, and other dependents of verbs as functors. By adopting Kaplan's idea of functional uncertainty (floating types), we extend this solution for cases in which the elements of an infinitival clause are interspersed among the constituents of the main sentence. This phenomenon can also be described by introducing a rule of type-changing, but we prefer Kaplan's technique. In the final section, we point out that standard phrase-structure rules cannot account for either grammatical relations or discourse structure in Finnish. A radical lexicalist approach is a better alternative.

4

Asymmetries in Long-Distance Extraction in a Tree-Adjoining Grammar

ANTHONY S. KROCH

In recent papers (Kroch & Joshi 1985, Kroch 1987) we claimed that, if one adopts the Tree-Adjoining Grammar (TAG) formalism of Joshi, Levy, and Takahashi (1975) as the formal language of syntax, the ungrammaticality of extractions from *wh-* islands can be made to follow in a straightforward way from the nonexistence of multiple *wh-* fronting in simple questions. The analysis we gave was oversimplified, however, because it wrongly predicted all *wh-* island extractions to be ungrammatical, and we know that certain of them are well-formed, not only in languages like Swedish or Italian, but also in English (Chomsky 1986, Grimshaw 1986). Nevertheless, the analysis we gave had the attraction of providing a simple structural explanation for the *wh-* island effect, and it generalized directly to such other manifestations of subjacency as the Complex NP Constraint. In this paper we show that the analysis presented in our earlier paper can be extended in a reasonable way to several cases that were not accounted for in the original discussion. In particular, we discuss such well-known examples as the following:

(1) a. *Who_i does he think that $[e_i \, left]$?
    b. $When_i$ does he think that $[we \, left \, e_i]$?
(2) $On \, Thursday_i$, $what_j$ will you buy $e_j \, e_i$?
(3) a. ?$On \, that \, shelf_i$, how many $books_j$ can you fit $e_j \, e_i$?
    b. *$That \, many \, books_i$, on what $shelf_j$ e_i can fit e_j?
(4) a. ?$What_i$ were you wondering $[how_j \, to \, say \, e_i \, e_j]$?
    b. *How_i were you wondering $[what_j \, to \, say \, e_j \, e_i]$?

This paper is based on work supported in part by NSF grants DCR 84-11726 and CER MCS-8219196, Aravind Joshi, principal investigator. I would like to express my thanks to the many people who have discussed the issues involved. Special thanks are due to the members of the TAG research group at the University of Pennsylvania: Sharon Cote, Caroline Heycock, Aravind Joshi, Megan Moser, Beatrice Santorini, K. Vijay-Shankar, and David Weir.

66

Accounting for some of these cases will require an extension of the TAG formalism as presented in our 1985 paper, but we hope to show that under this extension the principles governing all the above contrasts receive a natural formulation.

In a recent squib, Baltin (1986) has pointed out that topicalized sentences like (5) are grammatical, although the corresponding *wh-* question in (6) is ungrammatical:

(5)   *After the party$_i$, I wonder who$_j$ e$_j$ will stay e$_i$.*
(6)   **When$_i$ do you wonder who$_j$ e$_j$ will stay e$_i$?*

Baltin uses this contrast to argue that preposed adverbs may not leave traces, since under standard Government-Binding theory assumptions the trace of the adverb in (5) would not be properly governed. We, on the contrary, would take the significance of the above contrast to lie in the fact that it recapitulates the contrast between (7) and (8):

(7)   *After the party$_i$, who$_j$ e$_j$ will stay e$_i$?*
(8)   a. **When who will stay?*
      b. **I know when who will stay.*[1]

Since, as will become evident, our TAG analysis derives the ungrammaticality of (6) from the ungrammaticality of the simple sentence (8), it follows that we predict the grammaticality of (5), since the simple sentence (7) is grammatical.

1. A Sketch of the TAG Formalism

The analysis that makes the above predictions is based on the formal theory of TAG grammar in Kroch and Joshi (1985). The reader is referred to that paper and others that have appeared since for a detailed introduction to the formalism (Joshi 1985, Joshi 1987b, Vijay-Shankar, Weir, & Joshi 1986). To review briefly, the TAG formalism derives complex sentences by composing simple structures. These structures are phrase-structure trees, called in the theory ELEMENTARY TREES, and they come in two varieties, INITIAL TREES, which are representations of simple sentences, and AUXILIARY TREES, which are the recursive structures of the language. Auxiliary trees are composed with other trees, both elementary and derived, by a tree combining operation called ADJUNCTION, which inserts the auxiliary tree into another tree. A TAG consists simply of a finite set of elementary trees with the adjunction operation defined on it. The trees below illustrate how a derivation proceeds in a TAG. In these trees and in those to follow only the details relevant to the points under discussion are given.

(9) Initial tree:

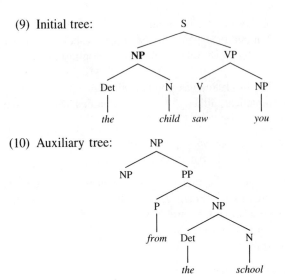

(10) Auxiliary tree:

As the tree in (10) illustrates, auxiliary trees have a root node which may be any phrasal category; and on their frontier, all their nodes are expanded to terminal symbols except one, called the FOOT node, which is identical in category to the root node. Adjunction works by first breaking an elementary tree at a phrasal node in such a way that the two pieces each contain a copy of the node at the break point. In (11) we illustrate this by breaking the tree in (9) at the boldface NP:

(11)

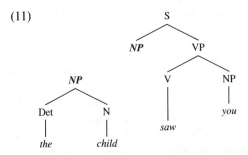

Then an auxiliary tree, in this case the tree in (10), whose root node is identical in category to this doubled node, is inserted at the broken node. This insertion occurs by the identification of the root and foot node of the auxiliary tree with the two instantiations of the doubled node. In our example the result of this insertion is the tree in (12), which corresponds to a sentence whose subject NP is modified by a prepositional phrase:

(12) Tree resulting from adjunction:

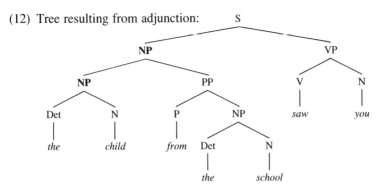

In the simplest case of adjunction, an auxiliary tree whose root node is of category XP may be adjoined at any node in another tree whose category label is also XP, but it is possible to constrain this adjunction further by associating with each node of an elementary tree a set of LOCAL CONSTRAINTS to specify which auxiliary trees may or must be adjoined at that node when the elementary tree appears in a derivation. In the application of Tree-Adjoining Grammar to linguistics, these local constraints should, of course, reflect linguistic generalizations and not be used in an ad hoc way to force otherwise inadequate analyses not to misgenerate.

As should be evident even from this simple example, the structures of complex sentences generated by any TAG are completely fixed by the inventory of elementary trees (initial and auxiliary). Since these trees are finite in number, it is possible to construct a TAG by simply listing the elementary trees it is to contain. Such a grammar would not be of linguistic interest, however, since it would contain no statement of the constraints governing the well-formedness of simple syntactic units. Hence, the TAG formalism must be supplemented with a substantive linguistic theory that defines well-formedness constraints for elementary structures, including the local constraints that they may contain. This theory must account for such linguistic constraints as those on phrase structure well-formedness (X-bar theory), on subcategorization and thematic role assignment, and on the appearance of empty categories. For reasons of space we cannot fully elaborate such a theory in this paper; but, as the reader will see, we largely assume, either directly or in modified form, the principles of Government-Binding theory for this purpose.

We also require, however, some constraints on the well-formedness of elementary structures that are particular to TAG; we assume without argument the following constraints: First, we require that the elementary trees be minimal; namely, that all initial trees be simple sentences and that auxiliary trees be minimal recursive structures. This minimality is expressed as a constraint that auxiliary trees rooted in a node of type XP contain no occurrences of nodes of that type on the path from the root to the required frontier node of type XP, except that Chomsky-adjunction structures in which the root node immediately dominates a node of its own type will not be considered to violate this constraint. Second, we restrict auxiliary trees to two types, which we designate ATHEMATIC TREES and COMPLEMENT TREES. The former have the structure of (13), with the order of the constituents variable:

(13) $X^n \rightarrow X^n \ldots (Y^{max}) \ldots$

An athematic tree introduces a modifying, complement, or dislocated phrase, and the crucial feature of such a tree is that its foot node is the head of the phrase dominated by the root node, giving the tree the Chomsky-adjunction structure illustrated above in (12). In previous TAG papers we have used athematic auxiliary trees to introduce such constructions as relative clauses and extraposed constituents. In the analysis below, examples like (40a) are licensed as athematic trees.

A complement tree serves to introduce a predicate that subcategorizes for and assigns a thematic role to a phrase of the category of its foot node. This type of tree has the structure in (14):

(14) $X^{max} \rightarrow \ldots Y^0 \ldots X^{max} \ldots$, where Y^0 governs X^{max}.

We require that the foot node of such a complement tree be lexically governed. As in the case of athematic trees, the order of constituents in complement trees is variable. But while the order in athematic trees is variable within languages, the order in complement trees will reflect the directionality of government and so will vary across but not within languages. Examples of complement trees used in the analysis in this paper are (21) and (40b), among others.

For reasons that will become apparent later, we require further that the foot node of a complement auxiliary tree have a certain government relationship to its root node. Let us define government as in (15):

(15) A minimal Y^0 GOVERNS a node X^{max} if and only if Y^0 is a sister of X^{max} and Y^{max}, the maximal projection of Y^0, dominates X^{max}. We call Y^{max} the GOVERNMENT DOMAIN of X^{max}. If the category of Y^0 is a lexical category (i.e., N, V, Adj, or P), then Y^0 LEXICALLY GOVERNS X^{max}, and Y^{max} is the LEXICAL GOVERNMENT DOMAIN of X^{max}.

Then we can define the transitive closure of the government domain relation as in (16):

(16) Let us say that the relation **G**(Y, X) holds of a pair of nodes if and only if Y is the government domain of X. We can then define **TG,** the transitive closure of **G,** as follows:
  (1) If **G**(Y, X), then **TG**(Y, X).
  (2) If **TG**(Y, X) and if Y′, the node immediately dominating Y, is a projection of Y, then **TG**(Y′, X).
  (3) For any W and Z, if **TG**(W, X) and **TG**(Z, W), then **TG**(Z, X). We define as the MAXIMAL GOVERNMENT DOMAIN of X in a given elementary tree that node W such that **TG**(W, X) and such that there is no Z for which **TG**(Z, W).

Given the definition in (16), we require, as a first approximation, that complement auxiliary trees meet the condition in (17).[2] Note that we are assuming, with Chomsky (1986), that S is a projection of Infl and that S′ is a projection of Comp.

(17) The foot node of a complement auxiliary tree must be lexically governed, and its maximal government domain must be the root node of the tree.

Note that the relation **TG** is similar to the notion of "extraction domain" of Huang (1982) and related to the concept of "g-projection" of Kayne (1983). In a sense, therefore, the foot nodes of complement auxiliary trees can be thought of as empty categories that must be "properly governed" in the sense of Chomsky (1981). If we define proper government as in (18), we can state a TAG version of the Government-Binding theory Empty Category Principle (ECP) as in (19):

(18) For any node X in an elementary tree α, initial or auxiliary, X is properly governed if and only if one of the following conditions is satisfied:
  i) the maximal government domain of X is the root node of α;
  ii) X is coindexed with a "local" c-commanding antecedent in α.
(19) For any node X in an elementary tree α, initial or auxiliary, if X is empty, then it must either be properly governed or be the head of an athematic auxiliary tree.

The utility of the requirement in (19) will become apparent in the course of the following section, where we discuss the mechanisms for capturing constraints on long-distance dependencies in a TAG.

2. *Wh-* Movement in a TAG

2.1. *Generating Unbounded* Wh- *Dependencies*

The sets of string languages and tree languages generated by TAGs have many interesting formal properties that have been explored by Joshi and his mathematical collaborators (Joshi, Levy, & Takahashi 1975; Vijay-Shankar & Joshi 1985; Vijay-Shankar, Weir, & Joshi 1986); and some of these formal properties make the formalism an interesting candidate for the formal syntactic apparatus of linguistic theory, a point we discuss in detail elsewhere (Kroch & Joshi 1985, Kroch 1987). It is sufficient for present purposes to note that the TAG formalism allows a strict separation of the statement of local co-occurrence restrictions from the statement of recursion. The result of this factoring is that elements linked by unbounded dependencies can be made to originate in single elementary trees and then to move apart as a result of the adjunction of auxiliary trees. The following trees illustrate how unbounded dependencies are created: [3]

(20) Initial tree:

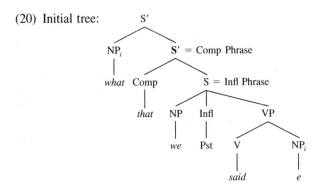

(21) Auxiliary tree:

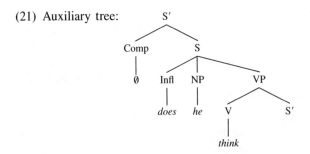

(22) Output of adjunction:

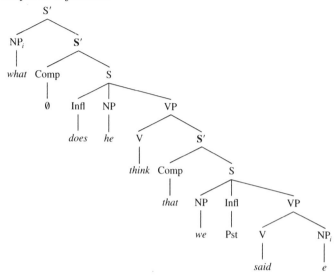

The *wh-* pronoun in (20) is in the same tree as the verb with which it is construed, and its interpretation as the object of the verb *say* is guaranteed by that fact. Following standard conventions, we represent the relationship between the fronted constituent and the position in which phrases with its grammatical role normally appear by coindexing the fronted *wh-* with an empty category. The relationship between an indexed empty category and the categorially identical, c-commanding node with which it is coindexed, we call LINKING. The adjunction of the auxiliary tree (21) at the boldface S' in (20) produces the tree (22), in which the *wh-* word is now initial in the matrix sentence.

2.2. ECP Effects

From the perspective of this analysis, let us now consider the cases in (1), repeated as (23):

(23) a. *Who_i does he think that [e_i left]?
      b. $When_i$ does he think that [we left e_i]?

The initial tree needed to derive sentence (23a) will have to be as in (24), which would combine with the auxiliary tree in (21):

(24)

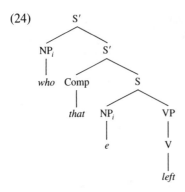

In this tree, however, the empty category in subject position is, under the standard Government-Binding (GB) assumptions we have adopted, not "properly governed." Being a subject, it is not "lexically governed" by a verb that subcategorizes it; and because the complementizer *that* intervenes between the fronted *wh-* and its trace in subject position, it is also not "antecedent-governed," as its c-commanding antecedent is not sufficiently local. Hence, since we have imposed the ECP as a constraint on the well-formedness of elementary trees, (24) is not a permissible initial tree and sentence (23a) is not derivable.

Unfortunately, this analysis runs into trouble in the case of a sentence like (23b). As Huang (1982) and Lasnik and Saito (1984) have pointed out, although adjuncts are thought to be properly governed in the same way as subjects (i.e., by antecedent government), they can be extracted out of subordinate clauses, as the grammaticality of (23b) shows. Under our derivation, the initial tree needed to derive (23b) would be as in (25):

(25)

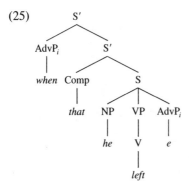

In this tree, as in (24), the trace linked to the preposed *wh-* is not properly governed; hence the analysis fails. This difficulty, we should note, is not particular to our TAG version of the analysis but rather has a counterpart in all treatments of these cases that are based on GB assumptions. Thus, in Lasnik and Saito (1984), the contrast between (23a) and (23b) leads those authors to stipulate a difference in the licensing conditions on subject traces and the traces of adverbial adjuncts. Because their analysis uses the GB level of representation known as "Logical Form" in a crucial way, we do not wish to incorporate it in our TAG treatment, one of whose strengths is that it seems able to state constraints on *wh-* extraction using only a single level of representation. If we consider additional data, moreover, we can find an alternative constraint on the licensing conditions on subject traces that produces the desired result. As the sentences in (2) and (3) (repeated as (26)–(27)) show, fronted PPs can occur adjoined to S′ to the left of a fronted *wh-* phrase:[4]

(26)   *On Thursday$_i$, what$_j$ will you buy e$_j$ e$_i$?*
(27) a. *?On that shelf$_i$, how many books$_j$ can you fit e$_j$ e$_i$?*
     b. **That many books$_i$, on what shelf$_j$ e$_i$ can fit e$_j$?*

Baltin (1982) argues on the basis of examples like (26) that adverb phrases can appear in this position, and example (27a) shows that even argument PPs can appear there. Subject NPs, on the other hand, cannot occur, as the ungrammaticality of (27b) shows. Sentences (26) and (27a) raise the question of how the traces of the fronted PPs are to be governed. In the case of the argument PP in (27a), one might treat the trace as lexically governed; but the adjunct PP in (26) cannot be so analyzed. We propose, therefore, the following difference between antecedent government of the traces of PPs or adverbs and subject NPs: Let us define local c-command (see Aoun and Sportiche 1983) so that the configuration in (24) and (25) does permit antecedent government of the trace bound by the moved *wh-*. This can be accomplished in a TAG simply by limiting the locality requirement to co-presence in the same elementary tree of an empty category and its antecedent governor. Then the extractability of adjuncts is predicted. To block the extraction of subjects, we require that the traces of subject NPs obey a stricter locality condition; namely, we require that they be adjacent to their antecedent governor. This stipulation will rule out the tree in (24) and so block the derivation of sentence (23a).

While we cannot claim to explain the source of the requirement that the traces of subject NPs, when antecedent-governed, be adjacent to their governors, we do think that it can be independently motivated. For one thing, it explains why English does not allow heavy–NP shift of subjects. Thus, we find a contrast between (28) and (29):

(28) a.   *I saw an old St. Bernard with a limp yesterday.*
     b.   *I saw e_i yesterday [an old St. Bernard with a limp]$_i$.*
(29) a.   *An old St. Bernard with a limp came by yesterday.*
     b.   **e_i came by yesterday [an old St. Bernard with a limp]$_i$.*

Given our expectation that extractions should be general, we might expect (29b) to be grammatical, as it is in many languages. From a structural point of view, moreover, the dislocated NP in (29b) is just as much a local c-commanding antecedent as the dislocated subject in a simple question like the following:

(30) [*Which old St. Bernard*]$_i$ e_i *came by yesterday?*

Apparently, the only relevant difference between the two cases is that in the latter the trace and its antecedent are adjacent.[5]

Consider next the fact, pointed out by Koopman (1984), that *do*-support cannot occur in subject questions. Thus, sentence (31) below is ungrammatical, unless *do* is stressed and so interpreted emphatically:

(31) **Who did come to town?*

Koopman assigns the structure in (32) to this sentence and argues that its ungrammaticality follows from the ECP, since the configuration in Comp is identical to that in the case of an extraction from the subject of an object complement clause with a lexical complementizer:

(32) [$_{S'}$ [$_{Comp}$ *Who$_i$ did$_j$*][$_S$ e_i [$_{Infl}$ e_j][$_{VP}$ *come to town*]]]

The difficulty with this analysis is that Baltin (1982) has given arguments that subject–aux inversion must be a local permutation of NP and Aux rather than a movement of Aux to Comp. If he is correct, as we believe him to be, then Koopman's explanation for the ungrammaticality of (31) is no longer available, since its structure will now be as in (33):

(33) [$_{S'}$ [$_{Comp}$ *Who$_i$*][$_S$ [$_{Infl}$ *did*] e_i [$_{VP}$ *come to town*]]]

If, on the other hand, we require that subject traces be adjacent to their antecedents, then (31) is ruled out as desired under the structural description in (33).

Finally, if we assume with Baltin (1982) and Lasnik and Saito (1984) that topicalized constituents are adjoined to S rather than to S′, the adjacency requirement will explain the contrasts in (34) and (35):

(34) a.   ?*Who$_i$ e_i thinks* [$_{S'}$ *beans$_j$ John will never eat e_j*]?
     b.   ?*Why$_i$ do you suppose* [$_{S'}$ *beans$_j$ John never eats e_j e_i*]?
     c.   **Who$_i$ do you think* [$_{S'}$ *beans$_j$ e_i will never eat e_j*]?

(35) a. *Who_i did they say [$_{S'}$ e_i would eat beans] and eat beans, e_i did?
      b. ?Who_i did they say e_i would eat beans and eat beans, he did?

The sentences of (34) differ unexpectedly in acceptability. While (34a) and (34b) are quite awkward, as topicalizations inside subordinate clauses generally tend to be,[6] they are more acceptable than (34c), which is completely out. Why this distinction should exist is unclear, unless the fact that the topicalized NP *beans* lies between the subject position and the original position of the fronted *wh-*, thereby preventing the antecedent governor of the subject from being adjacent to the subject position.[7] If we can assume that extraction from coordinate structures is constrained by some version of the "Across the Board Constraint" of Williams (1978), the sentences of (35) make the same point. Sentence (35a) is completely unacceptable, on our account because adjacency between the subject position and its governor is disturbed by the fronted VP *eat beans*. That this configuration produces an ECP violation is suggested by the fact that inserting a resumptive pronoun, as in (35b), improves the acceptability of the sentence, as is generally the case with such violations.[8]

3. Extraction from NP

3.1. Subject/Object Asymmetries in Extraction from NP

The treatment of *wh-* movement we have so far presented will not incorporate one important case of an unbounded *wh-* dependency, that known as "extraction from NP." Consider, for example, the following sentences:

(36) *Which painting$_i$ did you see e_i?*
(37) *Which painting$_i$ did you see a copy of e_i?*
(38) *Which painting$_i$ did you see a photograph of a copy of e_i?*

It is clear from examples like these that *wh-* phrases can be linked to empty categories embedded under any number of noun complements and hence that extraction from NP yields an unbounded dependency. If we wish to preserve a straightforward compositional semantics for our TAG, we cannot derive sentences like (37) and (38) from (36) by the adjunction of auxiliary trees rooted in NP to the NP node dominating the empty category. The problem is that under such a derivation, the preposed *wh-* phrase changes its thematic role with each adjunction, and the interpretation of the derived tree is not a simple function of the interpretations of its component elementary trees. Indeed, we never want to allow derivations under which thematic roles, once established, are altered by further adjunctions, and we will block such derivations by, in every tree, placing a particular local constraint on every node that is assigned a thematic role by a governor. This constraint limits adjunctions at that node to athematic auxiliary trees in the sense of §1 above (see Kroch and Joshi forthcoming for further details).[9] This general well-formedness constraint can be thought of as a TAG version of the GB constraint known as the "Projection Principle" (Chomsky 1981).[10] In order to permit the derivation of cases of extraction from NP in a way consistent with this constraint, it is necessary to extend the formalism beyond what we have been assuming. The extension we have in mind is one which is already defined in the original mathematical paper on TAGs and which we have made use of for linguistic purposes in our paper on extraposition (Kroch and Joshi 1987). In that paper we extended the definition of an auxiliary tree to include sets of such trees. An auxiliary tree is simply a set of elementary trees, each of which meets the definition of an auxiliary tree. When an auxiliary tree set is adjoined to another tree, each of its components is adjoined to a distinct node in the other tree. The only requirement on the adjunction of an auxiliary set is that all its components be adjoined into the same elementary tree. So long as the adjunction of auxiliary sets is defined in this way, all the mathematical properties of TAG are preserved (Joshi 1987b).

Once we allow auxiliary sets, we can define the linking relationship between nodes in different component trees of the same set. When two components contain nodes that are linked, however, we will require that, upon adjunction, the empty category wind up in a position where its coindexed antecedent c-commands it. With this machinery we can now derive sentences like (37) and (38). The initial and auxiliary trees needed to derive (37) are given in (39) below and (40) on the facing page:

(39)

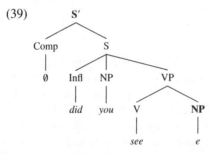

When the two components of the auxiliary set in (40) are adjoined to the boldface nodes in (39), the result is the proper tree for sentence (37). One interesting feature of these trees is the occurrence of an empty category in the initial tree not linked to any antecedent. The linking here is between nodes in the two components of the auxiliary set, those bearing the subscript *i;* and it is only when adjunction takes place that the empty category receives an interpretation by virtue of the index that adjunction supplies. It is because the empty category is uninterpreted until adjunction occurs that the semantic interpretation of the complex structure remains compositional. Since the empty category is uninterpreted in the initial tree, it has no thematic role; and so, rather than changing its thematic role as a result of adjunction, it merely acquires one for the first time.

(40) a.

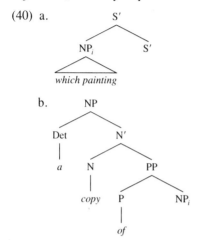

b.

The unbounded character of extraction from NP follows straightforwardly under the analysis we have given. Thus, if we add the following auxiliary tree to our grammar, we can derive sentence (38):

(41)

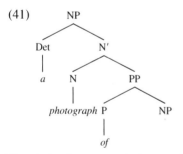

The derivation proceeds by simply adjoining the tree in (41) to the root node of (40b). Then the resulting derived auxiliary set, which consists of (40a) and the complex structure composed of (41) and (40b), is adjoined as before to the boldface nodes in (39). Clearly, the adjunction of structures like (41) into an auxiliary tree can be repeated any number of times before the set is adjoined to (39), ending the derivation. Thus, our analysis correctly allows extraction from NP to be unbounded.

Let us consider now the contrast between (37) and the following, ungrammatical, sentence:

(42) *Which painting$_i$ was a copy of e$_i$ seen by many people?

There have been many attempts to explain this contrast in the recent literature, and all of them in one way or another reduce it to the general contrast between subject and object extractions. The difficulty posed by this case is that, as standardly formulated, the ECP, which is usually responsible for subject/object asymmetries in GB analyses, appears not to rule out (42) (see Huang 1982). The trace in this sentence is lexically governed by a preposition; and the preposition, which one might want to say can transmit lexical government but is not by itself sufficient for proper government, is governed by the lexical head of a major category. Therefore, if, as is usual, proper government is stated on the most local domain to which it might apply, the ECP is not violated in (42). It was for this reason that Huang (1982) proposed his Condition on Extraction Domains. According to the CED, syntactic extraction from a properly governed position is possible only if there is a CHAIN of lexically governed positions linking the position of the empty category with a matrix predicate. In the case of (37) the empty category is lexically governed by the preposition *of,* which is in turn governed by the noun *copy,* which is in turn governed by the matrix verb *see;* and this chain of government licenses the extraction of *which painting.* In (42), on the other hand, the empty category is governed by *of,* which is governed by *copy* as before; but *copy* is not lexically governed, so the chain is broken before it reaches the matrix predicate. Hence, the extraction is not licensed.

The CED looks very much like an extension of the ECP, and the phenomena it covers have been analyzed by Kayne (1981, 1983) as ECP effects. Although various considerations have been invoked to argue that the two constraints should not be collapsed, we believe that the arguments for maintaining a distinction between the two principles are weak.[11] Hence we find it interesting that it is easy in a TAG to incorporate CED effects under the ECP in much the way that Kayne has, and it is such an analysis that we are developing in this paper. If it turns out that, for empirical reasons, the CED should appear as an independent stipulation in the theory of grammar, we can easily impose it in a TAG as a local constraint on the adjunction of the appropriate auxiliary trees. Even in this latter case, however, the effects of the CED would be linked to the ECP quite directly.

We can account in a natural way for the difference between (37) and (42) in our TAG analysis only if the initial trees for the two sentences differ appropriately, since the auxiliary set adjoined into the initial trees is the same in the two cases. Let us note then that the empty category in the initial tree for (37), namely (39), is lexically governed by the verb and that it is properly governed under the definition in (18) because its maximal government domain is the root of the tree in which it appears. On the other hand, in the initial tree for (42) (given as (43)) the empty category is in subject position, where it is not governed by the verb:

(43)

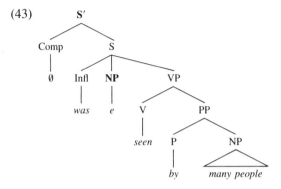

Since the initial tree (43) also does not contain an antecedent for the empty category, the empty category is neither antecedent-governed nor lexically governed, and hence it is not licensed by the constraints in §1. Once (43) is ruled out as a possible initial tree, (42) is excluded as ill-formed without further stipulation. Since (39) is licensed by the TAG version of the ECP, sentence (37) is correctly predicted to be grammatical.[12] This use of the ECP to rule out CED violations is made easy in a TAG because the natural domain of locality in a TAG, the elementary tree, is larger than that normally assumed in other approaches and because the adjunction operation allows the recursive extension of the constraints imposed on a local domain.

3.2. Lexical Government and Extraction from NP

The above analysis leads to a natural explanation for the contrast in acceptability between extraction from complement PPs and modifier PPs. As is well known, extraction from the latter is not possible, leading to the contrast between (37) (repeated as (44)) and (45):

(44)   *Which painting$_i$ did you see a copy of e$_i$?*
(45)   **Which town$_i$ did you see a boy from e$_i$?*

The reason for the unacceptability of (45), however, is apparent from the structure of the auxiliary tree set needed to derive it. The set would have to be as in (46):

(46) a.

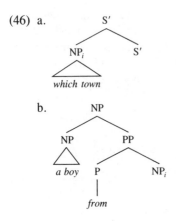

We see immediately that in tree (46b) the empty category of the extracted NP is not properly governed. It is lexically governed by the preposition *from,* but the preposition itself is not lexically governed, since it is not c-commanded by a zero-bar-level category. Hence, by the definitions in (15) and (16), the maximal government domain of NP_i is only PP and not the root of the auxiliary tree. Thus, NP_i is not properly governed and so the configuration in (46b) is ruled out by the ECP.

Once we have introduced auxiliary sets, we must alter our analysis of the Complex NP Constraint. We showed, in Kroch and Joshi (1985) and Kroch (1987), that in a TAG with only simple auxiliary trees, CNPC violations are not generable. In a TAG with auxiliary sets, however, it is possible to generate such violations unless the relevant tree sets are excluded. Thus, consider the following sentence:

(47) **Which book$_i$ did you reject the report which$_j$ e$_j$ mentioned e$_i$?*

Given the initial tree in (48), if we allow the tree set in (49), we can generate (47) by adjoining the tree set to the boldface nodes in the initial tree:

(48)

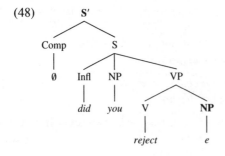

(49) a.

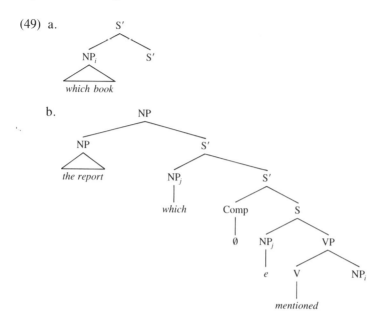

Since the tree in (49b) has the configuration that we have proposed for relative clauses (Kroch and Joshi 1985), the tree set (49) is basically well formed. Like the tree in (46b), however, the maximal government domain of the foot node of (49b) is only a daughter of the root node and not the root node itself. Thus, extraction from relative clauses reduces to an ECP violation, as in the analysis of Kayne (1981).

As has been noted by more than one author (see for example Chomsky 1986), the Complex NP Constraint does not apply with the same strictness to extraction from nominal complements as it does to extraction from relative clauses. The relative acceptability of (50) as compared to (47) is clear evidence of this difference:

(50) ?*Which book$_i$ did you reject the idea that students should read e$_i$?*

The analysis we are proposing relates the difference between these two sentences to the difference in the internal structure of relative clause and nominal complement NPs. Since the N^0 head of a nominal complement governs its complement clause, the maximal government domain of the foot node of the auxiliary tree in (51b) is the root node of the tree, so that the tree is well formed:

(51) a.

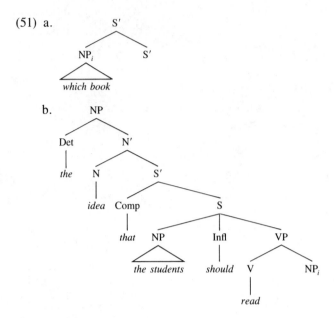

b.

When the tree set (51) is adjoined to the initial tree (48), the sentence (50) is generated.

4. Wh- Islands

4.1. Blocking Extraction from Indirect Questions

Restricting our attention for the moment to simple one-part auxiliary trees, we can insure the ungrammaticality of *wh-* island violations by imposing a well-formedness constraint on elementary trees to the effect that they can contain no more than one fronted *wh-*. This stipulation is needed in any case since multiple *wh-* fronting is impossible in English simple sentences. Since, by the definition of linking, the dislocated element in a *wh-* type dependency must originate in the same elementary tree as the empty category with which it is construed, there will be no way of generating *wh-* island violations. Thus, under a TAG analysis using only one-part trees, the ungrammaticality of the sentences in (52) follows directly from the ill-formedness of the initial trees that would enter into their derivation:

(52) a. *How_i did he wonder $what_j$ you had said e_j e_i?
     b. *Who_i did he wonder $what_j$ e_i had said e_j?

Thus, the initial tree for (52a) would be (53), in which both *how* and *what* are left adjoined to S':

(53)

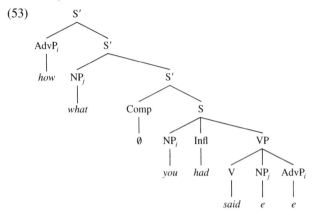

This analysis of the *wh-* island effect makes an interesting prediction that we are, fortunately, able to confirm. If we find a language which, like English, allows extraction freely from tensed clauses and in which multiple *wh-* fronting is possible, we expect extractions from indirect questions to occur freely. As it happens, there is at least one language of the sort needed to test this expectation. The language in question is Rumanian, which shares free extractability from tensed clauses with its Romance sister languages and which has borrowed multiple *wh-* fronting from the Slavic languages that it has for so long been in contact with. Comorovski (1986) reports that, in Rumanian, the multiple *wh-* fronted sentence in (54) is perfectly acceptable, as are *wh-* island extractions like (55), whose English counterpart would be completely unacceptable:

(54) *Cine$_i$ cui$_j$ ce$_k$ ziceai ca t$_i$ i$_j$-a promis t$_k$ t$_j$?* [13]
      'Who$_i$ did you say t$_i$ promised what$_k$ to whom$_j$?'

(55) *Pentru care clauza$_i$ vrei sa afli cine$_j$ t$_j$ nu a decis inca ce$_k$ va vota*
      t$_k$ t$_i$?
      'For which paragraph$_i$ do you want to learn who$_j$ t$_j$ has not decided
      yet what$_k$ he will vote t$_k$ t$_i$?'

As sentence (55) shows, Rumanian allows extraction out of an unbounded number of *wh-* islands, a fact that correlates with the, in principle, unbounded number of *wh-* phrases that can appear at the front of a given clause. Comorovski points out that this correlation is just what is predicted by the subjacency constraint; and the fact that our TAG analysis makes just the same prediction illustrates how directly subjacency follows from the factoring of recursion and local dependencies that the TAG formalism enforces.

4.2. Asymmetries in Extraction from Indirect Questions

Let us now consider the contrast in acceptability between the sentences of (4), repeated as (56):

(56) a. ?*What$_i$ were you wondering [how$_j$ to say e$_i$ e$_j$]?
     b. **How$_i$ were you wondering [what$_j$ to say e$_j$ e$_i$]?

Sentence (56a), while slightly unnatural, seems to us essentially grammatical, whereas (56b) is entirely unacceptable. Under the analysis of *wh-* islands that we have sketched, this difference cannot be accommodated, since in the derivation of either sentence the initial tree would have to contain two preposed *wh-* constituents, and such trees are ill-formed. However, the extension of the TAG formalism to allow auxiliary sets gives us a straightforward way of generating the acceptable sentence (56a) without admitting sentences like (56b). The initial and auxiliary trees needed to derive (56a) are given in (57) below and (58) on the facing page.

(57)

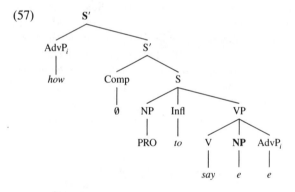

The component (58b) of the tree set is in a sense degenerate since it consists of only one node; but it fits the definition of an athematic auxiliary tree, and its use causes no formal difficulties. When it is adjoined to the NP node dominating the empty category in (57), its only effect is to add the index *j* to that node. The fact that it bears an index is enough to guarantee that it will only be adjoined to a node dominating an empty category, since otherwise the definition of linking would be violated. When the component (58a) is adjoined to the boldface S' node in (57) and the second component to the boldface NP node, the resultant tree (59) represents the sentence (56a).

(58) a.

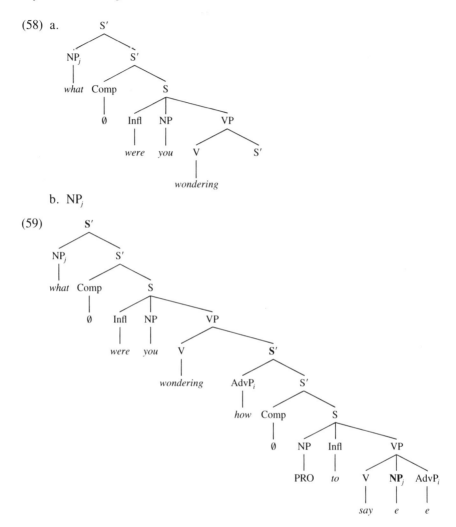

b. NP_j

(59)

Inspection of the elementary trees (57) and (58) makes it clear how to block the generation of (56b). In (57) there are two empty categories, one coindexed with *how* and the other not bearing an index. Both of these empty categories, however, are properly governed, since the indexed one is antecedent-governed and the other is lexically governed. In the trees needed to derive (56b), on the other hand, the initial tree corresponding to (57) would have an index on the lexically governed node, which would thus also be antecedent-governed, and no index on the node which was not lexically governed. Hence the second empty category would not be properly governed. Since we require that empty categories be properly governed in the elementary tree in which they appear, the initial tree needed to generate (56b) is not well formed. Thus, although we have had to use the extension of our formalism to auxiliary sets in order to generate (56a), we need make no changes in our linguistic constraints on the well-formedness of elementary trees to rule out (56b), a welcome result.[14] It should be obvious, moreover, that sentences like (52b), in which a subject is extracted from a *wh-* island, will be ruled out on an auxiliary set analysis just as (56b) is.

4.3. Extraction from Indirect Questions in Italian and English

In his well-known article on subjacency in Italian, Rizzi (1982) pointed out that Italian allowed extraction from indirect questions and so apparently differed from English. More recent work on English, however, has shown that the pattern of allowable extractions is quite similar in the two languages. Thus, the contrast between (56a) and (56b) discussed above is reproduced in Italian (Zanuttini, pers. comm.), and the pattern described by Rizzi can be reproduced in English (Grimshaw 1986). That pattern, whose analysis in a TAG we now propose to consider, is given in (60) and (61). These sentences are slightly modified versions of Grimshaw's sentences (3), (4), (5a), and (5b) respectively:

(60) a. (*I knew*) *which book$_i$ the students would forget who$_j$ e$_j$ wrote e$_i$.*
     b. (*I knew*) *which book$_i$ the TAs told us* (*that*) *the students would forget who$_j$ e$_j$ wrote e$_i$.*
(61) a. *(*I knew*) *which book$_i$ the students would forget who$_j$ e$_j$ told us* (*that*) *Dorothy Sayers wrote e$_i$.*
     b. *(*I knew*) *which book$_i$ the students would forget who$_j$ e$_j$ told us who$_k$ e$_k$ wrote e$_i$.*

As Grimshaw points out, the sentences of (60) are awkward in English but they are a great deal more acceptable than those of (61). Assuming that we wish to capture this contrast in our TAG grammar, we can do so fairly simply. Sentence (60a) is exactly parallel to (56a) and can be generated by adjoining the auxiliary tree set in (62) to the boldface nodes in the initial tree (63). Note that we are ignoring, for the sake of brevity, the inversion of subject and auxiliary. The proper statement of the constraints on this inversion are discussed in detail in Moser (1987).

(62) a.

b. NP_i

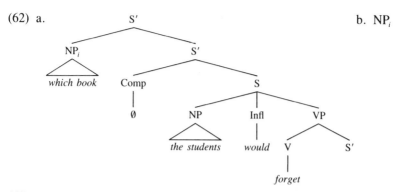

(63)

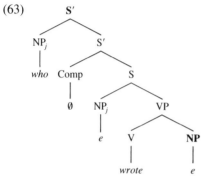

The resultant tree is (64):

(64)

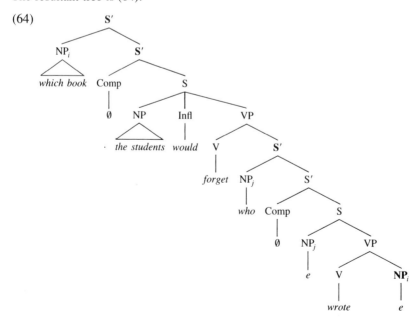

Sentence (60b) can now be generated from (64) by the adjunction of the object complement auxiliary tree in (65) at the second boldface node in the former:

(65)

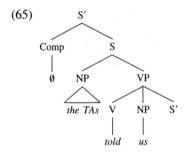

The structure of the resultant tree is obvious.

To avoid generating the sentences of (61), we must add a stipulation to our grammar in the form of a local constraint on all elementary trees with a *wh-* in Comp. The constraint will have the effect of blocking the adjunction of any other *wh-* tree if the result would be to produce a configuration with two *wh-* elements adjacent to one another. This stipulation is needed in any case to rule out sentences like the following: [15]

(66) *(*I know*) *which town$_j$ who$_i$ John persuaded e$_i$ to visit e$_j$.*

Without an appropriate local constraint to block it, sentence (66) will result from the adjunction of the auxiliary tree in (67) to the initial tree in (68):

(67)

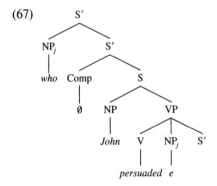

(68)

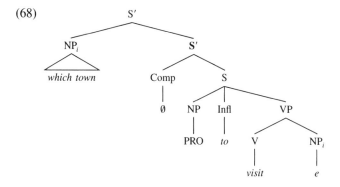

These trees are, of course, well formed and are needed to generate the grammatical sentences of (69) and (70) respectively:

(69) (*I know*) *who John persuaded to visit the town.*
(70) (*I know*) *which town John persuaded you to visit.*

The local constraint we are proposing is also needed to block the generation with two-part trees of simplex sentences with multiple fronted *wh*-elements like those that would correspond to the tree in (53). We have ruled out such structures as possible elementary trees; but with the addition of auxiliary sets, they can now be generated by adjoining an appropriate auxiliary set to a simple sentence with one fronted *wh*- and one unbound empty category. Needless to say, the fact that we must rule out structures with multiple *wh*- fronting at two different levels suggests that our analysis has missed a linguistic generalization. Rectifying this problem is beyond the scope of the present discussion because it requires a substantial reformulation of the notion of local constraint. The required reformulation has been worked out by Vijay-Shankar (1987); and under it, the desired unification of the two constraints is possible (see Moser 1987). This unified constraint remains, however, an independent, hence language-particular, stipulation. That this result is correct is demonstrated by the fact, stressed by Comorovski, that Rumanian shows none of the limitations on extraction out of *wh*- islands found in Italian and English. Further, the Rumanian counterpart of sentence (66) is entirely grammatical.

Once adjunctions are blocked that create structures with multiple fronted *wh*- elements, the sentences of (61) are ruled out whether simple auxiliary trees or auxiliary sets are used in their derivation. Thus, if we attempt to derive the sentences with simple auxiliary trees, the initial trees would have the structures in (71) and the auxiliary trees the structures of (72) and (73):

(71) a.

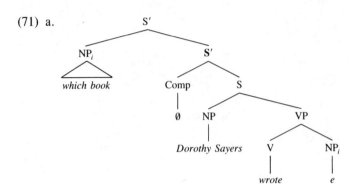

b.

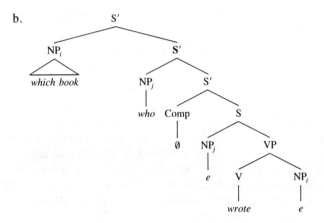

(72)

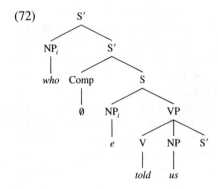

(73)

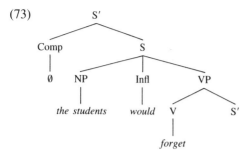

From these structures it is immediately clear that (61b) is ruled out because its initial tree (71b) contains two fronted *wh-* elements. Of course, (61a) is also ruled out, because the adjunction of (72) to (71a) produces the illicit configuration. Note that the derivation under which (73) is first adjoined to (71a) and then (72) is adjoined into the resulting structure is ruled out by the TAG version of the Projection Principle.

If we now try to derive the sentences of (61) using auxiliary sets, we find that the constraint against multiple *wh-* fronting continues to block the derivations. Because of the requirement that all member trees of an auxiliary set be adjoined into the same elementary tree, the auxiliary set containing the preposed *wh-* phrase *which book* must be adjoined to the initial tree containing the verb *wrote* as the first step in the derivations of both (61a) and (61b). As readers can easily check for themselves, this requirement means that any otherwise licit derivation of either sentence will run afoul of the constraint against multiple *wh-* fronting. As before, derivations which avoid violating this constraint are blocked by the local constraint that enforces the Projection Principle.

5. Conclusions

We hope to have shown in this paper that a very wide range of constraints on *wh-* extraction can be accommodated within the TAG formalism in a natural way. A major attraction of the formalism for a generative linguist is the fact that the effects of subjacency follow from the adjunction operation itself once the form of elementary trees is fixed. In an earlier paper (Kroch and Joshi 1985) we presented this result, demonstrating that a TAG would reflect such subjacency phenomena as the *wh-* island effect and the Complex Noun Phrase Constraint, although it contained no explicit reference to the bounding of long-distance dependencies. We were not able, however, to give a satisfactory account of the exceptions to subjacency that have been of concern in the recent transformational literature. In the present paper, by introducing the use of auxiliary tree sets as a supplement to simple auxiliary trees, we have been able to extend our earlier analysis to cover a wide range of apparently exceptional cases. Our earlier work also showed that the ECP could be stated easily as a constraint on the well-formedness of elementary trees, thus accounting for the simplest cases of subject/object extraction asymmetries. The present discussion has shown that the analysis can be extended to the range of cases covered by the CED. Moreover, this extension is made possible by extending the ECP, the major well-formedness constraint on empty categories, to the foot nodes of auxiliary trees, thereby pointing toward an explanation of CED effects along lines similar to Kayne's recent work.

The naturalness with which the TAG formalism incorporates the empirical results of work on constraining *wh-* movement provides, in our opinion, further evidence that the TAG formalism should be considered a serious candidate for the proper notation of universal grammar. This evidence has been accumulating since our first attempts to apply the formalism to linguistic description. In other work, we have shown, among other results, that TAG allows a natural syntactic treatment of subject-to-subject raising (Kroch and Joshi 1985), that it allows an elegant statement of the constraints on extraposition (Kroch and Joshi 1987), and that its additional generative capacity beyond context-free grammar can be exploited to provide a sound syntactic analysis of West Germanic verb raising (Kroch and Santorini forthcoming). The present paper should be seen as a contribution to a larger ongoing project, an attempt to establish the extent and limitations of the utility of TAG to the task of fixing the form of universal grammar.

NOTES

1. This sentence can be assigned two structural descriptions, one with two preposed *wh-* phrases and one with the subject *wh- in situ*. Both structures are ungrammatical but only the former is of interest for our discussion.

2. One of the advantages of stating the well-formedness constraints on auxiliary trees as we have is that they block extraction from sentential subjects. The type of auxiliary tree that would be required for such extractions would have a foot node S' in subject position, and such a tree would not be a possible complement tree since subject position is not lexically governed. Since the tree would not have a Chomsky-adjunction structure, it would also not be a possible athematic tree.

3. We assume in this paper that preposed *wh-* phrases are adjoined to S', as proposed in Baltin (1982).

4. Data from a certain marginal construction in English parallel the pattern in (26) and (27). In unplanned speech, doubly filled Comps sometimes occur in indirect questions, as in the following example taken from a corpus that we have gathered through informal observation:

(i) *That tells you [how many days]$_i$ that the car will be in the shop e$_i$.*

Such examples occur from time to time when the *wh-* element introducing the indirect question is a phrase rather than a simple pronoun, though whether they should be considered grammatical in the colloquial language is difficult to judge. It is striking, however, that, while examples like (i) or cases with lexically governed traces are possible, examples with subject gaps, like (ii), both fail to occur and are entirely unacceptable:

(ii) **I asked her [which car]$_i$ that e$_i$ was in the shop least often.*

It is clear that the difference between (i) and (ii) is due to a difference in the conditions under which subject and adjunct extractions are licensed.

5. This analysis has interesting implications for the analysis of Italian (Chomsky 1981, Rizzi 1982) and other languages that do allow the free inversion of subjects. It has been noted that these languages also allow subject pro-drop, have relatively rich subject–verb agreement, and do not display the *that*-trace effect in extraction from object complements. More than one attempt has been made to relate these features, and our adjacency requirement on the antecedent government of subject traces provides a new perspective on the problem of how to formulate this relationship. Suppose that the verbal agreement affix is sufficiently pronominal to be an antecedent governor of the subject position in a language like Italian but not in English. Then, since Infl is adjacent to the subject position, it will always function as such a governor in Italian, and so the appearance of inverted and extracted subjects will not be constrained by the adjacency requirement, which will always be met by the agreement affix. In English, on the other hand, movement of the subject will be highly constrained, since the moved subject itself must be the antecedent governor of the subject trace.

6. Sentences (34a) and (34b) would be more acceptable if the subordinate clause were introduced by the overt complementizer *that*. Unfortunately, the presence of an overt complementizer in (34c) would make it a violation of the ECP even if the topicalized NP had no effect.

7. In pre-*Barriers* GB analyses, this position is the Comp of the subordinate clause. In the TAG analysis presented here, it is the Chomsky-adjoined fronted position in the initial tree of the subordinate clause.

8. A further piece of evidence that adjacency with an antecedent is required for the government of subject traces is provided by such examples as the following:

(i) *a boss who$_i$ if you were late, e$_i$/he$_i$ used to yell at you*

In a corpus of relative clauses that we collected for another study (Kroch 1982), we found that resumptive pronouns were extremely common and highly acceptable in relative clauses of this type. Indeed, in speech, the resumptive pronoun occurs much more often than not. Moreover, while in other constructions, resumptive pronouns on subject position are very rare, in particular rarer than resumptive pronouns in VP, in this case they are more common on subject than object position. Thus, resumptive pronouns were more common in sentences like (i) than in sentences like (ii):

(ii) *a boss who$_i$ if you were late, you had to lie to e$_i$/him$_i$*

This pattern makes this sort of relative clause seem similar to relatives in which a resumptive pronoun amnesties an ECP violation, as in (iii):

(iii) *a problem that$_i$ I couldn't figure out how$_j$ it$_i$/*e$_i$ had been solved e$_j$*

These cases are clearly ungrammatical without a resumptive pronoun and are quite acceptable in colloquial speech with one. To see how these facts are related to the point under discussion here, note the following pair of sentences:

(iv) *When it rains, Mary likes to go for walks.*
(v) *Mary, when it rains, likes to go for walks.*

Both of these sentences are grammatical. In Baltin's (1982) terms, the adverbial clause in (iv) is adjoined to S and the one in (v) to VP. Assuming this description for the sake of concreteness, we can note that a relative clause on subject position based on the structure of (iv) will violate the adjacency requirement on the subject trace-antecedent link, as the following bracketing illustrates:

(vi) *a girl* [$_{S'}$ *who$_i$* [$_S$ *when it rains* [$_S$ *e$_i$ likes to go for walks*]]]

On the other hand, if the relative clause is based on the structure of (v), the adverbial clause, being adjoined to VP, will not intervene between the antecedent and trace. From these facts, the adjacency requirement predicts that relative clauses containing preposed adverbials should be possible both with and without resumptive pronouns, which is indeed the case. Furthermore, it is not surprising, given the highly marked character of the word order in (v), that the resumptive pronoun relative is the favored option in colloquial speech.

9. This constraint is not easily statable in the TAG formalism as we have presented it here. The addition of feature structures to nodes worked out in Vijay-Shankar (1987) makes possible the natural statement of this constraint as well as the other local constraints mentioned in the paper.

10. A TAG version of the Projection Principle is needed, among other reasons, to rule out an illicit derivation of a sentence like (i) from the initial tree in (9) (repeated here as the labelled bracketing in (ii)) and the auxiliary tree in (iii):

(i) *The child thought that I saw you.*
(ii) [$_S$ [$_{NP}$ *the child*][$_{VP}$ *saw you*]]
(iii)

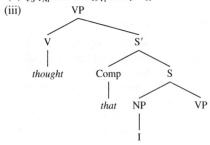

The tree in (iii) does not violate any of the well-formedness constraints on elementary trees that we have proposed, but its use in any derivation would lead to the sort of change in thematic relations that we want to rule out in principle. We thank Ken Safir for pointing out the problem posed by such unwanted structures.

11. Huang's argument for distinguishing the ECP from the CED is based on facts from Chinese, a language without syntactic *wh-* movement. Huang gives evidence that Chinese obeys the ECP but not the CED, and so he concludes that the ECP applies at the level of Logical Form while the CED is a constraint on syntactic movement. This argument depends on assumptions about the nature of Logical Form that seem to us not well established.

12. A TAG analysis of the sort we are giving agrees with Kayne (1983) in treating the subjects of the infinitive complements of exceptional case–marking (ECM) verbs as being antecedent-governed rather than lexically governed even though these subjects are case-marked by the matrix verb. The correctness of this approach is supported by the ungrammaticality of extractions from such subject NPs. Thus, note the contrast between (i) and (ii):

(i)   *Who$_i$ do you expect the parents of e$_i$?*
(ii) **Who$_i$ do you expect the parents of e$_i$ to visit Rome?*

Given the discussion of antecedent government in §2.2, our analysis also predicts that Heavy–NP Shift of the subjects of complements to ECM verbs should be ungrammatical. Here the facts are less clear, but there seems to be a contrast between the object control case in (iii) and the ECM case in (iv):

(iii) *I persuaded e$_i$ to tackle the problem [a friend of mine from school]$_i$.*
(iv) *?I believe e$_i$ to have made the discovery [a friend of mine from school]$_i$.*

To the extent that (iv) is better than expected, this may reflect a superficial process of reanalysis under which the phrase *believe to have made the discovery* becomes a complex verb.

13. The dative pronoun in this sentence is, as Comorovski shows, not a resumptive pronoun but an ordinary Romance doubled clitic.

14. For reasons that we do not understand, extractions that require the use of two-part auxiliary tree sets in a TAG share the feature that they are much more acceptable when the subject of the initial tree and the subject of the auxiliary tree are coreferential. Thus, the examples in the text are more acceptable than the following:

(i)   *?Which lines were you wondering how the actor said?*
(ii)   *?Which city did you buy John's picture of?*
(iii) *?Which novel were you wondering who wrote?*

Similarly, extractions from *wh-* islands, at least in English, are more acceptable when the embedded clause contains an infinitive or modal than when the embedded verb is tensed. Since the temporal interpretation of infinitive and modal verbs in indirect questions is usually controlled by the tense of the matrix sentence, this may also indicate that binding relations are relevant to extraction in two-part-tree cases.

15. We thank Polly Jacobson for pointing out the difficulties posed for us by sentences like (66).

5

Clitics and Phrase Structure

ALEC MARANTZ

Traditional phrase-structure (PS) rules describe the hierarchical arrangement and the left-right adjacency relations among constituents according to their syntactic categories. Recent work, however, has separated the hierarchical and ordering functions of PS rules. Hierarchical relations are constrained by general X-bar principles and, within a sentence, by some sort of Projection Principle that specifies how certain relations must be represented structurally. Linear order is constrained by principles regulating, for instance, the adjacency or direction of Government and Case-marking. Outside Government-Binding (GB) theory, similar assumptions are made about the nature of phrase structure. Hierarchical structure in Generalized Phrase Structure Grammar (and related theories) and Lexical-Functional Grammar determines or is determined by semantic and/or functional composition and feature percolation, while linear order is set independently, at least in principle, either by linear precedence statements or by stipulation within PS rules. What most contemporary syntactic theories assume is that (a) a residue of X-bar principles has some function in constraining constituent structure and (b) constraints on linear order have as their domain constituent structures obeying these X-bar principles.

This paper begins with the hypothesis that a slightly extended Projection Principle (Chomsky 1981) totally replaces any X-bar constraints on constituent structure. That is, the X-bar character of constituent structure, with the heads of phrases determining the category and features of these phrases, follows from the way that relations among constituents are projected into the syntax. Given this hypothesis, I argue that the distribution of clitics in constituent structure indicates that linear adjacency is a property of a level of syntactic analysis—call it surface structure, phonological structure, or PF—that does not obey X-bar constraints. Although the Projection Principle is obeyed at phonological structure, with its hierarchical structure projected from the relations that hold at this level of analysis, phonological structures do not conform to standard X-bar principles.

Consider first the problem that clitic constructions present for X-bar theory, or indeed any constrained system of phrase-structure rules or principles. Some representative clitic constructions are found in (1).

(1)   SYNTACTIC STRUCTURE   SURFACE PHRASE STRUCTURE
    a. [$_{PP}$ *de* [$_{NP}$ *le garçon*]   [$_{PP}$ [$_?$ *du*][$_?$ *garçon*]]
        of   the boy   of-the boy   (French)
    b. *Sa-sạ̰ạy Alchico* [$_{NP}$ *níí*   *Sa+sạ̰ạy Alchico+níí Rospita+rà*
        AGR-give Alchico   3sgOBJ   *pạ̰ạ*   (Yagua)
        Rospita][$_{NP}$ *rà   pạ̰ạ*]
        Rospita   InAnOBJ bread
    c. [$_{S'}$ *'o* [$_S$ [$_{V'}$ [$_{NEG}$ *pi*] *iam-hu cikpan*] *g*   [[[*pi+'o*] *iam-hu cikpan*] *g Huan*]
        AUX   NEG   there   work   ART   (Papago)
        Huan]]
        John
        'John is not working there'

The French prepositional clitic *de* 'of' in (1a) prefixes to the first constituent of its NP object. It shows a special suppletive form *du* 'of the (masc. sg.)' when it combines with the article *le* 'the (masc. sg.).' In Yagua (Payne 1986), as exemplified in (1b), certain definite specifiers on object NPs appear before the NPs that they specify, but phonologically they suffix to the last word that happens to come before the specified NP in the sentence. Payne (1986) carefully shows that these specifiers are in fact syntactically part of the phrases on their right but phonologically part of the word on their left. This sort of NP marker, phonologically bracketed outside the NP to which it belongs syntactically, is also found in Kwakwatl (Klavans 1985). In Papago (Pranka 1983), when the verbal constituent V' is the first major constituent of the sentence, the AUX clitic appears after the first element of V', as shown in (1c). The particles within the V' must occur in the order shown, and may be split up only by an AUX clitic in second position, as in the example. If some major constituent is topicalized or placed in sentence initial Comp position, then the AUX clitic remains in S-initial position, after the topic or Comp and thus in second position overall.

The essential disturbing feature of constructions containing clitics is that they do not directly obey any sort of X-bar constraints on syntax. It should be obvious that no directly motivated labeled bracketing of the strings in the right column of (1) will conform to the X-bar convention. For example, what sort of X-bar constituent is the combination of a preposition and a determiner such as French *du* in (1a)? Rather, clitic constructions in general conform to X-bar principles only with reference to some structure other than their surface phonological representation, some structure like the structures in the left column of (1). That is, given the X-bar–consistent structures on the left, we might imagine generating the structures on the right by a cliticization movement rule, moving the clitics into their surface phonological positions. The question for X-bar theory is whether the left-hand structures are motivated as linearly ordered surface structures in the derivations of the structures at issue. That is, do the clitic constructions on the right in (1) come from a level of analysis showing both X-bar constituent structure and linear order? I will show that clitic structures like (1) are derived directly from the unordered S-structure representations via the regular principles that map from these S-structures to linearly ordered surface structure representations. Moreover, the crucial information relevant to deriving the clitic constructions is present at S-structure but not in phrase-structure representations like those on the left in (1). If this conclusion is correct, then X-bar principles are not true of any structure displaying left-right linear order in the grammar.

The key to a grammar lacking PS rules is some sort of Projection Principle. Chomsky (1981) writes his Projection Principle as a constraint on constituent structure trees at D-structure, S-structure, and logical form, allowing phonological or surface structure (PF) to deviate from these other structures. Given the structure of the grammar in (2), I will claim that the Projection Principle applies at surface structure as well, directly constraining the phonologically interpreted representation of a sentence.

(2)

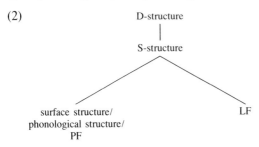

The Extended Projection Principle needed to project phonological structures is given in (3).

(3) For all pairs of constituents (X, Y), a relation $R(X, Y)$ at one level of representation of a sentence in the syntax must map onto a relation $R'(X', Y')$ at any other level of representation of the sentence, where X' and Y' are the constituents "corresponding" to X and Y at the other representation in a sense of "corresponding" made explicit in the theory (see (5) below).

The Extended Projection Principle may apply to surface structure because it recognizes that the lexical—D-structure—properties of θ-role assignment and semantic argument–taking correspond at each level of syntactic analysis to relations relevant at that level. For example, a θ-role–assigning relation at D-structure might correspond to a linear adjacency relation at surface structure, or perhaps to a morphological case-marking or agreement relation, where linear adjacency, case-marking, and agreement are relations characteristic of surface structures. The levels and relations relevant at each level are shown in (4).

(4) LEVEL OF ANALYSIS   RELATIONS AT THIS LEVEL
    D-structure   argument structure, θ-assignment
    │   Mapping: if Y bears a relation to X at D-structure, Y′ must bear a
    │   relation to X′ (or to a constituent headed by X′) at
    ↓   S-structure
    S-structure   Government, Case-assignment
    │   Mapping: if Y bears a relation to X at S-structure, Y′ must bear a
    │   relation to X′ at surface structure
    ↓
    PF   morphological case-marking and agreement,
                                 sisterhood in a surface PS tree (= structural
                                 government), linear (left- or right-)adjacency

In (4) I have also displayed the mapping principles that constrain the relationship between the levels of representation (see Marantz 1984 for detailed explanation of these mappings). The mapping principles in (4) connecting D- and S-structure and S- and surface structure realize the Extended Projection Principle (3). That is, to obey these mapping principles is to obey principle (3). These principles describe how relations at each level are to be connected—projected—to relations at neighboring levels.

In mapping from level to level, the D-structure relations of θ-assignment and semantic argument–taking—where to take an argument is often called "to subcategorize for"—must correspond at S-structure to relations of abstract Case assignment or syntactic Government. To extend the Projection Principle to surface structure, we require that the relations at S-structure map onto relations relevant to surface structure, notably the tree structure relations of left- or right-adjacency and structural government ("sisterhood") and the morphological relations of morphological case-marking and morphological agreement (if X morphologically case-marks Y, morphology determined by X appears on Y; if X morphologically agrees with Y, morphology determined by Y appears on X).

On the model of grammar in (4), a representation at each level consists of a set of constituents and relations, not a constituent structure tree. The constituents and relations of surface structure constrain the construction of a surface structure tree that will be phonologically interpreted, that is, serve as input to the phonological rules. Although the constituents and relations at each level may be represented by a tree at each level, the mapping between levels is defined over the list of constituents and relations, not over tree representations. In Marantz (1984) I discuss some of the implications of demanding that D- and S-structures be representable in trees.

Within the syntactic theory under consideration, X-bar principles reduce to principles of functional composition, as in a categorial grammar. Categories are defined according to their combinatorial potential. For example, argument-takers are functions from X to X', modifiers take constituents of type X to constituents of type X, and so forth. This categorial approach to syntactic categories combines our understanding of the way relations are projected into constituent structure with our knowledge of the correspondence between syntactic and compositional-semantic categories. For example, we project a verb's arguments as its sisters at D-structure, and we know it combines semantically with these arguments to produce a constituent that may assign the subject θ-role. Although it is possible to define a VP or V' independently within X-bar theory, I will claim that we should acknowledge that the VP is simply and essentially the combination of the verb and its arguments, with the V as the VP's functional and thus categorial head.

Although the categorial approach to constituent structure may appear foreign within canonical GB theory, it in fact accords with GB practice at D- and S-structure. That is, the projection of relations within GB theory conforms to the categorial interpretation of constituent labels. What is important to note about the theory in (4) and about GB practice is that there are not two distinct animals—relational constraints on argument-taking, θ-assignment, etc., on the one hand; and constituent structure constraints about hierarchical organization of head and complements, head and specifiers on the other. Rather, there is a single set of relational constraints, since relations are consistently mapped into constituent structures throughout the grammar by the Projection Principle.

The clitic constructions in (1) are directly analyzed within a grammar obeying the Extended Projection Principle. The S-structure of the constructions in (1) are mapped onto a set of relations satisfied by the surface structures on the right. No intermediate tree representations like those on the left in (1) are necessary to derive these structures. In explaining the distribution and behavior of clitics, it is necessary to appreciate their dual nature. As syntactic constituents, clitics are mapped by projection to bear certain surface structure relations—they are positioned as if they were phonologically independent constituents. However, as affixes, clitics have left- or right-morphological subcategorization frames, demanding to be attached to the left or right of a stem; that is, they superimpose their own left/right adjacency requirements over their syntactic positioning. For example, as determiners, the Yagua clitics in (1b) are ordered before the NPs they specify. However, as morphological suffixes, they must attach to the right of something. These dual constraints are met if the clitics appear before their NP complements but suffix to the last word of whatever constituent is ordered before these NPs.

To understand how the mapping of S-structure to phonological structure relations determines a phonological structure or PF tree, we imagine that the mapping of S-structure to phonological relations yields a set of restrictions on adjacency, surface case marking, and surface agreement that must be simultaneously met by the phonological structure tree. These requirements might be met by various possible phonological structure trees; however, independent constraints on the structure of phonologically interpreted trees conspire to narrow down the possibilities to just those that are grammatical. Still, various word orders or hierarchical structures might correspond to a single S-structure in some language.

As indicated in the statement of the Projection Principle (3), the mapping between levels in the grammar depends on a concept of how a constituent at one level can correspond to a constituent at a neighboring level. In Marantz (1984) I anchor the mapping between constituents at different levels to lexical items, which map themselves from level to level. That is, each lexical entry includes not an unstructured list of features for a morpheme, but rather a mapping between features of the morpheme relevant at each level of representation. Let's name the function that gives us the constituent corresponding to X at the next level of analysis COR(X). The lexicon itself determines COR(X) for all X that are lexical items. This property of lexical items allows us to define COR(X) recursively, depending on the notion of "head of a phrase" or HEAD(XP) at each level of analysis.

(5) COR(X) a. for X a lexical item, COR(X) is determined by the lexical entry for X;

b. for X a phrase headed by Y, that is, Y = HEAD(X), COR(X) = phrase headed by COR(Y), i.e., HEAD(COR(X)) = COR(Y).

That is, COR(X) for X a phrase is the constituent at the next level of analysis whose head is the constituent corresponding to the head of X at the next level of analysis.

In the mapping between S-structure and PF, applying the COR function blindly would yield a structural isomorphism between the two levels, disallowing the sorts of "bracketing paradoxes" or rebracketings between the levels that the clitic constructions in (1) display. However, a general principle of grammar taken with a particular understanding of the notion of "head" at phonological structure yields the observed mismatch between S-structure and PF bracketing in clitic constructions. Sproat (1985) explains this sort of mismatch by invoking the "associativity" of the adjacency relation at PF. He applies this understanding of adjacency to account for the sorts of morphological bracketing paradoxes discussed in Pesetsky (1985). Here we will see that the associativity of adjacency follows from more general principles on the nature of relations.

To see how the associativity of adjacency is derived, consider the situation schematized in (6a)–(6c), in which an S-structure constituent X whose phonological structure counterpart COR(X) must be left-adjacent to COR(Y), where Y at S-structure consists of Z and W, and COR(Z) is right-adjacent to COR(W). A concrete example of this situation could be the French clitic construction in (1a), which is analyzed in (6) alongside the schematic example. In what follows we use the asterisk to indicate the adjacency relation although this notation masks the fact that the adjacency relation is asymmetric—in the mapping to PF, if X * Y, then either X has been positioned to the left of Y to correspond to some relation in which the S-structure counterpart to X is the operator, or Y has been positioned to the right of X to correspond to some relation in which the S-structure counterpart to Y is the operator.

(6) a. $[_Y$ W Z], where Z = HEAD(Y)   Y = NP, Z = N, $[_{PP}$ *de*
                                                       $[_{NP}$ *le garçon*]]
    b. COR(X) * COR(Y)   COR(*de*) * COR(NP)
    c. COR(W) * COR(Z)   COR(*le*) * COR(*garçon*)
    d. COR(X) * [COR(W) *   COR(*de*) * [COR(*le*) *
       COR(Z)]   COR(*garçon*)]

Since, by the definition in (5), COR(Y) is the constituent headed by the COR(HEAD(Y)), that is, the constituent headed by COR(Z), COR(X) will be left-adjacent to the constituent headed by COR(Z), which will contain both COR(W) and COR(Z). We now appeal to the general principle that to govern a phrase is to govern the head of the phrase, where "govern" is taken in the general sense of "bear a relation to." Thus to be adjacent to a phrase at phonological structure is equivalent to being adjacent to the head of this phrase. But what is the head of a phrase at PF? For locating clitics and for describing generalizations about the direction of Case-marking and

about the location of S-structure heads in a PF phrase, a peripheral-head
definition seems appropriate for PF. That is, the head of a phrase is the
leftmost constituent if the grammar looks at it from the left, or the rightmost constituent if the grammar looks at it from the right. In a sense, then,
phrases are two-headed at PF but show a single head for purposes of working out adjacency relations, since adjacency involves the left or right edges
of phrases.

At the end of this paper, I return to how the peripheral-head notion at
phonological structure helps capture the apparent directionality of θ- and
Case-assignment. Here, I complete the demonstration that adjacency is
generally associative on this notion. Given that COR(X) is left-adjacent to
the constituent consisting of COR(W) and COR(Z), where COR(W) is left-
adjacent to COR(Z), then the adjacency constraints in (6d) are equivalent
to the constraints in (7a), which are satisfied by the structure in (7b).

(7) a. [COR(X) * COR(W)] *   [COR(*de*) * COR(*le*)] *
            COR(Z)   COR(*garçon*)
    b. [[X W] Z]   [[COR(*de*) COR(*le*)] *garçon*]

It should be clear that iterative applications to adjacency requirements
of the principle "to govern a phrase is to govern its head" taken with the
peripheral definition of head at PF will allow associative rebracketing of
constituents within the formal statement of these adjacency requirements,
like the statements in (6b)–(6d). Crucially, the rebracketings take place
within the relations that constrain the surface-structure tree, not within the
tree itself. Therefore, the associative rebracketings necessary to license
clitic constructions do not involve manipulations of constituent structure
but rather involve an interpretation of how to apply adjacency constraints
to a constituent-structure tree.

In (8) I show the critical constraints on PF derived via the mapping from
S-structure for the clitic constructions in (1). Informally, I indicate the adjacency requirements by using the asterisk notation to connect ortho-
graphic representations of the morphemes involved. So X * Y means that
the phonological representation of X is left-adjacent to the phonological
representation of Y, or Y is right-adjacent to X.

(8) a. *de* * [*garçon, le*]
           le * *garçon, de-* is a prefix
    b. *nii* * *Rospita, ra* * *paa*
           [*Alchico*] * [*nii, Rospita*] * [*ra, paa*]
           -nii, -ra are suffixes
    c. *'o* * [[*g, Huan*], [*pi, iam-hu, cikpan*]]

> *g * Huan, pi * iam-hu * cikpan*
> -'*o* is a suffix

In (8a), for example, as we saw in (6) and (7), the preposition *de* must be left-adjacent to the NP containing [*le, garçon*]. It meets this requirement by being left-adjacent to the leftmost constituent in this NP, *le,* i.e. by being left-adjacent to the phonological head of the NP at PF and by affixing to this head.

The Yagua case in (8b) is also straightforward. Although as suffixes the clitics must attach toward their left and thus to the right of some stem, the clitics must remain, associatively, left-adjacent to their NP complements. Suffixed, as they are in (1b), to the phonological head—the rightmost constituent—of the phrase preceding their NP complements, the Yagua clitics meet all the required adjacency constraints.

To derive the Papago clitic construction in (1c) from the constraints in (8c) we need an additional principle. By the associativity of adjacency, the clitic may adjoin to the first member (the PF head) of the V' constituent (itself the PF head of the S when V' is S-initial), even though the clitic is related to the whole S containing the V'. However, to satisfy the adjacency requirement between the AUX and the sentence, the AUX clitic should be a prefix on this leftmost word—the left-head of the sentence—and thus be associatively left-adjacent to the sentence. The AUX should not appear as a suffix to the leftmost word, because as a suffix it is no longer even associatively left-adjacent to the sentence. What happens in Papago is that the adjacency relation between the clitic and the first constituent of the V' is replaced by the affixation relation between these constituents, instantiating the principle of Morphological Merger given in (9).

(9) At any level of syntactic analysis, independent syntactic constituents X and Y standing in a relation at that level (or heading phrases standing in a relation) may merge into a single word, X + Y, projecting the relation between (the constituent headed by) X and (the constituent headed by) Y onto the affixation relation X + Y. In accordance with the Projection Principle, other relations involving X and Y (and constituents headed by X and Y) must continue to be projected in the usual way.

Marantz (1984) shows how Morphological Merger operates at every level of syntax, accounting, for example, for the syntax of derived causative constructions and applied verb constructions (see Marantz forthcoming b for a comparison of recent approaches to "syntactic affixation" like that involved in causative constructions). Crucially, Merger projects some relation in syntax onto the affixation relation between morphemes, removing this syntactic relation from projection onto other relations, like adjacency or case-marking at PF. In the Papago example, the adjacency relation between the AUX and NEG particles is replaced by the affixation relation between these elements. But, as an affix, the AUX is a suffix and thus appears to the right of NEG. The derived word, NEG plus AUX, takes over the relations of the NEG particle. In particular, the adjacency relation between the NEG and the locative particle to its right within the V' is satisfied by the adjacency of the NEG + AUX and this particle after Merger.

This analysis highlights an essential feature of Merger: only the relation between the merged constituents is projected onto the affixation relation in Merger; other relations borne by the merged constituents must still be met. For example, in the Papago case, the AUX could not suffix internal to the V' if it were involved in an adjacency relation with respect to a constituent on its left. Attached to the right of the NEG particle within the V', the AUX would not be adjacent to a constituent to the left of the V'. If we assume that the affix is always the head for determining features of derived words, the combination of NEG + AUX in Papago should take over the adjacency requirements of the AUX; thus, in principle, the derived NEG + AUX would meet the AUX's requirement to be to the right of the constituent to the left of V'. However, on such an analysis, the NEG particle would no longer be left-adjacent to the next particle in V': the NEG + AUX constituent would take over the AUX's adjacency requirements and, with the AUX between NEG and the next constituent of V', NEG would not even be associatively adjacent to this next constituent. If we assumed that the NEG + AUX constituent took over the adjacency requirements of NEG, then AUX would not meet its requirements with respect to the constituent to the left of NEG + AUX. As we shall see, when some constituent does appear to the left of AUX, in Topic or Comp position, then the AUX clitic may no longer appear internal to a phrase like V'.

Although for present purposes we need invoke Morphological Merger only in the analysis of the Papago AUX clitic, in Marantz (forthcoming a) I argue that Merger is always involved whenever a syntactically independent morpheme shows up as part of a word at surface structure, as in cliticization. Thus all clitic constructions involve the Merger of the clitic with the host word, replacing an adjacency relation between these constituents with the affixation of one to the other.

The present analysis of clitics, presented more fully in Marantz (forthcoming a), constrains the distribution of clitics to just that observed cross-linguistically (see Klavans 1985 for a survey of clitic positions and Marantz forthcoming a for a critique and explanation of Klavans's findings). In fact, the analysis allows the conceptually minimal theory of clitics—clitics are syntactically independent constituents that have morphological subcategorization specifications about direction of attachment. That is, beyond giving a clitic the usual lexical information that determines its syntactic function in a sentence, the clitic need only be specified as a prefix or a suffix. Independently motivated general principles completely determine the proper location for clitics given this information.

For example, all we need to say about the Yagua specifier clitics is that they are suffixes. Functionally, they mark definiteness of objects, i.e., they are governed by the verb and do not appear with subjects or obliques. To satisfy their adjacency relation with respect to their NP complement, these clitics could appear where they actually do appear, as in (10a), or, like the Papago AUX clitic, they could appear suffixed to the first word of their NP complement, as shown schematically in (10b). However, if they were positioned internal to the NP, the government relation between them and the verb determining their object status could not project onto any surface-structure relation, for internal to an NP, they would not be in a position to be structurally governed by the V. Alternatively, we might suppose that the affixation of the clitic to the first constituent of the NP (A in (10b)) causes this constituent (A + Det) to take over all the relations of the clitic and thus allows the V to govern the clitic by governing the NP, thus the head (the leftmost constituent) of the NP, thus the clitic as head of the NP. In that case, the affixation would prevent A from meeting its adjacency require- . ments with respect to the constituent on its right (B in (10b)). With the clitics suffixed to the leftmost constituent in the NP and with the derived word A + Det taking over the relations of Det, A + Det is no longer even associatively adjacent to B.

(10) a. . . . A + Det][$_{NP}$ B . . .
     b. . . .][$_{NP}$ A + Det B . . .

However, where the Yagua clitics actually show up, as the rightmost constituent of a phrase structurally governed by the V at PF as in (10a), they do stand in a surface-structure relation with respect to the verb. For the heads of a surface-structure phrase, as we have seen, are the left- and rightmost constituents in the phrase. And to govern a phrase is to govern its head. So, being the rightmost constituent of a phrase governed by the verb, the Yagua clitic is itself governed by the verb. Moreover, since the Yagua clitic attaches to the right of the last constituent in the host NP, this constituent remains associately adjacent to the constituent on its left, allowing it to maintain its PF relations after affixation of the clitic.

In Papago, the AUX clitic may be minimally specified as a suffix. In case no constituent is topicalized to the left of AUX or moved via *wh*-movement to Comp to AUX's left, neutral word order will place the V' constituent sentence-initial. As a suffix positioned left-adjacent to S, the AUX clitic must Merge with the first word in the sentence, i.e., the first morpheme in V', which is the head of the sentence at PF, given the peripheral definition of head. However, if some constituent is ordered before the AUX for syntactic reasons—say in topicalizations or *wh*-questions—then the AUX will simply suffix to the last element of the fronted constituent. Thus we find the sorts of structures in (11a)–(11c), where the XP is a Topic or other fronted constituent. Pranka (1983) gives prosodic evidence for fronting in these cases—the prosodic structure here differs from that in sentences showing neutral word order with V' as the initial constituent. Particularly interesting, and predicted by the present analysis, is the ungrammaticality of the structure in (11d). That is, even when the AUX finds itself adjacent to the V' according to syntactic requirements, it may not cliticize to the first member of the V' if there is some constituent to its left within the S', that is, if it has a left-looking adjacency requirement that it must meet.

(11) a.   XP+AUX V' . . .
      b.   XP+AUX XP . . .
      c.   *wh*+AUX XP . . .
      d.   *XP [$_{V'}$ *pi* + AUX . . .

Latin apparently shows a second-position clitic that confirms our relational analysis of the constraints on clitic positions. According to Sadock (1985), the Latin conjunction *-que* appears after the first word of the last conjunct, as shown in (12a). An example from Sadock is shown in (12b).

(12) a.

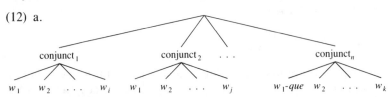

      b.   [*boni pueri*][*bellae-que   puellae*]
           good boys beautiful-and girls

All the grammar need specify here is that the Latin conjunction is a suffix and that it marks the last conjunct at PF. The important relational point about conjunction is that it is a relation among the conjuncts or between a conjunctive operator and all the conjuncts, not a relation between a conjunction and the last conjunct. Languages tend to mark the conjunction relation with a morpheme on all the conjuncts or just the last conjunct. In

Latin and English, the conjunctive morpheme phonologically marks the last conjunct and should be seen as having only PF features. This morpheme must be left-adjacent to the last conjunct in the conjunction at PF. The adjacency requirements on a structure like (12b) would be as shown in (13a), with the first conjunct required to be related to the second conjunct, and the *-que* required to appear adjacent to the second conjunct. A parallel case from English, the translation of the Latin example, is shown in (13b). Given that *-que* is a suffix, the structure in (14a) is the only one possible that meets the adjacency requirements. In particular, the structure in (14b), with *-que* suffixed to the last element of the first conjunct, would not conform to the adjacency requirements in (13a).

(13) a. COR([*boni, pueri*]) * COR([*bellae, puellae*])
         -que * COR([*bellae, puellae*])
     b. COR([$_{NP}$ *good boys*]) * COR([$_{NP}$ *beautiful girls*])
         and * COR([$_{NP}$ *beautiful girls*])
(14) a. [*boni pueri*][*bellae-que puellae*]
     b. [*boni pueri-que*][*bellae puellae*]
     c. [*good boys*][*and* [*beautiful girls*]]

In order to exploit the associativity of adjacency to allow for the structure in (14b), we would have to "unpack" the adjacency relation between the conjuncts in (13a) and find *-que* as the left head of the second conjunct adjacent to the right head of the first conjunct. But, since the positioning of *-que* is determined by an independent adjacency statement in (13a), the statement that places the conjunction before the last conjunct, no unpacking of the constituents and relations in (13a) will ever locate *-que* to the right of the first conjunct. Thus no computations over the adjacency requirements will allow the structure in (14b). Note that the English phonological structure in (14c), with *and* phonologically adjoined to the second conjunct, will satisfy the adjacency requirements in (13b) because the first conjunct will fall adjacent to COR([*beautiful girls*]) by being adjacent to the phrase [*and* [*beautiful girls*]]. The phonological phrase [*and* [*beautiful girls*]] is headed by COR(HEAD([*beautiful girls*])), as it must be according to the definition of COR in (5) because it is headed by COR([*beautiful girls*]) itself.

The Yagua and Latin examples discussed above are superficially identical. Both involve suffixal clitics that are positioned before the phrase to which they are related. However, the relational structures in which the clitics occur determine automatically that the Latin clitic will suffix to the first word of its relational dependent while the Yagua clitics suffix to the last word of the preceding constituent. Crucially, in Latin *-que*'s relational dependent, the last conjunct, is directly related at surface structure to the preceding constituent, the preceding conjunct, while in Yagua, the NP complement to the specifier clitics is not directly related at surface structure to the preceding phrase. On the other hand, Latin -*que* need only satisfy one PF relation, while the Yagua clitics bear relations with respect to both their NP complements and the governing verb. These relational differences determine the difference in the location of the clitics.

The main argument of the paper is now complete. The surface structures of clitic constructions do not obey X-bar principles, yet they are derived in accordance with the generalized Projection Principle directly from S-structures that do not encode linear order information. Moreover, the information necessary to correctly predict the behavior of clitics is S-structure —relational—information as mapped onto PF relations, not information encoded in some conceivable precliticization, linearly ordered tree. Therefore, linear order is a property only of a level that does not obey X-bar restrictions. Principles about the direction of Case-marking or θ-assignment must be principles involved in the mapping from S-structure to PF, not ordering principles constraining an X-bar–consistent level of representation at D- or S-structure.

To drive home this point, consider a movement analysis of cliticization, one that would derive the right-hand structures in (1) from an X-bar–consistent, linearly ordered tree structure like the left-hand structures. First note that, whatever Clitic Movement is, it is not a good candidate for an instantiation of a general trace-leaving Move-α. In most cases, the traces left by Clitic Movement would not be c-commanded by the moved clitic. Moreover, constraints on Clitic Movement seem strictly to involve linear adjacency, which is not associated with constraints on Move-α.

Therefore, to generate clitic constructions from linearly ordered precliticization tree structures, we would need to develop a special Clitic Movement rule. The simplest possibility for such a rule would involve specifying only whether the clitic is a prefix or a suffix. If it is a suffix, it would attach to the right of the word to its left in the precliticization structure; if a prefix, it would attach to the left of the word on its right. However, this sort of movement would not be sufficient to account for movement into a phrase, as in the Latin and Papago examples. But any specification we give to a clitic beyond its syntactically determined position and its status as prefix or suffix would allow clitics in places that they do not occur. That is, a movement analysis that allows clitics to move inside phrases will allow too much. In Marantz (forthcoming a) I show how one analysis along these lines, that in Klavans (1985), predicts clitic positions that are not observed. However, the guaranteed restrictive failure of any movement analysis of clitics should be clear from the analyses of this paper. I showed above that specifying a clitic's syntactic positioning and its status as a prefix or suffix is necessary and sufficient to predict its positioning at PF, but only given relational information not encoded in the dominance and precedence relations of a hypothetical pre-cliticization surface structure. Rather, the necessary relational information is available only in the S-structure and in the constraints on surface structure derived from S-structure via the Extended Projection Principle. A movement theory that is flexible enough to allow for the placement of the Latin conjunction could not prevent the Yagua clitics from appearing in a position within the NPs they modify, because the relational information that determines the actual positioning of these clitics is not represented at surface constituent structure.

Given that linear order is a property only of the surface-structure tree, all constraints on the linear positioning of syntactic heads and on the direction of syntactic relations such as Case-marking must involve the mapping from S-structure to adjacency constraints on PF. Our conclusion from the analysis of clitics that headedness at PF implicates the peripheral constituents in a PF phrase suggests the manner in which syntactically based linearity should be handled: heads at S-structure must correspond to heads at PF, as already indicated within the definition of "corresponding constituent" in (5). If Case-marking is to the right in a language, for example, then X^0 heads at S-structure must map onto left heads at PF. Ideally, we would like to fix a single linearity or "headedness" parameter for a language, stating whether S-structure heads correspond in general to either left or right heads at PF. However, there is an ambiguity in the notion of "head" at S-structure that suggests at least one more parameter for cross-linguistic variation. In an adjunction structure like (15), VP_1 is the categorial head of VP_2; however, if the PP in (15) is a modifier, taking VP_1 as its modifiee, PP is the relational head of VP_2.

(15) VP_2

In a language in which S-structure categorial heads are mapped onto left heads at PF, a verb would be followed by all it arguments and any VP adjuncts. However, in a language in which it is S-structure RELATIONAL heads that map onto PF left heads, modifier adjuncts, as relational operator heads, would appear before the V, which would be followed by its arguments.

Travis (1986) suggests the possibility of this split in location of arguments and adjuncts and illustrates it with examples from her research.

However, she also identifies languages whose arrangement of constituents seems to rely crucially on the distinction between direction of θ-assignment and direction of Case-assignment. On the model of grammar in (4), θ-assignment could not directly influence linear order, since θ-assignment is a D-structure relation and only S-structure relations are mapped onto linear adjacency. For languages that place all the Case-marked NPs on one side of the verb and all oblique arguments and adjuncts on the other, languages in which the direction of Case-assignment and θ-assignment seem dissociated, we might say that apparent oblique arguments of a verb actually involve the structure in (15), with the Case-assigner for the oblique argument acting as an S-structure operator to make oblique arguments relationally indistinguishable from adjuncts at S-structure. This possibility leads to the identification of a third parameter, that in (16c). The general directionality parameters for a grammar like that in (4) are summarized in (16).

(16) a. The DIRECTIONAL HEAD parameter: S-structure heads are {left, right} heads at PF
b. The SYNTACTIC HEAD parameter: for the mapping to PF, S-structure heads are {relational, categorial} heads
c. The OBLIQUE ARGUMENT parameter: oblique arguments are relational {operators, arguments} at S-structure

For the linear ordering of constituents, (16c) is only relevant if (16b) is set at "relational." A verb is always the categorial head of the VP regardless of the relational status of its arguments or of VP adjuncts.

Given the dependence of (16c) on (16b), there are only three typological possibilities for left-headed languages and three for right-headed languages. These are precisely the types of languages Travis (1986) claims are the only observed possibilities. Within a system that recognizes linear order at D- and S-structure, Travis is forced to ad hoc constraints on the independence of her ordering parameters to account for the limited range of variation in order she observed. On the other hand, the structure of the grammar in (4) yields Travis's typology without any special constraints on the independence of the parameters in (16). Given that linear order is a property only of a level of analysis, PF, at which X-bar principles do not hold, it is not surprising that theories in which linear order is explicitly represented at D- and S-structure must impose external constraints on ordering to limit the possibilities for ordering differences among the world's languages.

On the picture of grammar in (4), linearly ordered tree structures play a role only as input to the phonological rules. For the most part, what counts for the syntax on a model like (4) are the relations that are projected through the syntax. The conclusions reached in this paper, then, approach the thinking represented in *Barriers* (Chomsky 1986) within a more traditional generative framework. Within the *Barriers* framework, the relations that project into configurational structures and not the configurational structures themselves are shown to be relevant for the operation of S-structure principles. Government in *Barriers* is shown to be connected to relations like θ-assignment, Case-assignment, and agreement, not strictly to geometrical dominance relations in a tree. When relations like θ-assignment are represented in tree structures, information relevant to the operation of grammatical principles may, in a sense, be lost. For example, two constituents that are structurally sisters may or may not stand in a θ-assignment relation; whether the θ-assignment relation holds is not determinable from the geometry of the tree alone but only through examination of constituents' lexical properties. However, the presence of a θ-assignment relation may be important for the evaluation of the subjacency constraint on movement, for example, as Chomsky (1986) explains. Thus geometry alone is insufficient for the correct application of syntactic principles; relational information that may be projected onto configurational structure is required.

The conclusions of this paper lead the study of phrase structure in a number of directions. First, the approach to phrase structure suggested here should motivate a renewed investigation into the semantic basis of syntactic categories. Within traditional X-bar theories, the compositional semantics of a category was only indirectly relevant to its phrase-structural distribution. The interesting work on compositional semantics of syntactic categories took place within categorial syntax and Montague Grammar, but this work was hampered by the assumption of linguists in these frameworks of a single level of syntactic description. The assumption of a single syntactic level of analysis leads to a proliferation of syntactic category types and a lifting of constraints on the notion "possible syntactic category." Within the grammatical framework of this paper, we are ready to explore the compositional semantics of syntactic categories under a constrained theory of category types.

Second, following the trajectory of *Barriers*, we are also ready to investigate the relational basis of the S-structure Government relations relevant to Binding and Bounding theories (the theories of locality constraints on anaphora and movement). We may now abandon the last vestiges of purely configurational thinking—get down from the trees, so to speak—in determining the correct relational formulation of S-structure principles.

Finally, this paper leads to a pure study of phrase structure itself, where phrase structure is now seen as the hierarchical phonological structure that serves as input to the rules of phonology. Since, given the associativity of the adjacency relation, the projection of S-structure relations onto adjacency relations at PF is consistent with a variety of hierarchical structures, independent phonological constraints on constituent structure must constrain the possible PF realization of a set of S-structure relations. The present theory provides one account of what sort of constraints on PF the syntax—in particular, the Projection Principle—provides; we may now factor these constraints out in determining the contribution of autonomous PF constraints on constituent structure.

6

Individuation in and of
Syntactic Structures

JAMES D. McCAWLEY

1. Horizontal Individuation

In this paper I examine a number of cases in which alternative analyses of
the same phenomena differ with regard to individuation: with regard to
whether the units and relations that a linguistic entity is taken to be composed of are treated as making up a single syntactic structure or as making
up two or more separate structures; or with regard to whether parts into
which a unit could in principle be decomposed (e.g. morphemes compris-
ing a word) are allowed to participate in syntactic relations in addition to
those that the larger unit participates in.

Parenthetical expressions and vocatives can be argued to enter into discontinuous constituent structures and indeed do not even clearly combine
into a syntactic unit with the sentence that they interrupt. The following
argument, parallel to one that I offered (in McCawley 1982a) to show that a
parenthetical in the middle of a V′ is not a constituent of that V′, provides
evidence that a vocative is likewise not a constituent of a V′ that it occurs
in the middle of:

(1) *Tom: I think, my friend, that they're wrong.*
    Dick: Well, I don't ∅. (∅ = *think that they're wrong,* ≠ *think, my*
        friend, that they're wrong)

The vocative cannot be interpreted as part of the antecedent of the zero V′.
Under the assumption that any surface V′ is potentially an antecedent of a
zero V′, this provides evidence for a surface structure such as that in (2), in
which the vocative is not a constituent of the V′:

(2)

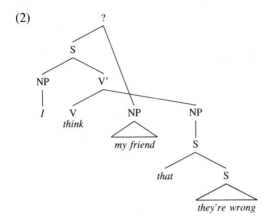

Let us turn our attention to one node in (2) whose existence might be thought uncontroversial, namely the topmost node. Is there justification for having such a node? That is, is there any respect in which the combination of S and vocative functions as a syntactic or semantic unit? The combination behaves as a phonological unit, at least to the extent that the intonation on the host S serves as a reference point for the assignment of an intonation to the vocative. However, given how common mismatches between syntactic and phonological structure are (cf. Sadock 1985), I do not regard this as much of an argument for treating the combination as forming a syntactic unit: the vocative might just stand in a relation to the host S that is like, say, that of a clitic to the word that it cliticizes onto. I thus do not wish to exclude from consideration a structure such as (3), in which the vocative and the host S (likewise, a parenthetical and its host S) simply do not form one syntactic unit:

(3)

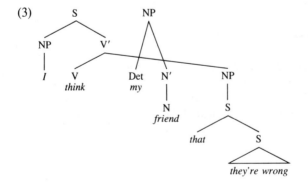

The vocative of course has SOME connection with the host S, in that it identifies the addressee of the S. But in saying that, I may be describing not the syntax of the sentence but its status as a device for performing speech acts. In McCawley 1985, I argued that speech acts can have the same sorts of complex internal structure that actions in general can have. In saying (4a), Tom is performing a complex act having a structure on the lines of (4b):

(4) a. *Mary, I'm sorry I behaved like such an idiot last night.*
     b. Tom discharges a debt to Mary by ADDRESSING TO MARY (locutionary act) an utterance in which he ASSERTS (illocutionary act) that he is sorry that he behaved like such an idiot last night.

In that view, illocutionary acts are normally embedded in locutionary acts, and the addressee has its status as addressee in virtue of the way that it is involved in the locutionary act. One might then describe the first sentence in (1) in terms of a structure that identifies the components of a complex act, roughly as in (5): [1]

(5)

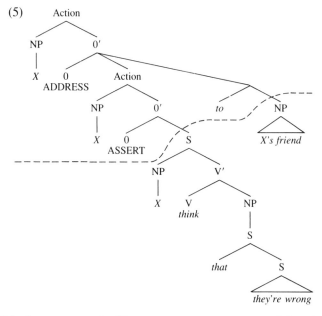

Whether one regards (5) as a SYNTACTIC structure of the given sentence depends on how far into the structure of action one is willing to go before one considers oneself to be out of the realm of syntax. I wish to emphasize, though, that a structure like (5) is related in straightforward ways to structures like (2) and (3), in that (leaving aside word order and taking only constituent structure into account), if one discards everything above the broken line in (5), one gets (3), and if one compresses everything above the broken line into a single node, one gets (2).

Two things are worth noting here. First, if one insists on doing syntax in terms of structures that have a single root, thus excluding in principle structures like (3), in which there are two roots, i.e. nodes not dominated by any other node, one should recognize that the inevitable structures like (2) have a root that is the syntactic projection of a unit of action rather than one of propositional content. And second, one should resist any temptation one might have to attach a label S (or S plus bars) to the root of a structure such as (2). Indeed, a combination of a host S and a vocative cannot be embedded as a subordinate clause the way that an S normally can:

(6) a. *Tom told Dick that he thought (*, his friend,) that they were wrong.*
    b. *We should stop making the noise that Edna said was driving her crazy (*, we pigs).*

In pointing out that combinations such as (2) are not Ss, I am making a plea not for the ad hoc creation of a new label (such as the "E" that has figured in such works as Banfield 1982 and Emonds 1976), but for identifying units of action or of discourse structure as such and not gratuitously assimilating them to already identified syntactic categories.

In this latter connection, I note that the familiar expressions of the form S *therefore* S, S *nevertheless* S, or S *so* S, which are virtually always claimed to be Ss, demonstrably are not. While these are often taken to be coordinate structures, as where Grice (1973) analyzes the *therefore* of (7) as *and* plus a conventional implicature, they behave neither like coordinate structures nor like structures with subordination, e.g. extractions are possible neither from both component Ss together (8a) nor from one of them by itself (8b, 8b').

(7)   *Rodney is English, therefore he is brave.*
(8) a. **What kind of movies does Tom like Ø, therefore Mary hate Ø?*
    b. **What did Tom do Ø, therefore Mary won't speak to him?*
    b'. **What did Tom spend all his money on video games, therefore Mary throw Ø at him?*

In fact, they cannot even be embedded, either:

(9) **I deny that [Rodney is English, therefore he is brave].*

(Versions of (8a) and (9) in which *and* appears before *therefore* are of course normal, but those are coordinate structures in virtue of the *and.*) I maintain that an expression like (7) is not a coordinate S but simply a paratactic combination of two Ss, the second of which happens to contain an S-modifying adverb that, because of its ANAPHORIC relation to the first S (*therefore* = 'because of that,' with the first clause the antecedent of *that*), is often mistakenly regarded as connecting the two Ss the way a "conjunction" might. An expression like (7) is probably some kind of syntactic unit, certainly also a phonological unit, but to the extent that I can find tests for whether that unit is an S, I find only grounds for saying that it is not.

2. Vertical Individuation

I have been talking so far about what might be described as "horizontal" individuation: the question of whether two units in the same level of structure form a single unit or are simply separate from one another. I now turn to the very different question of what one might call "vertical" individuation: that of whether different sets of relationships among underlying units count as making up multiple structures or as being parts of a single structure in which "underlying" and "surface" units and relationships occur together. Vertical individuation of syntactic structures is one of the most striking differences between Relational Grammar (RG, taken here as including Arc-Pair Grammar and the approach of Jespersen 1937) and the various incarnations of transformational grammar (TG). A syntactic structure such as is posited in RG can involve "strata" such as would correspond closely to the stages of a transformational derivation that includes applications of Passive, Raising, Tough Movement, and other transformations, but is conceived of as a single structure rather than as a sequence of separate structures.[2] It is this characteristic more than any other that provides justification for the oft-repeated claim that RG does without transformations.

I note here parenthetically that it is a mistake to assume that RG, Montague Grammar, Lexical-Functional Grammar (LFG), Brame's Base-generated Syntax, and the various other approaches to syntax that are claimed by their proponents to "do without transformations" share some property that is describable as "doing without transformations." The proponents of the different approaches assume quite different conceptions of "transformation," and there thus are great differences in what they are claiming to do without. Perhaps the only characteristic shared by all the various notions of "transformation" is that a transformation specifies a relationship between two classes of syntactic structures. Whether a putative linguistic rule satisfies even that minimal characterization of a "transformation," however, depends on one's answers to questions that are meta-

physical more than empirical: most notably, the question of whether the
things that the rule relates count as distinct structures or just as distinct
parts of a single structure; and the question of whether the things that the
rule relates are SYNTACTIC structures, rather than, say, semantic structures
or morphological structures. Consider a rule embodying the content of the
Quantifier Float transformation, that is, a rule relating structure containing
a quantified subject NP to a structure that is otherwise identical except for
having the quantifier not in the subject NP but as a modifier of the V' (10):

(10)

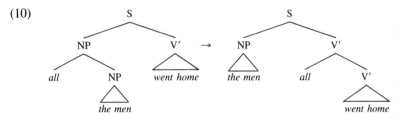

If the first structure is regarded as a semantic rather than a syntactic structure, the rule relating the two will not count as a transformation but rather
as something else, say, a semantic interpretation rule. The LFGian's version of Quantifier Float and the RGian's version of it are held by their proponents not to be transformations, but for completely different[3] reasons: in
the former case because one of the things that the rule relates is not syntactic, and in the latter case because the things that it relates, while both syntactic, are not separate structures.

   The RGian's policy on the vertical individuation of syntactic structures
is in fact a fairly natural extension of the conception of the identity of nodes
in syntactic structures that was developed in the late 60s by George Lakoff
(e.g. Lakoff 1971) as part of a conception of transformations and other
syntactic rules as DERIVATIONAL CONSTRAINTS: as conditions on the well-
formedness of derivations, regarded as sequences of trees. The notion of
derivational constraint presupposed a notion of CORRESPONDING NODE:
stated as a derivational constraint, a transformation specified that two
otherwise identical trees could be consecutive stages of a derivation if various conditions were met, each condition specifying that a node with some
property in the one tree have some other property in the other tree. The RG
policy is that of treating corresponding nodes as identical, e.g. of treating
the syntactic analysis of (11a) as involving only one occurrence of *John*
(rather than seven or eight), likewise only one occurrence of *Mary,* of
seem, etc., with each of those single occurrences of that item participating
in the multiplicity of syntactic relations that are implicitly also posited in a
transformational derivation that involves Passive, Raising, Tough Movement, etc.

(11) a. *John seems to have been easy to get Mary to want to be noticed by.*

b.

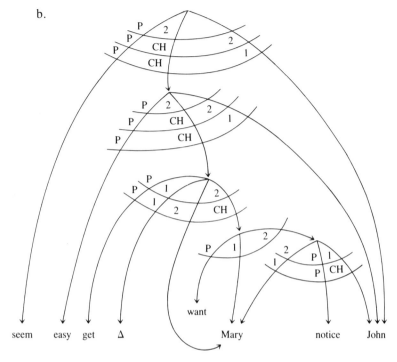

There are a couple of respects in which this identification of RG analyses with transformational analyses is inaccurate. First, transformational grammarians have almost always assumed that all syntactic structures in a derivation involve a LINEAR PRECEDENCE (LP) relation among their constituents and that that LP relation is relevant to the applicability of transformations. The unitary syntactic structures of RG allow for grammatical relations to differ from one "stratum" to another but not for LP relations to differ among the strata; indeed, RG has consistently taken LP to be significant only for, in effect, surface structure. Since LP is in fact not widely regarded as having much significance other than in surface structure (my impression is that TGians since the early 70s have included LP relations in deep structure more from force of habit than for any reason of substance), I will ignore the matter of LP relations and concentrate on the, to my mind, more interesting question of constituency relations.[4] Second, while TGians have usually recognized syntactic structures in which there is a considerable amount of branching, RG has generally been done in terms of quite "flat" structures, in which e.g. subject and direct object are sisters rather than aunt and niece.

These two characteristics of RG are in fact strongly reinforced by the most popular notational system for RG analyses, which provides a single horizontal line for each stratum in each nexus. This notational system provides for only as much constituent structure as is given by the embedding of nexuses as terms within other nexuses, and the diagrams in their pristine form allow at most for the representation of one set of LP relations per nexus (say, those of surface structure). It is of course not impossible to enlarge the combinatoric possibilities of relational diagrams so as to allow for VPs and other constituents that are intermediate between term and the nexus, but it requires considerable imagination to do so, and RGians have rarely exercised their imaginations in that particular regard.

The low cost of flat structures in RG is responsible for the popularity in RG of an analysis of passive Ss that in one important respect is counterintuitive, in that the derived subject is represented as not merely a subject but as the (derived) subject of the same thing that it is an underlying direct object of; e.g. in (11b), *Mary* is represented as the derived subject not of *be* or of *be noticed* but of *notice*.[5] In RG, derived subjects are commonly represented as derived subjects of the wrong thing. On the other hand, in orthodox TG, underlying subjects have often been represented as underlying subjects of the wrong thing—in underlying structures such as (12), which were popular in the late 1970s, the underlying subject of the main verb was represented as the underlying subject of passive *be,* to which it strictly speaking has no grammatical relation at all:

(12)

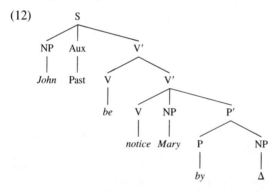

In both cases, a policy demanding a close match among the nodes on different strata favors analyses in which grammatical relations in one stratum are gratuitously projected onto another, the difference being which stratum is supplied with spurious instances of predicate elements that belong on a different stratum.

Good cases can be made for a number of types of deviation from a policy (like those of both RG and orthodox TG) requiring close parallelism among the strata.

  i. Fissions. Multiple nodes in a "later" stratum correspond to a single node in an "earlier" stratum, as in the treatment of coordinate conjunctions proposed in Ross 1967, in which each coordinate structure has a single conjunction, but that conjunction can have multiple realizations (e.g. one copy of it on each conjunct):

(13)

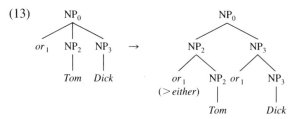

  ii. Fusions. A single node in a "later" stratum corresponds jointly to two or more nodes in an "earlier" stratum. I have argued (McCawley 1982a), for example, that Right Node Raising (RNR) consists in the fusion of identical constituents that occupy final position in all the conjuncts of a coordinate structure:

(14)

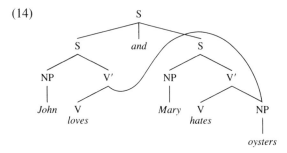

  iii. Chomsky-adjunction (fits the above definition of "Fission," but different in kind from the example given above). The "later" stratum contains two nodes, both of them counterparts of the same node in an "earlier" stratum, but one dominating an "adjunct" and the other not dominating it. The upper and lower nodes in a Chomsky-adjunction configuration can be thought of as looser and stricter versions of the same syntactic unit, i.e. as including vs. excluding something that is peripheral to the unit.

  iv. Insertion of lexical items, with concomitant creation of nodes corresponding to phrasal units headed by those items. The surface structure for passive Ss for which I have argued (McCawley 1981a, 1988)[6] illustrates both (iii) and (iv); here subscripts indicate what nodes are "equivalent" in

the extended sense in which multiple counterparts of a single node are
equivalent to one another:

(15)

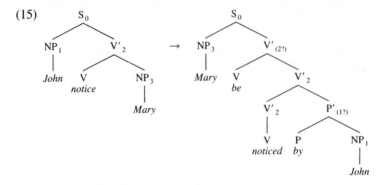

The derived structure in (15) contains five more nodes than appear in the
input structure: not only are the *be* and *by* inserted, but so also are nodes
corresponding to phrasal constituents headed by those words or formed by
adjunction of those constituents to underlying constituents.[7]

3. Lateral Individuation

I turn now to a different kind of individuation question, again a question of
whether various units and relations make up a single complex structure or
two simpler structures, but where the two structures are not an underlying
structure and a more superficial one but rather two structures that suppos-
edly are on the same structural "level."

Katsuhiko Momoi and I (McCawley & Momoi 1987) exhibit six phenomena in Japanese with regard to which participial complement constructions behave like single clauses in surface structure. For example, for
RNR, the combination of main verb and participial subordinate verb acts as
a unit, as it should if the main and complement verbs are combined into a
unit:

(16) a. *Taroo wa eigo   o   hanasi, Ziroo wa nihongo o
          Taro TOP English ACC speak Jiro TOP Japanese ACC
          hanasite mita.
          speak   try-PST
          'Taro tried speaking English, and Jiro speaking Japanese.'
     b. Taroo wa eigo   o, Ziroo wa nihongo o   hanasite
        Taro TOP English ACC Jiro TOP Japanese ACC speak
        mita.
        try-PST
        'Taro tried speaking English, and Jiro Japanese.'

However, we also exhibit four phenomena with regard to which the same complement constructions behave as if they have an embedded clause in surface structure; for example, a coordinate complement S is possible:

(17) a. *Taroo wa Tanaka-san ni   zitensya o   syuuzen-si, daidokoro*
        Taro TOP Tanaka   DAT bicycle ACC repair   kitchen
        o   soozi-site moratta.
        ACC clean   get-PST
        'Taro got Tanaka to repair the bicycle and clean the kitchen.'
     b. *Boku wa Borges ga   Nobel-syoo o   tori, Royko ga*
        I   TOP Borges NOM Nobel prize ACC take Royko NOM
        Pulitzer-syoo o   totte hosii.
        Pulitzer prize ACC take want
        'I want Borges to win a Nobel Prize and Royko to win a Pulitzer Prize.'

Interestingly, both types of phenomena are found among the constraints on anaphoric relations in Japanese. The nonreflexive pronoun *kare*, like English personal pronouns, is excluded when its antecedent is the subject of the same clause:

(18) a. *$*Tanaka-san_i$ wa $kare_i$ o hometa.*
        'Tanaka praised him.'
     b. *$Tanaka-san_i$ wa $zibun_i/*kare_i$ no koibito o hometa.*
        'Tanaka praised self's/his lover.'

Oddly, though, the reflexive pronoun *zibun* is also excluded in some of the same environments in which *kare* is. When *zibun* is in the same S as its antecedent (the andecedent is often in a higher S), it is not fully acceptable unless it is separated from *zibun* by an NP boundary, as in (18b), that is, a reflexive must not be a "peer" of its antecedent, in Postal's (1971) sense:[8]

(19) ?*$Tanaka-san_i$ wa $zibun_i$ o hometa.*

Consider now a participal complement construction in which the complement has a direct object coreferential with the main clause subject:

(20) *$Tanaka-san_i$ wa Taroo ga $zibun_i/*kare_i$ o   homete hosii.*
     Tanaka   TOP Taro NOM self/he   ACC praise want-PRES
     'Tanaka wants Taro to praise him.'

The unacceptability of *kare* provides evidence that that NP is a surface clausemate of *Tanaka-san* and thus that there is a single S in surface structure. However, the full acceptability of *zibun* provides evidence that the complement object NP is not a surface peer of the main subject and thus that it is within a subordinate S in surface structure.

The way in which Momoi and I proposed to resolve this seeming contradiction is by altering our conception of the derivational step that combines the verb of the complement S with the predicate element of the main S. Suppose that this step is taken not as severing the connection of the complement V to its S (and interacting with a principle of tree-pruning to yield a surface uniclausal structure (21a)) but as ADDING a connection of that element to the higher S without any concomitant change in its relation to the lower S (21b):[9]

(21) a.

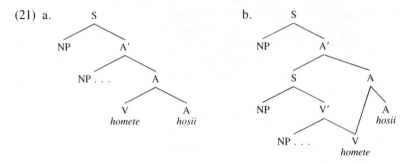

Adding a connection yields a structure in which the node in question has two mothers. When a graph contains nodes with multiple mothers, it also has multiple paths connecting such a node to higher nodes. The non-uniqueness of a path between two nodes in such a graph means that notions such as "clausemate" and "peer" (whose usual definitions presuppose that there is a unique path connecting the relevant nodes) will have to be redefined so as to allow for the extra paths. Each notion in fact splits into a "weak" and a "strong" version, e.g. two notes are WEAK CLAUSEMATES if there is some path joining them that does not cross an S-node and are STRONG CLAUSEMATES if no path joining them crosses an S-node. In (21b), the main subject and the object NP of the complement are weak clausemates because there is a path joining them that takes a detour via the V and thus avoids crossing the S-node, but are not strong clausemates because the other path that connects them does cross a S-node. We claim that *kare* is excluded even when it is a weak clausemate of a subject antecedent, whereas the restriction on *zibun* depends on a "strong" relation with the antecedent (it cannot be a "strong peer" of its antecedent, defined analogously to "strong clausemate").

I bring up this proposal here mainly to compare it with analyses in terms of "dual structures" such as are advanced in work on Japanese by Miyagawa (1987), on French by Zubizarreta (1985), and on West Flemish and Zürich German by Haegeman and van Riemsdijk (1986).[10] Miyagawa analyzes Japanese causative Ss in terms of a pair of structures (22) that represent the elements of such a sentence (here, a sentence meaning 'Taro made Hanako read the book') as simultaneously making up a uniclausal and a biclausal structure:

(22) [$_{S'}$ *Taroo ga Hanako ni* [$_{S'}$ PRO *hon o yom-*] *sase-ta*].
     [$_{S'}$ *Taroo ga Hanako ni hon o* [*yom-ase*] *-ta*]

If corresponding nodes in the two paired structures are treated as identical, one obtains a double mother structure of the sort proposed by McCawley and Momoi:

(23)

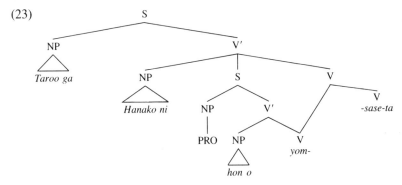

Not surprisingly, the descriptive possibilities of the two proposals overlap considerably, since both provide for multiple structural relations between the same elements in the same structural level. They differ principally in that the double mother proposal allows for structural relations (such as "command") between elements that, in the dual structure proposal, would not belong to the same structure and thus could not stand in any such relation to one another. Momoi and I provide a certain amount of evidence in support of our double mother structures and against Miyagawa's dual structures, though not what we would regard as a conclusive case for the one or against the other. For example, when the pronoun *kare* is used in a coordinate participial complement, the constraint on it is violated if it is in the second conjunct (24b) but not if it is in the first conjunct (24a):

(24) a.   *Tanaka-san$_i$ wa [Hanako ga   kare$_i$ o   home, Yosiko ga*
           Tanaka   TOP Hanako NOM he   ACC praise Yosiko nom
           Taroo o   sikatte] hosii rasii.
           Taro ACC scold   want seem
           'Tanaka seems to want Hanako to praise him and Yoshiko to
           scold Taro.'

b.   ?? *Tanaka-san₍ᵢ₎ wa [Hanako ga Setuko o home, Yosiko ga kare₍ᵢ₎
      o sikatte] hosii rasii.*
      'Tanaka seems to want Hanako to praise Setsuko and Yosiko
      to praise him.'

If we treat only the final conjunct as undergoing the addition of a link to the
main predicate element (i.e. if we treat the restructuring as affecting only
adjacent elements), we end up with a structure in which elements of the
second conjunct but not of the first are weak clausemates of the main subject, which implies that *kare* should be excluded from having the main
clause subject as its antecedent if it is in the final conjunct but not if it is in
an earlier conjunct:[11]

(25)

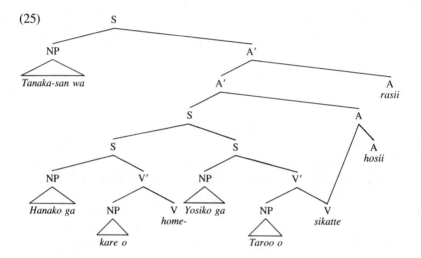

Note that this account requires that in a single structure the elements of the
second conjunct simultaneously stand in a clausemate relation to the main
subject and make up a separate clause so that there can be something for
the first conjunct to be conjoined with. It is hard to see how the distinction
in (24) could even be described in terms of a dual structure analysis, while
an account of it in terms of multiple mother structures is readily available.

4. Morphology and Syntactic Individuation

I have already acknowledged that word structure can conflict with syntactic
constituent structure. I accordingly do not accept the popular view that the

possibility of NPs as in (26) requires that restrictive relative clauses be taken as modifying NPs rather than N's:

(26) a. *someone that I admire*
     b. *anything that they ask for*

Since there is in fact a large amount of evidence that restrictive relatives modify N's (McCawley 1981b), I wish to treat *someone, anything,* etc. as consisting syntactically of two parts, a determiner (*some-, any-, . . .*) and an N' (*-one, -thing, -body, . . .*), and to treat (26a) as having the constituent structure (27):

(27)

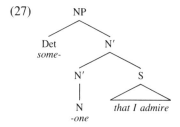

There is no solid morphemic analysis of *who* and *what* into a determiner and an N, though there are many published analyses (e.g. Katz & Postal 1964) that treat them as surface reflexes of underlying combinations of such elements. It is possible to form expressions similar to (26) in which the relative clause is attached to an interrogative pronoun:

(28) a. *Who that you know is likely to have noticed your absence?*
     b. *What that we have discussed so far do you think we should get Smith's advice on?*

Such examples present us with the following alternatives: (i) give up the idea that the relative clause modifies an N' in (28), which would presumably mean also giving up such an analysis for (26), since there is no apparent respect in which the syntax of relative clauses in the two cases differs; (ii) accept an analog to Sadock's (1985) analysis of Eskimo noun incorporation, i.e. treat the surface SYNTACTIC structure of (28a) as having separate elements that are, however, fused in the structure MORPHOLOGICAL structure of the sentence (29); or (iii) treat the surface syntactic structure as reflecting the morphological fusion, i.e. have a surface syntactic structure in which *who* corresponds to one of the terminal nodes (30):

(29)

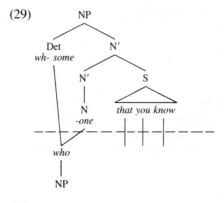

(30)

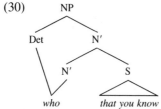

I have shown *who* in (30) as having a double mother, simply because I see
no reason why the morphological fusion would affect the syntactic constituent structure: *who* corresponds equally much to the determiner and the
noun that by hypothesis are fused in it, and it should thus inherit the structural relations of both unless some grounds can be found for saying otherwise. I have no idea whether the more transparent fusion that takes place in
something/anyone, etc. should be regarded as resulting in a similar fusion
of syntactic structure, i.e. I know of no grounds for choosing between (27)
and (31) as the surface structure of *someone that I admire:*

(31)

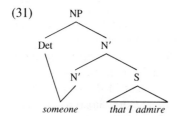

The choice between the two is again a question of individuation—what can
participate in surface syntactic relations: words, morphemic constituents of
words, or both?

5. Multiple Categorization and Syntactic Individuation

I turn finally to a class of questions that relate to multiple category membership and to whether particular elements count as part of a syntactic structure at all. I have argued (McCawley 1987) that "adjectival nouns" such as *bitch* are semantically adjectives but syntactically nouns and are used in such a way as to allow the surface syntax of nouns to mimic adjective constructions:

(32) a. *This is a bitch of a problem.*
     b. Ulysses *is a bitch to read.*
     c. *The schedule is a bigger bitch of a problem than the money.*

Here *bitch* appears as the apparent head of an NP (preceded by an article, followed by a P', etc.) but mimics the prenominal adjective construction, the Tough-Movement construction, and the comparative construction, in the sense that if one regarded *bitch* as an adjective and ignored the (here semantically empty) *a, of,* and *big,* one would get a well-formed construction of the type in question, with *bitch* filling the adjective position. This description suggests some sort of dual structure, but with some of the words of the one part of the structure not playing any role in the other part:

(33)

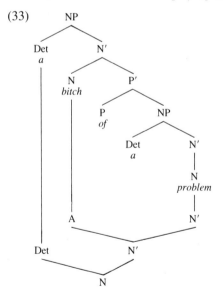

In (33), there are two syntactic structures, with *bitch* categorized as N in the one and as A in the other, and with *of* and the second *a* playing normal

syntactic roles in the upper structure but treated as morphological flotsam
in the lower structures. In (34), those two structures are superimposed:

(34)

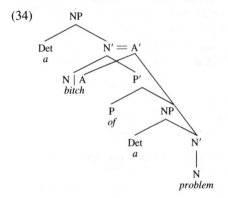

Presented as they are here, (33) is analogous to Miyagawa's dual structures
for the Japanese examples, while (34), a single structure involving double
mothers, is analogous to the McCawley-Momoi structure. Are there any
grounds for choosing between these two nearly equivalent ways of looking
at this structure?

There are in another case of a somewhat similar type that I discuss in the
same paper, where I argue that the color word of expressions such as *a pale
blue shirt* behaves simultaneously as a noun (thus, supporting as a modifier
the adjective *pale*) and as an adjective (thus, modifying *shirt*), as indicated
in (35):[12]

(35)

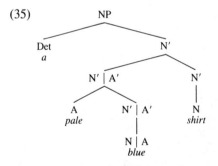

Note that in (35) the overlain structures are incomplete, in the sense that
pale blue as an N′ does not qualify to be a modifier of *shirt* and *pale* does
not qualify to be a modifier of *blue* as an adjective. I argued for such an
analysis by pointing out that the combination becomes unacceptable when
it is combined with material that would exclude one of the two overlain
structures:

(36) a. *a paler blue shirt than Ted was wearing
      b. *a more [pale blue] shirt than Ted was wearing

6. Conclusion

I will end by simply pointing out that while many of the syntactic structures
that I have given serious consideration above as possible analyses of the
various examples are "exotic" structures, i.e. they differ in significant
ways from the classical continuous labeled trees to which generative grammarians with few exceptions have been happy, even eager, to restrict their
conception of syntactic structure, the differences between the exotic structures and the commonplace ones have in most cases hinged on fairly arcane
questions that are often not really empirical in nature but relate to policies
about e.g. where one draws a boundary between syntactic structure and
structure of action, or whether one takes the relationship between corresponding parts of related syntactic structures to be that of identity or only
one of "correspondence." I thus hope in this paper to have gotten across
the idea that appearances of exoticness can be deceiving: telling the difference between an exotic structure and a more prosaic structure is often difficult. It is not impossible, though: differences are there and can be found if
one can figure out where to look. However, one is unlikely to look unless
one takes the exotic versions of the structures seriously, and I close by ad-
vocating precisely that.[13]

NOTES

1. Given the rudimentary nature of my understanding of the structure of actions, I have taken them to have what is arguably (cf. Simon 1962) the unmarked
sort of structure, namely that of a tree. My use of the label "NP" for the constituents with which "ADDRESS" and "ASSERT" are combined follows my account
(McCawley 1982b) of "NP" as a fuzzy category defined by the logical category
"argument of predicate." The 0 in (5) means 'predicate belonging to no lexical
category'; 0' thus means 'phrasal unit whose head belongs to no lexical category.'
The possibly jarring combination of units of language and of action in (5) merely
reflects the relatively uncontroversial proposition that speech acts have linguistic
units among their components.

2. I will ignore here an important individuation question that is internal to RG,
namely that of how many "nexuses" are involved in a particular syntactic structure. (I adopt Jespersen's (1924) term "nexus" for a combination of an item and
those things that stand in grammatical relations to it.) Davies and Rosen (1988), for
example, propose an analysis of "clause union" phenomena in which there are not
two nexuses, as in more orthodox relational analyses, but one, with one of the predicate elements taking over the role of predicate in some noninitial stratum.

3. To avoid possible misunderstanding, I alert the reader to the fact that in my dialect of English, the expression *completely different* is interpreted literally and is not (as it is in the dialects of most linguists, though not of most native speakers of English) synonymous with *different*. The rarity with which that expression occurs in my speech and writing reflects the rarity of cases in which two things that might be compared are COMPLETELY different.

4. In my own work, I regard LP relations as relevant only to the application of postcyclic transformations and surface structure constraints and accept Pullum's (1976) suggestion that precisely those transformations that are LOCAL in the sense of Emonds (1976) are postcyclic (McCawley 1988:167). Note in this connection the treatment of movement transformations in Baltin (1982), in which the formulation of transformations ignores LP in the input but specifies the LP relation that the moved constituent has in the output to the constituent to which it is adjoined.

5. The only works in which I have seen RGians make a real attempt to insure that derived grammatical relations involve the right predicate elements are Frantz (1985) and Davies and Rosen (1988). Davies and Rosen exploit the possibility of relational analyses in which one element takes over the Predicate relation from another, which allows the following analysis of English passive clauses:

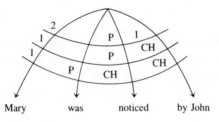

Even here there is a stratum in which *Mary* is represented as the subject of *notice* rather than of *be* (*noticed*); Rosen (pers. comm.), however, argues that such a stratum is required in the analysis of Italian passives if a generalization about agreement of adjectives and participles is to be captured.

Relational structures of the sort exploited by Davies and Rosen enable a RGian to compensate for some of the "flatness" of relational structures by distinguishing within what is technically a single nexus analogues to what for some linguists (e.g. McCawley 1988, chap. 8) are separate nexuses: for Davies and Rosen, each predicate in a nexus corresponds to a "P-sector" (the set of strata in which that element holds the predicate relation), and the P-sectors are more direct analogs to cyclic domains than are the nexuses themselves.

6. See also McCawley (1983) for an argument that, given some assumptions about language aquisition that I regard as plausible, such a structure would be imposed on passive sentences by children acquiring English even prior to their acquisition of the syntax of passives.

The extended sense of "equivalence" that is represented in (15) plays a role in the revised definition of c-command proposed in McCawley 1984, in which I attempt to revise Reinhart's (1983) analysis of anaphoric relations so as to make it

consistent with constituent structures that are otherwise defensible. My revised definition of c-command said that a constituent c-commands everything dominated by
its mother or by modifiers of its mother. Since I maintain that modifiers are always
Chomsky-adjuncts of the constituents that they modify, the revised definition takes
in almost the same cases as the following: a constituent c-commands all constituents that are dominated by a node equivalent to its mother, in the above sense.

7. The question marks on the mothers of *be* and *by* reflect my uncertainty as to
which property of those two nodes should determine their counterpart relations: are
they equivalent to the V′ and the subject NP of the input structure, on the grounds
that they result from Chomsky-adjunction of something to them, or do they constitute "new" V′ and P′ nodes because they have heads that do not correspond to
anything in the input structure? My inclination is to say the latter, but I do not at
present know of any respect in which it matters.

On the conception of syntactic category that I assume here, see McCawley 1982b.

8. This restriction was first noted by N. McCawley (1972).

9. The various syntactic structures discussed in this paper consist of nodes and
of relations of constituency and linear precedence between those nodes. Subject
perhaps to a qualification relating to items like (1), which may require deep structures having more than one root, I wish to assume that all DEEP structures are
TREES, in the sense that the constituency and linear precedence relations satisfy the
axioms given in McCawley 1982a (with the correction of an error in axiom (i),
which should have defined "root" as 'node that no node dominates'). The nontrees
that figure in the derivations sketched here are derived from trees by operations that
alter the set of nodes and/or the constituency and linear precedence relations, e.g.
(21b) is derived from a tree by replacing (*b, c*) in its constituency relation by the
pairs (*a, b′*), (*b, b′*), and (*b′, c*), where *a* is the node labeled V/*homete*, *b* is the
node labeled A/*hosii*, *c* is the node labeled A′, and *b′* is a node labeled A′ that is
hitherto not part of the structure. In this connection, see also note 12.

10. The term "DUAL structures" is not fully accurate, since e.g. Haegeman and
van Riemsdijk (1986:436–7) allow a reanalysed structure to be subjected to further
reanalysis and thus can obtain three or more parallel structures on the same stratum.

11. A different type of fusion that can affect one conjunct without affecting the
rest is the contraction *de + el → del* in Spanish, as in:

(i) *Puerto Rico . . . había salido victorioso **del** mal tiempo, la posible turbulen-
      cia política, y las dificuldades logisticas.* (*Américas* 39, no. 4, p. 63).
   'Puerto Rico had emerged victorious **from the** bad weather, the possible po-
      litical turbulence, and the logistic difficulties.'

12. There is an important difference between the two cases: with adjectival
nouns there is a sharp asymmetry in the roles of the two categories (noun surface
syntax is used to mimic adjective constructions, and not vice versa), whereas with
color words, each of the two categories licenses a different part of the surface syntactic structure in which the word occurs. I make no choice here between two alternative ways of interpreting diagrams like (35): either there are two nodes, one
labeled N′ and the other A′, that occupy the same position in linear order and share

some but not all constituency relations (e.g. A/*pale* would be a daughter of the N'
node but not of the A' node), or there is a single node bearing two labels and the
placement of the lines indicates not merely what nodes are dominated by what
nodes but also which of two or more categories to which a node belongs is the one
that licenses the presence of the node at that place in the structure (e.g. the node in
question can be a daughter of the upper N' node because it is an A' and can have
pale as a daughter because it is an N').

13. I am grateful to the participants in the NYU conference and to Carol Rosen
and two anonymous referees for valuable comments on earlier versions of this paper.

7

Subcategorization and Head-driven Phrase Structure

IVAN A. SAG AND CARL POLLARD

The most standard conception of phrase structure is based on the familiar notions of context-free phrase-structure grammars (CFPSGs), first developed for linguistic analysis in the 1950s. Context-free phrase-structure rules of the sort illustrated in (1), sanction trees like those in (2).

(1) a. S → NP VP
    b. NP → Det N
    c. VP → TV NP
    d. VP → IV

(2) a.

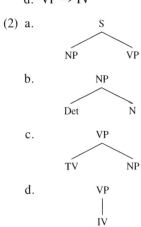

             S
      NP   VP

  b.   NP
      Det   N

  c.   VP
      TV   NP

  d.   VP
          IV

The contents of this paper are elaborated in several chapters of Pollard and Sag (in press). In addition to the people we thank there, we would particularly like to thank Peter Sells for comments on the material presented here. We also thank Dikran Karagueuzian and his staff for essential help with manuscript preparation. Our research was supported by grants from the National Science Foundation (BNS-8511687 and BNS-8718156) and by a gift from the System Development Foundation to Stanford's Center for the Study of Language and Information.

And a set of such rules, taken together with an appropriate set of lexical items, determines a set of phrase structures (terminated trees) like those in (3), by a process too familiar to warrant recapitulation here.

(3) a.

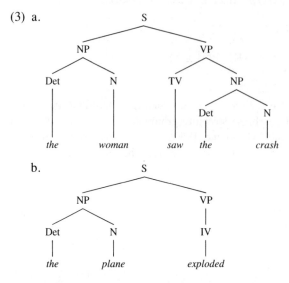

b.

Standard CFPSGs, as is well known, fail to express certain generalizations about the phrase structure of natural languages and have long since been abandoned in favor of theories that either augment context-free phrase-structure rules with ancillary devices (e.g. the transformations of Transformational Grammar or the functional structures of Lexical-Functional Grammar [LFG]), or else replace them with highly schematic rules and principles that interact in a modular fashion to define the phrase structures of a given language (as is done in Government and Binding theory [GB] and Generalized Phrase Structure Grammar [GPSG]). Among the generalizations that have been sought by proponents of the latter theories are (1) the systematic relation between phrases and their heads, loosely described by the slogan that "phrases are projected from their lexical heads" and (2) the general principles of constituent order that appear to hold across phrases of diverse types in a given language. The desire to explain such generalizations has led to the development of X-bar theory (Harris 1946, Chomsky 1970, Jackendoff 1977); the "Projection Principle" (Chomsky 1981); the "Head Feature Convention" (Gazdar et al. 1985); "Immediate Dominance/Linear Precedence" (IDLP) theory (Gazdar and Pullum 1981, Gazdar et al. 1985); as well as a recent revival of interest in categorial grammars (Bach 1983; Steedman 1985, forthcoming; Uszkoreit 1986; Zeevat et al. 1987).

In this paper, we sketch a theory of phrase structure that seeks to integrate a number of ideas from these diverse research traditions. Our "head-driven" approach to phrase structure, developed in greater detail in Pollard and Sag (1987; forthcoming; see also Sag & Pollard 1987), embodies a mathematically precise formulation of certain principles of universal grammar whereby properties of phrases are "projected" from lexical heads and generalizations about constituent order are succinctly expressed. As lexical structures bear much of the syntactic burden within our approach, we devote considerable attention to the nature of lexical information, in particular subcategorization information and its role in head-driven syntactic combination.

1. Signs, Categories, and Syntactic Structures

We take the fundamental objects of linguistic analysis to be signs, which we model by feature structures, in turn represented by attribute-value matrices (AVMs) such as (4).

(4) $\begin{bmatrix} \text{PHONOLOGY} & \text{/cookie/} \\ \text{SYNTAX} & \text{NOUN} \\ \text{SEMANTICS} & \text{COOKIE} \end{bmatrix}$

In fact, we use feature structures of various types to analyze linguistic entities of quite diverse sorts, including words, phrases, syntactic categories, semantic objects, principles of universal grammar, clusters of agreement information, and even (following Kay 1979, 1984, 1985) grammar rules. Through the use of recursive feature structures, where certain attributes have values that are themselves feature structures (or even lists or sets of feature structures), we can represent complex information of the sort commonly used in linguistic analysis. The phrase-structure tree in (5), for example, contains information that may also be rendered as the feature structure in (6).[1]

(5)

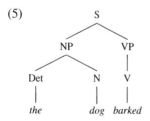

(6) $\begin{bmatrix} \text{PHON} & \textit{the dog barked} \\ \text{SYN} & \text{S} \\ \\ \text{DTRS} & \begin{bmatrix} \text{PHON } \textit{the dog} \\ \text{SYN NP} \\ \text{DTRS} & \begin{bmatrix} \text{PHON } \textit{the} \\ \text{DTRS } & \text{SYN} & \text{DET} \end{bmatrix}, \begin{bmatrix} \text{PHON } \textit{dog} \\ \text{SYN} & \text{N} \end{bmatrix} \end{bmatrix}, \\ \\ \begin{bmatrix} \text{PHON } \textit{barked} \\ \text{SYN VP} \\ \text{DTRS} & \begin{bmatrix} \text{PHON } \textit{barked} \\ \text{SYN} & \text{V} \end{bmatrix} \end{bmatrix} \end{bmatrix}$

In this simplified illustration, the attribute DAUGHTERS takes a list of signs as its value; order of elements in the list is used to encode the "surface order" of sister constituents (i.e. the temporal order of corresponding phonological realizations). There is an obvious redundancy here, for clearly the PHONOLOGY value of each constituent is predictable once the PHONOLOGY values of the "leaf nodes" are given; this redundancy will be absent from the structures we actually use, where the list order of elements within DAUGHTERS values reflects not surface order directly, but rather an abstract order of grammatical relations corresponding to the traditional notion of obliqueness. We shall be particularly concerned with the nature of both phrasal and lexical signs, which we analyze in terms of feature structures specified for values of the attributes PHONOLOGY, SYNTAX, and SEMANTICS. For the moment, we focus on the linguistic objects that serve as values of the SYNTAX attribute, which are called SYNTACTIC CATEGORIES, or simply CATEGORIES.

We begin by drawing a fundamental distinction between LOCAL features and BINDING features. Local features in general specify inherent syntactic properties of a sign, such as part of speech, inflection, case, subcategorization (including the traditional notion of government), and lexicality (whether a sign is lexical or phrasal). Binding features, on the other hand, provide information about dependent elements of various kinds contained as constituents within a sign, such as "missing" elements (often called GAPS or TRACES), relative pronouns, and interrogative expressions. Such information is nonlocal in the sense that the kinds of syntactic dependencies involved (e.g. between a gap and its "filler" or between a relative pronoun and the antecedent noun) may extend over arbitrarily long distances. The binding features include SLASH (denoting a gap within a constituent), REL, and QUE. These features (discussed in detail in Pollard and Sag forthcoming) are analogous to the FOOT features of Gazdar et al. (1985). These two types of grammatical information are governed by distinct grammatical principles and hence are propagated through linguistic structures along different kinds of paths.

Among the local syntactic features, a three-way distinction is to be drawn. First there are HEAD features, which specify syntactic properties that a lexical sign shares with its projections (i.e. the phrasal signs headed by that lexical sign). Second, the feature SUBCAT gives information about the valence of a sign, i.e. the number and kind of phrasal signs that the sign in question SUBCATEGORIZES FOR (or characteristically combines with). And third, the binary feature LEX is used to distinguish between lexical and nonlexical signs; this distinction plays much the same role as the distinction between X^0 categories and X^n categories with $n > 0$ in familiar versions of X-bar theory.

Thus the overall structure of a sign is as indicated in (7):

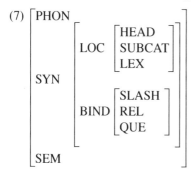

1.1. Head Features and Constituent Structure Types

The notion of the HEAD of a phrase is one with a long history, stemming from traditional grammar and playing a central role in recent syntactic frameworks such as GB and GPSG. The underlying intuition is simply that each phrase contains a certain word which is centrally important in the sense that it determines many of the syntactic properties of the phrase as a whole; that word is called the LEXICAL HEAD of the phrase. More generally, the HEAD of a phrase is that daughter (immediate constituent) of the phrase which either is or contains the phrase's lexical head.[2] For example, in the sentence *Sandy likes bagels,* the head daughter is the verb phrase *likes bagels.* The verb *likes* in turn is the head of the verb phrase, and it is also the lexical head of both the verb phrase and the sentence.

It is easy to see that the combinatory possibilities of a clause depend on the form of the head verb.

(8) a.
$$I \text{ believe that} \begin{Bmatrix} *John \text{ leave tomorrow.} \\ John \text{ leaves tomorrow.} \\ *John \text{ leaving tomorrow.} \end{Bmatrix}$$

b.
$$Bagels, \begin{Bmatrix} *John \text{ like.} \\ John \text{ likes.} \\ *John \text{ liking.} \end{Bmatrix}$$

(9) a.
$$I \text{ demand that} \begin{Bmatrix} *John \text{ leave tomorrow.} \\ John \text{ leaves tomorrow.} \\ *John \text{ leaving tomorrow.} \end{Bmatrix}$$

b.
$$With \begin{Bmatrix} *John \text{ leave tomorrow} \\ *John \text{ leaves tomorrow} \\ John \text{ leaving tomorrow} \\ John \text{ in New York} \\ John \text{ dead} \end{Bmatrix}, \text{ things sure will be dull.}$$

Thus, as (8a) and (8b) show, a clause headed by a finite verb (but not by a base form or present participle) can occur as complement to the verb *believe* and also in the topicalization construction. On the other hand, the verb *demand* takes a clausal complement only if it is headed by a base-form verb ((9a)). And (9b) shows that a clause headed by a verb in present-participial form (but not in finite or base form) shares with predicative prepositional and adjectival clauses the ability to function as a sentential adjunct marked by *with*. From these examples we see that verb form is not a property simply of the verb itself, but also of the entire clause headed by the verb. For this reason, we speak of finite clauses, present-participial clauses, etc.

Before proceeding, it may be instructive to sketch briefly how the sharing of head features between lexical signs and their phrasal projections is accounted for in our theory. In addition to the usual sign attributes PHONOLOGY, SYNTAX, and SEMANTICS, feature structures of type PHRASAL SIGN bear a fourth attribute DAUGHTERS that gives information about the (lexical or phrasal) signs which are the immediate constituents of the sign in question.

The DAUGHTERS attribute provides the kind of information about constituency (but NOT about relative order of constituents) that is contained in conventional constituent-structure tree diagrams. But in addition, it is important to distinguish the various daughters of a sign according to what kinds of information they contribute to the sign as a whole. Thus daughters are classified, inter alia, as HEADS (those which share their head features with the mother), COMPLEMENTS (those which discharge subcategorization requirements on the head), FILLERS (those which discharge binding requirements on the head), CONJUNCTS (coequal daughters in coordinate constructions), etc. Correspondingly, appropriate values of DAUGHTERS are feature structures of the type CONSTITUENT STRUCTURE, which have such attributes as HEAD-DTR (head daughter), COMP-DTRS (complement daughters), FILLER-DTR (filler daughter), CONJ-DTRS (conjunct daughters), etc.

Constituent structures are then classified on the basis of the kinds of daughters that appear in them. For example, one important subtype of constituent structure is COORDINATE STRUCTURE, one of whose attributes is CONJ-DTRS. Another important subtype of constituent structure, in fact the one that principally concerns us here, is HEADED STRUCTURE, which at minimum bears the attributes HEAD-DTR and COMP-DTRS. Headed structures in turn are subclassified according to what kinds of nonhead daughters they have; thus we have such subtypes of headed structure as HEAD-COMPLEMENT STRUCTURE (which bears the attributes HEAD-DTR and COMP-DTRS), HEAD-FILLER STRUCTURE (which requires the empty list ⟨ ⟩ as its value for COMP-DTRS and additionally bears the attribute FILLER-DTR), etc.

By way of illustration, the sign corresponding to the topicalized sentence *Bagels, John likes* is partially described by (10a):[3]

(10) a.

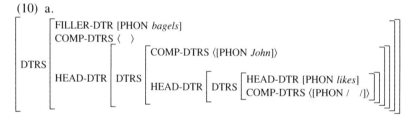

For emphasis, the SYNTAX and SEMANTICS attributes (as well as the PHONOLOGY attributes on phrasal constituents) have been omitted. The important thing to note here is that, in the description of a phrasal sign, the phrase's constituent signs (daughters) themselves are described by feature structures of type SIGN which occur as substructures within the DTRS attribute of the top-level description. Thus the values of FILLER-DTR and HEAD-DTR are just feature structures of type sign (since a sign has at most one filler daughter or head daughter), but the value of COMP-DTRS is a LIST of signs (since a sign may have several complement daughters). It is important to keep in mind that the order of elements in the COMP-DTRS value corresponds not to the temporal order of their phonological realizations (usually called "surface order"), but rather to the traditional notion

of obliqueness of grammatical relations, with more oblique elements occurring further to the left in the list. The correspondence between the
two kinds of order is determined by language-specific constituent-ordering
principles.[4]

For familiarity, we will often use an alternative notation to describe
phrasal signs, as illustrated in (10b):

(10) b.

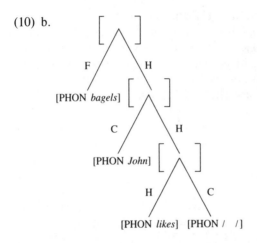

In this notation, which is intended to be suggestive of the tree diagrams
conventionally favored by syntacticians, the feature structure corresponding to the phrase under description appears at the top with all its attributes
indicated as in standard AVM notation, EXCEPT for the DTRS attribute.
Instead of being notated by an AVM in the usual way, the constituent structure which is the value of the DTRS attribute is indicated by the labeled
"branches" descending from the top AVM; the labels "F," "H," and "C"
on the branches correspond to the constituent-structure attributes FILLER-
DTR, HEAD-DTR, and COMP-DTRS respectively. The same descriptive
convention applies recursively, so that e.g. the AVM description (10a) with
multiple levels of recursive embedding takes the form of a labeled tree
(10b) with correspondingly many levels of branching. Of course, in the
labeled tree notation, the "leaves," which have no constituent structure,
simply appear as normal AVMs.

We call the longest path of branches labeled "H" leading upward from a
lexical sign its PROJECTION PATH; in terms of feature structures, a projec-
tion path is just a path of the form DTRS|HEAD-DTR . . . DTRS|HEAD-
DTR whose value is a lexical sign.[5] The PROJECTIONS of a lexical sign
within a phrase are just the phrases that lie on the projection path. Thus, in

the present example, the phrases *likes*, *John likes*, and *Bagels, John likes* are all projections of the lexical sign *likes*.

The sharing of head features between lexical heads and their projections is accounted for by a principle of universal grammar called the Head Feature Principle (HFP), stated in (11):[6]

(11) Head Feature Principle

$$\left[\text{DTRS}_{\;headed\;structure}\;[\;\;] \right] \Rightarrow \left[\begin{array}{l} \text{SYN} \mid \text{LOC} \mid \text{HEAD} \;\boxed{1} \\ \text{DTRS} \mid \text{HEAD-DTR} \mid \text{SYN} \mid \text{LOC} \mid \text{HEAD} \;\boxed{1} \end{array} \right]$$

(A historical note: the HFP is a reformulation in feature-structure terms of the Head Feature Convention of GPSG.) This says simply: If a phrase has a head daughter, then they share the same head features. In the case of the preceding example, the effect of the HFP is indicated in (12):

(12)

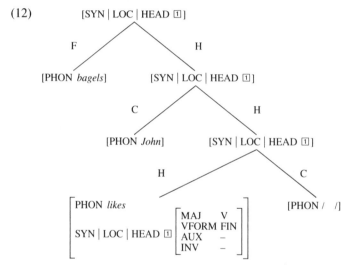

Speaking metaphorically, we sometimes describe such a situation by saying that the head features of the lexical head are "propagated," or "flow," up the tree along the projection path to all the phrasal projections. Of course, there is no actual MOVEMENT of information; what is really involved is a SHARING of information between the lexical head and its projections. (Similarly, the relationship between a filler and a gap is explained not in terms of movement, as in transformational grammar, but rather in terms of a sharing of information between the filler and the gap.)

We turn now to an inventory of the head features used in our analysis of English. With a few minor differences, these closely resemble the head features of GPSG.

The MAJ (major) feature corresponds to the familiar notion of part of speech. English MAJ values include those listed in (13) (as well as disjunctions thereof):

(13) MAJ Values:
    N   nominal signs, e.g. nouns and NPs, including pronouns
    V   verbal signs, e.g. verbs, VPs, and sentences
    A   adjectives, APs, and adjunct clauses headed by APs
    P   prepositions, PPs, and adjunct clauses headed by PPs
    D   determiners
    ADV   adverbs and adverb phrases

This list of MAJ values does not pretend to be exhaustive or definitive; the important thing is that part of speech be treated as a head feature. As we shall see in §2, this permits a highly schematic, cross-categorial formulation of the grammar rules that build head-complement structures, e.g. a single rule will do duty for a vast array of conventional phrase-structure rules such as VP → V NP, PP → P NP, AP → A PP, etc.

Another head feature is CASE. In numerous languages, the various inflected forms of nouns are specified in terms of differing values for CASE, and in virtue of the HFP the CASE specifications are inherited by the NPs that the nouns project. Thus when a given verb subcategorizes for an NP marked as [CASE GEN] or [CASE DAT] (the specifications corresponding to the traditional distinctions of genitive and dative case respectively), this has immediate consequences for the form of the head noun of the governed NP (as well as for the form of any determiners or modifiers whose CASE specifications are required to coincide with those of the head noun). In English, of course, the case system is highly degenerate. Only pronouns are lexically specified for CASE: *I, he, she, we,* and *they* are marked [CASE NOM] (nominative case); *me, him, her, us, them,* and *whom* are marked [CASE ACC]. We do not take a position here on the question of whether possessive NPs in Modern English should be analyzed in terms of a third (genitive) case value.

Major heads can be specified as selecting for complements of a particular grammatical form. This specification is accomplished by employing the features VFORM, PFORM, NFORM, etc. These features, which function roughly as outlined in Gazdar et al. (1985), are summarized in (14).

(14) Feature Values:
    MAJ   N, V, A, P, D, ADV, . . .
    CASE   NOM, ACC, (GEN?)
    VFORM   FIN, BSE, PSP, PRP, PAS, INF, GER
    NFORM   NORM, IT, THERE

PFORM   OF, ON, TO, FROM, . . .
AUX   +, −
INV   +, −
PRD   +, −

It should be noted, however, that familiar distinctions of person, number, and gender are not treated as head features. Rather, we assume that the features PER, NUM, and GEN serve to specify information about the variables of semantic indices. That is, variables (values of the path SEMANTICS|CONTENT|INDEX|VARIABLE) are feature structures specified for agreement features. The pronoun *he,* for example, is specified as in (15):

(15)
$$
\begin{bmatrix}
\text{SYN} \mid \text{LOC} \mid \text{HEAD} \mid \text{CASE} \quad \text{NOM} \\[2ex]
\text{SEM} \mid \text{CONTENT} \mid \text{INDEX} \mid \text{VARIABLE} \begin{bmatrix} \text{PER 3} \\ \text{NUM SING} \\ \text{GEN MASC} \end{bmatrix}
\end{bmatrix}
$$

On this view, articulated in Pollard and Sag (forthcoming), many agreement dependencies can be subsumed by the general mechanism for subcategorization, as outlined in §3.4.

1.2. The Subcategorization Feature

The subcategorization, or valence, of a lexical or phrasal sign is a specification of the number and kind of other signs that the sign in question characteristically combines with in order to become complete. For example, it is well known that different verbs combine with, or SUBCATEGORIZE FOR, different numbers of noun phrases in order to form a complete sentence. Thus an intransitive verb such as *sneeze* subcategorizes for only one NP (the subject) in order to make a complete sentence; a transitive verb such as *touch* subcategorizes for two NPs (the object and the subject); a di-transitive verb such as *hand* (as in *hand Kim a book*) subcategorizes for three NPs (the second object, the object, and the subject). The notion of subcategorization, of course, is relevant for phrases as well as words. Thus a VP such as *likes bagels* resembles a lexical intransitive verb in subcategorizing for a single NP; while a sentence such as *Kim likes bagels* is already complete, or SATURATED, i.e. it does not subcategorize for anything at all.

Verbs and their projections are not alone in bearing subcategorization specifications. For example, a predicative preposition such as *in* resembles a transitive verb in subcategorizing for two NPs (the prepositional object and the subject); a predicative PP such as *in New York* resembles a VP in subcategorizing for a single (subject) NP. Prepositional predicative clauses, such as the sentence-initial modifier in *Her father in New York, Kim took charge of the Duluth office* are saturated; thus they are analogous to sentences, except that their lexical heads are prepositions, not verbs. We also treat common nouns (and common noun phrases such as *tall man with an axe*) as subcategorizing for the determiners they combine with, while NPs such as *Kim* and *the tall man with an axe* are saturated. Determiners themselves, however, we consider saturated.

The repository of information about the subcategorization of signs is the local syntactic feature SUBCAT. Appropriate values of SUBCAT are lists of signs. Thus, a sign which subcategorizes for *n* other signs has as its SUBCAT value a list of *n* (partially specified) signs. An important special case is that of saturated signs (e.g. clauses, NPs, and determiners), whose SUBCAT value is the empty list $\langle\ \rangle$.

Equipped with the notions of head features and subcategorization, we are now in a position to DEFINE conventional grammatical symbols such as NP, VP, etc. in terms of feature structures of type sign. Thus, starting with saturated signs, we can define the symbol "DET" to be an abbreviation for the feature structure (16a), which partially describes a determiner sign such as *every*. Likewise, (16b) and (16c) define NP and S as the saturated signs headed by nouns and verbs respectively. Simple examples of unsaturated signs are N (common noun) and VP, defined as in (16d) and (16e). (Note: The symbol "N" is used both a value of the feature MAJ and as an abbreviation for a certain feature structure containing the specification [MAJ N]; which use is intended will always be clear from context.) Observe that the abbreviations are used recursively, e.g. "NP" is used in the SUBCAT specification in the definition of "VP."

(16)   Definitions of Conventional Grammatical Symbols

Symbol	Definition	Examples
a. DET	$\begin{bmatrix} \text{SYN} \mid \text{LOC} \mid \text{HEAD} \mid \text{MAJ D} \\ \text{SUBCAT} \langle\ \rangle \end{bmatrix}$	*every* *the*
b. NP	$\begin{bmatrix} \text{SYN} \mid \text{LOC} \mid \text{HEAD} \mid \text{MAJ N} \\ \text{SUBCAT} \langle\ \rangle \end{bmatrix}$	*Kim* *every cat*
c. S	$\begin{bmatrix} \text{SYN} \mid \text{LOC} \mid \text{HEAD} \mid \text{MAJ V} \\ \text{SUBCAT} \langle\ \rangle \end{bmatrix}$	*Kim left* *did Kim go*
d. N	$\begin{bmatrix} \text{SYN} \mid \text{LOC} \mid \text{HEAD} \mid \text{MAJ N} \\ \text{SUBCAT} \langle \text{DET} \rangle \end{bmatrix}$	*cat* *white cat*
e. VP	$\begin{bmatrix} \text{SYN} \mid \text{LOC} \mid \text{HEAD} \mid \text{MAJ V} \\ \text{SUBCAT} \langle \text{NP} \rangle \end{bmatrix}$	*sneezed* *liking cats*

In addition to such standard symbols, it is convenient to use certain complex symbols as abbreviations for more specific types of phrases bearing certain values for one or more additional head features as INV, CASE, NFORM, VFORM, PFORM, PRD, etc.

Of course, not just NPs are subcategorized for, as (17) illustrates:

(17) Values of SYNTAX|LOCAL|SUBCAT for representative lexical signs:
  a. *sneezed* ⟨NP[NOM, NORM]⟩
  b. *rained* ⟨NP[IT]⟩
  c. *ablaze* ⟨NP[NORM]⟩
  d. *touched* ⟨NP[ACC, NORM], NP[NOM, NORM]⟩
  e. *relied* ⟨PP[−PRD, ON], NP[NOM, NORM]⟩
  f. *tried* ⟨VP[INF, NP[NOM, NORM]⟩
  g. *fond* ⟨PP[−PRD, OF], NP[NORM]⟩
  h. *on* ⟨NP[ACC, NORM], NP[NORM]⟩
  i. *handed* ⟨NP[ACC, NORM], NP[ACC, NORM], NP[NOM, NORM]⟩
  j. *forced* ⟨VP[INF], NP[ACC, NORM], NP[NOM, NORM]⟩

It should be noted that, as with COMP-DTRS values, the order of occurrence of symbols on the SUBCAT list does not directly reflect the surface constituent order of complements, but rather corresponds to obliqueness of grammatical relations. Thus, in the case of NP complements, the last (least oblique) element corresponds to the grammatical SUBJECT; the next-to-last element corresponds to the DIRECT OBJECT, and the third-from-last element corresponds to the SECOND (or INDIRECT) OBJECT. (The connection between subcategorization in HPSG and the notions of grammatical relations embodied in theories such as LFG and categorial grammar are considered in more detail below.) The relationship between obliqueness order and surface constituent is mediated by the language-specific grammar rules and principles of linear precedence.

It should be intuitively clear that the SUBCAT value of a phrase ought to be the SUBCAT value of the lexical head minus those specifications that have already been satisfied by some constituent in the phrase. For example, the SUBCAT value of *touched Fido* is just ⟨NP[NOM, NORM]⟩, for the SUBCAT value of *touched* is lexically specified as ⟨NP[ACC, NORM], NP[NOM, NORM]⟩, but the specification NP[ACC, NORM] has already been satisfied within the phrase by the object *Fido*. Similarly, the SUBCAT value of *Kim touched Fido* is ⟨ ⟩ (the empty list), for now the remaining specification NP[NOM, NORM] has also been satisfied by the subject *Kim*. In HPSG, the transmission of subcategorization information up projection paths is governed by a principle of universal grammar called the Subcategorization Principle:

(18) Subcategorization Principle

$$\left[\text{DTRS}\underbrace{\quad}_{\textit{headed structure}}[\quad]\right]\Rightarrow$$

$$\begin{bmatrix}\text{SYN}\mid\text{LOC}\mid\text{SUBCAT}\ \boxed{2}\\[6pt]\text{DTRS}\begin{bmatrix}\text{HEAD-DTR}\mid\text{SYN}\mid\text{LOC}\mid\text{SUBCAT append}(\boxed{1},\boxed{2})\\\text{COMP-DTRS}\ \boxed{1}\end{bmatrix}\end{bmatrix}$$

It should be noted that for two lists L_1 and L_2, append (L_1, L_2) is the list obtained by concatenating the two lists in the indicated order. Thsu (18) means that for any sign with a head daughter, the SUBCAT value is the list obtained by removing from the SUBCAT value of the head those specifications that were satisfied by one of the complement daughters. In addition, the structure-sharing (indicated by the double occurrences of the tags " $\boxed{1}$ " and " $\boxed{2}$ ") indicates that the information from each complement daughter is actually UNIFIED with the corresponding subcategorization specification on the head. Thus a sign can satisfy a subcategorization specification on some head only if it is consistent with that specification; otherwise a unification failure will result, in violation of the Subcategorization Principle.

The resulting transmission of subcategorization information is illustrated by the partial description of the sentence *I appealed to him to leave* given in (19):

(19)

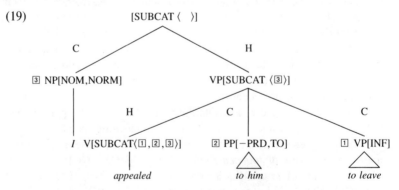

(Note: Here "SUBCAT" abbreviates "SYNTAX|LOCAL|SUBCAT.") In effect, as we move up the projection path from the lexical head, subcategorization requirements are canceled (removed from the SUBCAT list) as they are satisfied by appropriate complements. Readers familiar with categorial grammar should note that the Subcategorization Principle is analogous to the CANCELLATION of categories, with heads and complements corresponding to FUNCTOR CATEGORIES and ARGUMENT CATEGORIES respectively. However, unlike standard categorial grammars, HPSG grammar rules may allow constituent structures which are not BINARY BRANCHING; thus a phrase may have more than one complement daughter, as in the present example.

Finally, we should make clear that SUBCAT specifications may also make reference to semantic properties of dependent elements. In particular, agreement between a verb and its subject (or in certain languages between a verb and its direct object, indirect object, etc.) may be analyzed by restricting the SEM|CON|INDEX|VARIABLE value of the relevant dependent element on the verb's SUBCAT list. We return to this matter in §3.4.

2. Rules and Principles

2.1. The Logical Structure of Linguistic Theory

In the preceding sections we proposed two principles of Universal Grammar: the Head Feature Principle and the Subcategorization Principle. We conceive of universal grammar as a unification of principles:

(20) $UG = P_1 \wedge \ldots \wedge P_n$

where $P_1, \ldots, P_n$ is an exhaustive list of the universal principles.

Moreover, we assume that each natural language imposes additional language-specific constraints on its own. Thus there are principles P_{n+1}, $\ldots, P_{n+m}$ which must be satisfied by all signs of English. One such principle, the CONSTITUENT ORDERING PRINCIPLE, embodies all English-particular Linear Precedence rules.

In addition, each language presents a finite set of lexical signs and a finite set of GRAMMAR RULES. A grammar rule is just a very partially specified phrasal sign which constitutes one of the options offered by the language in question for making big signs from little ones. Let us suppose that $L_1, \ldots, L_p$ is an exhaustive list of the English lexical signs and $R_1, \ldots,$ R_q is an exhaustive list of the English grammar rules. Then our theory of English is (21):

(21) English $P_1 \wedge \ldots \wedge P_{n+m} \wedge (L_1 \vee \ldots \vee L_p \vee R_1 \vee \ldots \vee R_q)$

In other words, an object is an English sign token just in case (i) it satisfies all the universal and English-specific principles, and (ii) either it instantiates one of the English lexical signs or it instantiates one of the English grammar rules.

For reference, the two universal principles proposed so far, all of which take the form [DTRS $_{headed\ structure}$ [ ]] $\Rightarrow$ X, may be unified into the more compact form shown in (22):

(22) [DTRS $_{headed\ structure}$ [ ]] $\Rightarrow$

$$\begin{bmatrix} \text{SYN} \mid \text{LOC} \begin{bmatrix} \text{HEAD} & \boxed{1} \\ \text{SUBCAT} & \boxed{3} \end{bmatrix} \\ \\ \text{DTRS } \boxed{4} \begin{bmatrix} \text{HEAD-DTR} \begin{bmatrix} \text{SYN} \mid \text{LOC} \begin{bmatrix} \text{HEAD } \boxed{1} \\ \text{SUBCAT append}(\boxed{2},\boxed{3}) \end{bmatrix} \\ \text{SEM} \mid \text{CONT } \boxed{5} \end{bmatrix} \\ \text{COMP-DTRS } \boxed{2} \end{bmatrix} \end{bmatrix}$$

In the next two sections, we present three grammar rules which account for English head-complement structures.

2.2. Two Rules

Grammar Rule 1, given in (23a), corresponds to the rules standardly expressed in the forms "S → NP VP," "NP → DET NOM," and "NP → NP[GEN] NOM." It is also responsible for small clauses (sentence-like signs headed by predicative phrases or nonfinite verb phrases).

(23) a. Rule 1:

$$\begin{bmatrix} \text{SYN} \mid \text{LOC} \mid \text{SUBCAT} \langle\ \rangle \\ \text{DTRS} \begin{bmatrix} \text{HEAD-DTR} \mid \text{SYN} \mid \text{LOC} \mid \text{LEX } - \\ \text{COMP-DTRS} \langle [\ ] \rangle \end{bmatrix} \end{bmatrix}$$

The essential content of this rule is that one of the possibilities for a phrasal sign in English is to be a saturated (i.e. [SUBCAT ⟨ ⟩]) sign which has as constituents a single complement daughter (i.e. [COMP-DTRS ⟨[ ]⟩]) and a head daughter, which in turn is constrained to be a phrasal rather than a lexical sign. Recall that we treat VPs as the heads of sentences (unlike most work within GB theory); hence this rule legitimates the combination of VPs with subject complements to make sentences as well as the combination of unsaturated nominal constituents with Det or possessor phrase complements to form NPs.

For the sake of familiarity, we shall sometimes express a rule such as (23a) in a somewhat more standard "rewrite" notation, as in (23b):

(23) b. [SUBCAT ⟨ ⟩] → H[LEX −], C

Whenever we write rules in this way, however, it should be understood that this is just a shorthand for the official notation in (23a). Grammar rules are always to be conceived of as partially specified phrasal signs.

Of course, the rule in (23) does not tell all there is to know about the phrases that it subsumes; it does not contain any information that is predictable from universal principles (such as (22)) or English-specific principles (such as the Constituent Ordering Principle). For example, any phrasal sign subsumed by (23) must in fact be subsumed by the more specified version of Rule 1, given in (24), which is obtained by unifying (23) with the HFP and the Subcategorization Principle.

(24)
$$
\begin{bmatrix}
\text{SYN} \mid \text{LOC} \begin{bmatrix} \text{HEAD} & \boxed{1} \\ \text{SUBCAT} \langle \ \rangle \end{bmatrix} \\[3ex]
\text{DTRS} \begin{bmatrix} \text{HEAD-DTR} \mid \text{SYN} \mid \text{LOC} \begin{bmatrix} \text{HEAD} & \boxed{1} \\ \text{SUBCAT} \langle \boxed{2} \rangle \\ \text{LEX} \ - \end{bmatrix} \\[4ex] \text{COMP-DTRS} \langle \boxed{2} \rangle \end{bmatrix}
\end{bmatrix}
$$

Likewise, any phrasal sign subsumed by (23) (or, equivalently, by (24)) must also be subsumed by the still more specified version of Rule 1, given in (25), which is obtained by unifying (24) with the English Constituent Ordering Principle:

(25)
$$
\begin{bmatrix}
\text{PHON concat}(\boxed{3}, \boxed{4}) \\[1ex]
\text{SYN} \mid \text{LOC} \begin{bmatrix} \text{HEAD} & \boxed{1} \\ \text{SUBCAT} \langle \ \rangle \end{bmatrix} \\[4ex]
\text{DTRS} \begin{bmatrix} \text{HEAD-DTR} \begin{bmatrix} \text{PHON} & \boxed{4} \\ \text{SYN} \mid \text{LOC} \begin{bmatrix} \text{HEAD} & \boxed{1} \\ \text{SUBCAT} \langle \boxed{2} \rangle \\ \text{LEX} \ - \end{bmatrix} \end{bmatrix} \\[5ex] \text{COMP-DTRS} \langle \boxed{2} [\text{PHON} \boxed{3}] \rangle \end{bmatrix}
\end{bmatrix}
$$

The architecture of the theory is such that properties of phrases that follow from universal or language-specific principles need not be specified on individual grammar rules. Formula (25) differs from (24) in that it contains the information that the complement daughter precedes the head daughter in surface order.

Rule 2 is the rule that subsumes unsaturated phrasal signs such as VPs. It says that another one of the options for English is to be a phrasal sign one dependent short of being saturated (i.e. whose SUBCAT value is a list of length one) whose head daughter is an uninverted ([INV −]) lexical sign. This is shown in (26):

(26) Rule 2

$$
\begin{bmatrix}
\text{SYN} \mid \text{LOC SUBCAT} \langle [\quad] \rangle \\
\text{DTRS} \mid \text{HEAD-DTR} \mid \text{SYN} \mid \text{LOC}
\begin{bmatrix}
\text{HEAD} \mid \text{INV} - \\
\text{LEX} +
\end{bmatrix}
\end{bmatrix}
$$

The specification [INV −] in this rule prevents verbs marked [INV +], e.g. 1st person singular *aren't*, from being the head of a verb phrase (and hence accounts for the ungrammaticality of examples like *I aren't going to the store*). In the familiar rewrite notation, Rule 2 takes the form (27):

(27) [SUBCAT $\langle [\quad] \rangle$] → H[INV −, LEX +], C*

Again, this grammar rule says very little, since much of the structure of the phrases which it subsumes is obtained from the principles of Universal Grammar and the English Constituent Ordering Principle. The HFP will again enforce the identity of the phrase's head-feature values with those on the head daughter (in this case the lexical head); the Subcategorization Principle will guarantee that the lexical head have a SUBCAT list whose length is exactly one greater than the number of complement daughters, and that those complement daughters actually satisfy the subcategorization restrictions specified on the lexical head. In addition, the Constituent Ordering Principle will ensure that in the corresponding utterance tokens, the realization of the lexical head precedes the realization of the complements, that the direct object precedes the indirect object (if any), etc. Thus, for example, a transitive verb will combine with exactly one complement (the direct object) to form a verb phrase, i.e. a [MAJ V] phrasal sign that still requires one additional complement (the subject) in order to become saturated.

Because so many conventional phrase-structure rules are schematized by Rules 1 and 2, the two together account for a very substantial subtype ("fragment") of English: the noninverted head-complement structures. Such a structure is partially illustrated in (28):

(28)

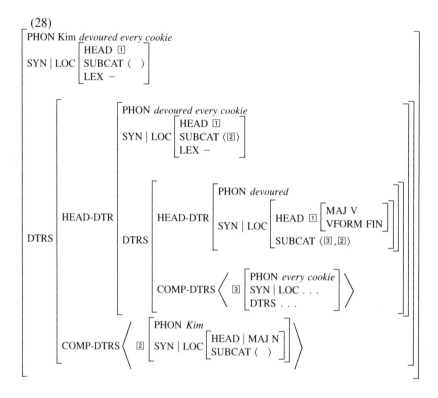

The connection between the structure of a complex sign according to HPSG theory and conventional constituent structure trees is seen at once by considering diagram (29), where the DTRS attributes have been notated by branches labeled "H" and "C" (for HEAD-DTR and COMP-DTRS respectively).

For ease of reference, each node of the tree is labeled by the number of the rule that subsumes it. To enhance readability, specifications for some head features are omitted. For the same reason, structure-sharing required by the HFP and the Subcategorization Principle (i.e. identity of HEAD between phrases and their head daughters, and identity of complement daughters with the subcategorization specifications that they satisfy) has not been explicitly indicated. Note that in the derivation of the nominal phrase *cookie*, the lexical sign *cookie* has combined according to Rule 2,

(29)

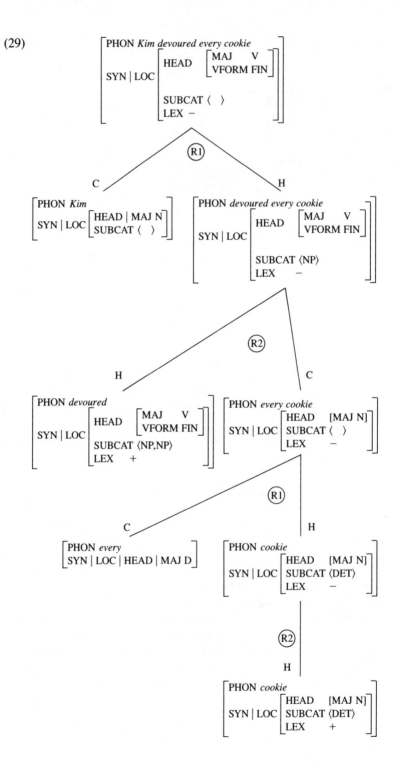

but with no complements. Intransitive verbs are built into verb phrases in similar fashion.

This same tree is displayed again in (30), this time with the relevant structure-sharing explicitly indicated.

(30)

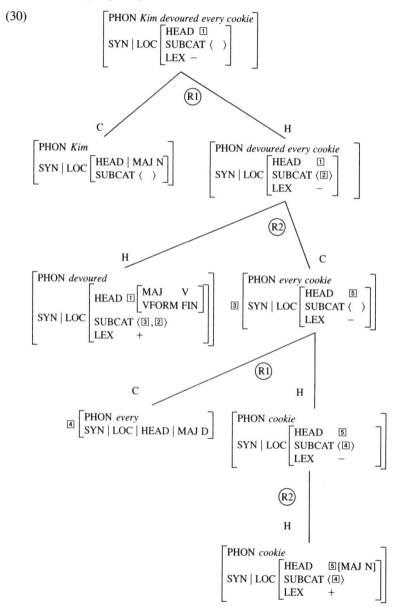

In similar fashion, Rules 1 and 2 interact to provide an account of possessor constructions (recall that common nouns also may be lexically specified as either [SUBCAT ⟨DET⟩] or as [SUBCAT ⟨POSP⟩], where "POSP" abbreviates whatever analysis is adopted for possessive NPs) and "small clauses" (sentence-like phrases whose heads are not finite verbs). This is illustrated by the partial descriptions in (31) and (32).

(31)

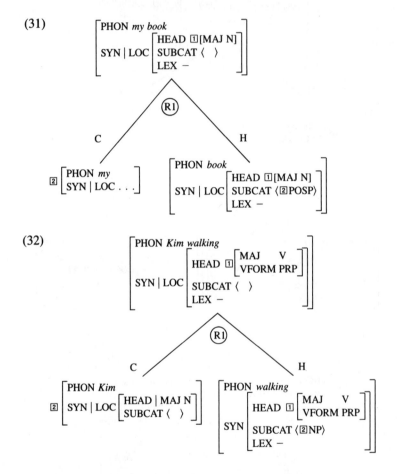

(32)

Small clauses like the one in (32) occur as predicative adjunct clauses (either marked by *with* or *not*), as in (33):

(33) *With Kim walking, we can throw away the crutches.*

2.3. *Inverted Structures*

Inverted clauses in standard varieties of English occur in a number of different main (or "root") clause construction types, some of which are illustrated in (34).[7]

(34) a. *Is Dana walking to the store?* (Polar ("yes-no") question)
    b. *Whose brother will Lou visit ____?* (Constituent ("*Wh*") question)
    c. *Never have I seen a taller tree.* ("Negative Adverb Preposing")
    d. *Did she ever ace the test!* (Exclamation)

The verbs that introduce such clauses are all compatible with the specification [INV +]. In fact, all invertible verbs in English (as opposed to other Germanic languages) are also specified as [AUX +].

To allow for this clause type, we posit the grammar rule given in its official form in (35) and in unofficial rewrite notation in (36).

(35) Rule 3:

$$\begin{bmatrix} \text{SYN} \mid \text{LOC} \mid \text{SUBCAT} \langle\ \rangle \\ \text{DTRS} \mid \text{HEAD-DTR} \mid \text{SYN} \mid \text{LOC} \begin{bmatrix} \text{HEAD} \mid \text{INV} + \\ \text{LEX} + \end{bmatrix} \end{bmatrix}$$

(36) [SUBCAT $\langle\ \rangle$] → H[INV +, LEX +], C*

In virtue of the HFP, the Subcategorization Principle, the English Constituent Ordering Principle, the fact that every lexical sign specified as [INV +] is a finite auxiliary verb, and the fact that auxiliary verbs always have SUBCAT lists of length 2, it follows that inverted phrasal signs will also be subsumed by the more specified version of Rule 3 shown in (37):

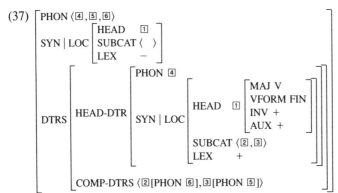

Thus Rule 3, taken together with universal principles and independently motivated English-specific constraints on constituent ordering, allows for inverted clauses of the sort sketched in (38):

(38)

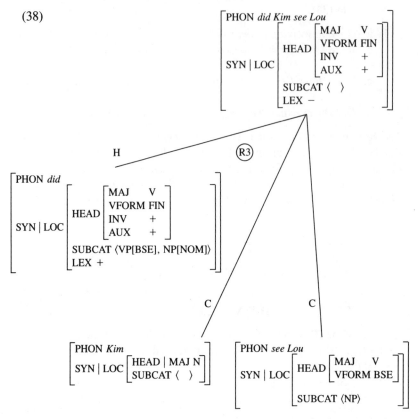

Since INV is a head feature, the specification [INV +] is inherited by clauses projected from [INV +] lexical heads. If we assume that verbs which take sentential complements subcategorize for S[INV −], we can then account for the fact that inverted clauses in standard English are always root clauses.

3. Subcategorization

In the previous sections we have outlined a head-driven conception of phrase structure that relies crucially on two principles of Universal Grammar: the Head Feature Principle and the Subcategorization Principle. These in turn rely on lexically specified information of two sorts: values of HEAD

and values of SUBCAT. In §1.1 we enumerated the various head features
we employ. The SUBCAT feature, outlined in §1.2, embodies a theory of
subcategorization that closely resembles that of categorial grammar and
differs in significant respects from those developed within frameworks like
GB or LFG. In this section, we discuss some of the motivation for our theory of subcategorization. Among the issues we address are: semantic role
assignment, why subcategorization cannot be purely semantic or purely
"functional," and subcategorization for subjects.

3.1. Subcategorization and Role Assignment

As we have seen, the feature SUBCAT is used to encode the various dependencies that hold between a lexical head and its complements (the signs
that it characteristically combines with). SUBCAT takes a list of (partially
specified) signs as its value; the position of an element on the list corresponds to the obliqueness of the complement sign which it describes, with
the rightmost element corresponding to the least oblique dependent sign
(subject). (It should be noted that we use the term "complement" to include subjects as well as NP and PP objects, VP and S complements, etc.
Thus, just as in LFG (but unlike GB and GPSG), we treat subjects as subcategorized-for; the reasons for this are discussed at some length below.)
As a head combines syntactically with a complement, the grammatical information specified in the appropriate position on the head's SUBCAT list,
as required by the Subcategorization Principle. In this way, grammatical
information is shared between heads and their complements, so that lexical
heads in effect impose restrictions on the number and kind of complements
they will combine with.

Significantly, the sign specifications that appear on the SUBCAT lists of
lexical signs bear values for both SYNTAX and SEMANTICS, but NOT for
DAUGHTERS; thus lexical signs can exert syntactic restrictions (e.g. subcategorization in the conventional sense, government, and case assignment)
and semantic restrictions (e.g. role assignment and sortal appropriateness
conditions of the kind often referred to as "semantic selection restrictions"); but such restrictions are strictly local in character (we return to this
point in §4). The semantic aspect of subcategorization is most simply illustrated by an intransitive verb such as *walk,* whose lexical sign is described in (39):[8]

$$(39) \begin{bmatrix} \text{PHON} & walk \\ \text{SYN} & \begin{bmatrix} \text{HEAD} & [\text{MAJ V}] \\ \text{SUBCAT} \langle \text{NP}_{\boxed{1}} \rangle \end{bmatrix} \\ \text{SEM} \mid \text{CONT} & \begin{bmatrix} \text{RELN} & \text{WALK} \\ \text{WALKER} & \boxed{1} \end{bmatrix} \end{bmatrix}$$

Here the variable $\boxed{1}$ associated with the SUBCAT element (which corresponds to the verb's subject) is identified (i.e. unified) with the variable corresponding to the walker role in the situation described by the verb itself. When the verb combines with its subject, the subject must unify with the partially specified sign on the verb's SUBCAT list in accordance with the Subcategorization Principle; in particular the variables of the subject and the SUBCAT element are unified. In consequence of these two unifications, the subject variable is unified with the variable filling the "walker" role in the verb's (and also the sentence's) described situation. Thus, information associated with a head is amalgamated with information associated with the complements of the head in the determination of the semantics of phrasal signs.

One essential function of the SUBCAT feature, therefore, is to set up the correspondence between grammatical relations (subject, object, etc.) and the roles in the described situation. This correspondence is reminiscent of the notion of "θ-role assignment under subcategorization," as discussed within the framework of GB theory; the fundamental difference is that HPSG treats roles not as syntactic entities but rather as constituents of semantic content. (Another difference is that HPSG does not require that every subcategorized complement be assigned a role.) It is important to understand the nature of this correspondence clearly, for out of it arises the whole communicative power of lexical signs. The point of role assignment is not to make syntactic objects well-formed; it is to establish a connection between the constituents of an utterance and the constituents of the thing the utterance is about.

To give a slightly more complex example, a ditransitive verb such as *give* will assign semantic roles to all three of its subcategorized-for dependents, as shown in (40):

$$(40) \begin{bmatrix} \text{PHON} & give \\ \text{SYN} & \begin{bmatrix} \text{HEAD} & [\text{MAJ V}] \\ \text{SUBCAT} \langle \text{NP}_{\boxed{1}}, \text{NP}_{\boxed{2}}, \text{NP}_{\boxed{3}} \rangle \end{bmatrix} \\ \text{SEM} \mid \text{CONT} & \begin{bmatrix} \text{RELN} & \text{GIVE} \\ \text{GIVER} & \boxed{3} \\ \text{RECEIVER} & \boxed{2} \\ \text{GIVEN} & \boxed{1} \end{bmatrix} \end{bmatrix}$$

Syntactic combination of this form with the required complements will yield the appropriate sentence semantics as the subject, direct object, and second object of the verb unify with the appropriate elements on the verb's SUBCAT list.

3.2. The Hierarchical Theory of Subcategorization

The theory of subcategorization presented here makes essential use of a HIERARCHICAL conception of grammatical relations. That is, notions such as SUBJECT and DIRECT OBJECT of a verb (or, more generally, of any lexical head) are defined in terms of the order of the corresponding elements on the head's SUBCAT list. The usage adopted here is a variant of the terminology employed within the categorial grammar approach of Dowty (1982a, b), which is keyed to the order of argument positions in Montague-style semantic translations. The underlying intuition is close to the ordered conception of grammatical relations adopted in relational grammar, where subject, direct object, and indirect object are identified as *1*'s, *2*'s, and *3*'s respectively.

To be more precise, we adopt the following usages with respect to grammatical relation terms. We begin by distinguishing two basic types of complements: (i) those which do not subcategorize for anything themselves, i.e. their SUBCAT values are ⟨ ⟩ (such as nonpredicative NPs and PPs, and sentential complements); and (ii) those with a nonempty SUBCAT value (such as predicative and VP complements). These two types are distinguished as SATURATED and UNSATURATED respectively. Saturated complements are then designated as SUBJECT, DIRECT OBJECT, and SECOND OBJECT according as the corresponding SUBCAT element appears last, next to last, or third from last on the SUBCAT list, as long as an unsaturated complement does not intervene. Following LFG usage, we often refer to an unsaturated complement as XCOMP. (The theory of CONTROL presented in Pollard and Sag (forthcoming) is concerned in large part with the semantic interpretation of the variables associated with the "missing" subjects of xcomps.) All other complements are simply lumped together as OBLIQUE OBJECTS.

Before turning to a detailed justification of the notion of grammatical hierarchy, it is worth pointing out that other conceptions of grammatical relations are broadly consistent with the general framework developed here. For example, within the JPSG system of Gunji (1986), SUBCAT values are treated as (unordered) sets rather than lists; subjects and objects are then distinguished by a feature whose values include SUBJ and OBJ. Evidently any notion of obliqueness is absent here. (Indeed, one imaginable theory of grammatical relations would hold that whether or not grammatical relations participate in an obliqueness ordering is a parameter of cross-linguistic variation.) In another variant of HPSG defended by Borsley (1987b), the SUBCAT feature involves nonsubjects only, as in GPSG; subject selection is then handled by a new SUBJECT feature. Elsewhere, Borsley (1987a) has suggested that determiners as well be split off from other dependent elements, to be treated by still another feature called SPEC. Of course, carrying this idea to its logical limit leads to a "keyword" theory of grammatical relations similar to that of LFG, wherein each grammatical relation is handled by a distinct feature. Within such a theory, SUBCAT values would resemble LFG f-structures, with the important difference that the value of each "grammatical relation feature" would be not an f-structure but rather a sign, as sketched in (41):

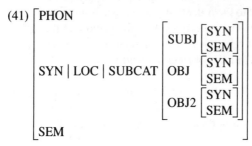

Any such variant theories of course require modification of our principles of Universal Grammar, in particular the Subcategorization Principle, which can no longer be formulated in terms of list cancellation.

But why assume that grammatical relations participate in an obliqueness ordering? There are at least four different classes of linguistic generalizations which, we claim, provide motivation for the hierarchical theory of grammatical relations. These are CONSTITUENT ORDER GENERALIZATIONS, GENERALIZATIONS INVOLVING THE THEORY OF CONTROL, GENERALIZATIONS ABOUT THE BINDING OF PRONOUNS AND REFLEXIVES, and GENERALIZATIONS ABOUT THE FUNCTIONING OF LEXICAL RULES.

In many—but by no means all—of the world's languages, the surface order of constituents (i.e. the temporal order of their phonological realizations) and their grammatical relations appear to be subject to mutual constraints. English, of course, is such a language: it is well known that the traditional notion of obliqueness corresponds closely to left-to-right order. In Sag (1987) it is argued that an array of facts about English constituent order follow from just such a HIERARCHICAL LINEAR PRECEDENCE CONSTRAINT, viz. that a complement must linearly precede any of its sister complements whose corresponding SUBCAT elements are earlier on the head's SUBCAT list.

Similarly, in Pollard and Sag (1987; forthcoming), it is argued that such long-standing problems as "Visser's Generalization" (Bresnan 1982a) find a natural solution in terms of the interaction of purely semantic control constraints and an Obliqueness Control Principle. This principle requires that whenever an "unsaturated" complement appears on the SUBCAT list of a lexical head, there must also be a less oblique controller (a dependent whose variable is unified with that of the complement's unexpressed subject) on the same SUBCAT list. This analysis, which we can do little more than mention here, relies crucially on the hierarchy of obliqueness as defined by the feature SUBCAT.

In virtually every current syntactic theory, some notion of "command" is assumed to play a central role in the formulation of linguistic constraints that govern the relationships (e.g. "coindexing," "disjoint reference") between anaphoric elements (such as personal and reflexive pronouns) and other constituents of the sentence. Depending on the theory, command is variously construed in terms of syntactic configuration (the "C-COMMAND" of GB), semantic predicate-argument structure (the "ARGUMENT-COM- MAND" of Categorial Grammar in the variant of Bach and Partee 1980), or functional structure (the "F-COMMAND" of LFG). In Pollard and Sag (forthcoming), we formulate constraints on the binding of reflexive and personal pronouns in terms of what might be called "O-COMMAND," where one constituent X O-COMMANDS another constituent Y provided X is a less oblique dependent (of the same head) than a constituent Z dominating Y (for the purposes of this definition, any constituent is assumed to dominate itself). Roughly: (i) a reflexive pronoun must be coindexed with (be associated with the same semantic variable as) a less oblique dependent, provided such exists; (ii) a (nonreflexive) pronoun must not be coindexed with any less oblique dependent; and (iii) no constituent can O-COMMAND a coindexed nonpronoun.[9] We argue that such a theory of anaphora is simpler and fits the facts better than alternative accounts.

Various generalizations about the application of lexical rules also provide motivation for a hierarchical conception of grammatical relations. Passivization, for example, applies in English so as to promote a next-to-last NP on a SUBCAT list to a SUBCAT-final element. But, as suggested by Dowty (1982b), passive in certain other languages should be formulated so as to generalize this "promotion" to other, more oblique dependents. Indirect objects, for example, may also passivize in a number of languages, including perhaps varieties of English where examples like (42b), as well as (42a) are grammatical.[10]

(42) a.   Sandy was given a book (by Lou).
     b.   %A book was given Sandy (by Lou).

Similarly, the analysis of languages that have impersonal passives, e.g. German *Es wird heute getanzt* 'there will be dancing today', may well motivate a schematic passivization rule that applies not just when a SUB-

CAT list ends in two NPs (as in standard varieties of English), but also when it ends in just one. Generalizations of this sort are naturally expressed under the assumption that subcategorization information is hierarchically represented, as with the SUBCAT feature, and that languages may set certain parameters on their lexical rules that let them apply to sublists of SUBCAT values.

We note in passing that there are a number of cross-linguistic generalizations proposed in the literature that are also naturally expressed in terms of a hierarchical view of syntactic dependents. Keenan and Comrie (1977) claim that there are generalizations about possible relative clause systems in the world's languages that have a hierarchical character; e.g. that any language permitting object relativization of the sort illustrated in (43a) also allows subject relativization as in (43b):

(43) a. *The man [who Kim likes _____]*
      b. *The man [who _____ likes Kim]*

They argue in fact that the hierarchy in (44) expresses the relative accessibility to relativization of NP positions (in simplex main clauses):

(44) Accessibility Hierarchy:

$$\text{SUBJECT} \Rightarrow \begin{matrix}\text{DIRECT}\\\text{OBJECT}\end{matrix} \Rightarrow \begin{matrix}\text{INDIRECT}\\\text{OBJECT}\end{matrix} \Rightarrow$$

$$\text{OBLIQUES} \Rightarrow \text{GENITIVES} \Rightarrow \begin{matrix}\text{OBJECTS OF}\\\text{COMPARISON}\end{matrix}$$

That is, they claim that any language allowing relativization of any of the positions in (44) will also allow relativization of all positions to the left of that position. (So, for example, no language could allow relative clauses like (43a) unless it also allowed those like (43b).) Within a hierarchical theory of subcategorization like the one we are proposing, the claim would be that languages set a parameter as to how far down a SUBCAT list relativization may apply.[11] A similar approach could be taken to explain Keenan and Comrie's observation that verb agreement, cross-linguistically, obeys the Accessibility Hierarchy (languages with object agreement also exhibit subject agreement, and so forth).

In sum, there appears to be considerable evidence that syntactic phenomena of diverse sorts obey generalizations that are hierarchical in nature. The theory of subcategorization we adopt here provides a direct encoding of hierarchical relations suitable for expressing these generalizations. This is not to say that alternative theories of subcategorizations such as those mentioned above are inconsistent with the available evidence, but only that a theory with no notion of obliqueness is inadequate. It may be possible to develop a hybrid theory that uses the keyword approach to subjects, objects, and other complements, but which uses other means to impose a hierarchical structure on syntactic elements, including optional modifiers not subcategorized for in the same sense.

3.3. Category Selection

It has sometimes been proposed that lexical dependencies can be accounted for without recourse to any notion of formal category selection. The analysis of English absolutive constructions proposed by Stump (1981), for example, would seem to suggest that subcategorization can be reduced to a matter of semantic selection, as does one nontransformational analysis of unbounded dependency (filler-gap) constructions due to Cooper (1983). Within the LFG framework, it is assumed that subcategorization is entirely a matter of selection for grammatical functions (such as subject, object, xcomp, etc.). But it is evident that there are subcategorization restrictions that crucially involve differences of syntactic category which cannot be reduced to semantic or functional distinctions.

First, subcategorization cannot be reduced to semantic selection. Natural languages abound with groups of verbs closely related in meaning which make different demands upon their complements with respect to either gross syntactic category or finer distinctions, such as inflectional form of the head verb in an xcomp, case of an object, or identity of the preposition which heads a prepositional phrase complement. Some examples involving gross category differences follow:

(45) a.   *Sandy trusts Kim.*
      b.   **Sandy trusts on Kim.*
(46) a.   *Sandy depends/relies on Kim.*
      b.   **Sandy depends/relies Kim.*
(47) a.   *Sandy spared Kim a second helping.*
      b.   **Sandy deprived Kim a second helping.*
(48) a.   *Sandy deprived Kim of a second helping.*
      b.   **Sandy spared Kim of a second helping.*

In our view, examples like these show that any adequate theory of lexical dependencies must recognize the syntactic distinction between NPs and PPs. Given the theory of syntactic features outlined in §1, the dependencies in question here are effected by positing lexical signs like the following:

$$
(49) \begin{bmatrix} \text{PHON} & \textit{trusted} \\ \text{SYN} \mid \text{LOC} & \begin{bmatrix} \text{HEAD} & \begin{bmatrix} \text{MAJ} & \text{V} \\ \text{VFORM} & \text{FIN} \end{bmatrix} \\ \text{SUBCAT} & \langle \text{NP, NP} \rangle \end{bmatrix} \end{bmatrix}
$$

$$(50) \begin{bmatrix} \text{PHON} & \textit{depended} \\ \text{SYN} \mid \text{LOC} & \begin{bmatrix} \text{HEAD} & \begin{bmatrix} \text{MAJ} & \text{V} \\ \text{VFORM} & \text{FIN} \end{bmatrix} \\ \text{SUBCAT} \langle \text{PP[ON], NP} \rangle \end{bmatrix} \end{bmatrix}$$

$$(51) \begin{bmatrix} \text{PHON} & \textit{spared} \\ \text{SYN} \mid \text{LOC} & \begin{bmatrix} \text{HEAD} & \begin{bmatrix} \text{MAJ} & \text{V} \\ \text{VFORM} & \text{FIN} \end{bmatrix} \\ \text{SUBCAT} \langle \text{NP, NP, NP} \rangle \end{bmatrix} \end{bmatrix}$$

$$(52) \begin{bmatrix} \text{PHON} & \textit{deprived} \\ \text{SYN} \mid \text{LOC} & \begin{bmatrix} \text{HEAD} & \begin{bmatrix} \text{MAJ} & \text{V} \\ \text{VFORM} & \text{FIN} \end{bmatrix} \\ \text{SUBCAT} \langle \text{PP[OF], NP, NP} \rangle \end{bmatrix} \end{bmatrix}$$

In each case the indicated feature specifications on the appropriate signs on the verb's SUBCAT list impose the relevant restrictions on the verb's complements.

In the foregoing examples, a verb that requires an NP object is contrasted with a semantically related verb that selects a particular PP. Similarly, verbs close in meaning vary with respect to the gross category selected for the xcomp. As is well known, forms of the English copula *be* can take NP, AP, VP, or PP complements, but *become* can be followed only by an NP or an AP. The purely syntactic nature of this selectional difference is underscored by the fact that a PP xcomp for *become* is ungrammatical even if it can be paraphrased by an NP or AP:

(53) a. *Terry is a complete madman.*
     b. *Terry is quite mad.*
     c. *Terry is out of his mind.*
(54) a. *Terry became a complete madman.*
     b. *Terry became quite mad.*
     c. **Terry became out of his mind.*

On the basis of such evidence, we further conclude that an adequate mechanism for lexical dependencies must be sensitive to the grammatical distinction between APs and PPs. Again, the relevant selections are enforced by a specification on the appropriate (here, the first) SUBCAT element: the xcomp of *become* must be specified as [SYNTAX|LOCAL|-HEAD|MAJ A$\lor$N].

A particularly vivid illustration of idiosyncratic variation in xcomp category selection is exhibited by a family of English verbs closely related in meaning to *become:*

(55) a. *Kim grew poetical.*
     b. **Kim grew a success.*
     c. **Kim grew sent more and more leaflets.*
     d. **Kim grew doing all the work.*
     e. *Kim grew to like anchovies.*
(56) a. *Kim got poetical.*
     b. **Kim got a success.*
     c. *Kim got sent more and more leaflets.*
     d. **Kim got doing all the work.*
     e. *Kim got to like anchovies.*
(57) a. *Kim turned out poetical.*
     b. *Kim turned out a success.*
     c. **Kim turned out sent more and more leaflets.*
     d. **Kim turned out doing all the work.*
     e. *Kim turned out to like anchovies.*
(58) a. *Kim ended up poetical.*
     b. *Kim ended up a success.*
     c. **Kim ended up sent more and more leaflets.*
     d. *Kim ended up doing all the work.*
     e. **Kim ended up to like anchovies.*
(59) a. *Kim waxed poetical.*
     b. **Kim waxed a success.*
     c. **Kim waxed sent more and more leaflets.*
     d. **Kim waxed doing all the work.*
     e. **Kim waxed to like anchovies.*

Evidently no semantic distinction will suffice to explain such lexical differences in category selection.

Similar variation is exhibited for finer syntactic selections. For instance, English verbs (including auxiliaries) differ with respect to the inflectional form required on the head verb of the xcomp, as the following examples show:

(60) a. *Sandy made Kim throw up.*
     b. **Sandy made Kim to throw up.*
(61) a. *Sandy forced Kim to throw up.*
     b. **Sandy forced Kim throw up.*

On our account, the corresponding lexical signs simply specify different values for the feature VFORM on the xcomp:

$$(62) \begin{bmatrix} \text{PHON} & \textit{made} \\ \text{SYN} \mid \text{LOC} \begin{bmatrix} \text{HEAD} \begin{bmatrix} \text{MAJ} & \text{V} \\ \text{VFORM FIN} \end{bmatrix} \\ \text{SUBCAT} \langle \text{VP[BSE]}, \text{NP}, \text{NP} \rangle \end{bmatrix} \end{bmatrix}$$

$$(63) \begin{bmatrix} \text{PHON} & \textit{forced} \\ \text{SYN} \mid \text{LOC} \begin{bmatrix} \text{HEAD} \begin{bmatrix} \text{MAJ} & \text{V} \\ \text{VFORM FIN} \end{bmatrix} \\ \text{SUBCAT} \langle \text{VP[INF]}, \text{NP}, \text{NP} \rangle \end{bmatrix} \end{bmatrix}$$

Precisely the same explanation accounts for variation in complement selection exhibited by English auxiliary verbs. Modal auxiliaries select VP complements whose lexical head is uninflected ([VFORM BSE]); (perfective) *have* takes complements headed by past participial phrases ([VFORM PSP]); and the verbal complements of *be* have heads that are present participial phrases ([VFORM PRP]) or passive phrases ([VFORM PAS]).

Likewise, in languages which inflect for case, semantically close verbs may require (or, in traditional terminology, govern) objects in different cases. An example of this kind is provided by the two German verbs for 'meet':

(64) a. *Wem* (DAT) *begegneten Sie?*
        'Who did you meet?'
     b. *Wen* (ACC) *trafen Sie?*
        'Who did you meet?'

More generally, idiosyncratic selection for case forms abound in inflected languages such as Latin, Greek, Russian, or Sanskrit, where the particular case governed by individual verbs or prepositions is not semantically predictable. Such facts are too familiar to warrant further documentation here. Under our approach, case assignment too is effected via the feature SUBCAT. Since CASE is a head feature, it follows (in virtue of the Head Feature Principle) that whenever a lexical form selects a phrasal complement specified as [SYNTAX|LOCAL|HEAD|CASE ACC] or [SYNTAX|LOCAL|HEAD|CASE NOM], the lexical head of that complement is also so specified.[12]

English, of course, lacks case inflection (except rudimentarily on pronouns), but an analogous situation obtains with respect to government of the particular preposition that heads a PP complement. It is well known that one and the same preposition can correspond to many distinct semantic roles, depending on the governing verb:

(65) a. *Kim relies/depends on Sandy.*
   b. *The authorities blamed/pinned the arson on Sandy.*
   c. *The search committee decided/settled on Chris.*

Conversely, as illustrated in (66), semantically related verbs may assign closely corresponding roles to different PP complements:

(66) a. *The authorities blamed Greenpeace for/*with/*of the bombing.*
   b. *The authorities accused Greenpeace *for/*with/of the bombing.*
   c. *The authorities charged Greenpeace *for/with/*of the bombing.*

On the basis of such examples, we conclude that government of particular prepositions is not semantically predictable; instead, different verbs which take PP complements require different values for the head feature PFORM on that complement.

If subcategorization restrictions cannot be reduced to semantics, might they be stated solely in terms of functional notions like subject, direct object, and second object? Precisely such an account is proposed within the LFG framework (Bresnan 1982), where subcategorization restrictions are stated in terms of "functional structure," a level of syntactic representation distinct from constituent structure (c-structure), where certain information about "grammatical functions" (e.g. subject, direct object), "discourse functions" (e.g. topic, focus), and possibly thematic role assignment is represented. However, there are several reasons why subcategorization restrictions cannot be stated in purely functional terms.

First, we have gross category selections of the sort considered above. For example, certain verbs like *become* select for an NP or AP xcomp, but not for PP or VP xcomps of the sort that may cooccur with the verb *be.* Such category distinctions are plainly nonfunctional (they are exclusively c-structure distinctions in LFG, for example).

Second, as Grimshaw, among others, has remarked, "a verb may govern case-marking on the head of its direct object" (Grimshaw 1982:35). One cannot reduce such dependencies to functional dependencies. For example, in Icelandic there are verbs that select for direct object NPs specified in the dative and genitive cases.

(67) a. *Ég hjalpaði honum* (DAT)
      'I helped him'
   b. *Ég mun sakna hans* (GEN)
      'I will miss him'

As demonstrated in detail by Zaenen, Maling, and Thráinsson (1985), the dative and genitive NPs that follow *hjalpaði* ('helped') and *sakna* ('miss') respectively in these examples must both be treated as direct objects. That

conclusion is based on standard kinds of syntactic arguments, e.g. pas-
sivizability of the postverbal NP. The verbs in question here must thus select the same grammatical function, yet they must assign distinct cases to
the NPs that perform that function. (Analogous examples of case government in Icelandic for subjects are discussed in the following section.)
Hence no purely functional account of subcategorization will suffice for
Icelandic, unless case distinctions are also treated a "functional" in nature
(as they are in Bresnan 1982, where case is regarded as an f-structure
attribute).

In our opinion, any attempt to render categories of inflectional morphology such as case and verb form as functional in nature is highly questionable, for it blurs the distinction between form and function traditionally
associated with such categories.[13] The formal category of dative NP, for
instance, is standardly juxtaposed to various functions that the dative NP
may serve, giving rise to such traditional "form-in-function" locutions as
the DATIVE OF INTEREST, the DATIVE OF PURPOSE, and so forth. Such distinctions of form and function in this domain reflect longstanding insights
into the nature of language that we are reluctant to abandon.

Analogous remarks apply to government of particular prepositions,
which is treated by LFG in terms of the "semantically restricted" "oblique
functions" OBL_θ (where θ ranges over some set of semantic roles). This
treatment strikes us as highly problematic, for—as our discussion of examples (65)–(66) above indicates—one and the same preposition can correspond to numerous distinct semantic roles (and, conversely, sementically
similar roles may correspond to PPs headed by different prepositions, depending on the governing verb).[14]

Indeed, if the difference in phonological form between distinct prepositions is not to be counted as a formal (as opposed to functional) difference,
it is difficult to imagine what should be. Once distinctions of morphological and phonological form, as well as such traditional functional notions as
subject and object, have all been subsumed under function, why not simply
abandon the notion of syntactic category altogether and distinguish NP, VP,
AP, etc. as nothing more than values of another "functional" attribute?

Of course, such a *reductio ad absurdum* is not what we propose. Rather,
we believe it is more illuminating to posit a limited notion of function (in
terms of the obliqueness hierarchy), in contradistinction to both selection for purely formal category distinctions (such as part of speech, verb
inflection, and government of case or prepositional form) and selection
for purely semantic distinctions (such as role assignment and sortal restrictions). The HPSG treatment of subcategorization dependencies allows
a uniform treatment of functional, formal, and semantic selections, for

the values of the feature SUBCAT contain all three kinds of information: functional information (e.g. the order of the elements on the SUBCAT list); formal information (specifications for values of the attribute SYNTAX); and semantic information (specifications for values of the attribute SEMANTICS).

3.4. Subject Selection

There can be little doubt that lexical dependencies of the type we have been discussing hold between verbs and their subjects. Subject–verb agreement, for example, is the agreement phenomenon par excellence. Our treatment of subject–verb agreement involves particular person and number specifications on the last member of a finite verb's SUBCAT list. Thus, a finite verb like *walks* requires that the variable of its subject's semantic index be third person singular in addition to imposing the syntactic requirement that the subject's case be nominative. This is illustrated in (68):

(68)
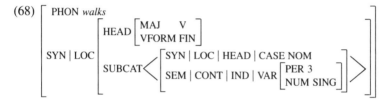

Assignment of semantic role is another respect in which verb–subject dependencies resemble the other subcategorizational dependencies we have been discussing.

Dependencies involving the selection of specific lexical forms, as we have seen, may involve prepositional heads and various inflected forms of nonsubject arguments. But there are certainly cases of form selection that involve subjects. Here we would include expletive (or "dummy") pronouns such as English *it* and *there* and their analogues (sometimes phonetically unexpressed) in many other languages. These must be viewed as lexical dependencies, as the class of lexical items that allows expletive subjects in any language is (sometimes highly) restricted.

Case assignment too can be shown to hold between subjects and verbs, rather than between subjects and abstract disembodied clusters of morphological information (e.g. INFL), as assumed in much recent work in GB theory (e.g. Chomsky 1982:50). In languages like English, where subjects of finite clauses uniformly appear in nominative case, this point is not evident, but in closely related languages like Icelandic, which have been carefully studied by Thráinsson (1979), Andrews (1982), Zaenen, Maling, and Thráinsson (1985), and others, subject case assignment is not uniform. As Thráinsson and Andrews show, there are various classes of verbs in Icelandic that differ as to the case they assign to their subject NP, as illustrated in (69). (The indicated cases are the only ones possible in these examples.)

(69) a. *Drengurinn   kyssti stúlkuna   i bílnum*
       the-boy (NOM) kissed the-girl (ACC) in the-car (DAT)
       'The boy kissed the girl in the car.'
   b. *Mig   langar að fara til Íslands.*
       me (ACC) longs   to to.go to Iceland
       'I long to go to Iceland.'
   c. *Honum   mæltist vel í kirkjunni.*
       He (DAT) spoke well in the church
       'He spoke well in the church.'
   d. *Verkjanna   gætir   ekki.*
       the-pains (GEN) is.noticeable not
       'The pains are not noticeable.'

The final kind of subject selection that we will discuss here involves sentential subjects. We should point out that the conclusions we draw, as well as some of the evidence adduced, are somewhat controversial. As noted by Kajita (1967) and independently by Janet Fodor (pers. comm.), there are verbs in English that subcategorize for NP rather than sentential subjects, despite the fact that they would appear to be semantically compatible with sentential subject arguments:

(70) a. *That we invested when we did made us rich.*
   b. *The fact that we invested when we did made us rich.*
(71) a. *That he was late resulted in his being dismissed.*
   b. *The fact that he was late resulted in his being dismissed.*
(72) a. *That he was going bald drove him to drink.*
   b. *The fact/idea that he was going bald drove him to drink.*
(73) a. *That images are waterproof is incoherent.*
   b. *The idea/claim/proposition that images are waterproof is incoherent.*

It might be thought that some subtle semantic distinction is at stake here; to the best of our knowledge, however, no precise semantic account of the facts has ever been provided. If the relevant distinction to be subcategorized for is indeed the distinction between NPs and Ss, then verbs that allow only the former are specified as [SUBCAT ⟨. . . , NP⟩], while those that allow both are specified as in (74):

(74) $\left[\text{SUBCAT} \left\langle \ldots \left[\text{SYN} \mid \text{LOC} \begin{bmatrix} \text{HEAD} \mid \text{MAJ N} \vee \text{V} \\ \text{SUBCAT} \langle \ \rangle \end{bmatrix} \right] \right\rangle \right]$

Alternatively, sentential subjects may well be NPs of a special type, in which case they may be distinguished from nonsentential NPs by some other syntactic feature, perhaps NFORM. In this case, it is NFORM that serves to distinguish the various kinds of subject NPs that verbs select. We leave this matter unresolved here, but under whatever analysis turns out to be correct, it is clear that the feature SUBCAT can be used effectively to provide an account of the selection in question.

To summarize, as far as the full range of subcategorizational dependencies is concerned (verb-complement agreement, role assignment, case assignment, selection for particular lexical forms or particular syntactic features), the behavior of subjects is no different in kind from that of nonsubject complements.

4. Conclusion

In this paper we have outlined a head-driven theory of phrase structure which expresses two kinds of generalizations about the syntactic structures of natural languages: (1) the systematic relation between phrases and their heads and (2) generalizations about constituent order. The inherent (HEAD) and dependency (SUBCAT) properties of words are seen to determine the properties of phrases in virtue of two principles of Universal Grammar, viz. the Head Feature Principle and the Subcategorization Principle. In Pollard and Sag (1987; forthcoming), we augment this theory of Universal Grammar with two additional principles: the Semantics Principle, which provides a general characterization of the interpretation of phrases (in terms of a version of Situation Semantics); and the Binding Inheritance Principle, which is the cornerstone of our analysis of "long-distance" (or "unbounded") dependency constructions.

We have said little here about the nature of our theory of Linear Precedence, which is developed in detail in Sag (1987) and in Pollard and Sag (1987, ch. 7). Rather, we have focused here on the nature of subcategorization and its role in head-driven syntactic combination. As we have seen, the feature SUBCAT provides the basis for the treatment of lexical dependencies in HPSG: subcategorized-for complements and their associated grammatical relations, category selection, case, agreement, semantic role assignment, and perhaps certain semantic selectional restrictions as well. Why should we seek to provide a single mechanism for analyzing all these seemingly diverse phenomena? There is a simple answer to this question: all the phenomena just listed share a certain LOCALITY property. Just as there are no verbs in any language we know of that select a sentential complement whose verb phrase is headed by a transitive rather than an intransitive verb, there are no verbs in any language that assign roles to a complement within a complement that they select. Likewise there are no verbs that assign case to or agree with some NP properly contained within one of their complements. Why should this be so? Our answer is that all of these locality restrictions follow from the assumption that THE SUBCAT ELEMENT OF LEXICAL SIGNS SPECIFIES VALUES FOR SYNTAX AND SEMANTICS BUT CRUCIALLY NOT THE ATTRIBUTE DAUGHTERS. This LOCALITY PRINCIPLE, we suggest, is a universal constraint on lexical signs.[15]

On the basis of the paradigm given in (75), Kajita (1967:103) has claimed that the verb *serve* must be subcategorized for a VP complement that contains a direct object NP (which would render it a counterexample to the Locality Principle):

(75) a. *The ice melted.*
      b. **The ice served to melt.*
      c. *The ice chilled the beer.*
      d. *The ice served to chill the beer.*

But this claim is suspect, as noted by R. Higgins (1973:173 n.5), who remarks as follows:

> One merely needs to strictly subcategorize the verb *serve* for an infinitival complement sentence. One has to say, in addition, that the subject of the complement verb must be interpretable as an instrument. (This is only a rough characterization and needs further precision.) Since any verb in English whose subject can be understood as an instrument of necessity has an object, the verb in the complement sentence must have an object. Clearly, the semantic nature of the subject of the complement sentence is not a matter to be regulated by strict subcategorization restrictions, and Chomsky's conjecture . . . that selection restrictions might be a more appropriate mechanism in this case, is confirmed.

Within our framework, it is possible for a verb to exert restrictions (including restrictions on role assignment) upon the "understood subject" of an unsaturated complement (xcomp), since those restrictions are internal to the SUBCAT value of the verb. Locality is not violated since there is no phonologically unrealized subconstituent ("empty category") corresponding to the complement subject; the restriction can be exerted without illicit access to the complement's DAUGHTERS value.[16]

Stuart Shieber (pers. comm.), who independently arrived at essentially the same conclusion as Higgins regarding the nature of the restriction on *serve,* points out that the semantic analysis is confirmed by the ungrammaticality of examples like (76), which should be grammatical if transitivity of the infinitival complement is the relevant constraining factor:

(76) **Kim served to break the window with the hammer.*

The deviance of this example is in complete accord with the semantic approach suggested by Higgins and Shieber. On the other hand, examples such as (77) suggest that (*pace* Higgins) verbs with instrument subjects need not be transitive:

(77) a. *A pair of nines can open in this game.*
     b. *You can open with a pair of nines in this game.*

Here (77a) is roughly paraphrasable by (77b). As our analysis predicts, (78) seems quite acceptable even though the complement verb is intransitive:

(78) *A pair of nines will serve to open in this game.*

The Locality Principle severely constrains the kind of elements that lexical signs may select. Nonlocal selection would require signs on SUBCAT lists to specify values for attributes such as HEAD-DTR or COMPLEMENT-DTR, as sketched in (79):

$$(79) \quad \text{SUBCAT} \; \langle \ldots \left[\ldots \text{DTRS} \begin{bmatrix} \text{HEAD-DTR} \quad \text{X} \\ \text{COMP-DTRS} \; \langle \ldots, \text{Y}, \ldots \rangle \end{bmatrix} \right] \ldots \rangle$$

It is precisely specifications like these that the Locality Principle rules out. In this way, the theory of subcategorization we have outlined makes strong empirical claims about the full range of lexical dependency phenomena.

NOTES

1. Here and throughout, we ignore most matters of semantics. These are treated at length in Pollard and Sag (1987; forthcoming). We also eschew serious consideration of phonological form, which we represent with standard English orthography to enhance readability. PHON, SYN, SEM, and DTRS are used as abbreviations for the features PHONOLOGY, SYNTAX, SEMANTICS, and DAUGHTERS respectively. In (6), the value of the attribute DTRS is a list of two signs.

2. Note that, in viewing phrases as possible heads (so that VP is the head of S,

in our system), we are departing from the terminology of Government-Binding theory, which restricts heads to lexical categories.

3. The symbol "/ /" denotes the empty phonological string.

4. The factoring out of ordering principles from grammar rules follows the tradition of work in GPSG originating with Gazdar and Pullum (1981). However, as argued in Sag (1987), a number of problems for the GPSG theory of linear precedence (LP) rules can be resolved in the context of HPSG. See also Pollard and Sag (1987, chap. 7).

5. Paths of attributes in AVMs thus have values just as attributes do.

6. An itcalicized left subscript, e.g. the subscript *headed structure* in (11), indicates an assignment of type to a given linguistic object. Tags, e.g. the ☐ that occurs twice in (11), serve to designate pieces of feature structures that are identical (unified). Note that this notion of identity is identity of tokens, not of types; thus (11) says not just that the HEAD values of mother and head daughter are specified analogously, but rather that the HEAD values of mother and head daughter are the selfsame object, namely a single feature structure. In this way, the objects of our theory are not just annotated phrase-structure trees, but rather directed graphs that do not actually satisfy a "single-mother" condition. For a systematic introduction to these notions, see Shieber (1986) and Pollard and Sag (1987).

7. There are nonstandard varieties of English where inverted clauses appear as embedded polar interrogatives as well, e.g. *I asked did he go* as a variant of *I asked whether he went.*

8. NP☐ abbreviates the following feature structure:

$$\left[\begin{array}{l} \text{SYN} \mid \text{LOCAL} \left[\begin{array}{l} \text{HEAD} \mid \text{MAJ N} \\ \text{SUBCAT} \langle \ \rangle \\ \text{LEX} - \end{array}\right] \\ \text{SEM} \mid \text{CONTENT} \mid \text{INDEX} \mid \text{VARIABLE} \ \boxed{1} \end{array}\right]$$

For a more complete discussion of roles, indices, and variables in HPSG, see Pollard and Sag (1987; forthcoming).

9. These constraints are analogous to GB's Binding theory principles A, B, and C respectively.

10. We use the symbol "%" to indicate that an example is acceptable in some but not all varieties of English.

11. This of course would provide no account of the behavior of genitives or objectives of comparison, for which, incidentally, the evidence offered by Keenan and Comrie is the most meager.

12. As with verb inflection, the correlation between overt case inflections and values of the feature CASE is determined by lexical rules.

13. Distinctions of verb inflection are treated in Bresnan (1982) in terms of the f-structure attributes TENSE (corresponding to our FINITE forms), PARTICIPIAL (our PRP, PSP and PAS forms), INF (our BSE), and TO (out INF).

14. The LFG treatment of PP [BY] phrases in passives in terms of the "oblique

agent function" OBL$_{AG}$ seems particularly infelicitous. As the following examples show, such phrases are by no means restricted to agentive semantic roles:

(i) *Kim was pleased/shocked/appalled by the report.*
(ii) *No even integer is exceeded/equalled by any of its factors.*
(iii) *Chris's cover was blown/goose was cooked by the ensuing chain of events.*
(iv) *Every proposition is entailed by a contradiction.*

Rather, the semantic role borne by the PP [BY] in a passive coincides with the role borne by the subject of the corresponding active form, be it agentive or not.

15. The point here is that no lexical sign inherently selects a particular value for the DAUGHTERS attribute of its complements; of course, in any token of a lexical sign, any SUBCAT element that is unified with a phrasal constituent bears a value for DAUGHTERS.

16. Similar considerations come into play in the control of subjects of xcomps, where under standard assumptions, a verb selects for a complement whose unexpressed subject is "coindexed" with either the subject or direct object of the matrix verb. Under our analysis of control (sketched in Pollard and Sag, forthcoming) the controlled complement is specified as [SYNTAX|LOCAL|SUBCAT $\langle NP_i \rangle$], where the variable i is unified with the variable corresponding to the controlling complement. Hence even if control were a lexical selection, a position which we argue against, the relevant variable would be locally available.

8

Scrambling as Semantically
Vacuous A'-Movement

MAMORU SAITO

As is well known, Japanese has scrambling, and word order is relatively free in this language. For example, (1a) and (1b) are both perfectly acceptable sentences of Japanese.[1]

(1) a. *Mary-ga   sono hon-o   yonda (koto)*
       Mary-NOM that book-ACC read   fact
    b. *sono hon-o   Mary-ga yonda (koto)*
       that book-ACC Mary-NOM read   fact
       'Mary read that book.'

It has been argued that scrambling is S-structure movement to A'-position, and further, that it is an adjunction operation. (See, for example, Whitman 1982, Saito 1985, and Hoji 1985.) According to this hypothesis, the S-structure representation of (1b) is as in (2):

(2) [$_S$ *sono hon-o$_i$* [$_S$ *Mary-ga* [$_{VP}$ t_i *yonda*]]] (*koto*)

On the other hand, it has also been suggested that scrambling is "stylistic" in nature. (See, for example, Ross 1967, N. McCawley 1976, Chomsky & Lasnik 1977.) As far as I can tell, the intuition behind this suggestion is that scrambling differs from other types of A'-movement, such as English topicalization and *wh*-movement, in that it does not establish a seman-

I would like to thank N. Fukui, A. Kroch, R. May, R. Washio, and especially H. Lasnik for helpful comments and suggestions. The research reported here was supported in part by a grant from Sumitomo Electric, U.S.A., to the University of Southern California Japanese Grammar Project.

The material in this paper was presented at the 1986 New York University workshop as a part of a joint work with Naoki Fukui titled "On Kuroda's Agreement Parameter." The analysis is revised in places, thanks to comments by participants in the workshop.

tically significant operator–variable relation.[2] Intuitive support for this suggestion can be found in the contrast between (3b) and (4b).[3]

(3) a.   [$_{S'}$ *who$_j$* [$_S$ *t$_j$* [$_{VP}$ *said* [$_{S'}$ *that* [$_S$ *that book$_i$* [$_S$ *John*
          [$_{VP}$ *bought t$_i$*]]]]]]]]

     b.   *[$_{S'}$ *who$_j$* [$_S$ *t$_j$* [$_{VP}$ *said* [$_{S'}$ *that* [$_S$ *which book$_i$* [$_S$ *John*
          [$_{VP}$ *bought t$_i$*]]]]]]]]

(4) a.   [$_S$ *sono hon-o$_i$* [$_S$ *John-ga* [$_{VP}$ *t$_i$ katta*]]] (*koto*)
          that book-ACC John-NOM   bought   fact
          'John bought that book.'

     b.   [$_S$ *dono hon-o$_i$* [$_S$ *John-ga* [$_{VP}$ *t$_i$ katta*]]] *no*
          which book-ACC John-NOM   bought
          'Which book did John buy?'

It is argued in Baltin (1982) that English topicalization can involve adjunction to S, as shown in the embedded clause of (3a).[4] Example (3b), on the other hand, indicates that a *wh*-phrase cannot be topicalized in English. The contrast between (3a) and (3b) suggests that the phrase adjoined to S by topicalization is in fact interpreted as a topic, and that the unacceptability of (3b) is due to the incompatibility arising from a *wh*-operator being a topic operator at the same time. Sentence (4b), in contrast, shows that a *wh*-phrase can be adjoined to S by scrambling. This fact suggests that a scrambled phrase is not interpreted as a topic, and further, that it may not be interpreted as any kind of semantic operator.

In this paper, I argue that the two hypotheses mentioned above concerning the nature of scrambling are both correct. That is, I argue that scrambling is S-structure A'-movement, and yet it does not, or at least need not, establish a semantically significant operator–variable relation. In §1 I briefly discuss Hoji's (1985) paradigm as evidence that scrambling is S-structure movement to A'-position. Then in §2 I argue that scrambling, an S-structure movement operation, can be freely undone in the LF component. If this conclusion is correct, then the LF representation of (2), for example, can be as in (5):

(5) [$_S$ *Mary-ga* [$_{VP}$ *sono hon-o yonda*]] (*koto*)

This in effect amounts to saying that scrambling can be merely "stylistic" in the relevant sense. If scrambling can be undone in LF, then it need not have any significant semantic import. Finally, in §3 I speculate on why scrambling, as opposed to English topicalization and *wh*-movement, can be merely "stylistic," despite the fact that it is S-structure movement to A'-position.

1. Hoji's Paradigm

Hoji (1985) discusses the following paradigm as evidence that scrambling is a subcase of S-structure Move-α:[5]

(6) a. (??)$[_S$ $dare_i$-ga $[_{VP}$ $[_{NP}$ $[_S$ pro_j e_i $hitome$ $mita]$ $hito_j]$-o
      who -NOM   once saw person-ACC
      $suki$-ni $natta]]$ no
      fell-in-love-with
      'who$_i$ fell in love with the person who took a glance at e_i'

  b. ?*$[_S$ $[_{NP}$ $[_S$ pro_j e_i $hitome$ $mita]$ $hito_j]$-ga $[_{VP}$ $dare_i$-o
                 once saw person-NOM who-ACC
      $suki$-ni $natta]]$ no
      fell-in-love-with
      'the person who took a glance at e_i fell in love with who$_i$'

  c. $dare_i$-o $[_S$ $[_{NP}$ $[_S$ pro_j e_i $hitome$ $mita]$ $hito_j]$-ga
    who-ACC   once saw person-NOM
      $[_{VP}$ t_i $suki$-ni $natta]]$ no
      fell-in-love-with
      'who$_i$, the person who took a glance at e_i fell in love with t_i'

  d. (??)$[_{NP}$ $[_S$ pro_j e_i $hitome$ $mita]$ $hito_j]$-o $[_S$ $dare_i$-ga
                once saw person-ACC who-NOM
      $[_{VP}$ t_j $suki$-ni $natta]]$ no
      fell-in-love-with
      '[the person who took a glance at $e_i]_j$, who$_i$ fell in love with t_j'

Japanese lacks syntactic *wh*-movement, and the *wh*-phrase *dare* 'who' is in situ in (6a), (6b), and (6d). In (6c)–(6d) the matrix object is scrambled to the sentence-initial position. In (6c), the matrix object is the *wh*-phrase *dare*, and hence the *wh*-phrase appears sentence-initially.

As Hoji points out, this paradigm is expected if we assume that scrambling involves S-structure movement to A'-position. The configurational relations of the *wh*-phrase and the coindexed empty category in (6a)–(6d) are as in (7a)–(7d) respectively.

(7) a. $[_S$ QNP_i $[_{VP}$ . . . e_i . . .]]
  b. $[_S$ $[_{NP}$ . . . e_i . . .]$[_{VP}$ . . . QNP_i . . .]]
  c. QNP_i $[_S$ $[_{NP}$ . . . e_i . . .]$[_{VP}$ . . . t_i . . .]]
  d. $[_{NP}$ . . . e_i . . .]$_j$ $[_S$ QNP_i $[_{VP}$ . . . t_j . . .]]

Japanese has null pronouns, and nothing seems to prevent e_i in (7a) from being a *pro*. In fact, since QNP_i c-commands e_i in (7a), the latter can be a bound pronoun.[6] Thus, the grammaticality of (6a) is expected, exactly as the English example in (8):

(8) *Everyone$_i$ loves his$_i$ mother*

The marginality of (6b) is also expected if we assume that e_i in this example is *pro*. This is so since if e_i is a pronoun, then (7b) is a configuration of weak crossover. More specifically, (7b) then contains a QNP that does not c-command a coindexed pronoun. Thus, (6b) is ruled out in exactly the same way as the English (9):

(9) ?*His$_i$ mother loves everyone$_i$*

The empty category e_i in (7c), unlike those in (7a)–(7b), is A'-bound. Further, it neither c-commands nor is c-commanded by t_i. Thus, it need not be a null pronoun but can be a parasitic gap. That is, the grammaticality of (6c) can be accounted for in the same way as that of (10), which is from Kayne (1983):

(10) *?a person who$_i$ close friends of e$_i$ admire t$_i$*

In (7d), e_i is neither c-commanded by QNP$_i$ nor A'-bound. However, QNP$_i$ c-commands the trace of the NP that contains e_i. Thus, as Hoji points out, (7d) has the configuration of "chain binding" in the sense of Barss (1984).[7] Hence, if e_i in (6d) is *pro*, we expect the example to be grammatical exactly like English examples such as the following, which are discussed in detail in Engdahl (1981):

(11) *[Which of his$_i$ poems]$_j$ would every poet$_i$ like to read t$_j$*

In (11) also, the QNP (*every poet$_i$*) c-commands the trace of the NP (*which of his poems*) that contains the pronoun (*his$_i$*).

Hoji's paradigm in (6) shows convincingly, I believe, that scrambling applies in the mapping from D-structure to S-structure, rather than in the PF component. The contrast between (6b) and (6c), for example, indicates that scrambling can save a sentence from a weak crossover violation. Given that PF does not have anything to do with weak crossover, we can conclude that scrambling must already be represented at S-structure.[8] Furthermore, in Hoji's account of the paradigm in (6) outlined above, it is assumed crucially that scrambling is movement to A'-position. Thus, if Hoji's account is correct, then scrambling must be A'-movement and not A-movement.

2. LF Effects of Scrambling

We saw in the preceding section that Hoji's (1985) paradigm provides evidence that scrambling is S-structure A'-movement. In this section, I argue that scrambling can be freely undone in the LF component. The argument is based crucially on the hypothesis that the Proper Binding Condition, which requires that traces be bound, is insensitive to "chain binding" in the sense of Barss (1984). I first provide evidence for this hypothesis in §2.1 and then come back to the discussion of scrambling in §2.2.

2.1. Proper Binding and Chain Binding

Let us first consider the widely discussed examples in (12).

(12) a. *[Which picture of himself$_i$]$_j$ does John$_i$ like t$_j$ best*
  b. *Himself$_i$, John$_i$ loves t$_i$*

The lexical anaphor *himself* is not bound in (12), yet these examples are perfectly grammatical. Similar examples in Japanese that involve scrambling are discussed in Muraki (1974) and Kuno (1973). Example (13) is grammatical despite the fact that it contains a free lexical anaphor.

(13) [$_S$ [$_{NP}$ *zibun$_i$-no   hahaoya*]-*o$_j$* [$_S$ *John$_i$-ga* [$_{VP}$ *t$_j$ aisiteiru*]]] (*koto*)
      self -GEN mother-ACC   John-NOM   love   fact
    'John$_i$ loves his$_i$ mother'

In this example, the object NP, which contains *zibun*, is adjoined to S by scrambling. Thus, the lexical anaphor *zibun* is not bound by its antecedent *John*.

I know of two hypotheses that have been proposed to account for examples such as those in (12)–(13). Langendoen and Battistella (1982) suggests that the moved phrases in these examples are lowered to the positions of their traces by a general reconstruction rule applying in the LF component. According to this hypothesis, the anaphors in (12)–(13) are bound at LF because of this general reconstruction rule and hence satisfy Binding theory at that level.[9] On the other hand, Barss (1984) argues, convincingly I believe, against the reconstruction approach and proposes that anaphors need not be bound as long as they are chain-bound. That is, according to Barss (1984), (14a) is too strong, and must be replaced by (14b):[10]

(14) a. Anaphors must be bound (in domain X).
    b. Anaphors must be chain-bound (in domain X).

For the purpose of the discussion here, I assume the following definition of chain binding:

(15) X CHAIN-BINDS Y = $_{df}$ X and Y are coindexed, and
    a. X c-commands Y, or
    b. X c-commands a trace of Z, where Z = Y or Z contains Y.

In (12a), for example, *John* chain-binds *himself,* since they are coindexed and *John* c-commands the trace of *which picture of himself,* which contains *himself.* Similarly, *John* chain-binds *himself* in (12b), since they are coindexed and the former c-commands the trace of the latter. Thus, if anaphors need not be bound as long as they are chain-bound, as Barss argues, then the grammaticality of (12)–(13) is expected.

Barss's (1984) arguments for the chain-binding account of (12)–(13) seem to be quite convincing. At the same time, there is evidence that traces, as opposed to lexical anaphors, cannot satisfy Binding theory by virtue of chain binding, but must be bound. That is, the relevant facts indicate that the Proper Binding Condition must be stated as in (16) in terms of binding and not in terms of chain binding.

(16) Traces must be bound. (Fiengo 1977, May 1977)

First, consider the following examples:

(17) a. ??*Who$_i$ do you wonder* [*which picture of t$_i$*]$_j$ *John likes t$_j$*
      b. *[*Which picture of t$_i$*]$_j$ *do you wonder who$_i$ John likes t$_j$*

Example (17a), which is due to Howard Lasnik (pers. comm.), is marginal, probably being a weak Subjacency violation.[11] Example (17b), on the other hand, is hopeless and contrasts sharply with (17a). This contrast indicates that (17b) is not a mere Subjacency violation, but violates the Proper Binding Condition as well because of the trace t_i. But note here that the offending trace t_i is chain-bound by *who$_i$* in this example. The latter c-commands the trace of the matrix *wh*-phrase, which contains t_i. On the other hand, the trace t_i is clearly not bound by *who$_i$* in this example. Hence, if (17b) violates the Proper Binding Condition, as seems to be the case, then this condition must be insensitive to chain binding, and must be stated in terms of binding.[12]

The same point can be made also on the basis of the examples in (18):

(18) a.   *Who$_i$ t$_i$ knows* [*which picture of whom*]$_j$ *Bill bought t$_j$*
      b. ??[*Which picture of whom*]$_i$ *do you wonder who$_j$ t$_j$ bought t$_i$*

It is pointed out in van Riemsdijk and Williams (1981) that (18a) is ambiguous; *whom* can take matrix or embedded scope. When *whom* has matrix scope, the LF representation of (18a) is as in (19):[13]

(19) [$_{S'}$ [*whom$_k$ who$_i$*][$_S$ t_i *knows* [$_{S'}$ [*which picture of t$_k$*]$_j$ [$_S$ *Bill bought t$_j$*]]]]

Example (18b), on the other hand, is clearly unambiguous. The sentence is a Subjacency violation and hence is marginal to begin with. But if we ignore its marginal status, it is clear that the sentence can have the interpretation in which *whom* takes matrix scope. The interpretation in which *whom* takes embedded scope, on the other hand, is simply impossible. This indicates that (18b) cannot have the LF representation in (20):

(20) $[_{S'}$ [*which pictures of* $t_k]_i$ $[_S$ *do you wonder* $[_{S'}$ [*whom*$_k$ *who*$_j$]
      $[_S$ t_j *bought* t_i]]]]

The structure in (20) can be ruled out by the Proper Binding Condition only if the condition is stated in terms of binding, not chain binding. The trace t_k is chain-bound by *whom*$_k$, since the latter c-commands t_i, whose A'-binder contains the former. Thus, (18b) also provides evidence that the Proper Binding Condition is insensitive to chain binding.

The contrast in (21) leads us to the same conclusion:

(21) a. ??*Who*$_i$ t_i *said that* [*the man that bought what*]$_j$, *John knows*
         whether Mary likes t_j
     b. **Mary thinks that* [*the man that bought what*]$_j$, *John knows*
         who$_i$ t_i *likes* t_j

Both examples in (21) are Subjacency violations, since the embedded topics are moved out of *wh*-islands. Example (21a) is only marginal, and hence does not seem to violate any other constraint. A possible interpretation, in fact the only possible interpretation, for this sentence is the one in which *what* takes matrix scope. This implies that (22) is a possible LF representation for (21a):

(22) $[_{S'}$ [*what*$_k$ *who*$_i$][$_S$ t_i *said* $[_{S'}$ *that* $[_S$ [*the man that bought* $t_k]_j$, *John*
      knows $[_{S'}$ *whether* $[_S$ *Mary likes* t_j]]]]]]

Example (21b), on the other hand, is hopeless, and clearly is not a mere Subjacency violation. Since *what* has to move to a [+ *wh*] Comp in LF, the LF representation of (21b) is as in (23):

(23) $[_S$ *Mary thinks* $[_{S'}$ *that* $[_S$ [*the man that bought* $t_k]_j$, *John knows*
      $[_{S'}$ [*what*$_k$ *who*$_i$][$_S$ t_i *likes* t_j]]]]]

Here, if the Proper Binding Condition is insensitive to chain binding, as I argued above, then (23) is straightforwardly ruled out by this condition. In (23), *what*$_k$ chain-binds t_k, since it c-commands t_i, whose A'-binder contains t_k. But it clearly does not bind t_k. Hence, the contrast in (21) provides us with additional evidence that the Proper Binding Condition should be stated in terms of binding, and not in terms of chain binding.

2.2. Scrambling and the Proper Binding Condition

We saw in the preceding section that while lexical anaphors can satisfy Binding theory by virtue of chain binding, traces cannot. This implies that while

Condition (A) of Binding theory should be stated in terms of chain binding, the Proper Binding Condition should be stated in terms of binding.[14]

Scrambling provides further evidence for the insensitivity of the Proper Binding Condition to chain binding. Before I introduce the crucial data, let me briefly go over some basic facts of scrambling. First, as shown in (24), multiple scrambling is possible, i.e., two constituents can be preposed by scrambling in a single sentence.

(24) a. [$_S$ *Mary-ga   John-ni sono hon-o   watasita*] (*koto*)
           Mary-NOM John-to that book-ACC handed   fact
           'Mary handed that book to John.'
     b. [$_S$ *sono hon-o$_i$* [$_S$ *John-ni$_j$* [$_S$ *Mary-ga t$_j$ t$_i$ watasita*]]] (*koto*)
     c. [$_S$ *John-ni$_j$* [$_S$ *sono hon-o$_i$* [$_S$ *Mary-ga t$_j$ t$_i$ watasita*]]] (*koto*)

Second, as pointed out by Haig (1976) and S.-I. Harada (1977), among others, scrambling is not clause-bound. For example, (25b) is perfectly grammatical:

(25) a. [$_S$ *John-ga* [$_S$ *Mary-ga   sono hon-o   yonda to*]   *itta*] (*koto*)
           John-NOM Mary-NOM that book-ACC read   COMP said fact
           'John said that Mary read that book.'
     b. [$_S$ *sono hon-o$_i$* [$_S$ *John-ga* [$_{S'}$ *Mary-ga t$_i$ yonda to*] *itta*]] (*koto*)

In fact, multiple "long-distance" scrambling is possible, as shown in (26):[15]

(26) a. [$_S$ *Mary-ga* [$_{S'}$ *John-ga   Bill-ni sono hon-o   watasita to*]
           Mary-NOM John-NOM Bill-to that book-ACC handed   COMP
           omotteiru] (*koto*)
           think   fact
           'Mary thinks that John handed that book to Bill.'
     b. [$_S$ *sono hon-o$_i$* [$_S$ *Bill-ni$_j$* [$_S$ *Mary-ga* [$_{S'}$ *John-ga t$_j$ t$_i$ watasita to*]
           omotteiru]]] (*koto*)
     c. [$_S$ *Bill-ni$_j$* [$_S$ *sono hon-o$_i$* [$_S$ *Mary-ga* [$_{S'}$ *John-ga t$_j$ t$_i$ watasita to*]
           omotteiru]]] (*koto*)

Finally, not only NPs and PPs but also S's are subject to scrambling. This is shown by the examples in (27):

(27) a. [$_S$ *John-ga* [$_{S'}$ *Mary-ga   sono hon-o   yonda to*]   *itta*] (*koto*)
           John-NOM Mary-NOM that book-ACC read   COMP said fact
           (= 25a)
           'John said that Mary read that book.'
     b. [$_S$ [$_{S'}$ *Mary-ga sono hon-o yonda to*]$_i$ [$_S$ *John-ga t$_i$ itta*]] (*koto*)

Despite the properties of scrambling discussed above, examples such as those in (28)–(29) are ungrammatical.

(28) *[$_S$ [$_{S'}$ *Mary-ga* t_i *yonda to*]$_j$ [$_S$ *sono hon-o$_i$* [$_S$ *John-ga* t_j *itta*]]]
     Mary-NOM read   COMP that book-ACC John-NOM said
     (*koto*)
     fact
     'John said that Mary read that book.'
(29) *[$_S$ [$_{S'}$ *Bill-ga* t_i *sundeiru to*]$_j$ [$_S$ *sono mura-ni$_i$* [$_S$ *John-ga* t_j
     Bill-NOM reside   COMP that village-in John-NOM
     omotteiru]]] (*koto*)
     think   fact
     'John thinks that Bill lives in that village.'

Example (28), for example, is derived from (25a), by first scrambling the embedded NP object to the sentence-initial position as in (25b), and then, by adjoining the embedded S' to the matrix S. Since multiple scrambling, "long-distance" scrambling, and scrambling of S' are all possible, there is nothing wrong with the movement operations involved in the derivation of (28). Hence, it is reasonable to assume that (28) is ruled out by the Proper Binding Condition, t_i being the offending trace. But t_i in (28) is chain-bound by *sono hon-o*. The latter c-commands t_j, and t_j's antecedent contains t_i. On the other hand, t_i is not bound by *sono hon-o*. Thus, the ungrammaticality of (28)–(29) also indicates that the Proper Binding Condition is insensitive to chain binding.

2.3. LF "Reconstruction" of Scrambled Constituents

We have seen in §2.2 that traces created by scrambling are constrained by the Proper Binding Condition exactly as expected, provided that the condition is insensitive to chain binding. That is, we have seen that traces created by scrambling and those created by *wh*-movement in English behave in exactly the same way with respect to the Proper Binding Condition. In this section, I discuss the traces created by LF *wh*-movement in Japanese and examine how they are constrained by the Proper Binding Condition.

First, it is shown convincingly in K. I. Harada (1972) that the traces created by LF *wh*-movement in Japanese are subject to the Proper Binding Condition.[16] For example, (30a) and (31a) contrast sharply with (30b) and (31b):

(30) a. [$_S$ *John-ga* *Mary-ni* [$_{S'}$ [$_S$ *dare-ga* *kuru*] *ka*] *osieta*] *koto*
      John-NOM Mary-to   who-NOM come Q taught fact
      'the fact that John told Mary Q who is coming'
   b. *[$_S$ *John-ga* *dare-ni* [$_{S'}$ [$_S$ *Mary-ga* *kuru*] *ka*] *osieta*] *koto*
      John-NOM who-to   Mary-NOM come Q taught fact
      'the fact that John told who Q Mary is coming'

(31) a.   [$_S$ *John-ga* [$_{S'}$ [$_S$ *dare-ga   sono hon-o   katta*] *ka*]
           John-NOM   who-NOM that book-ACC bought Q
           siritagatteiru] *koto*
           want-to-know fact
           'the fact that John wants to know Q who bought that book'
      b. *[$_S$ *dare-ga* [$_{S'}$ [$_S$ *John-ga   sono hon-o   katta*] *ka*]
           who-NOM   John-NOM that book-ACC bought Q
           siritagatteiru] *koto*
           want-to-know fact
           'the fact that who wants to know Q John bought that book'

In Japanese, an embedded Comp is [+*wh*] if and only if it contains the
Q-morpheme *ka*. Hence the *wh*-phrases in (30)–(31) must move to the
most deeply embedded Comp in LF. Consequently, the LF representations
of (31a)–(31b), for example, are as in (32a)–(32b):

(32) a.   [$_S$ *John-ga* [$_{S'}$ [$_S$ t_i *sono hon-o katta*] *dare-ga$_i$*] *siritagatteiru*]
           koto
      b.   [$_S$ t_i [$_{S'}$ [$_S$ *John-ga sono hon-o katta*] *dare-ga$_i$*] *siritagatteiru*]
           koto

Here, t_i is bound by *dare-ga$_i$* in Comp in (32a), but not in (32b). Hence,
(32b) is ruled out by the Proper Binding Condition at LF. The contrast in
(30) is accounted for similarly. That is, (30b), but not (30a), violates the
Proper Binding Condition at LF. According to this analysis, the contrast in
(30)–(31) is treated in exactly the same way as that between the English
(33a) and (33b).

(33) a.   *I urged Bill to find out* [$_{S'}$ *who$_i$* [$_S$ *Mary saw t_i*]]
      b.   **I urged t_i to find out* [$_{S'}$ *who$_i$* [$_S$ *Mary saw John*]]

The trace t_i is free in (33b), and hence is in violation of the Proper Binding
Condition.

Let us now turn to slightly more complicated cases. As we saw in (4)
above, a *wh*-phrase can be scrambled to the sentence-initial position in
Japanese. Interestingly enough, it can be scrambled, although somewhat
marginally, even to a position outside the c-command domain of the Comp
where it takes scope at LF. Example (34b) is somewhat marginal, but is far
better than (30b)–(31b).

(34) a.   [$_S$ *Mary-ga* [$_{S'}$ [$_S$ *John-ga   dono hon-o   tosyokan-kara*
           Mary-NOM   John-NOM which book-ACC library-from
           karidasita] *ka*] *siritagatteiru*] *koto*
           checked-out Q   want-to-know fact

'the fact that Mary wants to know Q John checked out which
book from the library'
b. ?[s *dono hon-o_i* [s *Mary-ga* [s′ [s *John-ga t_i tosyokan-kara
karidasita*] *ka*] *siritagatteiru*]] *koto*

Dono hon-o 'which book-ACC' in (34) moves into the most deeply embedded Comp marked by *ka* in LF, and takes scope there. In (34b), the *wh*-
phrase is clearly scrambled out of the c-command domain of this Comp.[17]
   A still more interesting example for our purpose is (35b):

(35) a.   [s *Mary-ga* [s′ [s *minna-ga* [s′ [s *John-ga   dono hon-o*
            Mary-NOM   all-NOM   John-NOM which book-ACC
            tosyokan-kara karidasita] *to*]   *omotteiru*] *ka*]
            library-from   checked-out COMP think   Q
            siritagatteiru] *koto*
            want-to-know fact
            'the fact that Mary wants to know Q everyone thinks that John
            checked out which book from the library'
      b. ??[s [s′ [s *John-ga dono hon-o tosyokan-kara karidasita*] *to*]_i
            [s *Mary-ga* [s′ [s *minna-ga t_i omotteiru*] *ka*] *siritagatteiru*]]
            koto

Example (35b) is derived from (35a) by scrambling the most deeply embedded S′ to the initial position. The scrambled S′ contains a *wh*-phrase,
dono hon 'which book,' and is scrambled out of the c-command domain of
the Comp where this *wh*-phrase takes scope at LF. Example (35b) is also
marginal, and is somewhat worse than (34b). But it is still far better than
(30b) and (31b), which indicates that it is not a Proper Binding Condition
violation.
   Let us examine (35b) more closely. The structure of the relevant part of
the example is shown in (36):

(36) [s [s′ . . . *wh* . . .]_i [s . . . [s′ [s . . . t_i . . .] Q] . . .]]

Although the S′ containing the *wh* is scrambled to the sentence-initial position, the *wh* must still take scope at the position of the Q-morpheme.
Hence, the *wh* must move to the position of Q in LF. If we directly apply
this LF *wh*-movement to (36), we obtain the structure in (37):

(37) [s [s′ . . . t_j . . .]_i [s . . . [s′ [s . . . t_i . . .] wh_j] . . .]]

But we know that the LF representation of (35b) cannot have the structure
in (37). In (37), the trace t_j is not bound, and hence is in violation of the
Proper Binding Condition. The trace is chain-bound since it is contained in

S'_i and the *wh* c-commands t_i. But this is irrelevant, since, as we saw above, the Proper Binding Condition is insensitive to chain binding. Note that the structure in (37) is in relevant respects identical to that of (23), the LF representation of the ungrammatical English example (21b).

What, then, is the structure of the LF representation of (35b)? We know that the *wh* has to move to the position of Q. Furthermore, since the example is not a Proper Binding Condition violation, the trace of the *wh* must be within the c-command domain of the *wh* at LF. It then must be the case that the scrambled S' in (35b) is moved back to a position within the c-command domain of Q in LF. That is, it must be the case that in LF, not only does the *wh* move to the position of Q, but also the scrambled S' moves to a position within the c-command domain of the moved *wh*. Then, the structure of the LF representation of (35b) will be as in (38), and not (37):

(38) $[_S \ldots [_{S'} [_S \ldots [_{S'} \ldots t_j \ldots] \ldots] wh_j] \ldots]$

In (38), the trace t_j is bound, and hence satisfies the Proper Binding Condition. Since the LF in (38) can be obtained only by lowering the scrambled S', we are led to the conclusion that scrambling can be freely undone in the LF component.

The conclusion drawn here implies that the reconstruction hypothesis of Langendoen and Battistella (1982) holds in essence for scrambling, although not for *wh*-movement and topicalization in English. Let us consider again (12a), repeated as (39):

(39) [*Which picture of himself$_i$*]$_j$ *does John$_i$ like t$_j$ best*

As mentioned in §2.1 Langendoen and Battistella (1982) suggests that *which picture of himself$_j$* in (39) is lowered to the position of t_j in LF by a general reconstruction rule, so that *himself$_j$* is bound by *John$_i$* at LF. The example in (18b), repeated as (40), provides evidence against this approach and hence for Barss's (1984) chain-binding analysis of (39), which I have been assuming in this paper.

(40) ??[*Which picture of whom*]$_i$ *do you wonder who$_j$ t$_j$ bought t$_i$*

As pointed out above, this sentence cannot have the interpretation in which *whom* takes scope at the embedded Comp. And this fact is straightforwardly accounted for by the Proper Binding Condition, since if *whom* is moved to the embedded Comp in LF, then its trace will not be bound at LF. But if there is a general reconstruction rule that lowers *which picture of whom$_i$* in LF to the position of t_i, then it is not clear how to prevent *whom* from taking scope at the embedded Comp. Thus, (40) indicates that there is no "general reconstruction rule" of the kind suggested in Langendoen and Battistella (1982). However, our conclusion that scrambling is freely undone in the LF component in effect amounts to saying that scrambled constituents, in particular, can be "reconstructed" in LF. Since nothing seems to prevent us from supposing that this LF lowering or "reconstruction" is achieved by application of Move-α in LF, I will assume that this is the case.[18]

I argued above that scrambling differs from *wh*-movement and topicalization in English in that it can be freely undone in the LF component. According to this hypothesis, the D-structure of (41) is as in (42), and its LF can be as in (41) or as in (42):

(41) $[_S$ *sono hon-o$_i$* $[_S$ *John-ga* $[_{VP}$ *t$_i$ katta*$]]]$ *(koto)* (= (4a))
　　　　 that book-ACC John-NOM　　　bought　fact
　　　'John bought that book.'
(42) $[_S$ *John-ga* $[_{VP}$ *sono hon-o katta*$]]$ *(koto)*

Since LF is the level that feeds into semantic interpretation in the relevant sense, this conclusion implies that scrambling does not, or at least need not, establish a semantically significant operator–variable relation.[19]

3. Summary and Speculations

I have argued in this paper that scrambling is S-structure A'-movement and, further, that it can be freely undone in the LF component. The latter conclusion implies that scrambling need not establish a semantically significant operator–variable relation, as already suggested in Ross (1967), N. McCawley (1976), and Chomsky and Lasnik (1977), among others.

If the conclusions arrived at in this paper are correct, then a question naturally arises as to why scrambling, but not *wh*-movement and topicalization in English, can be freely undone in LF. Before I conclude this paper, I will briefly speculate on this difference between scrambling on the one hand and *wh*-movement and topicalization on the other.

First, it is well known that a *wh*-phrase that is already in Comp at S-structure must be in the same Comp at LF. Consider the following example:

(43) $[_{S'}$ *Who$_i$* $[_S$ *t$_i$ wonders* $[_{S'}$ *where$_j$* $[_S$ *we bought what t$_j$*$]]]]$

As Baker (1970) points out, (43) is only two ways ambiguous. *What* can take scope either at the matrix Comp or at the embedded Comp. But *where* can only have the embedded sentence as its scope, i.e., it must be in the embedded Comp at LF. Thus, descriptively, the scope of the *wh*-phrases that underwent syntactic *wh*-movement is determined at S-structure.[20] This description may be generalized to cases of topicalization. Let us consider again (21b), repeated as (44):

(44) *Mary thinks that [*the man that bought what*]$_j$, *John knows who$_i$ t$_i$ likes t$_j$*

If the scope of the topic, *the man that bought what,* is determined at S-structure, then it cannot lower in LF to the position of t_j or to any other position within the scope of the most deeply embedded Comp. Thus, when *what* moves to the most deeply embedded Comp in LF, its trace violates the Proper Binding Condition.

Now the question is why scrambled phrases need not stay at their S-structure positions in LF. If one assumes Baltin's (1982) analysis of English topicalization, as I do here, then both scrambling and English topicalization can involve adjunction to S. Thus, the peculiarity of scrambling in question cannot be attributed to some universal property of adjoined positions. It seems then that the difference between scrambling and English topicalization, i.e., the fact that only the former can be undone in LF, must be attributed to some independent difference between Japanese and English. For this I do not have a definite proposal to make at this point. In the remainder of this paper, however, I would like to suggest a possible first step toward the solution of this problem. More specifically, I will try to relate the peculiarity of scrambling in question, descriptively, to the fact that Japanese, but not English, has what is called the multiple subject construction.[21]

Some examples of the multiple subject construction, which are taken from Kuno (1973), are shown in (45):

(45) a. [$_S$ *yama-ga*   [$_S$ *ki-ga*   *kirei-desu*]]
          mountain-NOM tree-NOM pretty-be
          'It is the mountains where trees are beautiful.'
      b. [$_S$ *bunmeikoku-ga*   [$_S$ *dansei-ga* [$_S$ *heikinzyumyoo-ga*
          civilized country-NOM male-NOM   average lifespan-NOM
          mizikai]]]
          is short
          'It is in civilized countries that men are such that their average lifespan is short.'

In (45a), for example, the embedded sentence functions as a "predicate" and licenses the additional subject *yama* 'mountain,' which appears in nominative Case. It is argued in Shibatani and Cotton (1976–77), Hoji (1980), and Saito (1982), among others, that these "additional subjects" are base-generated in the position adjoined to S. If this analysis is correct, then in Japanese an NP can appear in the position adjoined to S at D-structure. However, if scrambling is A'-movement, as I have been assuming in this paper, then a phrase adjoined to S by scrambling is in A'-position. In order to ensure that the position adjoined to S is in general an A'-position, let us adopt the following definition of A/A'-positions:

(46) An A-POSITION is a position in which an NP can appear at D-structure and to which a θ-role can be assigned provided that there is an appropriate θ-role assigner. An A'-POSITION is one that is not an A-position. (See Chomsky (1981:47).)

Let us assume here, as seems reasonable, that the "additional subjects" in (45) are not assigned a θ-role, but are licensed by some sort of aboutness relation. Then (46) implies that the position adjoined to S is an A'-position even in Japanese, since it is not a potential θ-position. The fact that an NP can be base-generated in that position does not suffice to make it an A-position. Thus, given (46), we can maintain both the analysis of the multiple subject construction, mentioned above, and the analysis of scrambling as A'-movement. The position adjoined to S is an A'-position in general, in both English and Japanese.

But at the same time it is clear that the nature of the position adjoined to S differs in English and Japanese. An NP can be base-generated in that position in Japanese as shown in (45), but not in English. In order to capture this difference, let us now define D/D'-positions as follows:

(47) A D-POSITION is a position in which an NP can appear at D-structure and can be licensed as a nonoperator. A D'-POSITION is one that is not a D-position.

The "additional subjects" in (45) are nonoperators in the sense that they need not bind a variable (or anything else) at any level. Hence, the position adjoined to S is a D-position in Japanese. In English, since an NP cannot appear in this position at D-structure, it is a D'-position.

Given (47), the fact that *wh*-movement and topicalization cannot be undone in LF may be described as in (48)–(49).

(48) At S-structure, a constituent in D'-position binding a trace must be licensed as an operator.

(49) If X is licensed as an operator at position Y, then it must take scope at that position.

Statement (48) ensures that *wh*-phrases in Comp and topics adjoined to S are licensed as operators at S-structure. Statement (49), on the other hand, states that a constituent that is licensed as an operator at S-structure must take scope at its S-structure position, and in particular, cannot be lowered in LF. Statements (48)–(49) are irrelevant for scrambling, since scrambled constituents adjoined to S are in D-position. Thus, scrambling can be undone in LF without contradicting (48)–(49). Statements (48)–(49) are mere descriptive statements at this point, and if they are correct, they themselves must be explained in a principled way. However, as noted above, it seems that the fact that scrambling in Japanese, but not *wh*-movement and topicalization in English, can be undone in LF must be explained in terms of some independent difference between the two languages. Statements (48)–(49), I believe, suggest a possible direction to pursue in this research.

NOTES

1. *Koto* 'the fact that' is added to the end of some of the example sentences to avoid the unnaturalness resulting from the lack of topic in a matrix sentence. I ignore *koto* in the translations of those examples.

2. Chomsky and Lasnik (1977), for example, assumes that scrambling applies in the PF component and hence that its application has no effects on the LF representations. The nonconfigurational analysis of the Japanese "free word-order phenomenon" proposed by Hale (1980) and Farmer (1980) is also based on the assumption that scrambling, as a phenomenon, does not have any significant semantic import.

3. There is considerable variation among speakers' judgments with respect to the acceptability of sentences involving embedded topicalization. In this paper, I assume the judgments of those who allow embedded topicalization relatively freely. To them, the contrast between (3a) and (3b) is quite clear.

4. See Lasnik and Saito (in preparation) for further evidence that English topicalization can involve adjunction to S.

5. The strongly preferred reading for (6a) and (6d) is the one in which *dare* is coindexed with the relative clause subject, and the relative head with the relative clause object. These examples are somewhat marginal under the intended interpretation. But I assume, following Hoji (1985), that the explanation of this marginality falls outside the domain of sentence grammar. See also Kornfilt, Kuno, and Sezer (1980) for relevant discussion. For an attempt to provide a syntactic account for the marginality of (6a) and (6d), see Hasegawa (1985).

6. We assume the following definition of "bind" throughout this paper:

X BINDS Y $=_{df}$ (i) X and Y are coindexed, and (ii) X c-commands Y.

See Chomsky (1981) and the references cited there. "C-command" is defined as follows:

X C-COMMANDS Y = $_{df}$ the branching node most immediately dominating X
also dominates Y.

See Reinhart (1981) and the references cited there.

7. "Chain binding" is defined in (15) below. This relation is discussed in detail
in §2 of this paper.

8. Note that given the standard account of weak crossover, the contrast between
(6b) and (6c) provides further evidence against the functional approach to empty
categories (Chomsky 1982). Suppose that weak crossover rules out the following
configuration at LF:

(i) . . . QNP$_i$ [. . . pronoun$_j$ . . . t_i . . .] . . . (order irrelevant),

where QNP binds the pronoun and the trace, and the trace does not bind the pronoun. The LF of (6b) has the configuration in (7c) after QR (Quantifier Raising)
takes place. Thus the example is ruled out as a weak crossover violation only if e_i
cannot become a parasitic gap and must remain a pronoun at that level. Hence, (6b)
shows that an S-structure null pronoun must remain a pronoun at LF and cannot
become a parasitic gap at that level. See Safir (1984) and Chomsky (1986) for additional arguments against the functional approach to empty categories.

9. See also Chomsky (1981:345) for relevant discussion. It is assumed in
Langendoen and Battistella's approach that lexical anaphors are subject to Binding
theory only at LF.

10. "Chain binding," as opposed to "binding," seems to be the relevant relation not only for lexical anaphors but also for bound pronouns, as we saw in (6d)
and (11). Discussing examples such as those in (12), Barss (1984) proposes "chain
binding" as a substitute for "binding" in general, and hence, as the only binding
relation in Binding theory. Although this assumption is quite attractive conceptually, I do not adopt it here for reasons that will become clear immediately below.

11. See Chomsky (1986:26) for similar examples in Spanish, which he attributes to Esther Torrego.

12. Maggie Browning has independently come up with a pair similar to (17)
which involves VP proposing. (ia) is clearly better than (ib), which is hopeless.

(i) a. . . . *ready to marry John, I wonder whether Mary is*
    b. . . . *ready to marry t$_i$, I wonder who$_i$ Mary is*

13. Since (19) is well formed, it must be the case that t_k satisfies the Proper
Binding Condition. That is, *whom* must c-command t_k in this example. However,
given the definition of c-command in note 6, it is not clear how this is possible. I
assume here that such c-command, i.e., "c-command out of Comp," is possible for
the purpose of Proper Binding, because of absorption in the sense of Higginbotham
and May (1981).

14. In the discussion of the Proper Binding Condition so far, I have considered
only traces of *wh*-movement, and not those of NP-movement. There are well-
known examples such as (i), which suggest that traces of NP-movement can satisfy
Binding theory by virtue of chain binding.

(i) [*How likely t_i to win*]$_j$ *is John*$_i$ t_j

In (i), the NP-trace t_i is not bound, but is chain-bound, by *John*$_i$. Given examples such as (i), I proposed in Saito (1986) that chain binding is relevant for A-binding, but not for A'-binding.

However, Anthony Kroch (pers. comm.) pointed out to me that there are similar but completely ungrammatical examples, due originally to Mark Baltin, such as those in (ii)–(iii), and these examples, as opposed to (i), clearly involve NP-movement.

(ii) *[*How likely t_i to be a riot*]$_j$ *is there*$_i$ t_j
(iii) *[*How likely t_i to be taken t_i of John*]$_j$ *is advantage*$_i$ t_j

Examples (ii)–(iii) suggest that the Proper Binding Condition, which constrains traces of NP-movement as well as those of *wh*-movement, is insensitive to chain binding in general, as assumed in the text of this paper, and that examples such as (i) should be explained in some other way. See Lasnik and Saito (in preparation) for detailed discussion. Since traces of NP-movement are subject to both Condition (A) and the Proper Binding Condition, I assume here that (ii)–(iii) satisfy the former but violate the latter. A question, of course, remains as to why chain binding is relevant for Condition (A) but not for the Proper Binding Condition.

15. Examples (26b)–(26c) are awkward for some speakers. Scrambled phrases, especially those that are scrambled "long-distance," often receive some sort of focus interpretation. The awkwardness of (26b)–(26c) may be due to this effect. That is, these sentences may be interpreted as having two focused constituents, and this may be the reason for the awkwardness.

16. K. I. Harada (1972), of course, does not presuppose Trace theory, and hence does not explicitly make use of the Proper Binding Condition as such. But her analysis can be easily translated into one in terms of this condition, and her insight, I believe, is not affected by such translation.

17. The marginality of (34b) may be in part due to Subjacency. The scrambled NP in this example is moved out of a *wh*-island. Further, it seems likely that there is a weak S-structure constraint requiring *wh* to be within the c-command domain of the Q-morpheme that it is "associated with."

18. I assume here, following Lasnik and Saito (1984), that a moved constituent need not leave a trace unless the trace is required by independent principles. The analysis proposed in the text implies that no principle requires the LF lowering of a scrambled constituent to produce a trace. Otherwise, the LF lowering will result in a Proper Binding Condition violation.

19. Given that scrambling can be freely undone in LF, the analysis of (28)–(29) proposed above implies that the Proper Binding Condition applies at S-structure as well as at LF. There will be no trace in (28)–(29) violating the Proper Binding Condition after scrambling is undone in LF.

20. Aoun, Hornstein, and Sportiche (1981) state that *wh*-raising (LF *wh*-movement) can take place only from A-position. Lasnik and Saito (1984) discuss the relevant cases in detail and propose an account for the phenomenon in question

in terms of Comp indexing. But this account does not cover the case of topicalization discussed immediately below.

21. See Kuroda (1965, 1984), Kuno (1973), Shibatani and Cotton (1976–77),
Hoji (1980), and Saito (1982) for discussion of the multiple subject construction in
Japanese. Interesting attempts to relate the possibility of scrambling to that of the
multiple subject construction are found in Kuroda (1985) and Fukui (1986). They
are concerned not with the peculiarity of scrambling discussed in this paper, but
with the more general issue of why scrambling and multiple subject construction
are allowed in Japanese. See also Kitagawa (1986) for relevant discussion.

9

Constituency and Coordination in a Combinatory Grammar

MARK STEEDMAN

The present paper modifies and extends an earlier proposal to explain the syntax and semantics of unbounded dependency and coordination in natural language using a generalization of the Categorial Grammars (CGs) of Ajdukiewicz (1935) and others (cf. Lyons 1968). The theory follows traditional CG in assigning lexical and phrasal grammatical categories a syntactic and semantic type defining them either as atomic ARGUMENTS or as (directional) FUNCTIONS from one type into another. However, whereas CG categories define legal syntactic structures (and the associated interpretations) solely via the operation of Functional Application, the present theory departs from "pure" CG in including certain further "combinatory" operations for combining grammatical entities. The combinatory rules notably include Functional Composition and Type-raising. The inclusion of these operations dramatically changes what is meant by the notion "surface constituent." The present paper examines the consequences for the grammar of coordination.

Thanks to Peter Buneman, Wynn Chao, David Dowty, Joyce Friedman, Jack Hoeksema, Polly Jacobson, Aravind Joshi, Tony Kroch, Dale Miller, Michael Moortgat, Glynn Morrill, Dick Oehrle, Remo Pareschi, Ellen Prince, K. Vijay-Shankar, Anna Szabolcsi, Bonnie Lynn Webber, David Weir, Mary Wood, and the students in my graduate seminars at the University of Pennsylvania in 1986/87. Portions of the work were presented in 1987 in talks at Chicago, Boston, Amherst, Ohio State, and Brown universities, and at the ASL/LSA Conference on Language and Logic, and the LSA Institute Workshop on Mathematical Theories in Language, Stanford, July–August 1987. I thank the participants for comments and advice. Parts of the research were supported by grants from ESPRIT (project 393) to CCS, University of Edinburgh; from the Cognitive Science Program at the University of Pennsylvania sponsored by the Alfred P. Sloan Foundation; and from NSF grant IRI-10413 A02, ARO grant DAA6-29-84K-0061 and DARPA grant N0014-85-K0018 to CIS, University of Pennsylvania.

201

Functional composition is a very simple example of a class of operations on functions and arguments called "combinators," which were proposed by Curry and Feys (1958) in order to define the class of "applicative systems" that includes the lambda calculi. An applicative system is simply a calculus which defines the notions of functional application and functional "abstraction," where the latter term simply means the definition of a function in terms of some other(s). Applicative systems like the lambda calculus are of interest to linguists because the syntax and the semantics of natural constructions like the topicalised sentence (1a) are strongly reminiscent of a lambda abstraction which might be written as (2b), in which a function with a bound variable x is defined by the abstraction operator λ, and then applied to the displaced object:

(1) a. *This dog,   I think I like!*
    b. λx [THINK((LIKE x) PERSON13) PERSON13]
    c.   **B (B (B (C_* PERSON13) THINK) (C_* PER-
                 SON13)) LIKE**

However, the absence in (1a) of any explicit linguistic realization of the variable-binding lambda operator and the bound variable itself makes it interesting to ask whether other less familiar applicative systems might have a more transparent relation to such expressions in natural language. The interesting feature of Curry's combinators for this purpose is that they allow us to define the equivalent of abstraction using operations that are entirely local and operate only on adjacent, linguistically realized, entities, without the use of bound variables. Example (1c) is the expression of the same abstraction as (1b), using two typed combinators called **B** and **C_*,** whose definitions are discussed below. The theory therefore holds out the promise of a very transparent relation between the syntax and the semantics.[1] Steedman (1988, 1987a) discusses some possible computational advantages of applicative systems which avoid the overheads of variable-binding via the use of combinators.

The combinatory rules dramatically generalize the notion of surface constituent, if what we mean by the term is any grammatical entity which is (a) operated on by grammatical rules, and (b) interpretable. Not only are verbs and verb phrases constituents under this analysis, but also sequences like *might have* and *Mary might*. (The former arises because verbs like *might* are functions and are allowed to compose with other functions into categories of the appropriate type, like *have*. The latter arises via type-raising of the subject and composition with the verb.) One result of this generalization is that surface syntactic analyses tend to proliferate. However, the associativity of functional composition ensures that all the novel constituents receive appropriate interpretations, and that all the alternative analyses for a given set of function–argument relations deliver EQUIVA-LENT interpretations. This property is crucial to the proposals of Pareschi (1986, in preparation) and Pareschi and Steedman (1987) concerning efficient parsers for these grammars.

One source of linguistic support for this controversial notion of surface constituency comes from the fact that these nonstandard surface constituents allow a large number of otherwise puzzling "reduced" coordinate constructions to be subsumed under a simple GPSG–style rule paraphrasable as "conjoin constituents of like type." Dowty (1988) and Steedman (1985; hereafter D&C) show that such grammars capture as theorems a number of well-known constraints on coordination.

The present paper summarizes and revises the earlier work in the light of three Principles of "Adjacency," "Consistency," and "Inheritance" which in Steedman (1987a; hereafter CGPG) are claimed to limit the form of combinatory rules in Universal Grammar. The principles explain further constraints on coordinate structures.

1. Combinatory Grammars

Categorial grammars consist of two components. The first is a categorial lexicon, which associates each word of the language with at least one syntactic and semantic CATEGORY. This category distinguishes between elements like verbs, which are syntactically and semantically FUNCTIONS, and elements like NPs and PPs, which are syntactically and semantically their ARGUMENTS. The second component is a set of rules for COMBINING functions and arguments, which are here called COMBINATORY RULES because of their close relation to Curry's combinatory logic. In the "pure" categorial grammar of Bar-Hillel (1953), this component was restricted to rules of functional application and made the grammar context-free, equivalent to the more familiar phrase-structure grammars. Later versions (Lambek 1958, 1961; Geach 1972; Bach 1979, 1980; Dowty 1979, 1982a; Ades & Steedman 1982; Szabolcsi 1983; CGPG; Hoeksema 1985; Huck 1985; Oehrle 1988) have included more abstruse operations. However, many of these extensions conform to the following limiting principle, as does the original operation of functional application.[2]

(2) The Principle of Adjacency:
      Combinatory rules may only apply to entities which are linguistically realized and adjacent.

This principle embodies the central assumption of the present theory. It expressly excludes the postulation of any "empty" categories whatever and embodies a very strong form of localism. We are thereby already committed to some class of combinators. Unbounded operations like abstraction operators, movement, or coindexing are excluded under the principle. Moreover, the combinators are restricted to apply only to terms, as in the variable-free logic of Quine (1960; 1982:283–8).

1.1. Categorial Grammar

1.1.1. The Categorial Lexicon. Some syntactic categories, such as nouns, are naturally thought of as arguments, and bear straightforward categories like N. In the present theory, functions which combine with arguments to their right bear a category of the form X/Y, denoting a rightward-combining function from category Y into category X. For example, determiners are NP/N and transitive verbs are VP/NP. Other functions which combine with their arguments to the left are distinguished by the use of a backward slash, with a category of the form X\Y denoting a leftward-combining function from Y into X.[3] For example, VP-adverbial phrases like *quickly* bear the category VP\VP, and predicate phrases like *arrived* bear the category S\NP.[4]

Both types of function may of course have more than one argument and may mix the two types of slashes, combining with different arguments in different directions. However, all function categories are unary or "curried." For example, the ditransitive verb *give* will bear the category (VP/NP)/NP—a (rightward-combining) function from (indirect) objects into (rightward-combining) functions from (direct) objects into VPs. This restriction has no great significance. Unary *n*th-order curried functions are equivalent to *n*-ary first-order functions, as first noted by Schönfinkel (1924; cf. Dowty 1982a for a brief discussion). Where convenient, I shall exploit this equivalence, referring to a function like (VP/NP)/NP as "binary" and to VP as its "range."

The categories of all expressions, including the lexical categories, conform to the following principle, which embodies an assumption of the strongest possible "type-driven" relationship between syntax and semantics (cf. Klein & Sag 1985):

(3) The Principle of Transparency:
    The information in the syntactic type of an expression includes the information in its semantic type.

In other words, if an expression bears the syntactic category of a function from objects of syntactic type α into those of type β, then it is also semantically a function over the corresponding semantic types. The syntactic type will also of course determine a number of additional factors, such as linear order and agreement, which are not represented semantically. Such categories can be represented by a single data structure uniting syntactic type and semantic interpretation in unification-based implementations like those of Zeevat, Klein & Calder (1986), Pareschi & Steedman (1987), and Pareschi (in preparation). (Cf. Karttunen 1986, Uszkoreit 1986, Shieber 1986, and Wittenburg 1986 for related approaches.) However, the principle embodies some strong assumptions about the nature of semantic representations in the present grammar. For example, if we wanted to follow Montague in accounting for ambiguities of quantifier scope by changing the type of NP arguments into functions, then we would probably have to do it at some other level of semantic representation. (See Kang 1988 for an interesting discussion of this point.)

The combinatory rules govern the combination of function categories with other adjacent categories to yield new categories conforming to the above principle. The simplest such rules are the ones which apply a function to an argument.

1.1.2. Functional Application. Because of the assumption enshrined above in the Principle of Transparency, we can write the syntactic and semantic combinatory rules in one, associating each syntactic category in a rule with the semantic interpretation that it transparently reflects. Indeed, the only point of distinguishing the two at all is to make explicit the relation that the interpretation of the result bears to that of the inputs. The following obvious rules are required:

(4) a. $X/Y:F \quad Y:y => X:Fy \qquad (>)$
     b. $Y:y \quad X \backslash Y:F => X:Fy \qquad (<)$

In this and the other combinatory rules that follow, X and Y are variables which range over any category, including functions, so X/Y is any rightward-combining function and X\Y is any leftward-combining function. Upper-case F, G, etc. are used for the interpretations of functions, while lower case $x, y,$ etc. are used for the interpretations of arguments. The application of a function F to an argument x is represented by left-to-right order, as "$Fx.$" Semantic interpretations appear to the right of the syntactic category that identifies their type, separated by a colon.

The first of these rules, called "Forward Application," allows rightward-combining functions like transitive verbs to combine with arguments to their right, as in the following derivations, in which the operation of combinatory rules is indicated by underlining the operands, indexing the underline with a mnemonic symbol identifying the rule (in this case "$>$"), thereby determining the interpretation of the result, whose type is written underneath:

(5) a. *Take*   *the*   *cake*   b.   *Put*   *the book*   *on*   *the desk*
        ‾‾‾‾‾‾‾ ‾‾‾‾‾‾ ‾‾‾‾‾‾   ‾‾‾‾‾‾‾ ‾‾‾‾‾‾‾‾‾ ‾‾‾‾‾‾ ‾‾‾‾‾‾‾‾
        VP/NP   NP/N   N   (VP/PP)/NP   NP   PP/NP   NP
                ‾‾‾‾‾‾‾‾‾‾‾‾‾>   ‾‾‾‾‾‾‾‾‾‾‾‾‾‾‾‾‾> ‾‾‾‾‾‾‾‾‾‾‾‾‾>
                      NP   VP/PP   PP
        ‾‾‾‾‾‾‾‾‾‾‾‾‾‾‾‾‾‾‾>   ‾‾‾‾‾‾‾‾‾‾‾‾‾‾‾‾‾‾‾‾‾‾‾‾‾‾‾>
                      VP   VP

(Such diagrams are equivalent to the trees associated with phrase structure grammars, of course.)

The second instance of the rule of functional application, (4b), allows a leftward-combining function X\Y to combine with an argument Y to its left. This instance of the functional application rule is indicated in derivations by an underline indexed by "<." Not many function categories of English are backward-combining, but certain non-subcategorised-for adverbials are, as in

(6) *Come quickly*
    ‾‾‾‾‾ ‾‾‾‾‾‾‾
    VP   VP\VP
    ‾‾‾‾‾‾‾‾‾‾‾‾‾<
          VP

The above two rules are the ONLY two rules of functional application that the theory allows. In particular, application of a function to an argument is by definition subject to their left-to-right order being consistent with the directionality of the function, because that is what the slashes MEAN. Obvious though this restriction is, it will be useful to enshrine it under the title of the principle of "Directional Consistency," as follows:

(7) The Principle of Directional Consistency:
    All syntactic combinatory rules must be consistent with the directionality of the principal function.

The "principal" function is the one whose range is the same as the range of the result. (Since there is only one function concerned in functional application, the adjective is redundant in the case at hand.)

The above principle is not a stipulation, for it could be shown to follow from the semantics of the metalanguage in which the grammar is couched. Informally, directionality is a property of the argument of a function. The direction of a slash on a particular argument of a function denotes the position of the entity with which it may combine. The consistent rules are limited by the categories themselves.

1.1.3. The Category of Subject and Verb.   Another apparent example of an argument occurring to the left of a function, and hence seeming to require backward application, is the subject of a sentence. It seems natural to assume that tensed verb phrases bear the category S\NP, so that tensed transitive verbs like *eat* are (S\NP)/NP, while ditransitives are ((S\NP)/NP)/NP and so on, giving rise to derivations like the following:

(8) *Harry   eats   apples*
$$\frac{\cfrac{\text{NP} \quad \cfrac{\text{(S\NP)/NP} \quad \text{NP}}{\text{S\NP}}>}{\text{S}}<}$$

This derivation assigns an interpretation of type S which we might write EAT APPLES HARRY, where functional application "associates to the left," so that the result is equivalent to ((EAT APPLES) HARRY). It is the interpretation of the verb, EAT, which determines the grammatical relations of the first argument, HARRY, and the second, APPLES, as subject and object respectively.[5]

1.2. Combinators, Right Node-raising, and Leftward Extraction

The two central problems for any theory of natural language grammar are posed by "reduced" coordinate constructions, exemplified in (9a), and "extractions," exemplified in (9b):

(9) a. [*I know Harry will cook*] *and* [*I think Betty might eat*] *the mushrooms we picked in the dank meadows behind the Grange.*
     b. *These mushrooms, I think Betty might eat.*

Both constructions appear to separate elements like objects and verbs which belong together in semantics. Both may separate them by unbounded amounts, including clause boundaries. They therefore appear to force us to abandon simple assumptions like the Principle of Adjacency (2), or the assumption that rules of grammar should apply to constituents. According to the present theory, however, both of these phenomena can be explained without abandoning either assumption, under some simple extensions to the combinatory rules and a consequent extension of the concept of a constituent to include entities corresponding to strings like *might eat* and *I think Betty might eat.*

1.2.1. Functional Composition. Like any context-free grammar, the present one will allow atomic categories like NPs and verbs to coordinate under the following schema, which can be paraphrased as "conjoin like categories," and which is inherited from Dougherty (1970) via Gazdar (1981).[6]

(10) Coordination:
      X CONJ X => X

For example, transitive verbs can coordinate as follows:

(11) *I*   *cooked*   *and*   *ate*   *the beans.*
      ‾‾   ‾‾‾‾‾‾   ‾‾‾   ‾‾‾   ‾‾‾‾‾‾‾‾
      NP (S\NP)/NP CONJ (S\NP)/NP   NP
      ————————————————————————————COORD
                (S\NP)/NP
      ————————————————————————————>
                        S\NP
      ————————————————————————————<
                     S

The following sentence, on the other hand, will block in a pure categorial grammar:

(12) *I*   *will*   *cook*   *and*   *might*   *eat*
      ‾‾   ‾‾‾‾   ‾‾‾‾   ‾‾‾   ‾‾‾‾‾   ‾‾‾
      NP (S\NP)/VP VP/NP CONJ (S\NP)/VP VP/NP

      the mushrooms we picked.
      ‾‾‾‾‾‾‾‾‾‾‾‾‾‾‾‾‾‾‾‾
                NP

Functional application will not help us here. But the earlier papers propose a comparably simple rule which will. It is the following (we will ignore the question of how the interpretations are related for the moment, and just treat it as a rule relating syntactic/semantic categorial types):

(13) Forward Functional Composition:
      X/Y Y/Z => X/Z

This rule, which has the appearance of the "cancellation" rule of fractional multiplication, and which for reasons that will be apparent directly will be indexed ">**B**," allows the following derivation for the coordinate sentence (12):

(14)

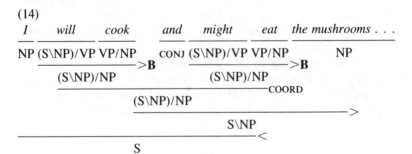

The categories of the adjacent functors *will*$_{(S\backslash NP)/VP}$ and *cook*$_{VP/NP}$ match the rule, as do the parallel categories *might* and *eat*. The result has the same type (S\NP)/NP as the transitive verb in (12), so the rest of the derivation is the same as the earlier one. Repeated application of Forward Composition to the verb sequences in examples like the following will allow coordination of indefinitely long strings of verbs, on the assumption that each is a function over the result of the one to its right:

(15) *She* [*may have seemed to have wanted to meet,*]$_{(S\backslash NP)/NP}$ *but* [*actually turned out to dislike,*]$_{(S\backslash NP)/NP}$ *the man you brought to the party.*

The semantics of this rule is almost as simple as functional application. It is in fact functional COMPOSITION.[7] The combinator which composes two functions F and G is called **B** by Curry, and can be defined by the following equivalence:

(16) $\mathbf{B}FGx = F(Gx)$

A convention that application associates to the left is again followed, so that the left-hand side is equivalent to $((\mathbf{B}F)G)x$. It follows that we can consider the application of **B** to F and G as producing a new function equivalent to abstracting on x in the above expression, thus:

(17) $\mathbf{B}FG = [x] F(Gx)$

(Curry's "bracket abstraction" notation "$[x] \langle$expression$\rangle$" means much the same as the lambda notation "$\lambda x \langle$expression$\rangle$." It is used here to remind us that the combinators are the primitives, not the abstraction operator.) It will be convenient to distinguish the two functions F and G in the above example as the "principal" and the "subsidiary" function respectively. Like the rule of Functional Application (4), this rule is subject to the Principle of Directional Consistency (7): the subsidiary function must occur to whichever side is consistent with the slash on the principal function. The rule is also subject to a less obvious principle, which is claimed in CGPG to limit all combinatory rules in Universal Grammar which produce a function as their output, as follows:[8]

(18) The Principle of Directional Inheritance:
     If the category that results from the application of a combinatory rule is a function category, then the slash defining directionality for a given argument in that category will be the same as the one defining directionality for the corresponding argument(s) in the input function(s).

(There is only one argument of the function which results from composition, and it is only inherited from one input function, so we can ignore the plural possibilities here. However, Szabolcsi 1983 and CGPG propose combinatory rules which identify the arguments of more than one function in order to cope with certain multiple extractions.)

The functional composition rule therefore potentially gives rise to four instances, distinguished by the left-to-right order and directionality of the principal and subsidiary functions, as follows:

(19) a. $X/Y:F\ Y/Z:G\ =>\ X/Z:BFG\ (>\mathbf{B})$
      b. $X/Y:F\ Y\backslash Z:G\ =>\ X\backslash Z:BFG\ (>\mathbf{B}x)$
      c. $Y\backslash Z:G\ X\backslash Y:F\ =>\ X\backslash Z:BFG\ (<\mathbf{B})$
      d. $Y/Z:G\ X\backslash Y:F\ =>\ X/Z:BFG\ (<\mathbf{B}x)$

As with all combinatory rules, natural languages are free to include rules on any of the four patterns, to restrict variables in any given rule to certain categories, such as S or maximal categories, or even to entirely exclude some of them. All four rules have been used to account for various phenomena in English.[9] For example, a second instance of the composition rule, on the pattern of (19d), must be included in the grammar of English if examples like the following are to be accepted:

(20)

I	shall	buy	today	and	cook	tomorrow	the mushrooms	etc.
NP	(S\NP)/VP	VP/NP	VP\VP	CONJ	VP/NP	VP\VP	NP	

$$\underline{}<\mathbf{B}x \qquad \underline{}<\mathbf{B}x$$

VP/NP   VP/NP

$$\underline{}\text{COORD}$$

VP/NP
$$\underline{}>$$
VP

The rule in question, which is discussed more fully in CGPG, is the following:

(21) Backward Functional Composition (Crossing):
      $Y/Z:G\ X\backslash Y:F\ =>\ X/Z:BFG$
      where $Y = S\backslash NP$

(The language-specific restriction on Y, that it be the category S\NP, is required to prevent overgeneralizations like $*the_{NP/N}\ walks_{S\backslash NP}\ dog_N$. This restriction is an alternative to Morrill's (1987) restriction of Z to a class of categories he calls MOVABLE.)

1.2.2. An Aside on Generalized Composition and Coordination.[10] Examples like the following show that natural-language grammars require a slight generalization of the notion of composition:[11]

(22)

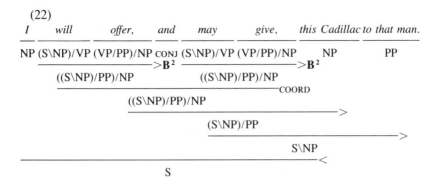

This derivation requires a combinatory rule indexed ">B^2," closely related to function composition, and which would be written

(23) $X/Y:F (Y/Z)/W:G => (X/Z)/W:B^2FG$

The semantics of the rule corresponds to the combinator B^2, which is so called because in the notation of Curry and Feys, the combinator which results from the composition of any combinator X with itself is written X^2, and the operation in question is simply the composition of composition with itself. Thus $B^2 = BBB$. In general, the combinator written X^{n+1} is defined as the composition of X with X^n, under the following equivalence:

(24) $X^{n+1} = BXX^n$

The composition rule originally proposed by A&S had the full generality of B^n and can be written in present terms as in (25) below, where the following conventions are assumed:

(25′) a. In each instance (25a)–(25d), the expression $Y/. . . Z$ or $Y\backslash. . . Z$ stands for a function of n arguments whose first argument is of type Z (and whose direction is unspecified), and whose LAST argument (which will of course be Z itself if the functor is unary) is to be found to the right.

b. In each instance, the expression $X/. . . Z$ or $X\backslash. . . Z$ stands for the ONLY corresponding resulting function permitted by the Principle of Inheritance and the combinator in question, namely the one in which the type and direction of all arguments are exactly as in the corresponding function into Y.

The universally permitted rules are then written as follows:

(25) a. $X/Y:F$ $Y/. . . Z:G => X/. . . Z:B^nFG$ $(>B^n)$
       b. $X/Y:F$ $Y\backslash. . . Z:G => X\backslash. . . Z:B^nFG$ $(>B^nx)$

c. $Y\backslash \ldots Z:G$ $\quad$ $X\backslash Y:F => X\backslash \ldots Z:B^nFG\ (<B^n)$
d. $Y/ \ldots Z:G$ $\quad$ $X\backslash Y:F => X/ \ldots Z:B^nFG\ (<B^nx)$

Individual languages are as usual allowed to further restrict these rules, and English probably only requires B^n to a value of n bounded by the maximum valency in the lexicon. However, the Dutch "crossed dependency" construction discussed in D&C requires rules with something like the generality of the above schemata. In particular, the existence in principle of sentences of the following form demands this generality under the analysis of D&C (cf. p. 559, ex. (50e)):

(26) (dat) *ik Cecilia Marie . . . Henk$_n$ zag [helpen leren . . . zwemmen$_n$*
$\qquad$ *en leren helpen . . . zingen$_n$]*
$\qquad$ 'that I saw Cecilia help Marie teach . . . Henk$_n$ to swim$_n$ and
$\qquad$ (Cecilia) teach (Marie) to help . . . (Henk$_n$) to sing$_n$'

The ellipses indicate that the construction can involve indefinitely many noun phrases followed by indefinitely many verbs requiring that number of arguments. The brackets indicate that coordination of a correspondingly indefinitely long sub-sequence of verbs, for which composition can build a function of unboundedly many arguments, followed by composition with a preceding tensed verb such as *zag,* can force the use of arbitrarily high order composition.

The introduction of "families" of combinators of the form X^n related in this way also provides us with a semantics for the operation implicit in the coordination rule (10). As the last example shows, this rule must apply to functions with one, two, or arbitrarily many arguments. In each case its semantics corresponds to a different combinator. In the basic case of unary functors, this combinator is Curry and Feys's Φ applied to a notoriously problematic function corresponding to the semantics of the conjunction in question. The present theory has nothing to say about this function, which will simply be written as $\&$. Φ is defined as follows:

(27) $\Phi FGHx = F(Gx)(Hx)$

In the case of functors taking n arguments, the requisite combinator is Φ^n (cf. Curry & Feys 1958:165). The rule can therefore be written as follows, where $X \ldots Z$ stands for functions of arity $n > 0$ and unspecified (but equal) directionality into X:

(28) $X \ldots Y:G$ CONJ $X \ldots Y:H => X:\Phi^n\&GH$

For discussion of the power engendered by generalized composition and coordination, see Friedman and Venkatesan (1986), Friedman, Dawei, and Wang (1986), Joshi (1987a), and Weir (1988).

1.2.3. Type-raising. The following examples require something more than functional composition.

(29) a. [*I will cook*] *and* [*Betty may eat*] *the mushrooms we picked in the dismal glens above the Grange.*

  b. [*I think I will cook*] *and* [*you think that Betty may eat*] *the mushrooms* etc.

The problem with examples like these is that the subject(s) cannot combine with the tensed verb(s) or the composed verb group(s), whose categories dictate that they have to combine with something else first:

(30) I *will*   *cook* . . .

    $\overline{\text{NP}}$ $\overline{\text{(S\textbackslash NP)/VP}}$ $\overline{\text{VP/NP}}$

            $\overline{\hphantom{xxxxxxxxxxxx}}$**>B**

           (S\NP)/NP

   $\overline{\hphantom{xxxxxxxxxxxxxxxxxx}}$ *

Functional composition alone does not help—composition is for combining FUNCTIONS, not arguments. However, there is an operation of "type-raising" which is widely used in the Montague Grammar literature to map arguments (such as subjects) into functions over functions-which-take-such-arguments (such as predicates).[12] Type-raising is indexed **C∗**, for reasons given below, and the instance of the rule that is relevant here is the following "forward" version:

(31) Subject Type-raising:
    X => S/(S\X) (>**C∗**)

It will permit the following derivation for (29a):

(32)

   I *will*   *cook* *and* *Betty*   *might*   *eat*   *the mushrooms* . . .

  $\overline{\text{NP}}$ $\overline{\text{(S\textbackslash NP)/VP}}$ $\overline{\text{VP/NP}}$ CONJ $\overline{\text{NP}}$ $\overline{\text{(S\textbackslash NP)/VP}}$ $\overline{\text{VP/NP}}$ $\overline{\text{NP}}$

$\overline{\hphantom{xxxxxx}}$>**C∗** $\overline{\hphantom{xxxxxx}}$>**C∗**

S/(S\NP)   S/(S\NP)

$\overline{\hphantom{xxxxxxxxxxxxxx}}$>**B** $\overline{\hphantom{xxxxxxxxxxxxxx}}$>**B**

   S/VP   S/VP

$\overline{\hphantom{xxxxxxxxxxxxxxxxxx}}$>**B** $\overline{\hphantom{xxxxxxxxxxxxxxxxxx}}$>**B**

     S/NP   S/NP

   $\overline{\hphantom{xxxxxxxxxxxxxxxxxxxxxxxxxxxxxxx}}$COORD

             S/NP

   $\overline{\hphantom{xxxxxxxxxxxxxxxxxxxxxxxxxxxxxxxxxxxxx}}$>

               S

The subject NP in the example raises into the category S/(S\NP). This category can in turn compose with the verb by the standard forward composition rule. Further iteration of composition and application completes the derivation. No other raised category for the subject NP will allow this or any other derivation. The more complex unbounded right node–raised example (29b) is accepted in a parallel manner, since the embedded subjects can also raise under the rule, and repeated composition can again assemble two constituents of type S/NP. However, right node–raising which violates the "across-the-board" condition is not permitted, because the grammar does not yield categories of like type:

(33) *[*I will cook*]$_{S/NP}$ and [*Betty might eat potatoes*]$_S$
        [*the mushrooms . . .*]$_{NP}$

Even across-the-board extraction may not combine subject- and object-extraction, for the same reason:

(34) *[*I will meet*]$_{S/NP}$ and [*will marry Mary*]$_{S\backslash NP}$ [*your best friend*]$_{NP}$

And of course, the following example is excluded, because only adjacent categories can coordinate:

(35) *[*I will cook*]$_{S/NP}$ [*the mushrooms*]$_{NP}$ and [*Betty will eat*]$_{S/NP}$

Like composition, this type of rule has a simple and invariant semantics. The semantics corresponds to another of Curry's basic combinators, called $\mathbf{C}_*$, defined by the following equivalence:

(36) $\mathbf{C}_* x \mathbf{F} = \mathbf{F} x$

It follows that $\mathbf{C}_*$ applied to an argument creates the following abstraction over the function (again, Curry's "bracket abstraction" notation is used):

(37) $\mathbf{C}_* x = [\mathbf{F}]\ \mathbf{F} x$

Type-raising is here assumed to be a "direction-preserving" property proposed by Dowty, such that arguments may only raise into RIGHTWARD-looking functions over leftward-looking ones, or into LEFTWARD-looking functions over rightward ones. There are therefore just two possible direction-preserving type-raising rules, of which (31) is one special case, and which can be written as follows:

(38) Direction-preserving Type-raising:
        a. $X : x => T/(T\backslash X) : \mathbf{C}_* x\ (>\mathbf{C}_*)$
        b. $X : x => T\backslash(T/X) : \mathbf{C}_* x\ (<\mathbf{C}_*)$

I follow D&C and Zeevat, Klein, and Calder (1987) in using a polymorphic type variable T in this rule. T can match any category that the grammar permits.[13] In derivations, this variable will be expanded to the category which instantiates it, as in the last derivation.

The possibility of type-raising embedded subjects potentially allows the assembly via forward composition of nonstandard constituents like *I think that Harry,* bearing the same category S/(S\NP) as a subject, thus:

(39)

I	*think*	*that*	*Harry*
NP	(S\NP)/S′	S′/S	NP

$$\frac{}{\text{S}/(\text{S}\backslash\text{NP})} >\mathbf{C}_*$$

$$\frac{}{\text{S}/\text{S}′} >\mathbf{B}$$

$$\frac{}{\text{S}/\text{S}} >\mathbf{B}$$

$$\frac{}{\text{S}/(\text{S}\backslash\text{NP})} >\mathbf{C}_*$$

$$\frac{}{\text{S}/(\text{S}\backslash\text{NP})} >\mathbf{B}$$

If these constituents are permitted, they will allow ill-formed coordinates like the following to mean the same as the conjunction of *Mary will lend you the money* and *I think that Harry will lend you the money*

(40) a. *[*Mary and I think that Harry*] *will lend you the money.*
      b. *[*I think that Harry and Mary*] *will lend you the money.*

(Example (40b) is of course only ill-formed under the indicated bracketing.)

One way of preventing this overgeneralization which we will tentatively adopt here is to apply a similar restriction to the forward composition rule as was applied earlier to the Backward Crossing rule (21), so that the rule becomes [14]

(41) Forward Functional Composition:
      $X/Y:F \; Y/Z:G => X/Z:\mathbf{B}FG$
      where $Z \neq$ S\NP

The restriction is again related to the type proposed by Morrill (1987) and prevents composition into subjects. It therefore also rules out the following questionable sentence:

(42) ?*I* [*believe that Harry*] *but* [*doubt whether Barry*] *will lend you the money.*

In D&C I somewhat doubtfully accepted a similar sentence, noting that it was much worse than related sentences with nonsubjects, like

(43) *I saw Harry, and heard Mary, feed the elephants.*

The restriction also rules out the following overgeneration permitted by the analyses in D&C and CGPG, and noted by Dowty (1988), which would also otherwise be permitted on the analysis of relatives in the next section. According to these analyses, nouns can type-raise over relative modifiers, and subject relative pronouns have a category like that of a subject (see below). The restriction nevertheless forbids constituents like *man who*, saving the CGPG proposal.

(44) **a man who and robot which can solve this problem*

However, the following is still allowed (cf. exx. (57) and (58) below):

(45) *people who can solve, and robots which ignore, these very fundamental and obvious problems*

1.2.4. Leftward Extraction. The two combinatory syntactic rules of functional composition and type-raising provide all that we need in order to solve the second problem introduced at the start of §1.2, namely that of leftward extraction in "*wh-* movement" constructions. Thus, in the following example the subject NP can again raise over the predicate category, and iterated composition can again assemble the subject and all the verbs in the entire sequence *Harry must have been eating* to compose into a single function, thus:

(46)

These apples	Harry	must	have	been	eating
NP	S/(S\NP)	(S\NP)/VP	VP/VP*en*	VP*en*/VP*ing*	VP*ing*/NP

$$\text{S/VP} \quad \text{---->B}$$

$$\text{S/VP}en \quad \text{---->B}$$

$$\text{S/VP}ing \quad \text{---->B}$$

$$\text{S/NP} \quad \text{---->B}$$

The important result is that the entire clause has been assembled into a single function adjacent to the extracted argument. Technically, this function still cannot combine, because the directionality of the slash forbids it. There are a number of ways of handling this detail consistent with the Principles of Adjacency and Consistency. We shall use the following rule, which is related to type-raising, but which is (obviously) NOT direction-preserving, and which marks its result as "S*t*"—an S marked with a feature, say +TOPIC, distinguishing it from other species of S. Since the rule is not pure type-raising, and its semantics is obscure, we omit the latter entirely.[15] The fact that this rule is exempt from the order prescribing constraint is presumably related to the fact that topicalization is a construction of spoken language, marked by intonation, so that this operation is not truly syntactic at all.

(47) Topicalization:
$$X => St/(S/X)$$
where $X \in \{NP, PP, VP, AP, S'\}$

Such topics can combine with the remainder of the sentence by the forward application rule, thus:

(48)

Apples,	Harry	must	have	been	eating
St/(S/NP)	S/(S\NP)	(S\NP)/VP	VP/VPen	VPen/VPing	VPing/NP

$$\underline{\hspace{8cm}}\text{(as before)}$$
$$\underline{\hspace{6cm}}$$
$$S/NP$$
$$\underline{\hspace{6cm}}>$$
$$St$$

A similar analysis holds for relativization as for topicalization. We shall assume here that restrictive relative clauses are noun adjuncts of type N\N. Object relative pronouns are then functions parallel to the topic category from S/NP into relative clauses N\N, written as follows:[16]

(49) $who(m)$: $= (N\backslash N)/(S/NP)$

This category is again related to, but not the same as, a type-raised category. We assume that it is assigned in the lexicon, not in free syntax.[17] A simple relative clause is analysed as follows:

(50) (apples)   which   Harry   eats

    (N\N)/(S/NP)   S/(S\NP)   (S\NP)/NP
$$\underline{\hspace{5cm}}>\mathbf{B}$$
$$S/NP$$
$$\underline{\hspace{5cm}}>$$
$$(N\backslash N)$$

The subject relative pronoun will bear the category (N\N)/(S\NP), allowing derivations like the following:

(51) (a man)   who   left

    (N\N)/(S\NP) S\NP
$$\underline{\hspace{5cm}}>$$
$$(N\backslash N)$$

The rules of functional composition and type-raising provide a general mechanism for unbounded extraction. On the assumption that one category for the tensed verb *believe* is $(S\backslash NP)/S'$, and that the complementiser *that* is S'/S, repeated application of the forward composition rule allows extractions across clause boundaries:

(52)   *Apples,   I   believe   that   Harry   eats.*

$St/(S/NP)$ $S/(S\backslash NP)$ $(S\backslash NP)/S'$ S'/S $S/(S\backslash NP)$ $(S\backslash NP)/NP$

$$\underline{\hspace{5cm}} >\mathbf{B}$$
$$S/S'$$
$$\underline{\hspace{6cm}} >\mathbf{B}$$
$$S/S$$
$$\underline{\hspace{7cm}} >\mathbf{B}$$
$$S/NP$$
$$\underline{\hspace{6cm}} >\mathbf{B}$$
$$S/NP$$
$$\underline{\hspace{8cm}} >$$
$$St$$

However, the corresponding SUBJECT extractions are excluded as a consequence of the English-specific restriction against slash-crossing forward composition, so that the Fixed Subject Constraint or *that*-trace Filter of Bresnan (1972) and Chomsky and Lasnik (1977) follows automatically:

(53) *   *Harry   I believe   that   eats   apples*

$St/(S\backslash NP)$ S/S' S'/S $(S\backslash NP)/NP$ NP

$$\underline{\hspace{3cm}} >\mathbf{B}$$
$$S/S$$
$$\underline{\hspace{3cm}} >$$
$$S\backslash NP$$
$$\underline{\hspace{4cm}} >*\mathbf{B}$$
$$S\backslash NP$$
$$\underline{\hspace{5cm}} >$$
$$St$$

The problem then arises of how to ALLOW subject extraction in examples like

(54) *Harry, I believe eats apples.*

CGPG shows that it is not possible merely to assume a further category VP/S for verbs like *believe,* and to allow the hitherto forbidden "slash-crossing" forward composition into the predicate category, excluding (53) by a restriction on such composition into S'. This expedient would permit the following sort of derivation, closely related to the earlier examples of object extraction, except that the topic receives a category resembling that of a type-raised subject:

(55)   *Harry   I believe   eats   apples.*
       ──────── ────────── ──────────── ────
       S*t*/(S\NP)   S/S   (S\NP)/NP   NP
                            ──────────────────>
                                  S\NP
                            ──────────────────>*B
                                  S\NP
       ──────────────────────────────────>
                     S*t*

However, the inclusion of composition on this pattern fails to acknowledge the exceptional character of subject extraction. It also threatens to allow overgeneralizations like the following:

(56) * *I   he   think   left*
       ── ── ────────── ────
       NP NP (S\NP)/S   S\NP
               ──────────────────>*B
                   (S\NP)\NP
               ─────────────────<
                     S\NP
       ───────────────────<
               S

This derivation is parallel to the analysis of Dutch infinitival clauses like (. . . *dat*) *ik Cecilia zag zwemmen* 'that I saw Cecilia swim' in D&C, so it is reasonable that it should potentially be allowed by the theory of grammar. (For example, its inclusion in Dutch may give rise to the possibility of subject extraction in that language; Perlmutter 1971.) But it must continue to be excluded from English. The only degree of freedom that the theory leaves us at this point is to assign a different lexical category to bare-complement verbs like *believe*. Such a proposal is developed in CGPG, but we shall pass over it here, together with a number of matters, such as "pied piping" of *wh*- categories, and other restrictions on *wh*- movement and "empty categories" that are considered in that paper, and in Szabolcsi (1987).

It will be clear by now that the theory predicts a conspiracy between the domains of left extraction and right node–raising. Both arise from the composition of the residue into a single function, so if something can left-extract then it should be able to right node–raise as well. In particular, there should be no independent "right roof constraint" (Ross 1967) on right node–raising of arguments of the verb, a condition which Gazdar (1981) has convincingly argued to be artifactual.[18] The converse does not apply: the limitations on the topicalizable and relativized categories, and limitation of their domain to S, means that more categories can right node–raise, both within S and within NP. For example, the following example has been argued to illustrate an asymmetry in the possibilities for left- and right-extraction:

(57) a.   *There will always be some people who like, and some people who dislike, algebraic semantics.*

    b.   ?*Which kind of semantics will there always be some people who like and some people who dislike?*

However, the possibility of (57a) arises from the possibility of right node–raising within NP—that is, of forming *some people who like and some people who dislike algebraic semantics* as follows:

(58)

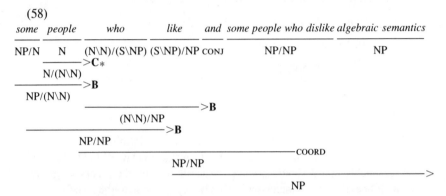

These NPs can take part in the (a) sentences as usual. The unacceptability of the (b) sentence above arises from quite different sources. In the case of the former example, it arises from the restrictions on the topicalization rule (47). In the latter case it arises from the same source as the difficulty of extracting out of a NP. Whatever that source may be, it does indeed apply equally to rightward movement, as the unacceptability of the following example shows:

(59)   ?*I love people who like, and you loathe people who dislike, algebraic semantics.*

(See Dowty 1988, D&C, and CGPG for further discussion.)

It should also be clear by now that the theory implies a very unusual view of surface structure. If strings like *I believe that Harry eats* are constituents for the purposes of conjunction and extraction, then they must also be possible constituents of canonical sentences like *I believe that Harry eats these apples* as well. It follows that the following derivation is only one among several possible "surface structures" for this sentence, under the present account:

(60)

I	believe	that	Harry	eats	apples.
S/(S\NP)	(S\NP)/S′	S′/S	S/(S\NP)	(S\NP)/NP	NP

$$
\begin{array}{l}
\underline{\qquad\qquad\qquad} {>}\mathbf{B} \\
\quad S/S' \\
\underline{\qquad\qquad\qquad\qquad} {>}\mathbf{B} \\
\quad\quad S/S \\
\qquad\qquad\qquad\qquad\qquad\underline{\qquad\qquad\qquad} {>}\mathbf{B} \\
\qquad\qquad\qquad\qquad\qquad\qquad S/NP \\
\qquad\qquad\underline{\qquad\qquad\qquad\qquad\qquad\qquad} {>}\mathbf{B} \\
\qquad\qquad\qquad S/NP \\
\qquad\qquad\underline{\qquad\qquad\qquad\qquad\qquad\qquad\qquad\qquad} {>} \\
\qquad\qquad\qquad\qquad\qquad S
\end{array}
$$

In fact, for each reading of a sentence, there will typically be many different surface analyses, corresponding to different orders of applying composition and application. The consequences for processing seem potentially grave.

However, if we assume a level of interpretation which is neutral with respect to aspects of meaning which are not solely structure-dependent, such as quantifier scope, then the associativity of functional composition ensures that all the derivations that arise from composing functions in different orders for a given set of given function-argument relations will produce the SAME interpretation.[19] This fact both sanctions the coherence of the grammar itself and points to a solution to the parsing problem: If these analyses are equivalent, it clearly doesn't matter WHICH of them we find, just so long as we find ONE. A couple of simple strategies immediately suggest themselves as the basis for a parser that just finds one analysis in each equivalence class, paraphrasable as "combine as soon as you can," or "only combine when you have to." A&S suggested that a "reduce first" strategy for a shift-reduce parser, augmented by a means for simulating nondeterminism, would be the basis for an algorithm to do this. This regime favors predominantly left-branching analyses like the above, rather than the standard right-branching surface structures. Pareschi (1986; in preparation) and Pareschi and Steedman (1987) discuss a potentially efficient and grammatically transparent solution to the processing problem.

2. Nonstandard Constituent Coordination

2.1. Contiguous Nonstandard Constituents

D&C and Dowty (1988) point out that Combinatory Grammars not only offer an account of coordinations of verb-groups, but also of the "nonconstituent" coordination of sequences of arguments, because arguments are allowed to type-raise into functions, and then to compose, as in the following example, adapted from Dowty:

(61)

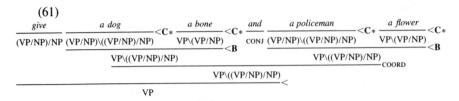

While this derivation invokes the second instance, $<\mathbf{C}_*$, of type-raising, and a third version, $<\mathbf{B}$, of composition, the constraints of Adjacency, Consistency, and Inheritance will not permit rules which would license arbitrary nonconstituent coordinations like the following:

(62) a. *give a bone a dog and a flower a policeman
      b. *a policeman a flower and give a dog a bone

Dowty points out that a combinatory grammar also allows such right node–raised nonstandard constituents to "strand" prepositions, just as standard constituent coordinates can, as in

(63)

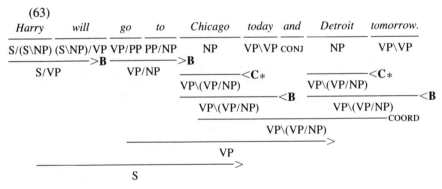

He also points out that the acceptability of such strandings appears to be precisely parallel to island constraints on leftward extraction, as would be predicted on the present model, in which both rightward and leftward extraction depend on the possibility of assembling the residue into a single entity via the composition rule. The following two examples from Dowty illustrate the parallel:[20]

(64) a. *Who did you read a book about?*
      b. **Who did you read Sue's book about?*
      c. **Who did you lose a book about?*

(65) a. *John read a book about Nixon on Monday and Reagan on Tuesday.*

    b. *John read Sue's book about Nixon on Sunday and Reagan on
       Tuesday.
    c. *John lost a book about Nixon on Sunday and Reagan on Tuesday.

2.2. Gapping

Both Dowty and D&C point out that the tactic of type-raising arguments,
composing them, and then conjoining the resulting nonstandard constituents permits the "backward gapping" construction found in coordinate
clauses in SOV languages. Thus, a subject and an object NP can compose,
via the forward type-raising rule and forward composition:

(66) SOV (TV = $(S\backslash NPs)\backslash NPo$):

$$
\begin{array}{ccc}
\textit{Barry} & \textit{potatoes} & \textit{brought} \\
\rule{2cm}{0.4pt}\!>\!\mathbf{C}_* & \rule{3.5cm}{0.4pt}\!>\!\mathbf{C}_* & \rule{2cm}{0.4pt} \\
S/(S\backslash NP) & (S\backslash NP)/((S\backslash NP)\backslash NP) & (S\backslash NP)\backslash NP
\end{array}
$$

$$
\begin{array}{c}
\rule{8cm}{0.4pt}\!>\!\mathbf{B} \\
S/((S\backslash NP)\backslash NP)
\end{array}
$$

$$
\rule{11cm}{0.4pt}\!> \\
S
$$

The resulting nonstandard constituent can therefore conjoin:

(67) $[Barry\ potatoes]_{S/((S\backslash NP)\backslash NP)}$ and $[Harry\ bread]_{S/((S\backslash NP)\backslash NP)}$ $eats_{(S\backslash NP)\backslash NP}$

What is more, the Principles of Adjacency, Consistency, and Inheritance
again limit the possible constituent orders. They do not permit any raised
categories or rules of composition that would produce a LEFTWARD-looking
function, so that no other constituent orders, in particular the corresponding "forward gapping" construction, are allowed on the SOV lexicon:[21]

(68) a. *Bread Harry and potatoes Barry eats.
     b. *Harry bread eats, and Barry potatoes.

    As Dowty pointed out, the position is reversed for verb-initial languages.
Again a subject and object can raise and compose to yield a single function
over the verb, this time via leftward type-raising and composition:[22]

(69) VSO (TV = $(S/NPo)/NPs$):

$$
\begin{array}{ccc}
\textit{Eats} & \textit{Barry} & \textit{potatoes} \\
\rule{2cm}{0.4pt} & \rule{3.5cm}{0.4pt}\!<\!\mathbf{C}_* & \rule{2cm}{0.4pt}\!<\!\mathbf{C}_* \\
(S/NP)/NP & (S/NP)\backslash((S/NP)/NP) & S\backslash(S/NP)
\end{array}
$$

$$
\begin{array}{c}
\rule{8cm}{0.4pt}\!<\!\mathbf{B} \\
S\backslash((S/NP)/NP)
\end{array}
$$

Again, the nonstandard constituent can coordinate:

(70) $Eats_{(S/NP)/NP}$ $[Barry\ potatoes]_{S\backslash((S/NP)/NP)}$ and $[Harry\ bread]_{S\backslash((S/NP)/NP)}$

Again, the three principles exclude any other constituent orders, including the "backward gapping" construction which appears to be universally disallowed in verb-initial languages:

(71) a. *Eats bread Harry and potatoes Barry.
    b. *Harry bread, and brought Barry potatoes.

According to the present combinatory theory of grammar, verb-initial "forward gapping," verb-final "backward gapping," and "right node–raising" reduce (as Maling's 1972 article implicitly suggests they should) to simple constituent coordination, together with the earlier examples of "coordination reduction." But what about sentence-MEDIAL ellipsis? In particular, what about gapping in SVO languages like English?

It is striking that the theory so far affords almost everything we need in order to account for gapping in English. For a start, both the residues and the gapped element itself in each of the following well-known family of gapped sentences are all constituents under one or other of the possible analyses of *you want to try to begin to write a play:*

(72) *I want to try to begin to write a novel, and . . .*
    a. *you,*   *to try to begin to write a play.*
    b. *you,*   *to begin to write a play.*
    c. *you,*   *to write a play.*
    d. *you,*   *a play.*

For example, the following example, adapted from D&C, is the analysis that goes with version (72c), in which the nonstandard constituent *want to try to begin,* of category (S\NP)/VP', is built by the composition rule:[23]

(73)

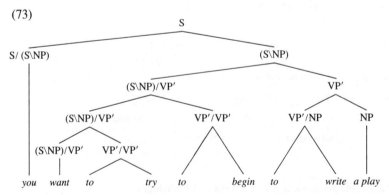

What's more, in all the earlier examples the coordination of sequences of arguments was brought under the general mechanism of constituent coordination by type-raising the arguments and composing to yield a function over verbal and sentential functors—as in the English example (61), repeated here:

(74) $give_{(VP/NP)/NP}$ [$a\ dog\ a\ bone$]$_{VP\backslash((VP/NP)/NP}$ and [$a\ policeman\ a$
      $flower$]$_{VP\backslash((VP/NP)/NP}$

It is therefore tempting to believe that the sequence of arguments that is left behind by gapping is also a constituent assembled by type-raising and composition, and that gapping is also an instance of constituent coordination under the extended sense of the term implicated in combinatory grammar. Such a proposal raises two questions: Do the degrees of freedom that the theory allows in fact permit the formation of the requisite nonstandard constituent on the right of the conjunction-word? And, if so, how can the LEFTMOST conjunct be decomposed to yield another constituent of the same type, despite the fact that the noun phrases (or other arguments) are not contiguous?

Such a constituent would semantically be a function over a tensed verb, so its syntactic category would have to follow suit, as in:

(75) ($A\ dog\ likes\ a\ bone,\ and$) [$a\ policeman,\ a\ flower$]$_{S\backslash((S\backslash NP)/NP}$

It is therefore immensely interesting that the four rules of composition (19) and the two rules of type-raising (38) allow exactly ONE way of assembling such a constituent, given the lexical category of the English verb.[24] The only one of the four composition rules that has hitherto remained unused, the "Forward-crossing" composition rule (19b), will allow the English type-raised subject category to compose with the English type-raised object caegory to its right to yield the desired category:

(76) SVO (TV = $(S\backslash NPs)/NPo$):

$$\ldots and\ \frac{\overline{\qquad Barry \qquad}}{S/(S\backslash NP)}{>}\mathbf{C}_* \frac{\overline{\qquad potatoes \qquad}}{(S\backslash NP)\backslash((S\backslash NP)/NP)}{<}\mathbf{C}_*$$
$$\frac{\qquad\qquad\qquad\qquad\qquad\qquad\qquad\qquad\qquad\qquad}{S\backslash((S\backslash NP)/NP)}{>}\mathbf{B}x$$

The result is the LEFTWARD-looking functor characteristic of the gapped conjunct in verb-initial languages. Universal Grammar will not permit the derivation of the parallel rightward-looking functor characteristic of verb-final languages.

For reasons that were noted in §1.2.3, the forward slash-crossing composition rule cannot apply freely, or wild overgeneration will result. One way of accomplishing the requisite restriction is to restrict it to apply only when Y is S\NP, as follows:

(77) English Forward Mixing Composition ($>$**B**x):
CONJ   X/Y:F   Y\Z:G $=>$ CONJ   X\Z:**B**FG
where Y $=$ (S\NP)

The rule is further restricted so that it can only apply to functions that are immediately to the right of a conjunction like *and*, in order to prevent derivations like the following:[25]

(78) * | *Eats* | *Harry* | *beans.* |

$$\frac{\frac{\text{(S\NP)/NP}\quad\text{S/(S\NP)}\quad\text{(S\NP)\((S\NP)/NP)}}{\text{S\((S\NP)/NP)}}*}{\text{S}}<$$

More important than the restrictions that hedge this rule about in English is the fact that the three principles of Adjacency, Consistency, and Inheritance, in conjunction with the SVO category of the English tensed verb, will not permit any OTHER type of function over tensed verbs to be constructed. In particular, the Principle of Inheritance requires that the composite function be BACKWARD-looking, just as in the case of a VSO language (cf. exs. (69)–(70)). A constituent of this category must occur to the right of the verb, so the fact that English and other SVO languages follow VSO languages in gapping on the right seems likely to be explained according to the present theory in terms of independently motivated universal properties of grammar. This result seems striking, regardless of what may be the solution to the second problem of decomposing the LEFT conjunct into an adjacent nonstandard constituent of the same type, together with the gapped verbal element.[26]

2.3. Constraints and Nonconstraints on Gapping

Of the constraints on gapping proposed by Hankamer (1971), Jackendoff (1971), Langendoen (1975), Stillings (1975), and Sag (1976), summarized by Neijt (1979), the most robust is exemplified by the following nonsentence:

(79) *I know that Harry brought bread, and [I think that Barry]$_{*\text{S/(S\NP)}}$, beans.*

This sentence is excluded by the present grammar for the same reason as the examples in (40), repeated here:

(80) a. *[Mary and I think that Harry] will lend us the money.*
     b. *[I think that Harry and Mary] will lend us the money.*

That is, the restriction of forward composition to functions in which Z is not S\NP (see ex. (41)) forbids the construction of the constituent *I think that Harry,* which all of these sentences would require. Nor can *I think that*$_{S/S}$ compose with *Barry, beans*$_{S\backslash((S\backslash NP)/NP)}$, because of the restrictions on the rule of forward mixed composition.

Examples like the following have been held by some of the above authors not to permit readings in which everything but the subject and the final NP(s) are gapped:

(81) a. *Harry thinks that hedgehogs eat mushrooms, and Barry, frogs.*
      b. *Harry went to London, and Barry, Detroit.*
      c. *Harry gave a bone to a dog, and Barry, a flower to a policeman.*
      d. *Harry gave a dog a bone, and Barry, a policeman a flower.*

However, Kuno (1976) has shown that similar sentences are merely very contextually demanding, and are acceptable when preceded by sentences establishing appropriate "open propositions" (in the sense of Prince 1986), such as the following:[27]

(82) a. *What do Harry and Barry think that hedgehogs eat?*
      b. *Which cities did Harry and Barry go to?*
      c. *What did Harry and Barry give to whom?*
      d. *What present did Harry and Barry give which animate being?*

They are accepted by the present grammar.

3. Conclusion

Since Curry's Bracket Abstraction Algorithm (Curry & Feys 1958: ch. 6) guarantees that we can accomplish ANY abstraction using small sets of combinators, the mere capture of a grammatical fragment in combinatory terms is not in itself remarkable. What IS interesting is the simplicity of the present fragment, and the fact that there is such a direct fit between natural language coordination phenomena and the unorthodox constituents that are engendered by the inclusion of a small and restricted set of typed combinators, particularly composition. In particular, the principles of Consistency and Inheritance seem to constrain constituent order in keeping with known universal tendencies among natural languages. In this respect, the theory may represent an advance on the related categorial analyses of van der Zee (1982), Cremers (1983), Dowty (1988), Wood (1986), and Oehrle (1987), which also extend the notion of constituency. While many constructions have not been considered in this short paper, it seems likely that all the nonstandard constituents permitted by the combinatory rules for English (which is a great many) can coordinate. It is not yet clear whether the converse holds, and that everything that can coordinate can be handled similarly straightforwardly by combinatory rules. The verb-medial gapping construction discussed here is a crucial test case. There appear to be clear hints that it too will prove amenable to analysis within combinatory grammar.

NOTES

1. Curry himself followed Ajdukiewicz and others in suggesting the existence of a close link between applicative systems and natural language syntax (see Curry & Feys 1958:274–75; Curry 1961).

2. The "wrapping" operation of Bach and Dowty is adjacent in the sense used here, since it can be regarded as an operation on three adjacent items.

3. The present theory follows Lambek and others including CGPG in this respect and differs from predecessors like Ades and Steedman (1982; hereafter A&S) and D&C, which used NONdirectional slashes, constraining order in the combinatory rules.

4. The reader is warned that some authors, including Lambek and Bach, use an opposite convention, under which this function would be written "NP\S," with the leftward-combining argument on the left. This alternative is less readable with the multiple argument function categories used in the present theory. Still others, such as Moortgat and van Benthem (1986), use the third possible convention, under which both rightward and leftward arguments appear to the left.

5. We may note in passing that the last, subject, argument of the verb must be defined for plural or singular number by the inflection of the verb, and that the subject argument must be compatible with this specification, to capture basic subject–verb agreement using an obvious unification-based mechanism of the kind proposed for this problem by Shieber (1986). See CGPG for further remarks on agreement and Pareschi and Steedman (1987) for further remarks on unification-based implementations.

6. The notion of "like category" is of course problematic for any theory of syntax, as well-known examples like Sag et al.'s (1985)

(i) *Pat is a Republican and proud of it.*

reveal. We shall not discuss such problems here, assuming that some finer-grained feature-based categorization of atomic categories like NP such as the one offered by them can be applied to the present theory. We also ignore the question of multiple coordination here and return to the semantics of the rule at the end of the section. It might seem that a more natural expedient for a categorially based approach would be to entirely eschew such syncategorematic rules, and to associate the following categorial type with conjunctions:

(ii) *and* = $(T\backslash(*T)/T$

where the lexical category itself includes a "polymorphic type" variable, written T. However, such a category won't quite do, for conjunctions do not in fact behave like a normal category. Most obviously, they cannot conjoin. They also cannot compose.

7. The reader is directed to the earlier papers for further discussion of the sense in which functional composition is "simple." There is a precedent for the inclusion of rules of composition in CG in the work of Lambek (1958, 1961) and Geach (1972). See Wall (1972) for a brief introduction to the concept of functional composition.

8. Again this principle could be shown to follow from the fact that directionality is a feature of ARGUMENTS, and from the fact that the operations of combinatory grammar are elementary combinators like functional composition.

9. Besides the forward rule (19a), Dowty (1988) has used the backward rule (19c) in his account of English "nonconstituent" coordination. While Dowty suggested that "slash-crossing" composition should be excluded, the slash-crossing backward rule (19d) is introduced in CGPG and has also been proposed by Moortgat (1988) and Morrill (1987) to account for right extraposition, and a very restricted version of the forward crossing rule (19b) is discussed below.

10. This section is somewhat technical and may be skipped on a first reading.

11. The example involves a double right-node raising and is therefore a little clumsy. However, given the account of left extraction sketched below, the same point could be made with less pragmatically loaded examples like

(i) (*a Cadillac*) *which I will offer, and may give, to that man*

12. I do not intend to suggest that the present syntactic use of type-raising is related in any way to Montague's account of quantifier scope phenomena. Again, there are precedents for including type-raising in natural-language grammars in the work of Lambek (1958, 1961), Lewis (1970), and Geach (1972). See CGPG for remarks on subject–verb agreement and the type-raised subject category.

13. D&C, CGPG, and Zeevat, Klein, and Calder (1987) use different notations, but they all amount to the same thing.

14. The present rule continues to allow examples like the following:

(i) a. *Eat apples, I will!*
    b. *I will, and you won't, lend Harry the money.*
(ii)   *One big, and two little, cups of coffee.*

15. The restriction on X is needed because not everything that we can right node–raise out of can we leftward-extract over. For example, compare *Harry and Barry went home* and **went home Harry and Barry*.

16. The assumption of an N modifier analysis of relatives is a mere notational convenience. See D&C for remarks on the equivalence of N–modifier and NP–S analyses in grammars using functional composition.

17. See Szabolcsi (1987) for an account of "pied piped" *Wh-* items like *in pictures of whom.*

18. That is not to say that ALL phenomena which have been gathered under the right roof constraint are artifactual. In particular, certain constraints on scope of relatives extraposed from subjects and objects noted by Baltin (1981) do not fall

under the above generalization and arise in the present theory because relatives are functions, not arguments.

19. This is not to say that composition will induce no new semantically distinct readings from a pure categorial grammar. The inclusion of the nonassociative operation of application, together with the presence of higher-order functions, may actually induce new function–argument relations.

20. Some apparent possibilities for extraction from nonstandard constituents are not explained by the apparatus introduced so far. Examples like the following, which are a type discussed by Morrill (1987) within a different but related framework, appear to require a generalization of type-raising:

   (i) a. *Which famous linguist did you put a book by on the table and a picture of on the mantlepiece?*
        b. *Which table did you put a book on and a chair beside?*
        c. *Which famous linguist did you give a book by Harry to and a portrait of to Barry?*

While the account of parasitic gaps offered in CGPG has not been discussed here, the following coordinate structure, also of a type discussed by Morrill, presents similar problems for that account:

   (ii) *Which famous linguist will you present a picture of to today, and an article about to tomorrow?*

21. Like other Germanic languages, Dutch, as discussed in D&C, DOES allow coordinations on the pattern of (68b) in subordinate clause conjunctions. This exception to the SOV pattern, which is discussed briefly below, is presumably related to the fact that these languages possess an SVO clause constituent order as well.

22. The alert reader will note that the derivation assumes that the subject is the FIRST argument of the VSO verb, not the last, as in the Germanic languages. This assumption seems to be a forced move under the present theory, at least for VSO languages that permit gapping.

23. The realization that such widely assumed conditions on rules as the Constituent Condition of Chomsky (1976) imply surface structures like (73) appears from time to time in the literature, only to be as quickly suppressed—cf. Neijt (1979:20–22).

24. For the present we are only considering gapped sentences which leave two arguments. More generally, for any *n* arguments and any function category over those arguments, the theory allows just one gapped category.

25. This restriction might appear to introduce context sensitivity into the rules. In fact, it is just a clumsiness in the notation induced by the use of the (notationally transparent but inelegant) syncategorematic coordination rule 10—cf. n. 6. We shall ultimately want to make conjunction words like *and* into functions, whose output category will be distinguished by some feature to which the application of the Forward Mixing Composition rule can be made sensitive in the usual way. The fact that the restriction is language-specific implies that other languages with simi-

lar lexicons will allow sentences like (77). The phenomenon of subject-verb inversion in Germanic languages may offer a confirmatory example. (Cf. Hepple, in preparation.)

26. Of course, everything hinges on there actually BEING a constrained way to effect the decomposition of the left conjunct. Any addition to the grammar that is introduced to accomplish such a decomposition must conform to the principles of Adjacency, Consistency, and Inheritance if it is not to compromise the result that has just been outlined. In particular, any such addition must continue to exclude examples like (35) (repeated here):

(i) *I will cook the mushrooms, and Betty will eat
    ─────────────────────────── ──── ──────────────
                 S   CONJ   S/NP

See Steedman (1987b) for a proposal.

27. The unexplained difficulty of the last of these may explain the similar difficulty of (81d). See D&C and Abbott (1976) for remarks on the pragmatic complexity of the related right-node-raised constructions.

10

Subjects, Specifiers, and X-Bar Theory

TIM STOWELL

1. Introduction

This paper deals with two related issues. The first is the relationship between the Subject position and the Specifier position in terms of X-bar theory. Are these positions distinct in X-bar terms, or are Subjects simply one of a number of types of Specifiers? Do these positions generalize across syntactic categories, or are they restricted to some categories and not others? The second issue concerns the relation between a determiner and a noun within a common noun phrase such as *the man* or *a man*. From a syntactic perspective, the issues are (i) whether the determiner (D) or the noun (N) is the X-bar head of a common noun phrase, and (ii) why nouns typically require Determiners.

Since the first issue calls into question the categorial status of common noun phrases (i.e. whether they should be analyzed as NPs or as DPs), I use the term CNP ("common noun phrase") to refer to these constituents in theory-neutral terms. As for the second issue, it is unclear whether the syntactic relation between D and N is responsible for the fact that nouns typically need determiners (and vice versa), or whether this follows in some way from semantic properties of D and N, especially with respect to their referential properties.

1.1. Adjectives and Nouns

As a point of departure, consider the difference between the categories A and N in English. Adjectives function as purely predicative categories; A may be a one-place or a two-place predicate. Like verbs, adjectives may

I would like to thank the following people for valuable discussion of the material in this paper: Steve Abney, Mark Baltin, Tom Ernst, Carlos Otero, Anne Rochette, Mamoru Saito, and Peggy Speas. The paper is based on talks given in 1986 at New York University and the University of Ottawa, and in 1987 at the University of California, San Diego. In addition, the usual disclaimers apply.

take complements, thus forming an A′ predicate that assigns the adjective's external θ-role to some NP outside A′.

(1) a. *John is* [$_{A'}$ *angry at Bill*].
   b. *I consider Frank* [$_{A'}$ *responsible for this*].

The exact location of the subject is controversial. For some theories, the subject is within a maximal projection AP, as in the Small Clause theories of Stowell (1981, 1983) and Manzini (1983). For other theories, e.g. that of Williams (1983), the subject must be external to AP. On the former view, the maximal projection of A is a clausal structure (a Small Clause); on the latter view, the maximal projection of A is an open one-place predicate phrase.[1] I will not choose between these approaches at this point.

   The status of nouns is less clear. It has often been suggested that nouns, like verbs and adjectives, are predicative categories. For instance, some nouns seem to function as two-place predicates:

(2) a. *a* [$_{N'}$ *father of two children*]
   b. *the* [$_{N'}$ *employee of John*]
   c. *John's* [$_{N'}$ *picture of David*]

And CNPs appear to function predicatively in copular and Small Clause constructions:

(3) a. *John is a good doctor.*
   b. *I consider Frank a genius.*

Adjectives are sometimes said to differ from verbs in terms of the types of predicates they denote: verbs function as names for actions or states of affairs, whereas adjectives function as names for properties. In this respect, common nouns like *book* and *genius* presumably resemble adjectives, whereas derived nominals like *destruction* presumably resemble verbs.

   In other contexts, CNPs seem to function neither as open predicates nor as clauses (closed predicates), but rather as referential expressions. Thus in examples like (4), the CNP is neither predicated of some other NP nor construed as a clause; instead, it refers to an individual or to a group of individuals:

(4) a. *The woman met those men.*
   b. *A comet hit the earth.*

Thus nouns seem to have a dual nature: like adjectives and verbs, they seem to have an internal argument structure (θ-grid); but unlike adjectives and verbs, they seem to be able to function as referring expressions.

1.2. Nouns and Specifiers

It is plausible to suppose that this difference between nouns and adjectives is related to another difference: nouns normally require specifiers (quantifiers, numerals, determiners, or possessive CNPs), whereas adjectives do not:

(5) a.   *John is (quite) daft.*
(6) a.   **(The) man read *(one) book.*
   b.   **(Bill's) sister read *(every) book.*

A question arises immediately concerning the syntactic position of the required determiner in (6). The traditional Extended Standard Theory analysis places D in the Spec position. But, as Abney (1986) and others have observed, this allows a head (X-zero) category to occur in a position that is defined as a phrasal XP position in the X-bar theory proposed by Chomsky (1986):

(7)

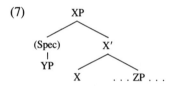

If all lexical items must function as heads of XPs, then D must appear as the head of DP. The structural relation between the DP and the NP projection of the noun is therefore either (8a) or (8b):

(8) a.   [$_{NP}$ DP N']
   b.   [$_{DP}$ D NP]

In (8a), DP occurs as the specifier of NP, as in Jackendoff (1977); in (8b), NP occurs as a complement of D, as in Abney (1986), on analogy to VP as a complement of Infl in IP. According to (8a), NPs require Specifiers obligatorily for some reason, whereas Abney's structure in (8b) claims that NP functions as an (obligatory) complement of D.

   It is not obvious that either of these approaches is intrinsically preferable as a basis for explaining why many nouns, unlike adjectives, typically require Specifiers. The structure in (8b) could be forced directly by stipulating that most verbs select DP arguments rather than NP arguments, and that NP is normally selected as a direct complement of D or Q—just as VP usually shows up as the structural complement of Infl (I). But this hardly amounts to an explanation in itself, since it begs the question of why these verbs select DPs and not NPs in the first place. In other words, it restates a

noun's syntactic dependence on D indirectly, using the selectional properties of the verb as a medium, without any obvious gain in explanatory
power.

The structure in (8a) could be forced by stipulating that NP must have a
Specifier position and that DP, QP, and genitive NP are the only categories
that may occupy this position. But the claim that NP requires a Specifier is
basically a restatement of the fact that we wish to explain. Suppose that this
category-specific stipulation were eliminated in favor of a category-neutral
version of Chomsky's (1982) Extended Projection Principle, such as (9):

(9) Every XP must contain a Specifier position.

If the Subject of a sentence is analyzed as the Specifier of IP, and if the
Subject of a Small Clause is treated in a parallel fashion as the Specifier of
the Small Clause XP, then (9) would have the potential of treating the obligatoriness of Specifiers in NP as part of the same phenomenon. Note that I
am assuming that Subjects are Specifiers, i.e. that there is no X-bar theoretic distinction between the Subject position and the Specifier position.
I question this assumption later on, but for present purposes assume that it
is correct. The obligatory Specifier position in NP would no longer be
exceptional, but a new problem would arise: why are null Specifiers permitted in AP but not in NP in examples like (6)?

It is doubtful that the module of phrase structure is directly implicated in
this apparent categorial asymmetry. First of all, determiners may sometimes be required even in AP (i.e. with superlative adjectival predicates).
Conversely, overt determiners are not required with certain classes of
nouns, including mass nouns and bare plurals (as well as proper names,
which might be classified as nouns). It is hard to determine how much importance to attribute to this fact, since these same types of nouns require
determiners in some languages (e.g. mass nouns and generic plurals in
French), whereas in other languages determiners are never required with
any nouns. Thus it is conceivable that from the perspective of the theory of
phrase structure, the Specifier position is always available as an option, and
that when it is required obligatorily, this is a function of other factors (e.g.
semantic conditions on the referential properties of nouns).

1.3. Outline

I do not attempt to account for the cross-linguistic variation in determiner
selection in this paper, and confine my attention to English. In §2, I provide some syntactic evidence that supports the DP structure proposed by
Abney in (8b) as the correct structure for CNPs. In §3, I propose a semantically based distinction between DP and NP, based on the idea that N is

uniformly predicative and D is uniformly referential. I then discuss evidence for and against this view, involving c-selection and the internal structure of nominal Small Clauses. In §4, I discuss an alternative account of the DP/NP distinction, based loosely on Carlson's (1977) theory of reference to kinds. This overcomes the major objection to the theory proposed in §3.

2. In Support of DP

For Abney (1986), Fukui (1986), and Speas (1986), the chief motivation for the DP hypothesis is structurally based: they seek to treat all X (X-zero) categories as heads of their own projections, and to unify the X-bar theoretic treatment of the functional categories C (Comp), I (Infl), and D. According to their version of the DP hypothesis, every functional category X takes a single XP phrase as its complement, forming a functional category X' (X-single bar); thus D combines with NP to form D', just as C combines with IP to form C', and I combines with VP to form I'. In each case, X' then combines with a specifier to form a maximal projection XP (X-max).[2] In this section, I discuss some evidence that appears to lend empirical support to the DP hypothesis, based on the distribution of PRO in CNPs (2.1) and on the behavior of CNPs with respect to constraints on extraction (2.2). I defer until §3 the issues of why CNPs should be DPs rather than NPs and why nouns require Ds in the first place.

2.1. PRO in NP and the DP Hypothesis

2.1.1. PRO in IP. The occurrence of PRO in NP provides the basis of an argument for the DP hypothesis. The argument here is based on the theory of the distribution of PRO developed in Chomsky (1981). According to this theory, the fundamental distributional property of PRO is that it must appear in an ungoverned position. (This follows as a theorem of Binding theory under the assumption that PRO is a pronominal anaphor, but I will not concern myself here with the issue of how the ungoverned status of PRO is derived.)[3]

When PRO occurs as the subject of an infinitival IP, as in control structures, the subject position must be ungoverned. This contrasts with the distribution of lexical NP or trace, which must appear in governed positions in order to satisfy principles of Case theory and the Empty Category Principle (ECP) respectively. With infinitival complements, this seems to be determined by whether a CP node dominates IP. If IP occurs as a direct complement of V (as in Exceptional Case Marking (ECM) and raising structures), then the subject of IP is governed by V; if IP occurs as the structural complement of a null C in CP, then the subject is ungoverned.

There are different theories about the IP/CP distinction and the status of infinitival clauses as barriers to government. Chomsky (1981) took S′ (CP) to be the maximal projection of S (IP) and claimed that all maximal projections are barriers to government, thus treating S′ (CP) as the crucial barrier protecting the subject of IP from government, as in (10a). On the other hand, Chomsky (1986) treats both IP and CP as maximal and develops a more complex theory of barrierhood to distinguish between infinitives with PRO subjects (as in (10b)) and ECM and raising infinitives (as in (10c)):

(10)

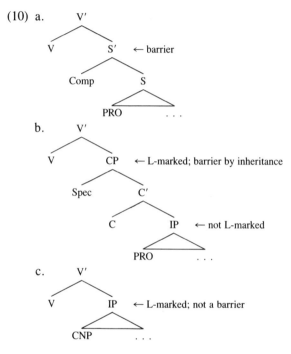

Chomsky's theory claims that maximal projection XPs may become barriers to government in one of two ways. First, XP is an INTRINSIC barrier to government of Y if XP is not L-marked, where L-marking usually corresponds to θ-marking under government by a lexical head. The only exception to this is IP, which is not an intrinsic barrier. Second, XP is a barrier for government of Y by INHERITANCE if XP dominates a non–L-marked ZP category, where ZP dominates Y. In (10b), CP is not an intrinsic barrier for government of PRO by the matrix V, since CP is L-marked by V; but it is a barrier by inheritance, since CP dominates a non–L-marked IP that dominates PRO. In (10c), IP is L-marked by the governing V, and no barrier intervenes between the subject of IP and the governing matrix verb.

Thus IP, like any other category, is transparent to government when it occurs as a complement of V.[4]

2.1.2. PRO in Small Clauses.   My (1983) theory of the X-bar structure
of Small Clauses forced me to assume that XPs are not always intrinsic
barriers to government. This followed from the theoretical claim that Small
Clauses are maximal projections (XPs) of the heads of their predicates. The
basic empirical observation is that the Subject position of a θ-marked
Small Clause always seems to be governed by the matrix verb. In the Small
Clauses in (11a)–(11b) the matrix verb governs and assigns Case to the
Small Clause subject; in (11c)–(11d) the verb lexically governs the subject
trace for the ECP:[5]

(11) a. *I consider [John fascinating].*
      b. *I made [them angry/leave the room].*
      c. *Who did you hear [[e] leave the room]?*
      d. *John seems [[e] angry].*

Furthermore, PRO is always prohibited from appearing in the Subject position of a Small Clause complement:

(12) a. **Kevin heard* [PRO *read the lesson*].
      b. **Sam considers* [PRO *fascinating*].
      c. **It/there was heard* [PRO *read the lesson*].   (*it* = expletive)
      d. *It/there was considered* [PRO *fascinating*].   (*it* = expletive)

Chomsky (1981) accounted for (12) by assuming that the head of the Small
Clause governs its own Subject position. But given that L-marked XPs are
normally transparent to government (*pace* inheritance), we are free to assume that the subject of the Small Clause in (11) and (12) is governed by
the matrix verb, even if the Small Clause is treated as a maximal XP projection of its predicate, as in Stowell (1983).[6]

2.1.3. PRO in NP.   Now consider the category N. In certain nominal
Small Clause constructions, NP is unexceptional; V governs the subject
of the NP Small Clause across the L-marked NP boundary, as shown by
the occurrence of accusative NP subjects and NP-trace subjects, and by
the exclusion of PRO subjects in (13) and (14):

(13) a. *They elected [him president of the class].*
      b. *He was elected [t president of the class].*
      c. **They elected* [PRO *president of the class*].
(14) a. *Mary considers [him heir to the throne].*
      b. *He is considered [t heir to the throne].*
      c. **Mary considers* [PRO *heir to the throne*].

The barrier status of referential CNPs is much less clear. Tests based on Case-marking and ECP do not indicate unambiguously that the subject of a referential CNP may be governed by an external verb, and if anything they seem *prima facie* to point in the opposite direction (see §2.2).

With respect to the distribution of PRO, the evidence seems contradictory; in some cases PRO is excluded, while in others it is apparently allowed. Interestingly, this apparent contradiction can be resolved if the DP hypothesis is assumed, and this is what I argue here. Chomsky (1981) claimed that PRO is excluded in CNPs, pointing to examples like (15a), where the lack of an overt determiner is supposed to allow PRO to occupy the Spec position of NP, under the implied assumption that either PRO or a determiner (but not both) can occupy this position:

(15) a. *John bought [PRO *('s) book*]. (= *'John bought his (own) book.'*)
      b. *John bought* [*a/the shoe*]. (*not* = *'John bought a/the shoe of his.'*)

This latter assumption may not be correct, and indeed it is incompatible with the DP hypothesis. Still, (15a) ought to be allowed on analogy with *John bought Bill's book,* where the head D is null. The exclusion of (15a) could be explained if the θ-marked DP is transparent to government by V, thus preventing PRO from occurring in the subject (Spec) position in DP—provided that other factors conspire to exclude any other type of empty category in this position too. The interpretation of the grammatical example (15b) also indicates that PRO may not occur as the subject of DP. With or without a determiner, CNPs headed by nouns such as *book* do not allow the sort of control interpretation that would be expected if PRO were allowed to function as the unexpressed Possessor of the book. Thus (15) suggests that the subject position of the CNP is governed—by the matrix verb, by the head noun, or by both.

But other data suggest that PRO may occur as the subject of a CNP. Many arguments for PRO in CNPs have appeared in the literature; I will not review them here in detail, but a representative sample of the relevant data is provided in (16):

(16) a. *John disapproves of* [*the* PRO *hatred of oneself*].
      b. *John needs* [*a* PRO *talking to t*].
      c. *Bill resented* [*the* PRO *destruction of the city* [PRO *to prove a point*]].
      d. *The boys told* [*a* PRO *story about them*].
      e. *The boys heard* [*a* PRO *story about them*].

In (16a), arbitrary PRO in the CNP is needed to serve as an antecedent of the reflexive *oneself* (Stowell 1983); in (16b), controlled PRO is needed to serve as the antecedent of NP-trace (Clark 1986); in (16c), PRO in the CNP is needed to serve as the antecedent of the controlled PRO in the rationale clause (Roeper 1986). In (16d)–(16e), PRO in the CNP is needed to account for the fact that *them* may be coindexed with *the boys* in (e) but not (d). Assuming that *them* may not be A-bound by PRO in the subject position of NP by virtue of Condition B of Binding theory, the distinction follows if PRO is itself controlled by *the boys* in (d) but not in (e) (Chomsky 1986).

Thus PRO may occur as the subject of an L-marked CNP in at least some cases, indicating that this position is governed neither by the head noun nor by the matrix verb. Government by the head noun can be excluded on general grounds if the government relation holds in only one direction (left-to-right in English), as in Horvath (1981), Kayne (1983), and Stowell (1983). This would ensure that the head of a Small Clause predicate never governs the subject of the Small Clause in English, even if the subject occurs within a projection of the head. Note that essentially the same result would follow if government is restricted in hierarchical terms (e.g. to within X′), as assumed in Lasnik and Saito (1984).

But given Chomsky's (1986) theory of barriers, the matrix verb should govern the prenominal genitive subject position if referential CNPs are simple NPs, since the L-marked NP ought to be transparent to government by V, and this should exclude the possibility of a PRO subject. How, then, should we account for the fact that PRO subjects are allowed in (16)?

2.1.4. *Referential CNPs as Barriers.*   In Stowell (1983), I accounted for the paradigms in (13)–(16) by appealing to the stipulative principles in (17) and (18):

(17) A referring phrase is opaque (to government).

(18) The Possessor θ-role may not be assigned to PRO.

Assuming that N cannot govern the Subject or Specifier position in NP, the crucial issue concerns the status of the CNP as a barrier to government by V. Principle (17) ensures that a referential CNP is opaque to government, even by a verb that θ-marks (L-marks) it. In (13)–(14), the CNP is non-referential, hence transparent to government by V; in (15)–(16) the CNP is referential, hence opaque to government by V. Therefore the contrast between (13)–(14) and (16) follows. Principle (18) comes into play to rule out Chomsky's examples in (15), since these should otherwise be permitted, given (17). A PRO subject in (15) would have to be assigned a Possessor θ-role, since nouns like *shoe* have no true θ-roles other than this to assign. Given (18), PRO violates the Theta Criterion in (15) but not in (16), where the θ-grid of the head N (or its morphological head V) makes another θ-role available.

But (17) and (18) are entirely stipulative, and it would be preferable to deduce their desirable empirical effects as theorems of more general principles. I see no simple account of these effects in a theory which treats CNPs as simple projections of N, but the DP hypothesis offers a way out.[7]

2.1.5. PRO in NP vs. PRO in DP. Suppose that CNPs have Abney's structure in (8b). Then if the Subject position generalizes across syntactic categories, there are two Subject positions available within a CNP: the Subject of DP and the Subject of NP. The structure of NP within DP in (8a) is closely analogous to that of IP within CP. Given that θ-marked (L-marked) XPs are transparent to government, any verb that governs and θ-marks DP should govern its Subject position too, analogous to government across a θ-marked CP, IP, or Small Clause XP complement. But NP within DP, like IP within CP, is not θ-marked by D, so it should be a barrier to government if NP can be an intrinsic barrier. Furthermore, a non–L-marked NP should make the dominating DP node a barrier (via inheritance) for government of the subject of NP, as in (19) (cf. 10b)):

(19)

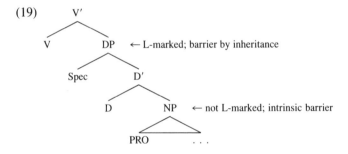

Hence PRO should be able to occur in the ungoverned subject (Spec) position in NP but not in the governed subject (Spec) position in DP.

Suppose now that the Possessor θ-role is assigned only to the subject of DP, by a null or overt head D, while the subject of NP is assigned the external argument of the N′ predicate. The effects of (17) and (18) now follow. PRO may occur in the ungoverned subject position of an NP within DP, since it is protected from government by the NP and/or DP barriers. Here PRO is assigned the external θ-role of N′. The Possessor θ-role is assigned only to the Subject position of DP, which is governed by the matrix verb and therefore excludes PRO. This accounts for (13)–(16) in a unified fashion, deriving the effects of the stipulative exception clause (18).

Suppose that (13)–(14) have essentially the same structure as other Small Clauses, as in (20):

(20)

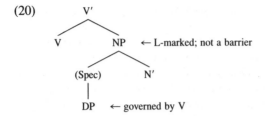

Since PRO may not occur as the subject of any XP that is directly θ-marked by V, these nominal Small Clauses may not function as control complements. There is only one subject position available, and it is governed, thus excluding PRO.

But (15)–(16) have the structure in (19), where one of the two subject positions is ungoverned (the subject of NP). PRO may occur here, as in (16), where it is θ-marked by the N'. Theoretically, PRO could also occur as the subject of NP in (15), but this would result in a Theta Criterion violation, since a determinerless N' of this type has no appropriate θ-role to assign to PRO, for reasons that I examine in more detail in §4. This derives the effects of (17) with respect to (16).

The nominal Small Clauses in (13)–(14) are not fully representative, and other types of nominal Small Clause complements are problematic for this theory in some respects. I will set these aside for the moment, but I will discuss them in more detail in §§3–4. For the facts discussed so far, the distribution of PRO supports the DP hypothesis.

2.2. Case, ECP, and the DP Hypothesis

2.2.1. Case-Marking and Subject Extraction from CNPs. If the subject of an L-marked DP may be governed by a matrix verb, then the data in (21) are potentially problematic:

(21) a. **Bill shot [him father]*. ('Bill shot his father.')
      b. **He was shot [t father]*. ('Bill's father was shot.')
      c. **Whose did Bill shoot [t father]?* ('Whose father did Bill shoot?')
      d. **Who did Bill shoot [t 's father]?* ('Whose father did Bill shoot?')

Apparently, no higher verb may assign (accusative) Case to the subject of a referential CNP complement (21a), and neither raising (21b) nor *wh*-movement (21c)–(21d) may leave a trace in the subject position of a CNP complement. This would follow if a referential DP is a barrier for government by V, as in (17), so Case would be assigned illegitimately in (21a) and an ECP effect would arise in (21b)–(21d). But given Chomsky's (1986) theory of barriers, the paradigm in (21) is unexpected if CNPs are simple

DPs or NPs, since the verb θ-marks the CNP and should be able to govern across it.

Some of the facts in (21) follow independently from other factors. Assuming that the matrix verb may only Case-mark one DP, (21a) is excluded, since the verb cannot Case-mark both a DP complement and the subject of that DP, even if it governs them both, so one of the DPs in (21a) must violate the Case filter (or the Visibility Condition; cf. Chomsky 1981). The unacceptability of (21b) follows from the usual assumption that passive morphology blocks the verb's Case-assigning ability, concomitant with its absorption of the external θ-role; cf. Burzio (1981), Jaeggli (1986). Thus the object of the verb in (21b) violates the Case filter. (This implies that nominal Small Clauses like those in (13) and (14) are not dependent on the matrix verb for Case, i.e. that only referential arguments require Case.)[8]

But (21c)–(21d) remain unexplained if V may govern the subject of DP, since one or the other should be grammatical, depending on whether DP + 's forms a constituent. If 's (POSS) is the head of DP, as Abney (1986) suggests, then the subject of DP should be free to move, as in (21d); if 's is just a genitive Case marker, then the entire DP + 's should be free to move, as in (21c). Therefore either the subject of DP is not governed after all, contrary to our assumption based on the distribution of PRO, or some other factor is responsible for blocking movement here.

2.2.2. Object and Adjunct Extraction from CNPs. It is worth noting in this context that while object extraction from a CNP is possible, as in (22), adjunct extraction is not, as in (23):

(22) a. *Who did you sell [a picture of t]?*
     b. *Who does Jane regret [the dismissal of t]?*
     c. ??*Who did you sell [Mary's picture of t]?*
     d. ??*Who does Jane regret [Bob's dismissal of t]?*
(23) a. *Frans sold [a picture by Rembrandt].*
     b. *Jane regrets [Bob's dismissal of her for incompetence].*
     c. **By whom did Frans sell [a picture t]?*
     d. ***Why does Jane regret [Bob's dismissal of her t]?*

There seem to be at least two factors determining the grammaticality of extraction from a CNP. The first involves the presence or absence of a prenominal genitive, distinguishing between (22a)–(22b) and (22c)–(22d). Torrego (1986) accounts for analogous effects in Spanish by assuming that *wh-* movement proceeds through the Spec position in NP in (22a)–(22b), which is unavailable in (22c)–(22d). She suggests that the ECP is violated in the latter examples, under the assumption that all NP-internal traces are dependent on antecedent government.

But there are two problems with extending this approach to English. First of all, if the prenominal Spec position in NP is supposed to function as an escape hatch for movement in (22a)–(22b), while being filled by the genitive CNPs in (22c)–(22d), then extraction of the genitive CPs ought to be possible in (21c)–(21d). Second, the ECP-based account of (22c)–(22d) leaves unexplained the significant contrast between these examples involving object extraction and those in (23c)–(23d) involving adjunct extraction. The DP hypothesis provides a possible basis for a partial resolution of these facts.

2.2.3. The Specifier of DP as an Escape Hatch for Subjacency. Suppose that nouns, like verbs, may function as "antecedent governors" for θ-marked objects, by virtue of coindexation with a θ-grid in the sense of Stowell (1981). Then the object traces in (22c)–(22d) satisfy ECP, and Subjacency must be responsible for the degraded status of these examples. According to Chomsky's (1986) Bounding theory, movement across a single barrier is basically permitted, but movement across two barriers is not. If CNPs are DPs dominating D and NP, then NP and DP should both function as Subjacency barriers for direct movement out of NP to the matrix Comp: NP, because it is not L-marked; and DP, because it immediately dominates NP. Examples (22a)–(22b) do not violate Subjacency, because *wh* may move through the vacant Spec position in DP. The initial movement crosses just one barrier (NP), and DP is not a barrier for subsequent movement since it is L-marked by V and does not dominate any other barrier for movement from the Spec of DP. (NP, which does not dominate the Spec of DP, does not count.)

Still, successive cyclic movement of an adjunct *wh-* phrase is not permitted, even when the Spec position in DP is vacant, as in (23c). The adjunct/object asymmetry realized in (23) vs. (22) suggests that the ECP is at work in (23). In this respect adjunct extraction from NP and DP differs from adjunct extraction from IP and CP in (24):

(24) a. *By whom did you say* [(*t*) *that this picture was painted t*]*?*
     b. *Why did John say* [(*t*) *that Mary fired her assistant t*]*?*

To distinguish (23c)–(23d) from (24), it seems that we must appeal either to a distinction between NP and IP or to a distinction between DP and CP with respect to barrierhood. A reviewer suggests that we might draw the desired distinction simply by assuming that NP, unlike IP, may function as an intrinsic barrier to government when it is not L-marked, thus blocking adjuncts from moving across NP to the Spec of DP, for ECP (antecedent-government) reasons. This crucially assumes, however, that all DP-internal adjuncts originate within NP at D-structure; otherwise the NP barrier would be irrelevant. Furthermore, this would leave (21c)–(21d) unexplained, assuming that Possessor subjects originate in the subject position of DP, as suggested above.

This suggests that the crucial barrierhood distinction between (24) and (21c)–(21d)/(23c)–(23d) must involve DP and CP. But in fact not all CPs behave the same in this respect, since adjunct extraction from factive CP complements is uniformly prohibited (cf. (24)):

(25) a. *Why do you regret [that John resigned t]?
      b. *When did it surprise you [that John left t]?

It is natural to assume that factive CPs—like referential DPs, but unlike nonfactive CPs—are referential, in which case the prohibition against adjunct extraction could be attributed to (26):

(26) A referential category is a barrier to antecedent government.

Given (26), adjunct extraction is prohibited from the referential DPs in (23c)–(23d) and the referential CPs in (25), since either the original adjunct trace or the intermediate trace in the Spec of DP is not antecedent-governed across the referential DP boundary, resulting in an ECP violation.

Assuming that intermediate traces must be antecedent-governed (Lasnik and Saito 1984), it must be possible for an intermediate trace in the Spec position of a referential DP to be deleted, or else this trace would violate the ECP antecedent-government requirement in the examples involving object extraction from NP in (22a)–(22b); cf. Chomsky (1981), Stowell (1981), Lasnik and Saito (1984).

Returning now to (21c)–(21d), the obvious move to make is to adopt the usual assumption that subjects have the same status as adjuncts with respect to antecedent-government requirements, at least in English. If subjects, like adjuncts, are dependent on antecedent government at LF, then (21c)–(21d) will violate ECP even if the matrix verb governs the Spec of its DP complement. This is true regardless of whether the subject originates as the agentive subject in the Spec of NP (21d) or as the possessive subject in the Spec of DP (21c). Note that (26), unlike the more general (17), leaves our account of the distribution of PRO intact, since referential categories do not block government by a lexical head.

2.2.4. Subjacency and the Strict Cycle Condition.   The subject of NP and the subject of DP may behave alike in terms of their dependence on antecedent government, but there is an interesting fact supporting our contention that the Spec position in DP is the relevant escape hatch for object extraction in (22a)–(22b). As Chomsky (1986 class lecture) has observed, (22c) is marginally acceptable only if the prenominal genitive CNP is interpreted as an Agent, i.e. as the D-structure subject of NP; it can't be interpreted as the Possessor subject of DP. This suggests a refinement of our analysis of object extraction in (22c), so that object extraction is completely impossible unless the Spec of DP is vacant at D-structure and available as an escape hatch for movement.

If the object must move through the Spec position in DP in order to avoid crossing the barriers NP and DP in a single step, it follows immediately that the genitive subject cannot be construed as a Possessor in 22c–22d. (When it is so construed, it originates in the Spec of DP itself.) The intermediate trace in the Spec of DP would still have to disappear in order to avoid an ECP violation, as in (21c)–(21d). Note, however, that this derivation satisfies Subjacency on par with (22a)–(22b), so we could no longer account for the marginality of these object extraction examples in terms of a Subjacency violation. Instead, we would have to relate the contrast between (22a)–(22b) and (22c)–(22d) to the fact that the Spec of NP is filled.

It is unlikely that the Spec of NP is needed as an escape hatch, for reasons already given. It is more probable that the problem arises because the D-structure subject of NP must undergo movement to the Spec position of DP. Abney (1986) suggests that this movement is forced by Case considerations, under the assumption that the Spec of DP, but not the Spec of NP, is a case-marked position. Presumably object extraction through the Spec of DP interferes with this in (22c). If object extraction depends on making use of the Spec of DP position in the (marginal) derivation of (22c), then the Subject of NP could not move to this position until after it is vacated by the subsequent application of *wh-* movement. The derivation would thus violate the Strict Cycle Condition (SCC) proposed by Chomsky (1973) in his original account of the *wh-* Island Condition. (It would also cover the intermediate trace, but since this can be deleted anyway, intermediate trace erasure is presumably nonproblematic; cf. Freidin 1978.)

Thus we can capture the distinction between Possessor subjects and Agent subjects in (22c) if we assume that Subjacency is absolutely inviolable, whereas a slightly weaker effect is incurred by an SCC violation. Suppose that the level of acceptability of a sentence is determined by its preferred derivation. Example (22c) can be derived by violating either Subjacency or the Strict Cycle Condition, but only the derivation violating SCC should be forced to interpret the prenominal genitive NP as an (agentive) subject of NP. The fact that this effect is noticeable in (22c) indicates that the preferred derivation is the one that violates the SCC; the derivation with a Possessor subject of DP violates Subjacency, and is completely impossible.

This indicates that Subjacency is inviolable, and suggests that the usual assumption that Subjacency violations have a weak effect on acceptability is wrong. Instead, it seems that the constraint with the marginal effect on acceptability is the SCC, a conclusion that has obvious implications for the analysis of object extraction from *wh-* islands.

2.2.5. Further Remarks. Principle (26) represents a partial return to our previous stipulation (17). Note that (17) applies to all forms of government, whereas (26) applies only to antecedent government. If (17) were assumed instead of (26), Possessor PRO subjects would no longer be excluded, and (18) would have to be resurrected. Although (26) remains a stipulation, it might conceivably be possible to reduce it to an effect of Rizzi's relativized version of Chomsky's (1986) Minimality Condition, if a referential D can block antecedent government (but not head government) into DP via Minimality.[9]

Principle (26) is reminiscent of the Specificity Condition (Fiengo & Higginbotham 1980), which prevents an open variable from occurring in a referring CNP. But (26) differs empirically from the latter insofar as it permits *wh* to bind a variable within a referring NP provided that the variable in question is not dependent on the *wh-* phrase for antecedent government. The practical effect of this is that direct object variables are free to occur within referential NPs, which would be prohibited by the Specificity Condition.

I should mention that (26) may not hold universally. It is well known that certain languages allow for possessor raising constructions; this is true, for instance, of Hungarian (Szabolcsi 1984) and many Muskogean languages (Carden, Gordon, & Munro 1982). Whatever proves to be responsible for allowing this, it is clear that this possibility is to be expected if L-marked DPs are transparent to government, abstracting away from the effects of (26).

The main point of §§2.1 and 2.2 has been that the postulation of a DP-level projection makes it possible to account for some otherwise problematic facts involving the distribution of PRO in CNPs and *wh-* extraction from CNPs. These facts cannot naturally be captured in terms of a theory that fails to recognize the extra level of structure. In particular, the structure in (8a) would fail to distinguish between Agentive and Possessive interpretations of PRO (and of prenominal genitives in structures like (22c)), and would fail to predict the barrier effects discussed in §2.2.

3. Reference and the DP Hypothesis

Assuming that the evidence discussed in §2 argues in favor of the DP hypothesis, we must now consider what principled basis there might be for this—i.e. why it should be that nouns need determiners in the first place, and why Abney's structure in (8b), rather than Jackendoff's structure in (8a), must be correct. In §1, I suggested that the special relation between D and N might be a function of the status of CNPs as referential expressions. In this section, I flesh out this idea and discuss some of its advantages and problems.

3.1. Predicative N and Referential D

On the basis of the discussion in §1, we might presume that the determiner serves two logical functions in a CNP: it closes the predicate (binding its open argument) and converts the phrase into a referential expression. It is difficult to see how the determiner's argument-binding function could be responsible for forcing Abney's DP structure in (8b), since Specifier XPs are capable of doing this; if DP were the Specifier of NP as in Jackendoff's structure (8a), the open argument of N' could presumably be bound by DP in Spec. Hence it seems that the most plausible basis for forcing the structure in (8b) involves exploiting the referential status of CNPs.

One way of achieving this would be to say that a referential phrase XP must have a referential head X. Suppose now that nouns are truly pure predicative categories, like adjectives and verbs, contrary to the suggestion in §1 that they are simultaneously predicative and referential. Suppose further that determiners, quantifiers, and so on are referential categories, and that they, unlike nouns, are eligible to function as the heads of referential XPs. In other words, DPs, but not NPs, may function as referential arguments of other predicates.

The status of proper names is obviously relevant to this issue. Although proper names are typically treated equivalently to nouns in terms of morphological processes, they clearly differ from nouns insofar as they are unambiguously referential, nonpredicative categories. I therefore assume that they belong to the same natural syntactic class of categories as DPs, despite the fact that they typically do not take NP complements. I will not discuss them further here.

3.2. NP, DP, and C-selection

If DPs are referential and NPs are nonreferential, it follows that whenever a governing predicate selects a referential expression as an argument, that argument must be a DP or QP, but not an NP, AP, or VP. On the other hand, when a governing predicate selects a Small Clause complement, it would have to be an NP, AP, or VP, and not a DP or QP. Thus Abney's DP structure in (8b) makes it possible in principle for verbs to be distinguished from each other in terms of their selectional properties, according to whether they select NP complements or DP complements. This provides the basis for a possible solution to a problem for the theory of Small Clause structure in Stowell (1981, 1983).

Hornstein and Lightfoot (1984) and Kuroda (1985) note that this theory treats both referential CNPs and nominal Small Clauses as maximal projections of N (i.e. NPs). But verbs must be able to distinguish between these two types of constituents in their selectional properties, since some verbs select one type but not the other:

(27) a. *We deemed **John a liar**.*
     b. *Mary considers **Bill a real friend**.*
     c. *They appointed **the elector of Hanover king of England**.*
(28) a. **Anne deemed **the elector of Hanover**.*
     b. *Mary considered **the guardian of her kids**.*
        (* on relevant reading of *consider*)
(29) a. *I met **the king of England** yesterday.*
     b. *Sally has a crush on **a friend**.*
(30) a. **I met **the elector of Hanover king of England** yesterday.*
     b. **Sally has a crush on **Bill a real friend**.*

As Kuroda (1986) observes, this subcategorization problem can be resolved by exploiting the distinction between NP and DP. Kuroda suggests that referential CNPs are selected as NP complements and that nominal Small Clauses are selected as DPs. However, if we assume that determiners are fundamentally referential and that nouns are fundamentally predicative, the opposite assumption seems more natural, namely that nominal Small Clauses are c-selected as NP complements, and that referential CNPs are c-selected as DP complements, in keeping with our previous idea. (This would obviously preserve Kuroda's intuition that the DP/NP distinction is involved.)

Pesetsky (1982) has argued that subcategorization (c-selection) is determined by semantic selection (s-selection), and that verbs do not actually select the syntactic category of their complements; this simply follows from properties of s-selection and Case assignment. In this respect, Pesetsky differs from Grimshaw (1978, 1981), who argues that s-selection and c-selection must be kept distinct, and that the general association between syntactic categories and semantic categories is simply a function of markedness theory and the theory of acquisition.[10]

If Pesetsky is correct, then the advantage offered by the DP/NP distinction in accounting for the c-selection patterns in (25)–(28) may be illusory. For instance, a verb such as *meet* selects an argument with the semantic type of "individual." It follows that only a phrase with a [+Referential] head will yield an interpretation that is consistent with this requirement. Hence DP rather than NP is required, if only DPs may refer (to individuals). Thus it might be technically correct that referential CNPs are DPs and that nominal Small Clauses are NPs, but this would not be directly relevant for selectional relations that are sensitive only to semantic categories. This point will be of some importance when we examine nominal Small Clause structures in more detail.

3.3. Determiners in Predicative CNPs

So far, I have tacitly been assuming (31):

(31) a. D functions only as the head of DP;
    b. DP is always referential;
    c. The predicate phrases of nominal Small Clauses are nonreferential categories.

Taken together, these assumptions predict that determiners should never show up in predicative CNPs, if these are nonreferential. But the facts suggest otherwise.

The problem arises with the internal structure of nominal Small Clauses. Given (31a) and (31b), determiners should only show up as the heads of referential CNPs. Then given (31c), determiners ought to be unnecessary (and perhaps impossible) within the predicate phrase of a nominal Small Clause. In a very narrow range of constructions, this prediction appears to be borne out. Consider (32) and (33):

(32) a. *We elected John **president of the class**.*
    b. *The queen appointed her lover **treasurer of the realm**.*
(33) a. **We elected John **the/some/this president of the class**.*
    b. **The queen appointed her lover **the/that treasurer of the realm**.*

The boldface determinerless CNPs in (32)–(33) are possible only in predicative environments of this restricted type, and may not serve as referring expressions:

(34) a. *_**President of the class** was at the meeting._
     b. *_The queen visited **treasurer of the realm.**_

The CNPs functioning as predicate phrases in (32) contain nouns belonging to a semantic class of "profession-denoting" predicates. Evidently these nouns need overt determiners only when they function referentially, as (31a)–(31c) predict.

But virtually all other types of Small Clauses behave differently; the nominal predicate phrase of a Small Clause usually has an internal structure that is not discernibly different from that of a referential CNP. Predicative NPs in these contexts contradict the expectations of (31), since the determiner must usually occur even when the CNP functions as a pure predicate as in (35):

(35) a. _Anne's death made George (**the**) **king of England.**_
     b. _Mary considers Bill ?(**the**) **guardian of her children.**_
     c. _Bob called Stan *(**a**) **fool.**_
     d. _This book will make John *(**the**) **most famous person I know.**_

The only predicative context where a determiner is problematic is in the predicate of a Small Clause complement to the _elect_ class in (33), which includes verbs such as _appoint, pronounce,_ and _select._ These verbs typically select profession-class complements, and in many cases their complements, unique among nominal Small Clauses, may contain nominal predicates preceded by the functional head _as._ For present purposes, I will concentrate on the paradigm in (35), which I take to be more representative of nominal Small Clauses than (32) or (33). (An account of the latter is suggested in §4.)

If the presence vs. absence of an overt determiner is a reliable test for DP vs. NP status, then the examples in (35) pose a problem for our referential/predicative distinction between DP and NP. The simple fact is that the occurrence of the determiner generally fails to correlate with the semantic function of the CNP; D is usually obligatory, even when the CNP containing it functions as a predicate.

Evidently, one of the assumptions in (31) must go; the only question is which one. We might reject (31a) and assume that D need not always function as the head of DP. Suppose instead that it can also be adjoined to a projection of N to serve some purpose other than that of heading a referential DP. This would allow us to maintain the assumption that nominal Small Clause predicates are headed by the predicative category N, as in (36):

(36)

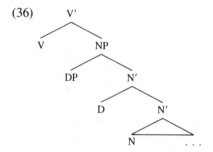

This would be consistent with a uniform interpretation for DP, but at the cost of allowing a functional head such as D to serve as an adjunct rather than as the head of its own XP. Since this would imply that D does not function referentially in (35), an account of its obligatory occurrence would still be called for.

A more serious problem with the solution in (36), as a reviewer reminds me, is posed by examples like (37); cf. Williams (1983):

(37) a. *We made Frank **our** new assistant.*
      b. *John considers James **his** friend.*

If the structure in (36) is assumed for examples like those in (35), then some provision must be made for the occurrence of the possessive pronouns in (37). If the subjects of these Small Clauses occupy the Specifier position in NP, parallel to the status of the subject of a sentence in the Specifier position in IP, then the position of the prenominal genitive pronoun is problematic.

A conceivable approach to (37) is to assume that these genitive pronouns are actually special types of determiners, and that they occur in the position occupied by D in (36). It should be noted in this context that there is a weak control relation holding between the prenominal genitive and the matrix subject in structures like (37), and examples like (38) with a full NP are somewhat marginal for some speakers:

(38) a. ?*We made Frank **the boss's** new assistant.*
      b. ?*John considers James **Mary's** friend.*

Nevertheless, examples like (38) should probably be considered grammatical, whatever is involved in the mild contrast between them and those in (37).[11] Since these are plainly phrasal XP categories, they presumably can't occupy the adjoined D position in a structure of the sort contemplated in (36).

This suggests that an additional Subject or Specifier position is called for within the Small Clauses in (37) and (38). This goes to the heart of an issue alluded to in §1, namely whether the Subject position and the Specifier position are one and the same, or whether they involve two distinct positions defined by the X-bar component. The answer to this question is dependent on whether the two "subjects" in the Small Clauses in (37) and (38) appear within the same maximal projection.

If they do, it follows that either (i) X-bar theory permits any number of specifiers to be adjoined to a lexical category, as Fukui (1986) and Speas (1986) suggest; or (ii) that the English X-bar component actually recognizes a further level of hierarchical structure (cf. Jackendoff 1977):

(39)   XC   ← (Small) Clause

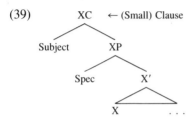

Note that XP in (39) must count as a "maximal projection" in the sense relevant to the theory of movement, at least if it is assumed that only lexical heads and maximal projections may move (Chomsky 1986), since the predicate phrase of a Small Clause may undergo movement, as Williams (1983) observed.

In Abney's (1986) theory of DP structure, prenominal genitives must occupy the Specifier position in DP at S-structure, even if they originate in the subject position of NP. This movement can be forced by assuming that the Spec position in NP is not Case-marked, whereas a head D assigns genitive Case to the Specifier position in DP. Abney's solution has the advantage of capturing the complementary distribution between overt determiners and prenominal genitives without assuming that they occupy the same position. (This is true regardless of whether we take 's to be D itself or a genitive Case marker assigned by a null D.) Moreover, his idea that "prenominal" genitive Case is assigned by D makes sense of gerund structures, which do not appear to involve NP categories. (Instead, IP seems to function as a complement of null D.)[12]

If this theory of genitive Case assignment is adopted, it follows that there must be a D within the Small Clause predicates in (38) to assign genitive Case. Thus the occurrence of the prenominal genitive specifiers in (37) and (38) suggests that the CNP predicate phrases in these structures have the same structure as referential CNPs, i.e. DP, as in (40):

(40)

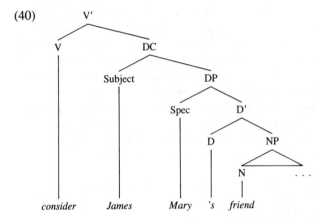

In order to maintain that the constituents labelled DP and DC in (40) are really projections of N, we would have to assume that even Ds that are adjoined to N' may assign genitive Case to a preceding DP in the Specifier of NP position, in a structure like (41):

(41)

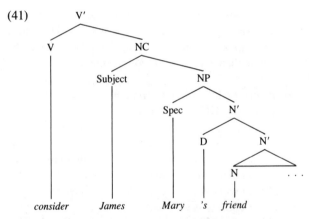

From the perspective of X-bar theory, the more conservative hypothesis that D always functions as a head is probably preferable. However, if we are forced on independent grounds to allow for X-zero operators to be adjoined to phrasal projections, e.g. to account for the placement of negative particles, then (41) might be correct.

It is unclear whether the choice between (40) and (41) can be decided on purely empirical grounds, since we have no pretheoretical basis for presuming that an adjoined D should be unable to assign Case to the Spec position in a structure like (41). On the other hand, our original reason for adopting (41)—the assumption that referential CNPs and predicative CNPs are categorially distinct—does not seem to have much empirical content if D must occur in both types of CNPs. Its only clear advantage lies in distinguishing between DP and NP for c-selectional purposes, but this may not be significant if Pesetsky's claims about c-selection are on the right track.

We are then left with two questions: (i) if the structure in (40) is correct, then why is DP allowed to function as the predicate of a small clause; and (ii) why is a bare (determinerless) NP unable to do so? These questions are addressed in §4.

4. Nouns as Predicates of Natural Kinds

4.1. DP Can Be a Predicate

If DPs really may occur as Small Clause predicates, then we might consider rejecting assumption (31c) in order to preserve the idea that DP is always a referential category, thus concluding that referential expressions may serve as predicates. Relevant to this issue is the contrast between the predicative and referential uses of the verb *be:*

(42) a. *John is a fool.*
     b. *The morning star is the evening star.*

When *be* takes a predicative NP complement, as in (42a), it presumably functions as a raising verb, as in Stowell (1978), Couquaux (1981), Burzio (1981). But when it takes a referential NP complement, as in (42b), it seems to function as a two-place predicate conveying a relation of identity holding between two referential NPs.

In the identificational structure, the two referential arguments are reversible, since identificational predicates are symmetric, as in (43). This is not possible with predicative *be* in (44), abstracting away from the stylistically marked construction of Preposing Around *be* (Emonds 1976):

(43) a. *That teacher over there is my great aunt.*
     b. *My great aunt is that teacher over there.*
(44) a. *Sam is a teacher.*
     b. **A teacher is Sam.*

This is also impossible with the Small Clause structures in (35) and (37), although here we must abstract away from the effects of Heavy NP Shift. Consider (45) and (46):

(45) a. *I made John **my assistant.***
     b. *John considers her **his/?Bob's** best friend.*

(46) a. *I made my **assistant** John.
     b. *John considers **his**/?**Bob's** best friend her.

When the matrix verb selects a nominal Small Clause complement, a CNP with definite reference is prohibited from appearing in the predicate position. Thus it seems that nominal Small Clause predicate phrases do not function as true referring expressions, and that DP must therefore be able to function as a genuine predicate phrase, contrary to the assumption in (31b), which I therefore reject.

Supporting evidence comes from the fact that the predicate phrases in (45) are questioned by *what* rather than by *who,* contrary to what we would expect if these structures were really analogous to those involving identificational *be* in (42b).

4.2. Predicates of Kinds

If DP can function predicatively, this forces us to ask why the DP-level projection is required at all in these contexts. Why can't a bare determinerless NP serve as the predicate of a small clause, as the predicative category AP can?

There is an important semantic distinction between adjectives and nouns that may be relevant here. Common nouns, unlike adjectives, specify membership in a class that constitutes a (natural) kind. Thus a boy can be *manly* without belonging to the natural kind *man,* but a *man* must belong to this natural-kind class. For this reason, the statement *This boy is a real man* is metaphorical in a way that *This boy is very manly* is not. I use the term "(natural) kind" here with some misgivings, since no direct correspondence is assumed with actual natural kinds in the real world; rather it reflects a sort of cognitive ontology underlying the intuition that the set of red things is not perceived as a *kind* in the same sense that the set of hammers is. Intuitions about membership in kinds are presumably provided by an extralinguistic cognitive system.

Carlson (1977) claims that bare plural CNPs are names for kinds, which accords rather naturally with their use as generics, as in *Geese like to fly.* But bare plurals can also be used referentially, as in *John shot geese yesterday;* Carlson argues that even here the bare plural CNP refers to the entire kind. He accounts for the intuition of existential quantification by providing a semantics which allows for indirect reference to groups of individuals belonging to a single kind. When such a group occurs at a particular time and place, the group is said to INSTANTIATE the entire kind at that time and place. This allows for groups to represent entire kinds in the model, while permitting bare plurals to refer to kinds in all cases.

In keeping with the idea that nouns are predicative categories, I would like to suggest that nouns function as predicates denoting the property of INSTANTIATING a kind, more or less in Carlson's sense. In the normal case, only nonsingular sets of individuals may instantiate a kind, as Carlson claims; hence a bare NP may normally be predicated only of a plural expression. This, I suggest, is why determiners are needed in nominal Small Clause predicates. (This proposal is theory-neutral with respect to (40) vs. (41).)

Suppose that the function of the determiner, when it is not used referentially, is to convert a predicate denoting INSTANTIATION of a kind into a predicate denoting MEMBERSHIP in the kind. Thus when D is not functioning as the head of a referential DP, it may still function as the head of predicative category of set-membership. Since an individual may be a member of a kind, no problem arises when a predicate of set-membership is predicated of a DP referring to an individual. Hence DP can function as a predicate phrase in contexts where NP may not. Presumably D also indicates membership in a kind when it occurs as the head of a referential DP. The end result is that the occurrence of a determiner is a reliable diagnostic for the property of set membership, but not for referentiality, since DP does not always function referentially.

4.3. Kinds with One Member

I now introduce a wrinkle in the notion of "instantiation of a kind" that is sensitive to the number of members in the kind that may occur at any given time. If only one member of the kind may exist at a given time, then the property of instantiating the kind may be true of an individual. Hence a predicate instantiating such a kind can be predicated of an individual.

This distinction enables us to explain the contrast between the "profession-class" nouns in (32) and their common-noun counterparts in (35). All the profession-class nouns in (32) denote instantiation of kinds that have a unique member at any given time. Thus there is only one king of England, one elector of Hanover, one class president, etc., at least at any given time. The determiner need not occur with the profession-class N′ predicates in (32) because the property of instantiating the kind can be directly predicated of the subject DP, which refers to an individual.

In contrast, the common nouns in (35) denote instantiation of kinds with an indeterminate number of members at any given time; any number of fools, hatmakers, or persons may in principle exist at once. The bare NP predicates in the Small Clauses in (35), unlike those in (32), are predicates of instantiation of non-singleton kinds that are being predicated of individuals.

This distinction between the two classes of natural kinds might appear to be needlessly complex. For instance, one might claim that the determiner is unnecessary with the profession-class NPs simply because they each have a unique referent. But this would be an oversimplification, since it would allow for examples like (47):

(47) a. *I find [that man **best hatmaker** in town].
     b. *I consider [John **only real friend I have**].

These examples are correctly excluded by our theory. Although a CNP such as *the only real friend I have* may indeed have a unique referent, there is no natural kind "only friend I have" for such a referent to instantiate. The ontology of natural kinds is fixed by an extralinguistic system and encoded into the language in terms of the nouns that it includes; it recognizes the natural kinds "man" and "king" but cannot be arbitrarily expanded to provide a new natural kind for every unique referent that can be picked out by a complex definite description. The crucial notion of uniqueness must be associated with a kind, as opposed to an individual with a particular collection of properties.

4.4. Number Agreement

Note that our theory does not distinguish between singular and plural nouns. Indeed, if nouns are predicates, then the occurrence of a plural morpheme on a noun must be seen as a reflex of agreement with the referential DP that it is predicated of, presumably as a subcase of subject-predicate agreement. This is relatively unsurprising in Small Clause contexts, such as (48):

(48) a. *I consider [that man **a fool**].
     b. *I consider [those men **fools**].

However, its implications are more interesting for determiner–noun agreement within a referential CNP. If nouns are always predicative, then the sourse of plurality in a CNP like *those men* must be the determiner, rather than the noun; thus we must assume that the noun is agreeing with the determiner, rather than vice versa. This presumably falls out as a special case of head–modifier agreement. The maximal projection of N may contain a null subject controlled by the referential head of the DP within which it occurs; then the null subject of NP will agree with the controlling head D, and the noun will agree with its null subject via Subject–Predicate agreement.

4.5. Summary

Whenever a CNP functions referentially, it must have a determiner, since NP cannot itself refer. This accounts for the uniform obligatoriness of D in referential CNPs (both singular and plural). When a CNP functions as a predicate, the obligatoriness of the determiner depends on two factors. If the noun predicates instantiation of a non-singleton set, then N′ cannot be predicated of a singular individual. Rather, a determiner is required to form a predicate of membership in the kind, which can be predicated of a singular individual.

This does not preclude N′ from being predicated directly of plurals, although the distinction between a plural N′ and a plural DP with a null determiner is not overt in English. But in languages like French, referential generic plurals must have overt determiners, as in *(Les) idiots sont innocents* 'fools are innocent,' and the determiner is absent when N′ is predicated of a plural subject, as in *Je crois ces hommes idiots* 'I consider these men idiots.' This conforms to the predictions of our theory.

Much more needs to be said about the status of determiners in CNPs—in particular about the choice between definite and indefinite determiners in nominal Small Clauses—but I will leave these matters for another time and place.

NOTES

1. The analyses in Stowell (1981, 1983) and Manzini (1983) agree insofar as they claim that the subject of a Small Clause is dominated by a maximal projection of the head of the Small Clause predicate. But they disagree on the status of the predicate phrase of the Small Clause. Manzini treats the Small Clause predicate phrase as a maximal projection, to which the subject is adjoined, whereas the Small Clause predicate is treated as a nonmaximal (X′) projection in Stowell (1981, 1983). These structures correspond to (i) and (ii) respectively:

(i)   XP   (ii)   XP
   Subject   XP   Subject   X′

A potential argument in favor of Manzini's analysis is the fact that the Small Clause predicate phrase may undergo movement, as noted by Williams (1983):

(iii) [*How stupid*] *do you consider* [*Bill* ____]?

If submaximal projections may not undergo movement, Manzini's structure must be preferred. Additionally, the existence of two "subjects" in nominal Small Clauses like (iv) appears to argue in favor of her structure:

(iv) *I consider Bill my best friend.*

On the other hand, the structure in (i) has the virtue of treating the subject of a Small Clause as structurally similar to the subject of IP, both of which behave like A-positions for the purposes of Binding theory. (Adjoined positions typically behave as A-bar positions in this respect.) For further discussion of these issues, see §3.

2. The idea that CNPs are DPs headed by D was suggested by Brame (1982) and was introduced into the GB literature by Abney (1986) and Kuroda (1985). See also Fukui and Speas (1985), Fukui (1986), and Speas (1986) for further development of this idea, especially with respect to parametric variation on the realization of functional categories such as D and Infl.

3. Bouchard (1982) and Koster (1984) provide an interesting account of some of the differences between arbitrary PRO and control PRO, by assuming that control PRO may (indeed, must) be governed. Our theory is incompatible with theirs, insofar as it ought to be possible for control PRO to occur in the (governed) Spec of DP position according to their analysis. Other problems with the idea that control PRO may be governed are discussed in Stowell (in preparation).

4. A similar approach to barrierhood was proposed by R. Kayne in a 1983 lecture at the UCLA Summer Institute, according to which a maximal projection is transparent to government iff it is θ-marked by the category governing it. This idea is incorporated into the theory of government in Stowell (1986), according to which a maximal projection is transparent to government by a category with which it is coindexed (where θ-marking is one means of achieving this).

5. Although the subject trace in (11c)–(11d) is antecedent-governed in the sense of Lasnik and Saito (1984), I assume that the ECP really consists of two distinct conditions, one of which requires government by a lexical (X-zero) head at S-structure. (See Jaeggli 1982, Stowell 1986, and Aoun et al. 1987.) Hence the existence of an antecedent-government relation in (11c)–(11d) does not affect the trace's dependence on the matrix verb for head-government. For further discussion of government in small clauses, see Stowell (to appear).

6. There is empirical evidence supporting the assumption that the head of the Small Clause predicate phrase does not govern the Small Clause subject. This comes from adjunct Small Clauses, which allow for PRO subjects:

(i) *John came home* [PRO *tired*].
(ii) *John ate the meat* [PRO *raw*].

The distinction between complement Small Clauses and adjunct Small Clauses is predicted by our analysis; adjunct Small Clauses are not L-marked and therefore function as barriers to government by any category external to the Small Clause. The inability of the head of the Small Clause predicate to govern its subject follows from the directional nature of the government relation, as discussed in the text. See also Stowell (1983, in preparation).

7. Abney (1986) also argues for the DP hypothesis on the basis of the possibility of PRO occurring within CNPs. His proposal works in the opposite way from ours, however. Abney assumes that the crucial potential governor for PRO within a

CNP is the head N in NP, and that when PRO occurs in a CNP, it must undergo movement to the Spec of DP so that the NP boundary will protect it from government by N.

I see two problems with this approach. First, the matrix verb ought to be able to L-mark a DP object and govern across the DP boundary into the Spec position of DP, excluding PRO. Second, this account is unable to distinguish between two types of PRO in the Spec of DP, i.e. a PRO that originates as the subject of NP and receives the external θ-role assigned by N (which is permitted), and a PRO that originates in the Spec of DP and receives a default Possessor θ-role (which is not permitted). The account developed in the text discussion avoids these problems.

8. This implies that only referential arguments must be Case-marked. I have no insightful explanation of this restriction; for a possible extension of Case-marking requirements to other categories, see Fabb (1984).

9. Chomsky's Minimality Condition states that whenever a position P is potentially governed by two categories A and B, where A asymmetrically c-commands B, the lower governor B always serves to block government of P by A. Rizzi's version of this relativizes the condition to be sensitive to the type of government involved; heads may only block government by other heads, while antecedent governors may block government by other antecedent governors.

Suppose, then, that a referential head D has the status of a potential antecedent governor—a reasonable assumption, if D, like Q and *wh,* functions as a referential operator. We could then assume that when D is present, as in (22), it creates a relativized minimality effect with respect to antecedent government. There are two ways in which this might work: (i) D might block antecedent government of the original adjunct trace in NP; (ii) D might block antecedent government of the intermediate trace in the Spec of DP. A problem with (i) is posed by the possibility of moving from the subject of NP to the subject DP; this is discussed in note 12 below.

A possible problem with (ii) is that it requires that antecedent government be less restricted than head government. Recall that head government must hold only within X', so that the head of a Small Clause does not govern its subject (see note 6). This may not represent a true problem if the "antecedent-government" relation is really a Binding relation rather than a Government relation, as argued in Stowell (1986) and Aoun et al. (1987).

10. Grimshaw (1981) suggests that syntactic categories are linked to semantic categories in the form of CANONICAL STRUCTURAL REALIZATIONS, which play a role in acquisition. The basic idea is that the acquisition of an s-selectional requirement for a given semantic category automatically implies c-selection for its associated CSR (i.e. the syntactic category to which it is linked). Subsequently the lexical entry may be complicated by stipulating additional alternative syntactic categories as a marked option. The theory developed here differs from Grimshaw's insofar as she assumes that in adult grammars, a given semantic category (e.g. "Question") may be associated with a syntactic category (e.g. NP) that does not correspond to its CSR. Our analysis assumes a tighter correlation between syntactic categories and semantic categories in the grammar itself.

11. In addition to the examples in (38), we find examples like (i) and (ii), which are somewhat better:

(i) *John considers James **Mary's** best friend.*
(ii) *Jim considers Mary **Bill's** only hope.*

The prenominal adjectives seem to be playing a role in improving the naturalness of the genitive subject. This might be captured by treating the prenominal genitive as the Subject of the AP rather than of the NP, which would allow for the subject of the Small Clause to count as the Subject of NP. I will not explore the mechanics of this possible solution here.

12. A problem arises with respect to the possibility of moving the Subject of NP into the Specifier position of DP. If the Subject of NP must be antecedent-governed, and if NP (not being L-marked) is a barrier for government, as our account of extraction suggests, then the trace of the moved Subject of NP should violate the antecedent-government requirement of the ECP. This movement is directly analogous to that of *wh-* movement from the Subject of IP to the Spec of DP. Chomsky (1986) solves the problem by stipulating that IP is never an inherent barrier, and we could adopt the same assumption. The DP dominating NP would still be a barrier by inheritance, so our account of extraction and the distribution of PRO in §2 would be preserved, for the most part.

This solution would have to assume, however, that IP and NP may both serve as intrinsic barriers for Subjacency, in order to force successive cyclic movement through the Spec of DP in the case of object extraction. This assumption is needed anyway for IP, since otherwise object extraction from a *wh-* island would not violate Subjacency in a sentence like (i), where CP is the only barrier crossed if IP cannot be an intrinsic barrier for Subjacency:

(i) **Who_i did you wonder [when_j [Bill saw t_i t_j]]?*

11

Parameters of Phrase Structure

LISA TRAVIS

In the enthusiasm to replace a system of rules with a system of principles and parameters, it is important not to lose sight of the reasons for this shift of formalism. The problem that the principles and parameters framework seeks to solve is: How can a grammatical system be flexible enough to account for language variation while at the same time be, to a large extent, restricted in order to account for the relative ease of language acquisition and the impossibility of certain language types? While rules were descriptively adequate, they were far too powerful. Not only were they capable of describing language structures that, while logically possible, were not intuitively plausible; they also raised the question of how a child was able to internalize such a system.

In an effort to restrict the power of rule type formalisms, more and more constraints on rules were introduced until, in Government-Binding (GB) theory (e.g. Chomsky 1981), there was nothing left to the rules beyond Affect-α. The grammar became a system of restrictions rather than a system of rules. In the transformational component, Affect-α has the more specific realizations of Move-α and Delete-α (see e.g. Lasnik and Saito 1986). In the base component, which is the subject of this paper, one could assume that Affect-α would appear in the form of Generate-α. The grammar of restrictions is broken down into principles and parameters. Restrictions which are common to all languages are encoded in principles of Universal Grammar (UG), and these restrictions (such as Subjacency, Case Filter, Theta Criterion, Projection Principle, etc.) are considered to be part of the innate language faculty. Language variation is allowed through parameters which introduce a limited flexibility to the system. For instance, while Subjacency may prohibit movement across more than one bounding node, language variation in extraction structures is accounted for through parameterization of which nodes are considered bounding nodes by any language (Rizzi 1982, Sportiche 1981). Within the base component, generation is restricted by universals such as X-bar theory, but language specific

263

variation of word order may be captured through parameters such as head-initial/head-final as well as those presented below.

This new framework has appealing consequences both in the field of language typology and in the field of language acquisition. Principles represent both what is common to all languages and what need not be learned by the child. Parameters represent the range of variation that can be found in natural languages as well as what has to be learned by the child.

There is a certain amount of tension in this system, however. While languages appear to vary in a large number of ways, children can acquire diverse languages with relative ease. In other words, if a child had to actually acquire each language-specific fact separately, the task of language acquisition would be much greater than evidence indicates. This tension may be relieved, however, by assuming that parameters account for a clustering of language specific properties. For instance, if a parameter P accounts for seven language properties, even though language A may differ from language B in seven ways, the child would only have to hear one bit of evidence to set the value for P which would then project six other language differences. Further, other predictive powers are gained by using parameters to account for a group of properties, since the range of possible languages is restricted. If parameter P incorporates properties 1 and 2, there should be no language which exhibits 1 without also exhibiting 2. It is important to note that this system is restrictive only when a parameter incorporates more than one language difference. As soon as there is a one-to-one mapping between language differences and parameters, we lose the explanations for the ease of language acquisition and the restrictions on language variation.

It is the aim of this paper to present a system of parameters which is powerful enough to account for the diversity of word order in natural language while being restrictive enough to provide an explanatory account for language acquisition and restrictions on language variation. Since further in-depth research needs to be done in this area and on the specific languages involved, the framework presented here is intended as a working model.

Word order is one of the more obvious ways in which languages differ. In an *Aspects* model of syntactic theory, word order was encoded in Phrase Structure Rules. The problem with this system was that the rules were too powerful and the range of possible word orders was not at all diminished. Phrase structure rules also encoded two disparate types of relationships: dominance relations and precedence relations. The latter may be further divided into the ordering of non-heads with respect to one another and the ordering of non-heads with respect to heads.

These different relations are being teased apart in the GB framework. Dominance relations are restricted by X-bar theory. The ordering of non-heads with respect to one another is restricted by subcomponents of the grammar such as Case theory (Stowell 1981). The order of non-heads with respect to heads is restricted by one of the first parameters proposed, the headedness parameter, although it was not so called. By setting a value for headedness, separate language-specific facts were collapsed. This headedness parameter captured Greenberg's (1963) observation that VO languages tended to be prepositional and OV languages tended to be postpositional. The problem with this system, however, is that it is not powerful enough to describe existing languages. While purely head-final and head-initial languages may be described with such a parameter, difficulties arise in languages such as German which are OV but prepositional, and in languages like Chinese and Kpelle which appear to have head-internal VPs.

In this paper I examine the headedness parameter and the relation of non-heads to heads.[1] First I discuss languages for which the headedness parameter is not sufficient and propose that smaller domains within a maximal projection may be determined by assuming that θ-role assignment and Case assignment create their own domains, and that head-internal constituents may be described by setting a direction for any of these subdomains. Such additions to the inventory of parameters, however, predict a wide variety of word orders that have not been reported. To solve this problem, in the second part of the paper I suggest a way of restricting the use of these parameters. The end result is that these parameters will represent a cluster of properties and thereby have the predictive power needed for explanatory adequacy.[2]

1. The Parameters

Two languages which present problems for the headedness parameter are Chinese and Kpelle. Both languages have head-internal VPs which suggests that distinctions finer than those provided by the headedness parameter are needed to explain head/non-head relations. As we see below, Chinese and Kpelle pose different problems for the headedness parameter and provide valuable insights into the ways in which word order may vary cross-linguistically.

1.1. Chinese

Beginning with Chinese, we can see that if one categorizes languages as being VO/OV, head-initial/head-final, one creates problems in describing languages where either the object does not speak for all of the complements of a verb, or where the logical object can appear on either side of the verb. Both of these problems occur in Chinese. As the examples in (1) show, even though the object appears to the right of the verb, other members of the VP appear to the left of the verb:[3]

> (1) a. *cóng yōu gú   chūlai* (Li & Thompson 1973:200)
>   from dark valley emerge
>   'emerge from dark valley'
>   b. *ta pian-le   Lisi.* (Huang 1982:27)
>   he cheat-ASP Lisi
>   'He cheated Lisi.'

Further, the object may also appear to the left of the verb in a *ba-* construction, as we can see in example (2):

> (2) *ta ba Lisi pian-le.*   (Huang 1982:27)
>   he *ba* Lisi cheat-ASP
>   'He cheated Lisi.'

This array of facts presents problems for typologists who see languages in the black and white categories of OV/VO and has created a discussion in the literature as to whether Chinese is OV or VO. As a first pass, we might say that bare NPs follow the verb while PPs precede the verb, presuming that *ba* is a preposition. However, as reported by Li and Thompson (1975), some PPs follow the verb while others precede. In fact, two prepositions, *zai* and *gei,* can both precede and follow but there are meaning differences depending on the position. The relevant distinctions are given in examples (3) and (4):[4]

> (3) a. *ta gěi wǒ mài le   chēzi le.* (Li & Thompson 1975:180)
>   he for me sell ASP car   ASP
>   'He sold a car for me.'
>   b. *tā mài gěi wǒ chēzi le.*
>   he sell to me car   ASP
>   'He sold a car to me.'
> (4) a. *Zhāng-sān tiào   zài zhuōzi-shang.* (Li & Thompson 1975:182)
>   Zhang-san jump at   table-on
>   'Zhang-san jumped onto the table.'
>   b. *Zhāng-sān zài zhuōzi-shang tiào.*
>   Zhang-san at   table-on   jump
>   'Zhang-san is jumping (up and down) on the table.'

In example (3) we see that *gei* is benefactive when preverbal and dative when postverbal. In example (4) we see that *zai* has a locational reading when preverbal and a directional reading when postverbal. I suggest the correct generalization is that post-verbal constituents are θ-marked by the verb, while preverbal constituents are VP-internal adjuncts. While benefactives and locational PPs may appear with any verb, datives and directionals depend directly on the lexical selection of a verb. This distinction has been noted by traditional grammarians. Li and Thompson (1981:409) write:

> In conclusion, we observe that the locative phrase may occur in either the preverbal position or the postverbal position. In the preverbal position, it has a general locational meaning and is essentially unconstrained with respect to the verbs with which it can occur: accordingly, the preverbal locative phrase is called *zhuanggyu* 'adverbial' by Chinese grammarians.
>
> Postverbal locative phrases, on the other hand, are restricted to certain types of verbs, just as direct objects are, and are designated by the term *buyu*, 'complement', which is also used for object, in traditional Chinese grammar. This distinction between these two grammatical terms captures the difference between the relatively free preverbal locative phrase and the more tightly restricted postverbal locative phrase in terms of semantic "intimacy" (p. 409).

The generalization proposed above (i.e. that only elements which are not dependent on the verb for θ-marking precede the V) requires the assumption that *ba* is capable of θ-marking the NP which follows it. At first this may seem problematic. Goodall (1986) points out that if *ba* in some way absorbs the Theme θ-role normally assigned by the verb, this would violate Williams's (1981a) claim that only lexical processes may affect the θ-structure of a head, and even then, only external θ-roles may be absorbed. Further, pairs like (5) and (6) seem to argue that the *ba* NP may be completely independent of the θ-structure of the verb.[5]

(5) *Wo ku de   Zhangsan hen shangxin*   (Goodall 1987, 233)
    I   cry so-that Zhangsan very sad
    'I cried so much that Zhangsan was very sad.'
(6) *Wo **ba** Zhangsan ku de hen shangxin.*

Cheng (1986), however, offers an account which solves both of these problems. First she proposes, following Higginbotham (1985), that the *ba* does not absorb the Theme θ-role, but rather identifies it through a linking process. Cheng further convincingly argues that the use of the *ba* construction is sensitive to θ-roles to the extent that not even all Themes may appear in this construction, but only what she calls "affected Themes." This would account for the distinction in (7)–(9).

268   Lisa Travis

(7) a. *Wo sha le Lisi.*   (Cheng 1986:36–7)
        I   kill ASP Lisi
        'I killed Lisi.'
    b. *Wo **ba** Lisi sha le.*
(8) a. *Ta bang le wo*
        he help ASP I
        'He helped me.'
    b. **Ta **ba** wo bang le.*
(9)   **Ta **ba** zhebu dianying ka le.*
        he *ba* this   movie   see ASP
        'He saw this movie.'

In (7), where the object is an affected Theme, the *ba* construction is possible. In (8) and (9), however, because the object is a benefactive and an 'unaffected' Theme respectively, the *ba* construction is not possible.

This characterization of the θ-role that *ba* assigns could also be used to account for the problem raised by Goodall. In the examples he gives (see (5) and (6)), the *ba* NP is arguably the affected theme of the action of the verb.

Passive is formed in a similar way, where *bei* can be used to identify an adversary/agent θ-role (see Cheng 1986 for details).

(10) *Ta **bei** Zhangsan sha le.*
      he by Zhangsan kill ASP
      'He was killed by Zhangsan.'

Cheng's conclusions, in fact, help to support the claim that *ba* is, in fact, a θ-role assigner, providing an explanation for why the *ba* phrase may appear to the left of the V.

The word order of Chinese is presented schematically in (11), where PP_1 is assigned its θ-role directly from the V and PP_2 is an adjunct PP or identifies an argument position through linking:

(11) PP_2 V NP PP_1

Assuming that all the elements to the right of the verb are directly θ-marked by the verb, one could describe this word order by having a directionality parameter for θ-role assignment. Chinese, then, would assign θ-roles to the right. To account for the placement of adjuncts to the left of the verb, there would be a default specification of head-final. The head-final parameter would have an effect only on those elements not already covered by a previously mentioned parameter.

1.2. Kpelle

We have seen that by supposing that θ-role assignment direction may be parametrically specified, overriding a parameter of headedness, one type of head-internal word order may be accounted for. However, there are head-internal word orders that cannot be described through the direction of θ-role assignment. In Kpelle, within the VP, only objects precede the verb while all PPs follow the verb. Examples are given in (12) and (13).[6]

(12)   *galoŋ a   pérɛ tɔ̂i.*   (Gay and Welmers 1971:5)
    chief AGR house build
    'The chief is building a house.'

(13) a. *e pa   dipɔ.*   (Gay and Welmers 1971:31)
    he come them-to
    'He came to them.'

    b. *e   sɛŋ-kâu tèe kâloŋ-pɔ́.*   (Givon 1975:50)
    AGR money   sent chief-to
    'He sent the money to the chief.'

This means that, unlike Chinese, argument and non-argument PPs fall on the same side of the head. Schematically, this word order is as shown in example (14).

(14) NP V PP_1 PP_2

The direction of θ-role assignment will not solve this problem, since θ-assigned elements appear both the left and to the right of the head. However, by assuming that the direction of Case assignment, like the direction of θ-role assignment, may also be set as a word order parameter, we will be able to capture these word order facts (see Koopman 1984 for a similar account for Mahou). What we would say about Kpelle, then, is that Case is assigned to the left, explaining the position of the object NP to the left of the V. Again, a default specification of headedness is needed. If we say that heads are initial, all the PPs will be placed to the right of the verb. The Case direction will have an effect only on those elements dependent on the verb for Case (i.e. the object), and the head-initial parameter will have an effect on all other elements with the VP (i.e. the PPs).

1.3. The Realization of the Parameters

The above view of word order parameters basically provides tools by which maximal projections may be divided into smaller domains. For instance, a VP can be seen as containing a Case domain and a θ-domain.

(15) [$_{VP}$ V   NP   PP$_1$ PP$_2$]

$\underbrace{}$

CASE

$\underbrace{}$

THETA

No new primitives have been introduced to the theory, since Case relations and θ-relations are needed independently in the grammar. By allowing parameters to be sensitive to these relations, however, the system has
become more powerful. Where before only non-heads could be positioned
with relation to the head, now the precedence relation between a Case-
assigner and a Case assignee, or a θ-role assigner and a θ-role assignee
may also be given a parametric value.

Before investigating the problems that this new power brings, I would
like to address the question of where the effect of any of these parameters
takes place. Following GB theory strictly, the parameter of direction of
θ-role assignment and the parameter of the direction of Case assignment
will affect different levels of syntax. Since D-structure is seen as the pure
representation of GF-θ, the direction of θ-role assignment will affect the
way in which a D-structure is constructed. In other words, the D-structure
of Chinese will have the same order as the S-structure. Elements θ-marked
by the verb will be base-generated to the right of the verb, while all other
elements will appear on the left. In Kpelle, however, the surface order will
not be directly base-generated. Objects will be generated to the right of the
verb in order to be θ-marked. However, since Case is assigned to the left,
they will not receive Case in their base-generated position and they will be
forced to move to a Case-marked position to the left of the verb. This is
shown in example (16):

(16) D-structure: V   NP   PP$_1$ PP$_2$

CASE   THETA

S-structure: NP$_i$ V t_i PP$_1$ PP$_2$

Seen this way, the direction of θ-assignment affects D-structure, while
the direction of Case assignment affects S-structure.[7]

2. Restricting the System

By introducing these two new parameters, we have increased the power of
our system and are running the risk of raising the same problems as those

raised by the system of Phrase Structure Rules. In other words, while accounting for a larger number of word orders than allowed by the headedness parameter, we may also be predicting the possibility of word orders that are, in fact, nonexistent. With three parameters having two values each, we predict eight possible word orders within the VP. These are given below in terms of the parameters and then in terms of word order.

(17) Parameters:

	HEADEDNESS	THETA-DIRECTION	CASE-DIRECTION
a.	Final	Left	Left
b.	Final	Left	Right
c.	Final	Right	Left
d.	Final	Right	Right
e.	Initial	Left	Left
f.	Initial	Left	Right
g.	Initial	Right	Left
h.	Initial	Right	Right

(18) Word Orders:

a. PP_2 PP_1 NP V
b. PP_2 PP_1 V NP
c. PP_2 NP V PP_1
d. PP_2 V NP PP_1
e. PP_1 NP V PP_2
f. PP_1 V NP PP_2
g. NP V PP_1 PP_2
h. V NP PP_1 PP_2

Cases (17a) and (17h) are those that could be covered by the headedness parameter, since they are head-final and head-initial respectively. These are clearly evidenced in natural language by, for instance, Japanese (head-final) and English (head-initial). Cases (17d) and (17g) represent the languages already discussed in this paper, where (17d) is Chinese and (17g) is Kpelle. The question now is raised: are the other four predicted word orders exemplified in natural language? Cases (17b) and (17e) are the mirror images of Kpelle and Chinese respectively, suggesting that perhaps these orders should exist since they simply represent the opposite values for each parameter.

The two remaining orders, (17c) and (17f), however, are a type very different from the other six. In all the other six word orders, the same results may be achieved by stating the value of one or two parameters, (i) either Case or θ-direction, and/or (ii) the headedness parameter. For example, Chinese (17e) assigns θ-roles to the right but is otherwise head-final, and

Japanese (17a) need specify only head-final. All three parameters must be specified to describe the word orders in (17c) and (17f), however. Because of this difference, and the lack of evidence for languages of the type of (17c) and (17f), I propose that all six other orders are possible, but that (17c) and (17f) must be ruled out in principle. In order to support this proposal, I begin by discussing languages which exemplify (17b) and (17e) and then outline a means by which directionality parameters may be restricted so as not to produce languages like (17c) and (17f).

2.1. Possible and Impossible Languages

2.1.1. Chinese Future.
Within the context of the debate as to whether Chinese is SOV or SVO, Li and Thompson (1975) suggest that Chinese is in the process of changing from SVO to SOV and hence the possibility of both orders. Further, they claim that, although the change has been under way for two millennia, the shift is now nearly complete. As confirmation, Li and Thompson give the following evidence. First, the *ba* construction is becoming more and more common. Second, a definite versus indefinite distinction that used to hold of preverbal versus postverbal objects is being lost and replaced by the development of indefinite and definite determiners. Third, a semantic distinction between the preverbal and postverbal PPs is being lost and all PPs are appearing preverbally. Note, however, that bare NPs still may not precede the verb. Although the *ba* construction is becoming more common, bare objects still retain their ability to appear only postverbally. In sum, all PPs are beginning to appear preverbally.[8] If this change takes place, the word order of Chinese would be:

(19) PP_2 PP_1 V NP

This is the mirror image of Kpelle, and, like Kpelle, the relevant parameter would be Case directionality. Case would be assigned to the right and the default specification for headedness would be head-final.[9]

This projected shift in parameters is further supported by a comment made in Li and Thompson's (1981) grammar. They give three different classes of verbs which take dative NPs. Some verbs may take either the NP *gei* NP or the NP NP construction, while some must take NP *gei* NP and others must take the NP NP construction. Examples, taken from Li and Thompson (1981:374–9), are given in (20)–(22).

(20) *gei* obligatory:
    a. *Ta dai-le   yi bao tang **gei Zhangsan.***
        he bring-ASP one bag candy to Zhangsan
        'S/he brought a bag of candy to Zhangsan.'

    b.   *Ta dai **gei Zhangsan** yi bao tang.*
    c.   **Ta dai-le **Zhangsan** yi bao tang.*

(21) *gei* optional:
    a.   *wo song-le yi ping jiu   **gei ta.***
        I   give-ASP one bottle wine to he
        'I gave a bottle of wine to him/her.'
    b.   *wo song **gei ta** yi ping jiu.*
    c.   *wo song-le **ta** yi ping jiu.*

(22) *gei* impossible:
    a.   **wo wen-le ji-ge   wenti   gei ta.*
        I   ask-ASP several-CL problem to he
    b.   **wo wen **gei ta** ji-ge wenti.*
    c.   *wo wen-le **ta** ji-ge wenti.*

It is interesting in the context of the present investigation to see which of the above constructions are being affected by this alleged shift to SOV. Li and Thompson write:

> The indirect object marked by *gei* has begun to appear in the preverbal position . . . the appearance of the indirect object in the preverbal position, however, is confined to only a few verbs . . . that is, to those groups for which *gei* is either obligatory or optional (1981:386–7).

This is just the result that we would expect. Those NPs which are assigned Case independently of the verb (i.e. by the preposition) may appear preverbally, while in the double object constructions, NP NP, both must appear postverbally in order to be assigned Case.

2.1.2. Kpelle Past. As for the mirror image of Chinese, there is a possibility that an earlier form of Kpelle had this word order. Hyman (1975:128) describes modern Kpelle but adds that "there is good evidence that datives once preceded the verb." This suggests that in an earlier form of Kpelle, where dative PPs appeared preverbally, θ-marked elements were positioned to the left of the head. This would give the word order in (23):

(23) PP_1 NP V PP_2

Theta-roles would be assigned to the right and the default setting of headedness would be head-initial.

2.1.3. Impossible Languages. If one believes in Chinese future and Kpelle past, then these argue for the word orders given in (17b) and (17e) above. We might also say that we do not want to rule out these orders in principle since, in terms of parameter settings, they are not different in type from the needed parameter settings for the present day forms of Chinese and Kpelle. As noted above, word orders of types (17c) and (17f) are very different in kind, since *both* subdomain parameters must be specified as well as the headedness parameter. This raises one question: how many of these parameters may be set for any language? Another question that is raised, within this system as well as with the headedness parameter, is: Can parameters be set for every different category? What I claim is that only one subdomain parameter (i.e. Case or θ-direction) may be set per language, and that only the default parameter of headedness may vary from category to category. We will see below in more detail how this works. What is important is that the power of the parameters and the range of possible language types will be restricted.

2.2. The Restrictions

In talking of Chinese and Kpelle, we have been discussing two parameters for each language: Chinese assigns θ-roles to the right but is otherwise head-final. Kpelle assigns Case to the left but is otherwise head-initial. It was suggested above that perhaps only two parameters at most might be specified, a subdomain direction and then a default parameter of headedness. While this works and would rule out (17c) and (17f), it adds a complication to the framework. It is generally assumed that grammatical rules cannot "count." In other words, a grammatical rule could never refer to "three bounding nodes" or "the fifth Comp." A restriction could only refer to "one" or "many." For example, subjacency restricts movement to one bounding node.[10] If we were allowed to specify only one parameter, however, it would seem that we could not distinguish Chinese from English, or Kpelle from Japanese. The relevant word orders are given in (24):

(24)		CASE	THETA	HEADEDNESS
a.	PP_2 V NP PP_1 Chinese	———	right	final
b.	V NP PP_1 PP_2 English	———	right	initial
c.	NP V PP_1 PP_2 Kpelle	left	———	initial
d.	PP_1 PP_2 NP V Japanese	left	———	final

Without specifying the headedness parameter as well as the direction of θ-role assignment for Chinese and Case assignment for Kpelle, there would be no way to distinguish (24a) from (24b) or (24c) from (24d). However, one should also note that neither Japanese nor English needs to specify a subdomain, since their VPs are purely head-final and head-initial respectively. Let us assume, then, that subdomains need to be stipulated only when they are separated from other elements of the maximal projection. This means that a specification of Case assignment to the right carries with it the information that the language is otherwise head-final. If the language were head-initial, the Case domain would not need to be specified in a directional parameter.

We can now postulate the following restictions on word order parameters:

(25) a. If a subdomain direction is specified, this is all that may be specified. (This would be the marked case.)

   b. If no subdomain direction is specified, then a value must be given for headedness. (This is the unmarked case.) This value may vary across categories.

Below, the chart given in (17) is reinterpreted in the context of our restrictions. Possible word orders may all be distinguished by specifying only one parameter (capitalized in (26)). Further, word orders that are assumed to be impossible cannot be characterized using the restrictions above.

(26) Parameters:

	HEADEDNESS	THETA	CASE	LANGUAGE
a.	FINAL	Left	Left	Japanese
b.	Final	Left	RIGHT	Chinese (future)
c.	Final	Right	Left	*
d.	Final	RIGHT	Right	Chinese (present)
e.	Initial	LEFT	Left	Kpelle (past)
f.	Initial	Left	Right	*
g.	Initial	Right	LEFT	Kpelle (present)
h.	INITIAL	Right	Right	English

2.3. The Predictions

As well as ruling out certain word orders within a maximal projection, two other predictions follow from restriction (25a):

(27) I. Once a subdomain direction is set, it must be consistent throughout the language.

   II. If the value for the headedness parameter is determined only as a default parameter following the specification of a subdomain direction, then it must be consistent throughout the language.

2.3.1. Prediction I.

If the direction of a subdomain is set, since nothing more may be said, this relation must be constant in the language. To give this prediction some content, let us look at Kpelle and Chinese again. In Kpelle, where the verb assigns Case to the left, we expect that all structural

Case assigners will assign Case to the left. In other words, we expect to find postpositions. As shown in example (28), this is indeed what we find.[11]

(28) *bérɛi mà*   (Gay & Welmers 1971:30)
     house on
     'on the house'

Note that this is very different from saying that Case assignment is uni-directional in all languages (as suggested by Koopman 1984). For instance, German, which has head-final VPs and head-initial PPs, is not problematic for this system. Since Case need not be specified as a subdomain for German, no claims are made about the direction of Case assignment in any category. Languages like German, however, are the reason for the second part of Restriction (25b).[12]

In Chinese, where θ-direction is to the right, elements which can assign θ-roles directly exhibit the same head-internal facts. Adjectives, like verbs, can take bare NP complements to their right whereas the same complement to the left must have an accompanying θ-marker. We see an example of this in (29):

(29) a. *hen gaoxing zheijian shi.*   (Huang 1982:27)
        very happy   this   matter
        'very happy about this matter'
     b. *dui   zheijian shi   hen gaoxing*
        toward this   matter very happy

Since nouns do not assign θ-roles to their complements (see Rappaport 1983 for arguments), NPs will be head-final.

(30) a. *ta dui   guojia de re-ai*   (Huang 1982:29)
        he toward country *de* hot-love
        'his enthusiastic love of the country'
     b. **ta de re-ai guojia*

2.3.2. Prediction II.   A language which specifies a direction of a sub-domain sets its headedness parameter through a default specification. Since nothing further can be said, the value for the headedness parameter must be the same for all categories. Kpelle, for instance, must be head-initial across all categories, and Chinese must be head-final. There are arguments that this is true in both languages. Just looking at the Infl projection, if we assume that aspect is in Infl in Chinese and AGR (or what Gay & Welmers 1971 and Givón 1975 gloss as a pronoun) is in Infl in Kpelle, we can see in (31) and (32) that INFL' is head-final in Chinese and head-initial in Kpelle.[13]

(31) *tā gěi wǒ mài le chēzi le.*   (Li & Thompson 1975:180)
he for me sell ASP car ASP
'He sold a car for me.'

(32) *gâloŋ a   lónôi.*   (Gay & Welmers 1971:4)
chief AGR talk
'The chief is talking.'

In (31) above, where ASP appears both before and after the direct object, I am assuming the first occurrence is realized under the V while the second is realized under Infl. This is a matter which still requires further research but which, at this point, provides confirmation for our prediction.

2.4. *Unspecified Parametric Values*

One final note should be made concerning parameters, in particular parameters which have a possible setting but for which no value has been given. For example, in Kpelle Case direction has been set, and headedness direction follows; however, nothing has been said about the direction of θ-role assignment. My assumption is that unspecified parameters have the option of both possible values. This is important for languages like German, where θ-marked complements and Case-marked complements may appear either to the left of their heads (as in VPs) or to the right (as in PPs). Since German specifies neither subdomain, nothing restricts the direction in which Case-marking or θ-marking apply.[14]

This also allows for an alternative analysis concerning which level is affected by the setting of word order parameters (see §1.3). Davis (1987) suggests that Case assignment is just as important as θ-role assignment in creating initial phrase structures. In her view, the direction of Case assignment would be operative immediately in determining the placement of complements of the verb. Direct objects in Kpelle, then, would be base-generated in a position to the left of the verb. Since θ-roles can be assigned in either direction, no problem is created. Theta-assignment would take whichever direction was necessary in order to "find" the appropriate complement. This is shown in (33) (cf. (16)):

(33)   ← Case   ← specified (to the left)
    [$_{VP}$ NP   V   PP$_1$ PP$_2$]

        Theta   ← not specified (either direction)

3. Conclusion

In this paper I have investigated the headedness parameter with the intention of solving the problem of head-initial languages like Chinese and Kpelle. I began by proposing two new parameters. These broke maximal projections into smaller domains, created by relations already incorporated into the theory such as Case assignment and θ-role assignment. While adding enough flexibility to the system to account for head-internal orders, these new parameters created a problem of overgeneration. Not only could Chinese and Kpelle be described, but nonexistent word orders would be predicted as well. In order to avoid this problem, restrictions on word order parameters were proposed to constrain their generative power. By restricting parameters in this way, I hope to have not only solved the empirical problem of word order in Chinese and Kpelle, but also met my own requirements for a parametric system outlined at the beginning of this paper.

NOTES

1. This paper is a development of proposals made in Travis (1984). For a similar view of word order parameters, see Koopman (1984).

2. For further restriction to word order parameters, see Travis (forthcoming), where a proposal is made that parameters may affect only precedence relations but not dominance relations.

3. I am assuming that such PPs are part of the VP, as argued in Reinhart (1983).

4. Much has been written on whether prepositions exist in Chinese or simply co-verbs. I assume along with Li and Thompson and others that these elements are indeed prepositions.

5. Sentential complements also follow the verb. It is not clear to me what exactly accounts for this. It is not unusual, however, for languages to position sentential complements at the end of the sentence. See Koster (1978) and Stowell (1981) for different accounts for this.

6. The structural analyses of the following examples are mine, in particular the assignment of AGR to the pronominal element in the clause.

7. An alternate analysis is discussed in §2.4.

8. Li and Thompson give a fourth argument, that postpositions begin to appear in the language. In fact, these postpositions may be analyzed as nominal compounds. See Travis (1984) for details.

9. In this form of Chinese, *ba* could eventually lose its θ-role–assigning function and be demoted to simply a Case assigner. If this were to happen, we would expect to lose the restriction of the θ-role in *ba* constructions that was pointed out by Cheng.

10. Another example comes from metrical phonology, where branching must be either binary (one branching) or unbounded (multiple branching).

11. I assume that Infl assigns Case through coindexation, not through structural Case assignment. See Travis (1984) and Lamontagne and Travis (1986) for details.

12. Obviously, the grammar would be simpler without such a provision, yet until further research proves otherwise, headedness does seem to vary from category to category in some languages.

13. I am avoiding a discussion of the position of Specifier positions, including subject.

14. Piggott (1987) has proposed this independently for a parameter of nasal spreading.

12

Maximal Projections in Words and Phrases

EDWIN S. WILLIAMS

The most recent work in morphology has uncovered resemblances to the systems in phrasal syntax, again raising the question whether morphology is a distinct from syntax. The "lexicalist hypothesis" has a number of forms, not all of which are consistent with these discovered resemblances. But the simple atomicity of words in syntax is not inconsistent with there being notions and laws spanning both domains. In this paper I first enumerate the common elements of the theories of words and phrases, and focus on one essential difference between word and phrase as the source of a great many of the other differences between the two.

The rules of formation are similar. Both use concatenation as the basic operation. Furthermore, both identify a distinguished element of each composite form, the head, which determines many of the properties of the whole in a precise way. So, for example, -s makes the noun *boy* plural in the same way that the noun *boys* makes the NP *the boys* plural; and *-ion* makes *destruction* nominal in the same way that *destruction* makes *the destruction of the city* nominal. This role of the head in morphology is discussed in Williams (1981b).

In addition, both systems have free and bound forms. The bound forms in morphology are the affixes; in syntax, the clitics. Although it is sometimes difficult to tell clitics from affixes, it can in principle always be done; see Zwicky and Pullum (1983) and Di Sciullo and Williams (1986) for discussion.

Both morphology and word order have a θ-theory and certain common θ-theoretic notions, such as θ-role, argument structure, and internal/external argument. Part of the similarity is unavoidable—morphology produces words with certain argument structures, and these argument structures must be interpretable by the syntactic system. But much of the similarity goes beyond what this kind of consideration can explain.

The external argument of a lexical item is the particular argument in its argument structure that is realized outside the maximal projection of that item in syntax—that is, the "subject" argument. Here, the external argument is indicated by underlining.

The role of the external argument in morphological derivation can be seen in the rule for the suffix -*ness:* the rule is, make the external argument of X the internal argument of X-*ness* (and add a new nominal external argument "R"):

(1) *complete* + *ness*

    | |

  (*th*)   (*R*)

The two operations of θ-theory, θ-role satisfaction and function composition, occur in both systems as well. Satisfaction occurs in morphology in compounding:

(2) a. Syntax: *see Bill$_i$*

      (A th$_i$)

    b. Morphology: *bar$_i$ tend*

          (A th$_i$)

Indexation is used to indicate satisfaction: the argument in the argument structure is indexed with the NP that satisfies it. Function composition occurs regularly in affixation; in syntax, it occurs in the raising constructions in English:

(3) a. Morphology: *construct* + *ion* → *construction*

         (A th)   (R)   (R A th)

    b. Syntax: seem$_0$ + [$_{VP_i}$ sad] → [$_i$ seem sad]

Here, the arguments of the nonhead, as well as any arguments of the head, become arguments of the whole.

Control and binding occur in both systems as well. Syntactic control in the *want* construction in English is paralleled by morphological control in the -*ta* construction in Japanese:

(4) a. Syntax: *want*   *to read*

        (A$_i$ . . .) (A$_i$ . . .)

    b. Morphology: *yomi*   -*ta*

        (A$_i$ . . .) (A$_i$ . . .)

        read   want

        want to read

And binding occurs in both systems:

(5) a. Syntax: *see   himself$_i$*
            (A$_i$ . . .)

    b. Morphology: *self$_i$*-perception
                (A$_i$ . . .)

In sum, then, a great many of the concepts and rules of one system occur in the other. This concurrence might suggest that in fact we have really
just one unified system for the generation of words and phrases, and that
what differences there now appear to be will disappear on further inspection. In fact, though, there appear to be some quite systematic and deep
differences, which it is the purpose of this paper to explore.

These differences are seen to stem from the absence in morphology of
the syntactic notion "maximal projection." While morphology has the notion "head and projection" in common with syntax, it lacks the notion
"maximal projection." It consequently lacks in addition some of the notions
of Case and θ-theory that are pegged to the syntactic notion "maximal projection," such as case-marking, predication, reference, and opacity. The
differences that flow from these differences are so large as to encompass
most of the observed differences between syntax and morphology.

A precise meaning must be given to the term "maximal projection."
Morphology does have maximal projections in a trivial sense: in the compound *off-white paint*, the adjective *off-white* is a maximal projection of the
adjective *white* in the sense that there is no larger projection of that adjective
in this compound. However, there is nothing intrinsic about *off-white* that
makes it maximal; it is simply an A, and subject to further A-projection.
An AP, on the other hand, is subject to no further A-projection, in any
context.

One might argue that there are certain morphological processes that
make further projection impossible, and that therefore the outputs of these
processes qualify as morphological maximal projections. One such process
is the addition of certain inflectional endings, for example the third person
singular present verbal ending in English. I will not take the time here to
counter this proposal, which is treated in detail in Williams (1980) and Di
Sciullo and Williams (1986). There it is argued that the proper analysis of
inflectional endings is not arrived at by adding them on after derivational
endings, but rather by putting them in (ultimate) head position; and the
analysis of *bar-tends*, for example, is

(6)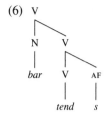

where the inflectional ending is added on *before* the compounding is done. If this is correct, then clearly the adding on of the inflectional ending cannot create a morphological maximal projection subject to further morphological rules. Further evidence against this proposal is that many inflectional endings which in some contexts seem to terminate morphological derivation, in other circumstances do not; for example, the plural in English can appear inside of compounds (*parts supplier;* T. Roeper, pers. comm.); and the Latin infinitive ending *-are* forms not only the infinitive, but also the base form for certain tenses. Again, these matters are dealt with in the references cited.

1. Predication

Theta-theory in syntax determines that maximal projections are interpreted as one-place predicates. So, whatever rules are used to construct maximal projections, from the θ-theoretic point of view, the result must be a one-place predicate. In one type of case, the head of the maximal projection has a designated argument (the external argument), which serves to make the maximal projection a one-place predicate:

(7)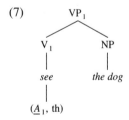

If the head lacks a designated external argument, then the nonhead can supply the argument that makes the maximal projection a one-place predicate, under function composition:

(8)

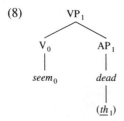

In either case, the result is a one-place predicate. Maximal projections in syntax are never two-place predicates, for example, regardless of the aclicity of the elements that make them up.

Morphology, on the other hand, regularly derives n-place predicates. For example, when a causative is formed in morphology by affixation, if the input form is n-place, then the output form is $(n + 1)$-place:

(9) yomi   -sase   ⇒   yomisase
     | | |
    ($\underline{A}$, th) ($\underline{A}$) ($\underline{A}$, A, th)
    read   make   make-read (Japanese)

In nominalization also, n-place predicates are taken to $(n + 1)$-place predicates—the verbal θ-roles are internalized, and the derived nominal is supplied a nominal external argument:

(10) donate   -ion   ⇒   donation
      | | |
     ($\underline{A}$, th, G) ($\underline{R}$) ($\underline{R}$, A, th, G)

In syntax, the maximal projection interpreted as a one-place predicate is the local of the subject opacity effects, at least according to Williams (1980). There it was proposed that the opacity ordinarily attributed to subjects was actually a fact about one-place predicates:

(11) PREDICATE OPACITY CONDITION (POC): an anaphor cannot occur free in XP, if XP is a predicate.

For almost all cases, this matches the ordinary Subject Opacity Condition (as in Chomsky 1973, or Principle A of the Binding theory of Chomsky 1981).

Under the POC, subject-bound reflexives can occur in a predicative XP if they are bound to the subject that the XP is predicated of, because they will then be co-indexed with the predicative XP itself, and that counts as being bound in the XP:

(12) John [$_{VP_i}$ saw himself$_i$]

Here, *himself* is bound in VP because it is co-indexed with VP. It should be easy to see why the POC matches the Subject Opacity Condition so closely in empirical prediction: wherever there is a subject, there is a predicate.

Recently though, some evidence favoring the POC has come to light. As observed by D. Lebeaux (pers. comm.) and K. Johnson, the difference in the following pair follows from the POC, but not from the Subject Opacity Condition:

(13) a.   *John_i wondered [which picture of himself_i] Mary would like*
     b.   **John wondered [_AP_i how mad at himself] Mary_i would be*

In (13a), the reflexive occurs in no predicative XPs except the one predicated of its antecedent, so the reflexive satisfies the POC; in (13b), however, the reflexive occurs in the AP predicated of *Mary* and so must be bound in that AP; co-indexation of the reflexive with the AP would satisfy the POC but would give the wrong meaning, for then the reflexive would be bound by *Mary*. So the POC correctly discriminates between the two cases, the important difference being that the *wh-* fronted XP is not predicative in (13a), but in (13b) it is.

The Subject Opacity Condition cannot discriminate these—in both cases, the reflexive has been moved out of the domain of the subject. It is not clear what prediction the Subject Opacity Condition makes here—it depends on whether it applies to the pre– or post–*wh-* movement structure—but whatever the prediction, it should be the same for the two cases.

If this is so, then it is strong evidence for the notion "predicate" in syntax, and for the definition of "predicate" in terms of maximal projection.

Since morphology does not have maximal projections, it does not have predicates. Since it does not have predicates, it should not show any POC effects. And in fact there is no evidence of any kind of POC, or Condition A, effects.

But there is a locality condition on binding in morphology, and appropriately, its domain is the *n*-place predicate, since this is what morphology is in the business of manufacturing; in morphology, every *n*-place predicate—that is, everything—is opaque. The following minimal pair illustrates the difference between syntax and morphology with respect to opaque domains:

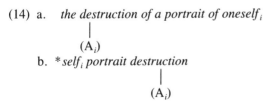

(14) a.   *the destruction of a portrait of oneself_i*

                 |
              (A_i)
     b.   **self_i portrait destruction*

                 |
              (A_i)

In (14a), we have a reflexive bound to the implicit agent argument of *destruction*. Since the NP *destruction of oneself* is not predicative, this binding satisfies the POC. In (14b) we see that the parallel binding in morphology is ungrammatical; apparently binding in morphology is subject to a tighter restriction: namely, bound forms, such as *-self*, must be bound in every *n*-place predicate in which they occur; in particular, *-self* in (14b) must be bound in the *n*-place predicate *self-portrait*. The symmetry is compelling: syntax builds opaque one-place predicates; and morphology builds opaque *n*-place predicates.

2. Reference

Like the notion of one-place predicate, the notion of reference is tied to the syntactic notion of maximal projection, and hence should play no role in morphology.

In fact, θ-theory relates reference to predication in such a way that if one played no role in morphology, the other could not either: The θ-structure of an XP is independent of its use as a referential or predicative expression.

The θ-structure of an XP, referential or not, involves the "percolation" of the external argument of the head up to the maximal projection of the XP:

(15)

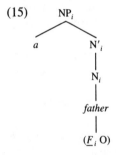

Father is a two-place relation, but the NP *a father* "refers to" only one end of this relation. The reason is, the external argument (F) is percolated, but not the other argument. What is of highest interest is that it is the same argument percolated whether the NP is used in a referential position or in a predicative position:

(16) a. *A father arrived*

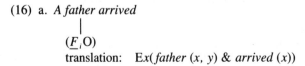

translation: $\text{E}x(father\ (x,\ y)\ \&\ arrived\ (x))$

b. *John is a father*
   translation: *father (John, y)*

It is in this sense that the θ-structure of an XP is autonomous from its use as a referential or predicative expression. The θ-structure of the NP *father* is that given in (15), and it is the same θ-structure used in both (16a) (referential) and (16b) (predicative).

It is far from obvious that this autonomy should hold. In fact, in a recent elaboration of θ-theory by Higginbotham (1986), this autonomy does not hold: the θ-structure of a predicative expression, in his view, is the same as I give in (7) in all respects relevant to the present discussion; however, the θ-structure of an NP used referentially is quite different—in such an NP the external argument of the head is "satisfied" or "discharged" by the specifier, so that the NP itself has no unsatisfied argument. Higginbotham's view has much to recommend it; for example, in his theory, the reason that predicative NPs need subjects is that they have an undischarged θ-role, whereas the reason referential NPs do not have (external) subjects is that they do not. I will not undertake here a systematic comparison of his and my views on this; this is done in a preliminary way in Williams (forthcoming) and more fully in Williams (in preparation). I mention it here simply to emphasize that the autonomy appealed to here is far from necessary, and in fact if Higginbotham is right, it is wrong.

Now, since the maximal projection is the locus of predication, that is, it is only maximal projections that have the special status as one-place predicates, and since reference also seems to attach to maximal projections, then we might expect morphology to lack certain aspects of reference, if it lacks maximal projections.

The first kind of reference that seems to be missing in words is specific time reference. Consider the lack of synonymy in the following pair:

(17) a. *John is a bank robber.*
      b. *John is robbing a bank.*

Example (17a) does not imply that John is robbing a bank at the moment; rather, it implies that he robs them in general. We may postulate that specific time reference is a feature only of a maximal projection in syntax, perhaps S (= tense-bar; or perhaps IP, in the terminology of Chomsky 1986).

Another kind of reference missing in words is illustrated in (17): in (17b) it is implied that there is a specific bank that John is robbing; in (17a), on the other hand, no specific bank is referred to; in fact, (17a) is compatible with John never having robbed a bank, so long as he has whatever properties are taken to warrant that designation—he may be plotting to rob a (nonspecific) bank, etc. So, parts of words seem to fail to have specific object reference. We may attribute this lack of specific object reference to the lack of maximal projections in word-formation, if the maximal projection is the locus of specific object reference.

There are however some cases where we seem to find specific object reference inside of words; in particular, compounds that include proper names:

(18) *Nixon-hater*
Anglophile
Nazi sympathizer

Even here, though, there are some distinctions to be drawn. As in the case of (17), we find that the compositional semantics does not give us the meaning of these expressions:

(19) a.   *John is a Nixon-hater, even though he does not hate Nixon.*
b.   **John hates Nixon, even though he does not hate Nixon.*

Sentence (19a) does not sound contradictory, the way that (19b) does: apparently, it is not necessary to actually hate Nixon to be called a Nixon-hater; (19a) implies that there are other criteria for membership in this group, but of course does not reveal what they are. This at least means that the reference of Nixon does not figure in the calculation of the meaning of the term *Nixon-hater* relevant for (19a), as it does in case of the phrase *hates Nixon* in (19b). In fact, though, this does not mean that the noun *Nixon* does not refer to Nixon in (19a); it simply means that this reference does not determine the meaning of the term *Nixon-hater* (I am indebted to A. Marantz for clarification here).

It is frequently observed that in such compounds, only names of famous people can be incorporated, a rather strange restriction:

(20) **a Bill-hater*

I think, though, this has a natural explanation under the assumption that definite object reference does not attach to parts of words. The reason is, it is difficult to attach generic reference to the resulting phrase, because it is difficult to know what the "other criteria" of membership (apart from hating Bill) might be.

In noun-incorporating languages, it appears that parts of words are capable of definite object reference, as incorporated nouns can be interpreted as having non-generic reference, and in fact may be used to introduce definite discourse referents:

(21) *Yao-wir-a'a   ye-nuhs-nuhwe'-s*
PRE-baby-SUF 3fS/3N-house-like-ASP
'The baby house-likes'   (Baker 1987:81)

In (21) the incorporated noun 'house' can be used to refer to a specific house, and apparently can be used as the first mention of a house. Such examples might at first suggest that definite object reference could attach to parts of words, at least in Mohawk, if not in English.

But Mithun (1984) directly argues against this view of noun incorporation: "It is the pronominal system . . . that differs from English, not the word formation process" (p. 871). And she gives the following to illustrate:

(22) *K-atenun-hah-kwe. Ah tis   yehetkv.*
I-watch-HAB-PAST   Ah how she ugly
'I was baby-sitting. Boy is she ugly.'
(Mohawk, ex. (112) from Mithun 1984)

In this example, 'watch,' which does not have a noun incorporated, nevertheless serves to introduce a referent, which the subsequent pronoun 'she' picks up. So this means that definite discourse referents can be introduced with no syntactically or morphologically overt signal. Naturally, then introduction of discourse referents will be possible with noun incorporation as well; this example simply shows that it is independent of noun incorporation.

Finally, variables are excluded from the interior of words. This no doubt follows from the exclusion of definite reference, for in syntax, variables are used to quantify positions in which definite reference holds. So, although the adjective *complete* has a "degree" interpretation in the N *completeness,* this degree cannot be questioned:

(23) *[How complete]-ness does John appreciate?*
    cf. *What degree of completeness does John appreciate?*

And the same of course holds for positions of definite object reference:

(24) *[Which bank] robber is John?*
    cf. *Which bank did John rob?*

Likewise, pronouns cannot occur in compounds, either bound by a quantifier or directly referential:

(25) a. *John is a him hater.*
    b. *Everyone_i thinks that John is a him_i-hater.*

The exception is the pronouns in such expressions as *he-man* or *she-whale,* but since in these uses the pronouns are not referential, they simply confirm that it is a kind of reference that is excluded from words, not any particular lexical items.

Again, the significance of these exclusions is that they will follow from the absence of maximal projections in morphology, if definite object reference attaches only to maximal projections. The lack of variables in morphology essentially means that the entire A-bar binding system will be lacking as well, as it depends on the presence of variables. So, there should be no evidence of operators or scope in the syntactic sense. This is not to say that there is not a very trivial sense of scope in morphology; for example, *mis-re-align* does not mean the same thing as *re-mis-align,* and the difference can be intelligibly described as a difference in scope of the two prefixes (which may in fact reasonably be called "operators"); but this scope is a trivial consequence of the compositionality of word-formation. What will not be found in morphology are cases in which a prefix, for example, has "scope" different from that given it directly in the phrase-structure tree (an affix has scope over what it is added onto). But in syntax, quantifiers do have scope different from that directly given by their syntactic position—hence the presence of QR and other scope assignment mechanisms in the theories of the logical structure of sentences.

Now, the absence of variables, operators, and nontrivial scope and scope assignment mechanisms from morphology is of course not a matter of necessity, and in fact, recent proposals by Pesetsky (1985) entail the presence of all of these in word structure. I have argued elsewhere against Pesetsky's proposals (in particular, in Di Sciullo & Williams 1988) and will not repeat those arguments here.

3. The Theta/Theta-Bar Distinction and the A-binding System

So far we have seen that in lacking the maximal projection, morphology also lacks predication, reference, and the entire A-bar binding system. In this section we postulate that some features of the A-binding system are lacking as well, and again the reason will be the lack of maximal projections in morphology.

We have already reviewed some parts of the A-binding system that are common to morphology and syntax: anaphors (*himself* in syntax, *-self* in morphology); θ-roles, θ-role satisfaction, and the internal/external argument distinction; function composition.

One feature of the A-bar system that is missing, however, is the θ/θ-bar distinction. The evidence for this the lack of expletives in morphology:

(26) a. **It-raining is nice.*
      b. **It-appearance that Bill left was disquieting.*

The role of the expletive in syntax is to fill θ-bar A positions: positions which in general can be argument positions, but which, for some particular verb, is not an argument position.

Now, the theta-bar positions in syntax are the "subject" positions:

(27) a. *It rained.*
      b. *It seemed that Bill was here.*
      c. *It being clear that Bill was here.*
      d. *I consider it clear that Bill was here.*

In (27a) we have Tensed Clause subject position; in (27c) and (27d) Small Clause subject positions. The important question for syntax is, what is the notion of subject that governs these cases? Elsewhere (Williams 1980 in particular), and in §2 above, I have argued that the correct notion of subject for θ-theory is "subject of a predicative XP," and that θ-bar positions are the structural subject positions of XPs which are not predicative. Since morphology lacks XPs, it lacks the distinction between predicative and nonpredicative XPs, and so must lack the θ/θ-bar distinction. Every "position" in morphology is in some sense a θ-position.

This is not to say that every morphological object is an instance of θ-role satisfaction; some are (as in (28a)) but others are not ((28b)):

(28) a. *nutcracker, churchgoer*
      b. *church pew, gopher hole*

The rule in morphology is that every element in a compound must contribute to the interpretation of the compound, and the examples in (28) conform to this rule, unlike the examples in (26). In syntax, subjects are exempt from this law; morphology does not have subjects in the relevant sense, and so has no exceptions.

References

ABBREVIATIONS

ACL	Proceedings of the Association of Computation Linguistics
BLS	Proceedings of the Annual Meeting of the Berkeley Linguistics Society
CLS	Papers from the Regional Meeting of the Chicago Linguistic Society
COLING	Proceedings of the International Conference on Computational Linguistics
ESCOL	Proceedings of the Eastern States Conference on Linguistics
FL	Foundations of Language
LA	Linguistic Analysis
Lg.	Language
LI	Linguistic Inquiry
LP	Linguistics and Philosophy
LR	Linguistic Review
NELS	Proceedings of [formerly Papers from] the North Eastern [formerly New England] Linguistic Society
NLLT	Natural Language and Linguistic Theory
WCCFL	Proceedings of the West Coast Conference on Formal Linguistics

Abbott, B. 1976. Right Node Raising as a Test for Constituenthood. *LI* 7:639–42.

Abney, S. 1986. Functional Elements and Licensing. Paper presented at GLOW, Barcelona.

Ades, A., & M. Steedman. 1982. On the Order of Words. *LP* 4:517–58.

Ajdukiewicz, K. 1935. Die syntaktische Konnexität. *Studia Philosophica* 1:1–27. English trans. by H. Weber in *Polish Logic, 1920–1930,* ed. S. McCall, 207–31. Oxford: Oxford University Press.

Andrews, A. 1982. The Representation of Case in Modern Icelandic. In Bresnan 1982a:427–503.

Aoun, J., N. Hornstein, D. Lightfoot, & A. Weinberg. 1987. Two Types of Locality. *LI* 18:537–77.

Aoun, J., N. Hornstein, & D. Sportiche. 1981. Some Aspects of Wide Scope Quantification. *Journal of Linguistic Research* 1:69–95.

Aoun, J., & D. Sportiche. 1983. On the Formal Theory of Government. *LR* 2:211–36.

Bach, E. 1979. Control in Montague Grammar. *LI* 10:515–31.

————. 1980. In Defense of Passive. *LP* 3:297–341.

————. 1983. Generalized Categorial Grammars and the English Auxiliary. In *Linguistic Categories: Auxiliaries, and Related Puzzles.* Vol. 2, *The Scope, Order and Distribution of English Auxiliary Verbs,* ed. F. Heny & B. Richards, 101–20. Dordrecht: Reidel.

Bach, E., & B. Partee. 1980. Anaphora and Semantic Structure. *CLS Parasession on Pronouns and Anaphora,* 1–28.

Baker, C. 1970. Notes on the Description of English Questions: The Role of an Abstract Question Morpheme. *FL* 6:197–219.

Baker, C., & J. McCarthy, eds. 1981. *The Logical Problem of Language Acquisition.* Cambridge: MIT Press.

Baker, M. 1983. Noun Incorporation in Iroquoian. MS, MIT.

Baltin, M. 1981. Strict Bounding. In Baker & McCarthy 1981:257–95.

————. 1982. A Landing Site Theory of Movement Rules. *LI* 13:1–38.

————. 1985. Review Article of Bresnan 1982a. *Lg.* 61:863–80.

————. 1986. Adverb Preposing and Extraction Constraints. MS, New York University.

————. 1987. Degree Complements. In Huck & Ojeda 1987:11–26.

Banfield, A. 1982. *Unspeakable Sentences: Narration and Representation in the Language of Fiction.* London: Routledge & Kegan Paul.

Bar-Hillel, Y. 1953. A Quasi-Arithmetical Notation for Syntactic Description. *Lg.* 29:47–58.

Barss, A. 1984. Chain Binding, MS, MIT.

Belletti, A., & L. Rizzi. 1981. The Syntax of "ne": Some Theoretical Implications. *LR* 1:117–54.

van Benthem, J. 1986. *Essays in Logical Semantics.* Dordrecht: Reidel.

Bloomfield, L. 1933. *Language.* New York: Holt, Rinehart & Winston.

Borsley, R. 1987a. A Note on HPSG. Bangor, Wales: University College of North Wales (Bangor Research Papers in Linguistics 1).

————. 1987b. Subjects and Complements in HPSG. Stanford: Center for the Study of Language and Information, Stanford University (CSLI Technical Report).

Bouchard, D. 1982. On the Content of Empty Categories. Ph.D. diss., MIT.

Brame, M. 1982. The Head-Selector Theory of Lexical Specifications and the Nonexistence of Coarse Categories. *LA* 10:321–25.

Bresnan, J. 1970. On Complementizers: Toward a Syntactic Theory of Complement Types. *FL* 6:297–321.

————. 1972. Theory of Complementation in English Syntax. Ph.D. diss., MIT.

————, ed. 1982a. *The Mental Representation of Grammatical Relations.* Cambridge: MIT Press.

————. 1982b. Control and Complementation. In Bresnan 1982a: 282–390.

Bresnan, J., R. Kaplan, & P. Peterson. In preparation. Coordination and the Flow of Information through Phrase Structure.

Burzio, L. 1981. Intransitive Verbs and Italian Auxiliaries. Ph.D. diss., MIT.

Carden, G., L. Gordon, & P. Monro. 1982. Raising Rules and the Projection Principle. Paper presented at LSA Annual Meeting.

Carlson, G. 1977. Reference to Kinds in English. Ph.D. diss., University of Massachusetts (Amherst).

Cheng, L. 1986. Clause Structure in Mandarin Chinese. M.A. thesis, University of Toronto.

Chomsky, N. 1957. *Syntactic Structures*. Mouton: The Hague. Janua Linguarum Series Minor 4.

———. 1965. *Aspects of the Theory of Syntax*. Cambridge: MIT Press.

———. 1970. Remarks on Nominalization. In *Readings in English Transformational Grammar*, ed. R. Jacobs & P. Rosenbaum, 184–221. Waltham, Mass.: Ginn.

———. 1973. Conditions on Transformations. In *A Festschrift for Morris Halle*, ed. S. Anderson & P. Kiparsky, 232–86. New York: Holt, Rinehart & Winston.

———. 1975. *The Logical Structure of Linguistic Theory*. Plenum.

———. 1976. Conditions on Rules of Grammar. *LA* 2:303–51.

———. 1980. On Binding. *LI* 11:1–46.

———. 1981. *Lectures on Government and Binding*. Dordrecht: Foris.

———. 1982. *Some Concepts and Consequences of the Theory of Government and Binding*. Cambridge: MIT Press.

———. 1986. *Barriers*. Cambridge: MIT Press.

Chomsky, N., & H. Lasnik. 1977. Filters and Control. *LI* 8:425–504.

Clark, R. 1986. Boundaries and the Treatment of Control. Ph.D. diss., University of California (Los Angeles).

Comorovski, I. 1986. Multiple *Wh* Movement in Romanian. *LI* 17:171–77.

Cooper, R. 1983. *Quantification and Syntactic Theory*. Dordrecht: Reidel.

Couquaux, A. 1981. French Predication and Linguistic Theory. In *Levels of Syntactic Representation*, R. May and J. Koster, eds., 33–64. Dordrecht: Foris.

Cremers, C. 1983. On the Form and Interpretation of Ellipsis. In *Studies in Modeltheoretic Semantics*, ed. A. ter Meulen, 145–60. Dordrecht: Foris.

Curry, H. 1961. Some Logical Aspects of Grammatical Structure. In R. Jakobson, ed., *Structure of Language and Its Mathematical Aspects*, 56–68. Providence: American Mathematical Society. Proceedings of the Symposia in Applied Mathematics 12.

Curry, H., & R. Feys. 1958. *Combinatory Logic*. Vol. 1. Amsterdam: North Holland.

Davies, W., & C. Rosen. 1988. Unions as Multi-Predicate Clauses. *Lg*. 64:52–88.

Davis, M. 1987. Base-generating NP-Structure. *McGill Working Papers in Linguistics* 1:85–120.

Di Sciullo, A., & E. Williams. 1986. Noun Incorporation vs. Cliticization. MS, University of Massachusetts.

———. 1988. *On the Definition of Word*. Cambridge: MIT Press.

Dougherty, R. 1970. A Grammar of Coordinate Conjoined Structures: I. *Lg*. 46:850–98.

Dowty, D. 1979. *Word Meaning and Montague Grammar.* Dordrecht: Reidel.

————. 1982a. Grammatical Relations and Montague Grammar. In *The Nature of Syntactic Representation,* ed. P. Jacobson & G. Pullum, 79–130. Dordrecht: Reidel.

————. 1982b. More on the Categorial Analysis of Grammatical Relations. In Zaenen 1982:115–53.

————. 1988. Type Raising, Functional Composition, and Non-Constituent Conjunction. In Oehrle, Bach, & Wheeler 1988:153–98.

Dowty, D., L. Karttunen, & A. Zwicky, eds. 1985. *Natural Language Parsing: Psychological, Computational, and Theoretical Perspectives.* New York: Cambridge University Press.

Emonds, J. 1972. Evidence That Indirect Object Movement Is a Structure-Preserving Rule. *FL* 8:546–61.

————. 1976. *A Transformational Approach to English Syntax: Root, Structure-preserving, and Local Transformations.* New York: Academic Press.

————. 1985. *A Unified Theory of Syntactic Categories.* Dordrecht: Foris.

Engdahl, E. 1981. The Syntax and Semantics of Questions in Swedish. Ph.D. diss., University of Massachusetts.

Fabb, N. 1984. Syntactic Affixation. Ph.D. diss., MIT.

Farmer, A. 1980. On the Interaction of Morphology and Syntax. Ph.D. diss., MIT.

Fassi Fehri, A. 1988. Agreement in Arabic, Binding and Coherence. In M. Barlow & C. A. Ferguson, eds., *Agreement in Natural Language: Approaches, Theories, Descriptions,* 107–58. Stanford: Center for the Study of Language and Information, Stanford University.

Fiengo, R. 1977. On Trace Theory. *LI* 8:35–61.

Fiengo, R., & J. Higginbotham. 1980. Opacity and NP. *LA* 7:395–422.

Frantz, D. 1985. Passive Verbal Morphology in Relational Grammar. Paper presented at LSA annual meeting.

Fraser, B. 1965. An Examination of the Verb-Particle Construction in English. Ph.D. diss., MIT.

Freidin, R. 1978. Cyclicity and the Theory of Grammar. *LI* 9.4:519–49.

Freidin, R., ed. Forthcoming. *Proceedings of the Princeton Conference on Comparative Grammar.* Cambridge: MIT Press.

Friedman, J., D. Dawei, & W. Wang. 1986. The Weak Generative Capacity of Parenthesis-free Categorial Grammars. *COLING* 11:199–210.

Friedman, J., & R. Venkatesan. 1986. Categorial and Non-Categorial Languages. *Proceedings of the 24th Annual Meeting of the ACL,* 75–77.

Fukui, N. 1986. A Theory of Category Projection and Its Applications. Ph.D. diss., MIT.

Fukui, N., & M. Speas. 1985. Specifiers and Projection. *MIT Working Papers in Linguistics* 8:128–72.

Gay, J., & W. Welmers. 1971. *Mathematics and Logic in the Kpelle Language; and a First Course in Kpelle.* Ibadan, Ivory Coast: Institute of African Studies, University of Ibadan. Occasional Publication 21.

Gazdar, G. 1981. Unbounded Dependencies and Coordinate Structure. *LI* 12: 155–84.

Gazdar, G., E. Klein, G. Pullum, & I. Sag. 1985. *Generalized Phrase-Structure Grammar.* Cambridge: Harvard University Press.

Gazdar, G., & G. Pullum. 1981. Subcategorization, Constituent Order and the Notion "Head." In *The Scope of Lexical Rules,* ed. M. Moortgat, H. van der Hulst, & T. Hoekstra, 107–23. Dordrecht: Foris.

Gazdar, G., G. Pullum, & I. Sag. 1981. Auxiliaries and Related Phenomena in a Restrictive Theory of Grammar. *Lg.* 58:591–638.

Geach, P. 1972. A Program for Syntax. In *Semantics of Natural Language,* ed. D. Davidson & G. Harman, 483–97. Dordrecht: Reidel.

Givón, T. 1975. Serial Verbs and Syntactic Change: Niger-Congo. In Li 1975: 47–112.

Goodall, G. 1987. On Argument Structure and L-Marking with Mandarin Chinese *ba. NELS.* 17, vol. 1 pp. 232–42.

Greenberg, J. 1963. Some Universals of Grammar with Particular Reference to the Order of Meaningful Elements. In *Universals of Language,* ed. J. Greenberg, 73–113. Cambridge: MIT Press.

Grice, H. 1973. Logic and Conversation. In *Speech Acts,* ed. P. Cole & J. Morgan, 41–58. New York: Academic Press. Syntax and Semantics 3.

Grimshaw, J. 1979. Complement Selection and the Lexicon. *LI* 10:279–326.

———. 1981. Form, Function, and the Language Acquisition Device. In Baker & McCarthy 1981:165–82.

———. 1982. Subcategorization and Grammatical Relations. In Zaenen 1982: 35–56.

———. 1986. Subjacency and the S/S' Parameter. *LI* 17:364–9.

Gunji, T. 1986. *Japanese Phrase Structure Grammar.* Dordrecht: Reidel.

Haddock, N., E. Klein, & G. Morrill, eds. 1987. *Categorical Grammar, Unification Grammar, and Parsing.* Edinburgh: Center for Cognitive Science, University of Edinburgh. Edinburgh Working Papers in Cognitive Science 1.

Haegeman, L., & H. van Riemsdijk. 1986. Verb Projection Raising, Scope, and the Typology of Rules Affecting Verbs. *LI* 17:417–66.

Haig, J. 1976. Shadow Pronoun Deletion in Japanese. *LI* 7:363–71.

Hakulinen, A. 1976. Suomen sanajärjestyksen kieliopillisista ja temaattisista tehtävistä. *Reports on Text Linguistics: Suomen kielen generatiivista lauseoppia* 2. Turku, Finland: Meddelanden fran Stiftelsens för Abo Akademi Forskningsinstitut 7.

Hale, K. 1980. Remarks on Japanese Phrase Structure: Comments on the Papers on Japanese Syntax. *MIT Working Papers in Linguistics* 2:185–203.

———. 1983. Walpiri and the Grammar of Non-configurational Languages. *NLLT* 1:5–49.

Halvorsen, P.-K. 1987. Situation Semantics and Semantic Interpretation in Constraint-based Grammars. Stanford: Center for the Study of Language and Information, Stanford University (Report CSLI-TR-87-101).

Hankamer, J. 1971. Constraints on Deletion in Syntax. Ph.D. diss., Yale University.

Harada, K. 1972. Constraints on WH-Q Binding. *Studies in Descriptive and Applied Linguistics* 5:180-206.

Harada, S.-I. 1977. Nihongo-ni 'Henkei'-wa Hituyoo-da. *Gengo* 6:nos. 10, 11 88-95; 96-103.

Harris, Z. 1946. From Morpheme to Utterance. *Lg.* 22:161-83.

Hasegawa, N. 1985. On the So-called "Zero Pronouns" in Japanese. *LR* 4:289-341.

Heinämäki, O. 1980. Problems of Basic Word Order. In *Proceedings of the Fourth International Congress of Fenno-Ugrists*. Turku, Finland: University of Turku, 1980.

Heny, F. 1979. Review of Chomsky 1975. *Synthese* 40-317-52.

Hepple, M. In prep. A Combinatory Categorial Grammar Account of Constituent Order in Germanic Languages. Ph.D. diss., University of Edinburgh.

Higginbotham, J. 1985. On Semantics. *LI* 16:547-93.

Higginbotham, J., & R. May. 1981. Crossing, Markedness, Pragmatics. In *Theory of Markedness in Generative Grammar*, ed. A. Belletti, L. Brandi, & L. Rizzi, 423-44. Pisa: Scuola Normale Superiore.

Higgins, F. 1973. On J. Emonds' Analysis of Extraposition. In *Syntax and Semantics 2*, ed. J. Kimball, 149-95. New York: Academic Press.

———. 1973. The Pseudo-Cleft Construction in English. Ph.D. diss., MIT.

Hoeksema, J. 1985. Wazdat? Contracted Forms and Verb-Secnd in Dutch. In *Germanic Linguistics: Papers from a Symposium at the University of Chicago, April 24, 1985*, ed. J. Faarlund, 112-24. Bloomington: Indiana University Linguistics Club.

Hoji, H. 1980. Double Nominative Constructions in Japanese: Lexically Based Syntax. M.A. thesis, University of Washington (Seattle).

———. 1985. Logical Form Constraints and Configurational Structures in Japanese. Ph.D. diss., University of Washington (Seattle).

Hornstein, N., & D. Lightfoot. 1984. Rethinking Predication. MS, University of Maryland.

Horvath, J. 1981. Aspects of Hungarian Syntax and the Theory of Grammar. Ph.D. diss., University of California (Los Angeles).

Huang, C.-T. J. 1982. Logical Relations in Chinese and the Theory of Grammar. Ph.D. diss., MIT.

Huck, G. 1985. Discontinuity and Word Order in Categorial Grammar. Ph.D. diss., University of Chicago.

Huck, G., & A. Ojeda, eds. 1987. *Discontinuous Constituency*. New York: Academic Press. Syntax and Semantics 20.

Hyman, L. 1975. On the Change from SOV to VSO: Evidence from Niger-Congo. In Li 1975:113-47.

Ishikawa, A. 1985. Complex Predicates and Lexical Operators in Japanese. Ph.D. diss., Stanford University.

Jackendoff, R. 1971. Gapping and Related Rules. *LI* 2:21-35.

———. 1977. $\bar{X}$ *Syntax: A Study of Phrase Structure*. Cambridge: MIT Press.

Jacobson, P. 1982. Comments on "Subcategorization and Grammatical Relations." In Zaenen 1982:57–70.

Jaeggli, O. 1982. *Topics in Romance Syntax*. Dordrecht: Foris.

———. On Certain ECP Effects in Spanish. MS, University of Southern California.

Jespersen, O. 1924. *The Philosophy of Grammar*. London: Allen & Unwin.

———. 1937. *Analytic Syntax*. London: Allen & Unwin. Reprinted 1984, University of Chicago Press.

Johnson, M. 1986. The LFG Treatment of Discontinuity and the Double Infinitive Construction in Dutch. *Proceedings of the West Coast Conference on Formal Linguistics* 5:102–18.

———. 1987. Regular Path Equations. MS, Stanford University.

Joshi, A. 1985. How Much Context-Sensitivity Is Required to Provide Reasonable Structural Descriptions: Tree Adjoining Grammars. In Dowty, Karttunen, & Zwicky 1985:206–50.

———. 1987a. The Convergence of Mildly Context-Sensitive Formalisms. Paper presented at CSLI Workshop on Processing of Linguistic Structure.

———. 1987b. An Introduction to Tree Adjoining Grammars. In Manaster-Ramer 1987:87–114.

Joshi, A., L. Levy, & M. Takahasihi. 1975. Tree Adjunct Grammars. *Journal of Computer and System Sciences* 10:136–63.

Kajita, M. 1967. *A Generative-Transformational Study of Semi-Auxiliaries in Present-Day American English*. Tokyo: Sanseido.

Kang, B. 1988. Functional Inheritance Anaphora and Semantic Interpretation in a Generalized Categorial Grammar. Ph.D. diss., Brown University.

Kaplan, R., & J. Bresnan. 1982. Lexical-Functional Grammar: A Formal System for Grammatical Representation. In Bresnan 1982a:173–281.

Kaplan, R., L. Karttunen, M. Kay, C. Pollard, I. Sag, S. Shieber, & A. Zaenen. 1986. Unification and Grammatical Theory. *WCCFL* 5:238–54.

Kaplan, R., & J. Maxwell. 1988. An Algorithm for Functional Uncertainty. *COLING* 12:297–302.

Karttunen, L. 1986. *D-PATR: A Development Environment for Unification-based Grammars*. Stanford: Center for the Study of Language and Information, Stanford University. CSLI Report.

Karttunen, L., & M. Kay. 1985. Parsing in a Free Word-Order Language. In Dowty, Karttunen, & Zwicky 1985:279–306.

Katz, J., & P. Postal. 1964. *An Integrated Theory of Linguistic Descriptions*. Cambridge: MIT Press.

Kay, M. 1979. Functional Grammar. *BLS* 5:142–58.

———. 1984. Functional Unification Grammar. *COLING* 10:75–83.

———. 1985. Parsing in Functional Unification Grammar. In Dowty, Karttunen, and Zwicky 1985:251–78.

Kayne, R. 1981a. ECP Extensions. *LI* 12:93–133.

———. 1981b. On Certain Differences between French and English. *LI* 12:349–71.

———. 1983. Connectedness. *LI* 14:223–49.

Keenan, E., & B. Comrie. 1977. Noun Phrase Accessibility and Universal Grammar. *LI* 8:63–99.

Kitagawa, Y. 1986. Subject in Japanese and English. Ph.D. diss., University of Massachusetts (Amherst).

Klavans, J. 1985. The Independence of Syntax and Phonology in Cliticization. *Lg.* 61:95–120.

Klein, E., & I. Sag. 1985. Type-driven Translation. *LP* 8:163–201.

Koopman, H. 1984. *The Syntax of Verbs: From Verb Movement Rules in the Kru Languages to Universal Grammar.* Dordrecht: Foris.

Kornfilt, J., S. Kuno, & E. Sezer. 1980. A Note on Criss-Crossing Double Dislocation. In *Harvard Studies in Syntax and Semantics* 3, ed. S. Kuno.

Koster, J. 1978. Why Subject Sentences Don't Exist. In *Recent Transformational Studies in European Languages,* ed. S. Keyser, 53–64. Cambridge: MIT Press.

———. 1984. On Binding and Control. *LI* 15:417–59.

Kroch, A. 1982. A Quantitative Study of Resumptive Pronouns in English Relative Clauses. Paper presented at 13th NWAVE Conference, University of Pennsylvania.

———. 1987. Unbounded Dependencies and Subjacency in a Tree Adjoining Grammar. In Manaster-Ramer 1987:143–72.

Kroch, A., & A. Joshi. 1985. The Linguistic Relevance of Tree Adjoining Grammar. Philadelphia: University of Pennsylvania Department of Computer and Information Sciences Technical Report MS-CIS-85-16.

———. 1987. Analyzing Extraposition in a Tree Adjoining Grammar. In Huck & Ojeda 1987:107–49.

Kroch, A., & B. Santorini. Forthcoming. The Derived Constituent Structure of the West Germanic Verb Raising Construction. In Freidin, forthcoming.

Kuno, S. 1973. *The Structure of the Japanese Language.* Cambridge: MIT Press.

———. 1976. Gapping: A Functional Analysis. *LI* 7:300–318.

Kuroda, S.-Y. 1965. Generative Grammatical Studies in the Japanese Language. Ph.D. diss., MIT.

———. 1984. Movement of Noun Phrases in Japanese. MS, University of California (San Diego).

———. 1985. Whether You Agree or Not: Rough Ideas about the Comparative Grammar of English and Japanese. MS, University of California (San Diego).

Lakoff, G. 1971. On Generative Semantics. In *Semantics,* ed. D. Steinberg & L. Jacobovits, 232–96. Cambridge: Cambridge University Press.

Lambek, J. 1958. The Mathematics of Sentence Structure. *American Mathematical Monthly* 65:154–70.

———. 1961. On the Calculus of Syntactic Types. In R. Jakobson ed., *Structure of Language and Its Mathematical Aspects.* Providence: American Mathematical Society (Proceedings of Symposia in Applied Mathematics 12), pp. 166–78.

Lamontagne, G., & L. Travis. 1986. The Case Filter and the ECP. *McGill Working Papers in Linguistics* 2:51–75.

Langendoen, D. 1970. The 'Can't Seem To' Construction. *LI* 1:25–35.

———. 1975. Acceptable Conclusions from Unacceptable Ambiguity. In *Testing*

Linguistic Hypotheses, ed. D. Cohen & J. Wirth, 111–27. Washington, D.C.: Hemisphere.

Langendoen, D., & E. Battistella. 1982. The Interpretation of Predicate Reflexive and Reciprocal Expressions in English. *NELS* 12:163–73.

Lasnik, H., & M. Saito. 1984. On the Nature of Proper Government. *LI* 15:235–89.

———. In preparation. Move-alpha: Conditions on Its Application and Output.

Levin, L. 1986. Operations on Lexical Forms: Unaccusative Rules in Germanic Languages. Ph.D. diss., MIT.

Lewis, D. 1972. General Semantics. In *Semantics for Natural Language,* ed. D. Davidson and G. Harman, 169–218. Dordrecht: Reidel.

Li, C., ed. 1975. *Word Order and Word Order Change.* Austin: University of Texas Press.

Li, C., & S. Thompson. 1975. The Semantic Function of Word Order: A Case Study in Mandarin. In Li 1975:163–95.

———. 1981. *Mandarin Chinese: A Functional Reference Grammar.* Berkeley & Los Angeles: University of California Press.

Lyons, J. 1968. *Introduction to Theoretical Linguistics.* Cambridge: Cambridge University Press.

Maling, J. 1972. On "Gapping and the Order of Constituents." *LI* 3:101–8.

Maling, J., & A. Zaenen. 1985. Preposition Stranding and Passive. *Nordic Journal of Linguistics* 8:197–209.

Manaster-Ramer, A., ed. 1987. *The Mathematics of Language.* Philadelphia: Benjamins.

Manzini, R. 1983. Restructuring and Reanalysis. Ph.D. diss., MIT.

Marantz, A. 1984. *On the Nature of Grammatical Relations.* Cambridge: MIT Press.

———. Forthcoming a. Clitics, Morphological Merger, and the Mapping to Phonological Structure. In *Theoretical Morphology,* ed. M. Hammond & M. Noonan. New York: Academic Press.

———. Forthcoming b. Apparent Exceptions to the Projection Principle. In *Morphology and Modularity,* ed. M. Eversert et al. Dordrecht: Foris.

May, R. 1977. The Grammar of Quantification. Ph.D. diss., MIT.

———. 1985. *Logical Form: Its Structure and Derivation.* Cambridge: MIT Press.

McCawley, J. 1968. Concerning the Base Component of a Transformational Grammar. *FL* 4:243–69.

———. 1981a. An Un-Syntax. In *Current Approaches to Syntax,* ed. E. Moravcsik & J. Wirth, 167–95. Syntax and Semantics 13. New York: Academic Press.

———. 1981b. The Syntax and Semantics of English Relative Clauses. *Lingua* 53:99–149.

———. 1982a. Parentheticals and Discontinuous Constituent Structure. *LI* 13:91–106.

———. 1982b. The Nonexistence of Syntactic Categories. In J. McCawley, *Thirty Million Theories of Grammar,* 176–203. Chicago: University of Chicago Press.

———. 1983. Towards Plausibility in Theories of Language Acquisition. *Communication and Cognition* 16:169–83.

———. 1984. Anaphora and Notions of Command. *BLS* 10:220–32.

———. 1985. Speech Acts and Goffman's Participant Roles. *ESCOL* 1:260–74.

———. 1987. A Case of Syntactic Mimicry. In *Functionalism in Syntax*, ed. V. Frid & R. Dirven, 459–70. Amsterdam: Benjamins.

———. 1988. *The Syntactic Phenomena of English.* Chicago: University of Chicago Press.

McCawley, J., & K. Momoi. 1987. The Constituent Structure of -*te* Complements in Japanese. *Papers in Japanese Linguistics* 11:1–60.

McCawley, N. 1972. A Study of Japanese Reflexivization. Ph.D. diss., University of Illinois.

———. 1976. Reflexivization: A Transformational Approach. In *Japanese Generative Grammar*, ed. M. Shibtani, 51–116. New York: Academic Press. Syntax and Semantics 5.

Mithun, M. 1984. The Evolution of Noun Incorporation. *Lg.* 60:847–94.

Miyagawa, S. 1987. Restructuring in Japanese. In *Issues in Japanese Linguistics*, ed. T. Imai & M. Saito, 273–300. Dordrecht: Foris.

Moortgat, M. 1988. Mixed Composition and Discontinuous Dependencies. In Oehrle, Bach, & Wheeler 188:319–48.

Morrill, G. 1987. Meta-Categorial Grammar. In Haddock, Klein, & Morrill 1987:1–29.

Moser, M. 1987. Some Feature Assignments in TAGs. MS, University of Pennsylvania.

Muraki, M. 1974. *Presupposition and Thematization.* Tokyo: Kaitakusha.

Neijt, A. 1979. *Gapping: A Contribution to Sentence Grammar.* Dordrecht: Foris.

Netter, K. 1986. Getting Things out of Order. *COLING* 11:494–96.

———. 1987. Nonlocal Dependencies and Infinitival Constructions in German. MS, University of Stuttgart.

Oehrle, R. 1987. Boolean Properties in the Analysis of Gapping. In Huck & Ojeda 1987:201–40.

———. 1988. Multi-Dimensional Compositional Functions as a Basis for Grammatical Analysis. In Oehrle, Bach, & Wheeler 1988:349–90.

Oehrle, R., E. Bach, & D. Wheeler, eds. 1988. *Categorial Grammars and Natural Language Structures.* Dordrecht: Reidel.

Pareschi, R. 1986. Combinatory Categorial Grammar, Logic Programming and the Parsing of Natural Language. DAI Working Paper, University of Edinburgh.

———. In preparation. Type-driven Natural Language Analysis. Ph.D. diss., University of Edinburgh.

Pareschi, R., & M. Steedman. 1987. A Lazy Way to Chart Parse with Categorial Grammars. Paper presented at 25th Annual Conference of the ACL.

Payne, D. 1986. Derivation, Internal Syntax, and External Syntax in Yagua. Paper presented at Milwaukee Morphology Meeting.

Perlmutter, D. 1971. *Deep and Surface Structure Constraints in Syntax.* New York: Holt, Rinehart & Winston.

Pesetsky, D. 1982. Paths and Categories. Ph.D. diss., MIT.

———. 1985. Morphology and Logical Form. *LI* 16:193–246.

Piggott, G. 1987. On the Autonomy of the Feature Nasal. *CLS Parasession on Autosegmental and Metrical Phonology*, 223–38.

Pollard, C. 1984. Generalized Phrase Structure Grammars, Head Grammars and Natural Language. Ph.D. diss., Stanford University.

Pollard, C., & I. Sag. 1987. *Information-based Syntax and Semantics*. Vol. 1, *Fundamentals*. Stanford: Center for the Study of Language and Information, Stanford University. CSLI Lecture Notes 14.

———. Forthcoming. *Information-based Syntax and Semantics*. Vol. 2, *Topics in Binding and Control*. Stanford: Center for the Study of Language and Information, Stanford University. CSLI Lecture Notes.

Postal, P. 1971. *Cross-over Phenomena*. New York: Holt, Rinehart & Winston.

———. 1976. Avoiding Reference to Subject. *LI* 7:151–82.

Pranka, P. 1983. Syntax and Word Formation. Ph.D. diss., MIT.

Prince, E. 1986. On the Syntactic Marking of Presupposed Open Propositions. *CLS Parasession on Pragmatics and Grammatical Theory*, 208–22.

Pullum, G. 1976. Rule Interaction and the Organization of a Grammar. Ph.D. diss., University of London. Abridged version pub. 1979, New York: Garland.

———. 1982. Free Word Order and Phrase Structure Rules. *NELS* 12:209–20.

Quine, W. 1960. Variables Explained Away. *Proceedings of the American Philosophical Society* 104:343–47. Reprinted in W. Quine, *Selected Logic Papers*, 227–35. New York: Random House.

———. 1982. *Methods of Logic*, 4th ed. Cambridge: Harvard University Press.

Rappaport, M. 1983. On the Nature of Derived Nominals. In *Papers in Lexical Functional Grammar*, ed. L. Levin et al. Bloomington: Indiana University Linguistics Club.

Reinhart, T. 1981. Definite NP Anaphora and C-Command Domains. *LI* 12:605–35.

———. 1983. *Anaphora and Semantic Interpretation*. Chicago: University of Chicago Press,

van Riemsdijk, H., & E. Williams. 1981. NP-Structure. *LR* 1:171–217.

Rizzi, L. 1982. *Issues in Italian Syntax*. Dordrecht: Foris.

Roeper, T. 1986. Implicit Arguments, Implicit Roles, and Subject/Object Asymmetry in Morphological Rules. MS, University of Massachusetts (Amherst).

Ross, J. R. 1967. Constraints on Variables in Syntax. Ph.D. diss., MIT. Pub. 1986 as *Infinite Syntax!*, Hillsdale, N.J.: Erlbaum.

———. 1969. Auxiliaries as Main Verbs. *Studies in Philosophical Linguistics* 1:77–102.

———. 1970. Gapping and the Order of Constituents. In *Progress in Linguistics*, ed. M. Bierwisch & M. Heidolph, 249–59. The Hague: Mouton.

Rothstein, S. 1983. The Syntactic Forms of Predication. Ph.D. diss., MIT.

Rouveret, A., & J. R. Vergnaud. 1980. Specifying Reference to the Subject: French Causatives and Conditions on Representations. *LI* 11:97–202.

Sadock, J. 1985. Autolexical Syntax: A Proposal for the Treatment of Noun Incorporation and Similar Phenomena. *NLLT* 3:379–439.

Safir, K. 1984. Multiple Variable Binding. *LI* 15:603–38.

Sag, I. 1976. Deletion and Logical Form. Ph.D. diss., MIT.

———. 1987. Grammatical Hierarchy and Linear Precedence. In Huck & Ojeda 1987:303–40.

Sag, I., G. Gazdar, T. Wasow, & S. Weisler. 1985. Coordination and How to Distinguish Categories. *NLLT* 3:117–71.

Sag, I., & C. Pollard. 1987. *HPSG: An Informal Synopsis*. Stanford: Center for the Study of Language and Information, Stanford University. CSLI Technical Report.

Saiki, M. 1985. On the Coordination of Gapped Constituents in Japanese. *CLS* 21:371–87.

Saito, M. 1982. Case Marking in Japanese: A Preliminary Study. MS, MIT.

———. 1985. Some Asymmetries in Japanese and Their Theoretical Implications. Ph.D. diss., MIT.

———. 1986. LF Effects of Scrambling. Paper presented at Princeton Workshop on Comparative Grammar. In Freidin, forthcoming.

Schachter, P. 1976. A Nontransformational Account of Gerundive Nominals in English. *LI* 7:205–41.

Schönfinkel, M. 1924. Über die Bausteine der mathematischen Logik. *Mathematische Annalen* 92:305–16.

Shibatani, M., & C. Cotton. 1976–77. Remarks on Double Nominative Sentences. *Papers in Japanese Linguistics* 5:261–77.

Shieber, S. 1986. *An Introduction to Unification-based Approaches to Grammar*. Stanford: Center for the Study of Language and Information, Stanford University. CSLI Lecture Notes Series 4.

Simon, H. 1962. The Architecture of Complexity. *Proceedings of the American Philosophical Society* 106:467–82. Reprinted in H. Simon, *The Sciences of the Artificial*, 84–118. Cambridge: MIT Press.

Speas, M. 1986. Adjunction and Projection in Syntax. Ph.D. diss., MIT.

Sportiche, D. 1981. Bounding Nodes in French. *LR* 1:219–46.

Sproat, R. 1985. On Deriving the Lexicon. Ph.D. diss., MIT.

Steedman, M. 1985. Dependency and Coordination in the Grammar of Dutch and English. *Lg.* 61:523–68.

———. 1987a. Combinatory Grammars and Parasitic Gaps. *NLLT* 5:403–39.

———. 1987b. Gapping as Constituent Coordination. MS, University of Pennsylvania.

———. 1988. Combinators and Grammars. In Oehrle, Bach, & Wheeler 1988:417–42.

Stillings, J. 1975. The Formulation of Gapping in English as Evidence for Variable Types in Syntactic Transformations. *LA* 1:247–73.

Stowell, T. 1978. What Was There Before There Was There. *CLS* 14:458–71.

———. 1981. Origins of Phrase-Structure. Ph.D. diss., MIT.

———. 1983. Subjects across Categories. *LR* 2:285–312.

———. 1986. Null Antecedents and Proper Government. *NELS* 16:476–93.

———. To appear. Small Clause Restructuring. In R. Freidin, forthcoming. Cambridge: MIT Press.

———. In preparation. Phrase Structure. MS, UCLA, Los Angeles.

Stump, G. 1981. The Formal Semantics and Pragmatics of Adjuncts and Absolutes in English. Ph.D. diss., Ohio State University.

Szabolcsi, A. 1983. ECP in Categorial Grammar. MS, Max Planck Institut (Nijmigen).

———. 1984. The Possessor That Ran Away from Home. *LR* 3:89–102.

———. 1986. Filters vs. Combinators. In I. Bodnár, B. Máté & L. Pólos, eds., *Intensional Logic, Semantics and the Philosophy of Science: In Honor of Imre Ruzsa at the Occasion of His 65th Birthday,* 81–90. Budapest.

———. 1987. Bound Variables in Syntax: Are There Any? Proceedings of the 6th Amsterdam Colloquium. In press.

Tesnière, L. 1959. *Élements de syntaxe structurale.* Paris: Klincksieck.

Thráinsson, H. 1979. On Complementation in Icelandic. Ph.D. diss., Harvard University. Pub. 1980, New York: Garland.

———. 1986. On Auxiliaries, AUX and VPs in Icelandic. In *Topics in Scandinavian Syntax,* ed. L. Hellen & K. Koch-Christensen, 235–65. Dordrecht: Reidel.

Torrego, E. 1986. On Empty Categories in Nominals. MS, University of Massachusetts (Boston).

Travis, L. 1984. Parameters and Effects of Word Order Variation. Ph.D. diss., MIT.

———. 1986. Paper given at the Phrase Structure Conference, Summer LSA Institute, New York City.

———. Forthcoming. Parameters of Phrase Structure and V2 Phenomena. In Freidin, forthcoming.

Uszkoreit, H. 1986. Categorial Unification Grammars. *COLING* 11:187–94.

Vergnaud, J.-R. 1974. French Relative Clauses. Ph.D. diss., MIT.

Vijay-Shankar, K. 1987. A Study of Tree Adjoining Grammar. Ph.D. diss., University of Pennsylvania.

Vijay-Shankar, K., & A. Joshi. 1986. Some Computational Properties of Tree Adjoining Grammars. *ACL* 11:82–93.

Vijay-Shankar, K., D. Weir, & A. Joshi. 1986. On the Progression from Context-Free to Tree Adjoining Languages. MS, University of Pennsylvania.

Vilkuna, M. 1986. Konstittuenttirakenteen ja sanajarjestyksen ongelmia: Suomen hajoavat infinitiivirakenteet ja lausekerakennekielioppi. *Kieli* 1:183–223.

Wall, R. 1972. *Introduction to Mathematical Linguistics.* Englewood Cliffs, N.J.: Prentice-Hall.

Weir, D. 1988. Characterizing Mildly Context-sensitive Grammar Formalisms. Ph.D. diss., University of Pennsylvania.

Whitelock, P. 1986. A Feature-based Categorial-like Morpho-Syntax for Japanese. Paper presented at the Workshop on Word Order and Parsing in Unification Grammars, Friedenweiler, West Germany.

Whitman, J. 1982. Configurationality Parameters. MS, Harvard University.

Williams, E. 1978. Across-the-Board Rule Application. *LI* 9:31–43.

———. 1980. Predication. *LI* 11:203–38.

———. 1981a. Argument Structure and Morphology. *LR* 1:81–114.

———. 1981b. On the Notions "Lexically Related" and "Head of a Word." *LI* 12:245–74.

———. 1982. The NP Cycle. *LI* 13:277–95.

———. 1983. Against Small Clauses. *LI* 14:287–308.

———. 1984. Grammatical Relations. *LI* 15:639–73.

———. Forthcoming. The Argument Bound Empty Categories. In Freidin, forthcoming.

———. In preparation. Theta Roles and Reference.

Wittenburg, K. 1986. Natural Language Parsing with Combinatory Categorial Grammar in a Graph-Unification-based Formalism. Ph.D. diss., University of Texas (Austin).

Wood, M. 1986. The Description and Processing of Coordinate Structures. Manchester: Centre for Computational Linguistics, University of Manchester. Report 86/4.

Zaenen, A. 1980. Extraction Rules in Icelandic. Ph.D. diss., MIT. New York: Garland, 1985.

———, ed. 1982. *Subjects and Other Subjects*. Bloomington: Indiana University Linguistics Club.

———. 1983. On Syntactic Binding. *LI* 14:469–504.

Zaenen, A., J. Maling, & H. Thráinsson. 1985. Case and Grammatical Functions: The Icelandic Passive. *NLLT* 3:441–83.

van der Zee, N. 1982. Samentrekking: Een Kategoriaal Perspektief. *Glot* 5:189–217.

Zeevat, H., E. Klein, & J. Calder. 1987. Unification Categorical Grammar. In Haddock, Klein, & Morrill 1987:195–222.

Zubizarreta, M.-L. 1985. The Relation between Morphophonology and Morphosyntax: The Case of Romance Causatives. *LI* 16:247–89.

Zwicky, A., & G. Pullum. 1983. Cliticization vs. Inflection: English *n't*. *Lg*. 59:502–13.

Author Index

Subject Index